Introduction to Comparative Politics

Introduction to Comparative Politics

First Edition

Edited by Joel D. Wolfe
University of Cincinnati

cognella®
SAN DIEGO

Bassim Hamadeh, CEO and Publisher
Jennifer Codner, Senior Field Acquisitions Editor
Alisa Munoz, Project Editor
Susana Christie, Senior Developmental Editor
Celeste Paed, Associate Production Editor
Emely Villavicencio, Senior Graphic Designer
Greg Isales, Licensing Coordinator
Natalie Piccotti, Director of Marketing
Kassie Graves, Senior Vice President of Editorial
Jamie Giganti, Director of Academic Publishing

3970 Sorrento Valley Blvd., Ste. 500, San Diego, CA 92121

Contents

Introduction Comparative Politics
Studying States in the Global Context

C OMPARATIVE POLITICS IS A POLITICAL SCIENCE subfield that focuses on the study of nation-states and uses comparative methods to explore similarities and differences in their forms and functions. In order to deal with this complex and inclusive topic, the readings will focus on the reach of the comparative method briefly, outline standard features of late twentieth-century states, and then examine the sources and patterns of the modern state, the debate about who rules, the challenges that are reshaping states, and finally the insurmountable challenges. The goal of this collection is to provide a sampling of comparative politics themes and also the key methods facilitating a search for insights into political issues.

Changing Topics in Comparative Politics

While political science founders go back to at least Plato and Aristotle followed by a long line of important contributors, the modern discipline began in the early twentieth century and developed into a major subfield of political science after World War II. The overall aim of seeking to understand all modes and effects of state power evident among the earliest scholars continue into the twenty-first century.

Comparative politics in its modern form took shape after World War II, when the postwar climate encouraged the formation of academic fields and methodologies studying patterns of democracy and development around the world. The new era encouraged a more quantitative and theoretically informed political science. It was in this era that comparative politics enhanced its own identity by exploring political and economic development, democratization, state building, and electoral politics across a wide range of developing and developed states.

The search for understanding the bases of democracy remains the major focus of research. A turn toward using the methods of the natural sciences flourished as hypothesis formation and empirical data analysis grew, particularly concerning the spread and stabilization of democratic institutions. Methods of data analysis found in the natural sciences became the standard model. But the study of elections, institutional stability, third-world political development, variations in political cultures, along with theories of economic and cultural modernization generated a diverse subfield. A small number of political scientists also studied the sources of communism and strategies for military defense. The overwhelming objective, however, was the idea that social and economic development was desirable and should be studied just as a scientist explores chemistry and biology.

With the collapse of Soviet communism after 1990, the US political model of liberal democracy and its study appeared triumphant. Nonetheless, serious challenges to free market liberal democracy emerged over the next thirty years. Important new political and economic challenges developed, such as an overall shift in patterns of economic growth, environmental crisis, and globalization. The shift, for example, from production-based capitalism toward finance capitalism contributed to an increasing disparity in the distribution of wealth. Between the end of World War II and the 1970s, democracy had spread, and populations experienced many benefits from the very strong economic growth. As global and domestic tensions mounted from the 1970s, the United States and many European countries abandoned the postwar Keynesian policy in favor of the neoliberal program of austerity and free market superiority. This economic program is still in place today.

From the beginning of the twenty-first century, the developed states experienced continuing economic problems, becoming more unequal and unstable, and faced important new international conflict. The tragedy of 9/11 in 2001, the stock market crash of 2008–2009, the inability to overcome massive public debt, and the failure of most manual and office workers to obtain rising incomes and higher living standards led to spreading fears of uncertainty, increasing hardship, and economic and political uncertainty. There was a rise and domination of finance and market speculation as well as growing inequality in which most of the population in America and Europe fell further behind the richest two percent. This trend continues to characterize the political economies of the American and European states. Worse, the prospects for a renewing economic growth in the United States of America and the European Union based on a return of manufacturing jobs would be unlikely.

In short, the increasing disparity between the extreme wealth of privileged entrepreneurs and the majority of wage earners in the West compelled the latter to live above their income by going into debt. The purchasing of property became a popular investment, as the rising value in property provided a large number of citizens with appearance of wealth and served to pacify many workers in North America and Europe. Even among the elite, the buying and selling of financial assets became central to wealth accumulation, as returns on stock markets investments became the key to wealth accumulation, more important than earned income.

Awareness of these shifts in history will help students to understand the readings and raise interesting questions about the past and the future. Studies in comparative politics will be helpful.

Book Chapters

Comparative Politics: Problems and Methods

Understanding political life depends on the ontology and epistemology guiding our empirical research. These philosophical concepts refer to nonempirical assumptions researchers use to inform their empirical research. Ontology refers to assumptions about the kinds of entities and processes to be studied. Epistemology denotes concepts determining what can be known and studied. Choices about these matters then lead to devising methods of empirical research best yield valid findings.

Chapters 1 and 2 provide detailed accounts of how empiricist research operations serve to control how the subject matter should be studied. These two chapters show the interdependence of empirical theory and method, in particular, how the criterion of research controls the formulation of research issues and findings. Chapter 1 is an overview of how comparison is the key philosophical tool when studying political phenomena. States and other political phenomena involve complex and variable phenomena that cannot be examined in laboratories. Instead, their complexity calls for research methods that come as close as possible to the processes of laboratory examination. Challenging circumstances often limit control over the substance being studied, the methods used, and the validity of the research findings.

The first chapter consists of two related readings laying out an empiricist view of comparative research. These readings provide an example of behavioralist model adapted to comparative politics research and serve as the ideal of the scientific model as used in political science. This first reading surveys the elements of empirical research, while the second reading applies these elements to types of research characteristic of comparative studies. The second reading emphasizes the adaptation of the model of laboratory research to political phenomena. While control of variables may be minimal or nonexistent, the aspiration for scientific insights compels the search for measurable links between causes and effects.

Yet, science consists of three levels or components, of which only one involves empirical testing. The first level is ontology, that is, the unobservable metaphysical foundations of things assumed to constitute nature. The second level is epistemology, that is, what can we know about the world and how do we know it. The third question is the research methodology, which refers to the collection and verification of what is knowable. These are the three analytical levels of knowing involved in scientific research. Collectively, scientific knowledge depends on philosophical theories about what exists, how it can be known, and what empirical research can support.

One Question, Different Answers: Power of Philosophical Methods

Chapter 2 includes two articles that go a step further in providing an overview of the steps or phases involved in empirical research, one targeting the bond between substantive cases and the second highlighting types of philosophical methodology. The first reading underscores the interdependence between research cases and philosophical method. These bonds start with a research problem, the selection of the case, hypothesizing credible inferences, research, and then further theorizing of in view of the research findings. In reading 2.1, Professor Landman highlights this interdependence between problems and methods. He illustrates that research questions entail ontology, epistemology, choice of research method, and case materials.

More significantly, reading 2.2 highlights how different philosophical starting points pose different problems and conclusions. In particular, it provides a comprehensive overview of three major philosophical methods and explains how they provide different views of research problems, thereby posing different questions and the use of different analytic tools. The authors of this reading go beyond Landman's emphasis on explication by means of behavioralist's investigation of variations among dependent and independent variables. The authors explain the different consequences of positivist, interpretivist, and critical realist philosophical traditions. In doing so, it becomes clear that the three different philosophical starting points expose differences about what the nature of the world is, what we can know about it, and what can be observed and recorded.

The research processes predetermine biases and conclusions. This involves two nonempirical stages of conceptualization: identifying the ontology (what the world is assumed to be like) and the epistemology (assumptions about what can be known) leading to the research examination of relevant empirical objects. For example, a forest ranger visits a section of a forest in order to check if there were prospects of it catching fire. While there he meets a group of native people who protest his presence. They assert that the land has been deemed a "sacred burial" ground, a special site to be visited exclusively by tribe members The first theme here is to realize that what we know is not given or fixed but constructed by research. The second proposition is the agent's dependence on these philosophical tools for making sense of particular issues or things, realizing that the analysis may not be final. Always identifying unspoken assumptions or using philosophical tools of analysis gives the reader deeper insight into variations in situations and control over what the conclusion might be and how it can be challenged.

These philosophical and empirical concepts presented in this text provide students with a more complete understanding of political analyses. The philosophical tools associated with comparative politics apply to all fields of political science research. They furthermore provide the fundamental analytical tools used in all science. Therefore, using these theoretical starting points contributes to developing the skills of critical evaluation. This is because understanding the intellectual sources and significance of various schools of thought underlying research in comparative politics will bring to light the sources of diverse viewpoints and so enable critical comparison.

The State: Power, Supremacy, Forms

Chapter 3 consists of four readings defining internal traits constituting the states. This chapter's four readings explain why states have power and the differences between democracy and authoritarianism. In doing so, the reading identifies and explains the resources of states that uniquely empower them with ultimate control within their realm. Readings 3.1 and 3.2 explain the sources of internal state authority, identified by the concepts of power, authority, and legitimacy. These societal phenomena enable states to have final authority over all activities within its territory.

States exercise power over their own territories, but the character of these social orders affects the type of rule, for example, whether democracy or authoritarianism exists. The composition of society, its political culture and wealth, affects the state's authoritative capacity to rule, though this may vary within regions. The ability of a state to exercise power within its territory ultimately depends on its legitimacy and other sources of political authority. Nonetheless, internal conflicts do arise from differences in the cultural and sociological variations within a polity.

The readings on democracy (reading 3.3) and on authoritarianism (reading 3.4) explore the question of who rules, how, and for what. The effect of such variation in operation of the power formation gives form to two very different patterns of "final authority," one backed by social traditions and interests practicing democracy and the other providing for an elite group capable of imposing its interests on state affairs. Readings in these chapters explain these two very different types of state formations and outline the criteria for identifying them. Regardless of the formal rules of the state, social foundations and values enable formation of these two diametrically opposed types of rule. These variations show the interdependence between state and society. This illustrates that the distributions of power within and between the societal and state spheres of political power are decisive in determining patterns of state stability and power. Such factors also determine who becomes leaders and determine different types of political challenges.

Embedded States: Social, Economic, and Global Substructures

The next group of readings complements those in chapter 3. Instead of focusing on the state itself, these readings are concerned with how the larger social system decides who controls the state itself. The societal foundations of states shape who rules and what matters and so are integral to the distribution of power in the state as well as its ability to exert foreign influence. Exploring societal organizations brings to light the major sources of indirect influence, affecting who can use the state for what purpose. The readings on nationalism, ethnic and cultural conflicts, the impact of economic growth, and the operations of global corporations will underscore the importance of the societal foundations of state policies. Often overlooked, societal organizations exercise significant influence over who or what decides whose interests are served.

Chapter 4 explores four of the most important sociological foundations of states. Reading 4.1 focuses on national identity or cultural element binding citizens together as constituting a group. Reading 4.2 explores the important role of ethnicity and its political functions and effects on democracy. The members of the group will bond as they advocate for acceptance of their own values, while rejecting those of the dominant culture. In reading 4.3, a third basis for creating an identity comes from placement within an economic system. As a collective identity it is a source of pride and solidarity that can strengthen the economy through solidarities that can press for better living standards and help generate social harmony. Finally, reading 4.4 explores the degree to which foreign firms, operating within a state, can influence social and political attitudes, for example, through the way they distribute their benefits to the community.

Theorizing Patterns of Domination and Conflict

The readings in chapter 5 explore the question of who rules and why? This starts with pluralism, an optimistic form of democracy in which citizens join together to influence state policymaking. Pluralism assumes that citizens voluntarily organize themselves into groups in order to correct an injustice or promote a needed social improvement. This provides a model idealizing American democracy, that is, as consisting of a government responsive to mobilized and active citizens.

The next reading, however, finds little existing or even potential democracy. The rationalization and bureaucratization of political institutions assures top-down control, the essence of modern politics. Using a review of David Graber's book on the rationalization (bureaucratization) of modern life, this article explains how rationalization of society eliminates any possibility of citizen control of political decision-making. The key message is that instrumental organization ensures elite control and prevents any hope of democracy.

The third reading considers how capitalists rule without the support of any class-consciousness among the ruling class. This is an application of instrumentalism to class analysis. As long as citizens feel satisfied with their living standard, the materialist motives driving society are satisfied and self-reproducing. Because of this, Fred Block argues that capitalism operates with an ideological backing built on rationality. In effect, capitalism controls because it fits into the Weberian model of a social order built on prioritizing a total rationalizing of all types of means-ends operations.

A fourth reading relies on an interpretivist approach to investigate whether growing Chinese power will become a threat to America's global power. As ideological conflict grows with the successful expansion of Chinese power, the author uses a fixed empiricist view of conflicting relations and so foresees growing conflict and an eventual war. In this article, ideology or cultural heritage becomes the most important causal factors guiding China and American toward war.

Factors Weakening State Formations

This set of readings in chapter 6 moves beyond standard explanations of state power to examine the sources of the conflicts generating divisive conflicts within and between modern states. These articles point to destabilizing social conflicts developing within and between states. David Lake explores the reasons for increasing growth of ideological conflict amid the diminishing capacity to increase economic growth and social cohesion. He points to the end of the postwar era of "embedded capitalism" that had effectively raised the living standard of most people and supported states' ruling capacities. As the Keynesian era ended during the 1970s, so did full employment. The era of rising incomes was ended by the Thatcherite neoliberalism economic formula that was adopted from 1979 onward. This fundamental change in the government's economic policy appeared to have some success for the first few years but led to unstable and limited growth for the majority of citizens. This economic paradigm was adopted in America and Europe, both of which suffered from the market crash of 2008–2010 and have had little growth since. Next, Frances Fox Piven turns our attention to the impact of neoliberalism's contradictions following the great crash of 2008. She points to the increasing ideological and social conflicts in the face of diminishing expectations of better living standards and intensifying cultural and ideological conflicts between groups. The effect of this ideological conflict was to further exacerbate and so weakening citizens' influence. A final reading by Matthias Matthijs explores how the flawed neoliberal program generated political conflict and division within the European Union. He points to the divisive impact of elite's capture of policymaking through its control of trade, policymaking, and European finance. The result has been a decline of economic growth, a rise in conflict within and between member states, and a failure to deal with important social and political problems.

Threats to the Current Political Order

This final chapter turns attention to several of the most significant and dangerous threats to political stability and social progress. These political issues pose serious challenges to the very existence and future of states and societies themselves. The first reading reviews recent books examining current economic issues and takes seriously the prospect that our modern economies may fail to find ways to survive the current economic crisis. In his book review, Mark Blyth reports that Jürgen Kocha contends that the capacity for self-adjustment disappeared once finance became the dominant economic system. A second book he reviews is by Wolfgang Streeck who argues that capitalism appears to be experiencing a slow decay with no signs of recovery. Finally, Mark Blyth reviews Paul Mason's prognosis of capitalism's total collapse. The effect of this future would be poverty and starvation, testing the ability of humans to survive.

A second reading examines population growth, arguing that the populations in the most productive and wealthy regions are declining, while population growth in unproductive but highly populated regions will continue to expand.

The last reading is the most unsettling. This summary of studies of efforts combating climate change contends that humans do not appear to be able to deal with the challenges of the complex coordination needed nor will they be able to contend with greater oncoming threats due to climate change. The scientific, political, and organizational challenges are just too great.

In short, these three readings point to unprecedented challenges that can be met only by new types of political systems. The implication is that human survival will depend on some type of yet to be found collective solidarity, framed by a complex of social organizations capable to ensuring collaboration.

Chapter 1

Comparative Politics
Problems and Methods

C OMPARATIVE POLITICS EXAMINES THE OBJECTIVES, PROCESSES, and results of decisions allocating collective values among actors within and between all political systems past and present. Classic writings date from the work of Plato and Aristotle on the nature of political life and the work of Hobbes and Locke among others on how political power regulates moral and distributive impacts for society. As a result, comparative politics is the most encompassing subfield in political science, claiming its origins in the great works of political thought and the founders of liberal democracy. As a major subfield of political science, comparative politics took shape with the emergence of new states between and after World Wars I and II.

Comparative politics examines the phenomena political theorist David Easton captures in his notion that politics involves the "authoritative allocation of values," that is, who or what controls the final decisions regulating community affairs. This requires a political system deciding contentious issues and enforcing order based on authorities' legitimate right to do so. If needed, these rights authorize the use of force to resolve international conflicts. While comparative politics includes all the world's states and peoples as subject matter for study, it is also open to all types of political analysis. What further distinguishes comparative politics is its focus on use of the "comparative method." This refers to research strategies approximating experimental methods, the method of natural science.

Our first reading, "Why Compare Countries?," emphasizes that contemporary comparative politics is one of the subfields of political science distinguished by using systematic comparisons aiming to mimic natural science. Comparison of countries strives to clarify differences among countries, fit countries into a limited number of comparable models, conduct empirical tests by examining the cases for similarities and differences, and then use reliable findings to make predictions. Description, classification into patterns, identification of "causal" hypotheses, and prediction for further testing enable the development of empirical theory. Yet, the comparative method falls short of the scientific ideal of natural science since comparativists cannot use experiments or replicate phenomena. This first chapter explains these scientific research methods, distinguishing theory and method, elements of method (ontology, epistemology, and methodology), variables (causes or effects), agency as involving individuals or structures, and the analytical importance of various types of data, in particular distinguishing between the quantifiable and the qualitative.

The second reading, "Common Themes and Different Comparisons," assesses the contributions to the field that have been discussed in previous chapter. The review reveals a wide diversity of topics, variations in the application of the comparative method, and how the findings contribute to political science. Landman's focus on research problems and forms of comparison finds that comparative politics in differentiated by rationalist, structuralist, and culturalist perspectives or schools of research. Even so, his overall conclusion emphasizes the care to be taken over the research process itself. Thus, Landman views comparative politics in terms of the use of comparative methods and how this affects the selection of cases, the limits of conclusions, and relevance to theory-building. In short, Landman proposes that comparative politics advances through refining the use of comparative methods in formulating research questions.

Reading 1.1

Why Compare Countries?

Todd Landman

M AKING COMPARISONS IS A NATURAL HUMAN activity. From antiquity to the present, generations of humans have sought to understand and explain the similarities and differences
they perceive between themselves and others. Though historically, the discovery of new peoples was often the product of a desire to conquer them, the need to understand the similarities
and differences between the conquerors and the conquered was none the less strong. Since
the new millennium, citizens in all countries continue to compare their position in society to
those of others in terms of their regional, ethnic, linguistic, religious, familial, and cultural
allegiances and identities; material possessions; economic, social and political positions; and
relative location in systems of power and authority. Students grow up worried about their
types of fashion, circle of friends, collections of music, appearance and behaviour of their partners, money earned by their parents, universities they attend, and careers they may achieve.

In short, to compare is to be human. But beyond these everyday comparisons, how is the
process of comparison scientific? And how does the comparison of countries help us understand the larger political world? In order to answer these important questions, this chapter
is divided into four sections. The first section establishes the four main reasons for comparison, including *contextual description*, *classification* and 'typologizing', *hypothesis-testing* and
theory-building, and *prediction* (Hague *et al.* 1992:24–27; Mackie and Marsh 1995:173–176). The
second section specifies how political science and the sub-field of comparative politics can be
scientific, outlining briefly the similarities and differences between political science and natural science. The third section clarifies the terms and concepts used in the preceding discussion
and specifies further those terms and concepts needed for a science of politics. The fourth section summarizes these reasons, justifications, and terms for a science of comparative politics.

Reasons for Comparison

Today, the activity of comparing countries centres on four main objectives, all of which are
mutually reinforcing in any systematic comparative study, but some of which receive more
emphasis than others, depending on the aspirations of the scholar. *Contextual description*
allows political scientists to know what other countries are like. *Classification* makes the
world of politics less complex, effectively providing the researcher with 'data containers' into

which empirical evidence is organized (Sartori 1970:1039). The *hypothesis-testing* function of comparison allows the elimination of rival explanations about particular events, actors, structures, etc. in an effort to help build more general theories. Finally, comparison of countries and the generalizations that result from comparison allow *prediction* about the likely outcomes in other countries not included in the original comparison, or outcomes in the future given the presence of certain antecedent factors and conditions.

Contextual Description

This first objective of comparative politics is the process of describing the political phenomena and events of a particular country, or group of countries. Traditionally, in political science, this objective of comparative politics was realized in those countries that were different to those of the researcher. Indeed, as the field developed in American political science, a comparativist was considered anyone who carried out research on a country other than the United States. Through often highly detailed description, scholars sought to escape their own ethnocentrism by studying those countries and cultures foreign to them (Dogan and Pelassy 1990:5–13). The comparison to the researcher's own country is either implicit or explicit, and the goal of contextual description is either more knowledge about the nation studied, more knowledge about one's own political system, or both. The comparative literature is replete with examples of this kind of research, and it is often cited to represent 'old' comparative politics as opposed to the 'new' comparative politics, which has aspirations beyond mere description (Mayer 1989; Apter 1996). But the debate about what constitutes old and new comparison often misses the important point that all *systematic research begins with good description*. Thus description serves as an important component to the research process and ought to precede the other three objectives of comparison. Purely descriptive studies serve as the raw data for those comparative studies that aspire to higher levels of explanation, and provide initial hunches about which topics of research may be of interest and which factors may be important to explain observed phenomena that are related to those topics.

In the field of Latin American politics, Macauley's (1967) *Sandino Affair* is a fine example of contextual description. The book is an exhaustive account of Agusto Sandino's guerrilla campaign to oust US marines from Nicaragua after a presidential succession crisis. It details the specific events surrounding the succession crisis, the role of US intervention, the way in which Sandino upheld his principles of non-intervention through guerrilla attacks on US marines, and the eventual death of Sandino at the hands of Anastasio Somoza. The study serves as an example of what Almond (1996:52) calls 'evidence without inference', where the author tells the story of this remarkable political leader, but the story is not meant to make any larger statements about the struggle against imperialism. Rather, the focus is on the specific events that unfolded in Nicaragua, and the important roles played by the various characters in the historical events. None the less, the account could provide a wealth of evidence for comparative and single-case studies examining the role of indigenous resistance to outside intervention, the history of the rise of military authoritarianism in Central America, the roots of revolutionary movements (the contemporary Sandinistas from whom President Daniel Ortega comes), among many other relevant topics found in comparative politics both inside and outside Latin America.

Classification

In the search for cognitive simplification, comparativists often establish different conceptual classifications in order to group vast numbers of countries, political systems, events, etc. into distinct categories with identifiable and shared characteristics. Classification can be a simple dichotomy such as that between 'authoritarianism' and 'democracy', which draws on a set of theoretically-derived criteria that help determine where particular countries would fall. Or classification can be a more complex array of regimes and governmental systems that provides greater differentiation. Like contextual description, classification is a necessary component of systematic comparison, but in many ways represents a higher level of comparison since it seeks to group many separate descriptive entities into simpler categories. It reduces the complexity of the world by seeking out those qualities that countries share and those that they do not share. Moreover, classification schemes can be the first step towards capturing cross-national variation in political phenomena, such as democratic and authoritarian countries, developed and underdeveloped countries, core and peripheral countries, military and civilian regimes, among many other distinctions.

The process of classification is not new. The most famous effort at classification is found in Aristotle's *Politics* (Book 3, Chapters 6–7), in which he establishes six types of rule. Based on the combination of their form of rule (good or corrupt) and the number of those who rule (one, few, or many), Aristotle derived the following six forms: monarchy, aristocracy, polity, tyranny, oligarchy, and democracy (see Hague *et al.* 1992:26). A more recent attempt at classification is found in Finer's (1997) *The History of Government*, which claims that since antiquity (*ca.* 3200 BC) all forms of government have belonged to one of the following four basic types: the palace polity, the church polity, the nobility polity, and the forum polity. Each type is 'differentiated by the nature of the ruling personnel' (ibid.: 37). In the palace polity, 'decision-making rests with one individual' (ibid.: 38). In the church polity, the church has a significant if not exclusive say in decision making (ibid.: 50). In the nobility polity, a certain pre-eminent sector of society has substantial influence on decision-making (ibid.: 47). In the forum polity, the authority is 'conferred on the rulers from below' by a 'plural headed' forum (ibid.: 51). Aristotle's classification was derived deductively and then 'matched' to actual city states, while Finer's classification scheme is based on empirical observation and inductive reasoning (see below for the distinction between these two types of reasoning).

Both scholars, however, seek to describe and simplify a more complex reality by identifying key features common to each type (see Briefing box 1.1.1).

Briefing Box 1.1.1 Making Classifications: Aristotle and Finer

Description and classification are the building blocks of comparative politics. Classification simplifies descriptions of the important objects of comparative inquiry. Good classification should have well-defined categories into which empirical evidence can be organized. Categories that make up a classification scheme can be derived inductively from careful consideration of available evidence or through a process of deduction in which 'ideal' types are generated. This briefing box contains the oldest example of regime classification and one of the most recent. Both Aristotle and Samuel Finer seek to establish simple classificatory schemes into which real societies can be placed. While Aristotle's scheme is founded on normative grounds, Finer's scheme is derived empirically.

Constitutions and Their Classifications

In Book 3 of *Politics*, Aristotle derives regime types which are divided on the one hand between those that are 'good' and those that are 'corrupt', and on the other, between the different number of rulers that make up the decision-making authority, namely, the one, the few, and the many. Good government rules in the common interest while corrupt government rules in the interests of those who comprise the dominant authority. The intersection between these two divisions yields six regime types, all of which appear in Figure 1.1.1. The figure shows that the good types include monarchy, aristocracy, and polity. The corrupt types include tyranny, oligarchy, and democracy. Each type is based on a different idea of justice (McClelland 1997: 57). Thus, monarchy is rule by the one for the common interest, while tyranny is rule by the one for the one. Aristocracy is rule by the few for the common interest, while oligarchy is rule by the few for the few. Polity is rule by the many for the common good, while democracy is rule by the many for the many, or what Aristotle called 'mob rule'.

		Those Who Rule		
		One	Few	Many
Form of Rule	Good	Monarchy (kingship)	Aristocracy	Polity
	Corrupt	Tyranny	Oligarchy	Democracy (mob rule)

FIGURE 1.1.1 Aristotle's classification scheme

Sources: Adapted from Aristotle (1958: 110–115); Hague *et al.* (1992: 26); McClelland (1997: 57)

Types of Regime

Finer (1997: 37) adopts an Aristotelian approach to regime classification by identifying four 'pure' types of regime and their logical 'hybrids'. Each regime type is based on the nature of its ruling personnel. The pure types include the palace, the forum, the nobility, and the church. The hybrid types are the six possible combinations of the pure types, palace–forum, palace–nobility, palace–church, forum–nobility, forum–church, and nobility–church. These pure and hybrid types are meant to describe all the regime types that have existed in world history from 3200 BC to the modern nation state. Finer concedes that there are few instances of pure forms in history and that most polities fit one of his hybrid types. These pure forms, their hybrids, and examples from world history appear in Figure 1.1.2. The diagonal that results from the intersection of the first row and column in the figure represents the pure forms, while the remaining cells contain the hybrid forms. Many regime types that were originally pure became hybrid at different points in history. Of all the types, the pure palace and its variants have remained the most common through history, and despite its popularity today, the forum polity that represents modern secular democracies is a relatively rare and recent regime type (Finer 1997: 46).

	Palace	Forum	Nobility	Church
Palace	*Pure Palace* Persian, Roman, Byzantine, Chinese, and Islamic Empires; 18th-century absolutisms	*Palace–Forum* Greek tyrants, Roman dictators, Napoleonic France, modern dictatorships and totalitarian regimes	*Palace–Nobility* Court of Louis XIV, Britain 1740–60, Poland, Mamluk Regime in Egypt, and pre-1600 Japan	*Palace–Church* Traditional Thailand: the *sangha*; European Middle Ages
Forum		*Pure Forum* Greek poleis, Roman republics, and medieval European city-states; modern secular democracies	*Forum–Nobility* Roman republic, Republic of Venice	*Forum–Church* Ephrata Mennonites 1725, Amish 1700–present,[†] both near Lancaster, Pennsylvania
Nobility			*Pure Nobility* 17th- and 18th-century Poland	*Nobility–Church* Teutonic Order 1198–1225
Church				*Pure Church* Vatican; Tibet 1642–1949

FIGURE 1.1.2   Pure and hybrid regime types with examples from history

Source: Adapted from Finer (1997: 34–58)

Note: [†] Author's addition

Hypothesis-Testing

Despite the differences between contextual description and classification, both forms of activity contribute to the next objective of comparison, hypothesis-testing. In other words, once things have been described and classified, the comparativist can then move on to search for those factors that may help explain what has been described and classified. Since the 1950s, political scientists have increasingly sought to use comparative methods to help build more complete theories of politics. Comparison of countries allows rival explanations to be ruled out and hypotheses derived from certain theoretical perspectives to be tested through examining cross-national similarities and differences. Scholars using this mode of analysis, which is often seen as the *raison d'être* of the 'new' comparative politics (Mayer 1989), identify important variables, posit relationships to exist between them, and illustrate these relationships comparatively in an effort to generate and build comprehensive theories.

Arend Lijphart (1975) claims that comparison allows 'testing hypothesized empirical relationships among variables'. Similarly, Peter Katzenstein argues that 'comparative research is a focus on analytical relationships among variables validated by social science, a focus that is modified by differences in the context in which we observe and measure those variables' (in Kohli *et al.* 1995:11). Finally, Mayer (1989:46) argues somewhat more forcefully that 'the unique potential of comparative analysis lies in the cumulative and incremental addition of system-level attributes to existing explanatory theory, thereby making such theory progressively more complete'. In other words, comparison of countries and testing hypotheses contributes to the progressive accumulation of knowledge about the political world. Multiple symposia on comparative politics in *World Politics* (Kohli *et al.* 1995), *American Political Science Review* (vol. 89, no. 2, pp. 454–481), and *Political Analysis* (Brady *et al.* 2006), as well as new monographs containing critical reflections on the state of comparative methodology suggest that questions of theory, explanation, and the role of comparison continue to be at the forefront of scholars minds (see, e.g., Flyvbjerg 2001; Brady and Collier 2004; George and Bennett 2005).

Furthermore, the publication of truly comparative books in the field continues to demonstrate the fruitfulness of this mode of analysis. For example, Luebbert (1991) compares Britain, France, Switzerland, Belgium, The Netherlands, Denmark, Norway, Sweden, Czechoslovakia, Germany, Italy, and Spain to uncover the class origins of regime type in inter-war Europe. Rueschemeyer *et al.* (1992) compare the historical experiences of the advanced industrial countries with those of the developing world to uncover the relationship between capitalist development and democracy. Wickham-Crowley (1993) compares instances of revolutionary activity in Latin America to discover the causal configuration of successful and unsuccessful social revolution in the region. Foweraker and Landman (1997) compare the authoritarian cases of Brazil, Chile, Mexico, and Spain to illustrate the relationship between citizenship rights and social movements. Dryzek and Holmes (2002) examines the ways in which citizens think and view democracy across eleven post-communist countries. Hawkins (2002) uses the single case of Chile to examine how international mobilization condemning human rights abuses led 'rule-oriented' factions of the Pinochet regime to push for a democratic transition, the inferences from which are applied to the cases of Cuba and South Africa (see Chapter 11). Finally, Inglehart and Welzel (2005) compare cross-national survey and other data to assess the complex relationship between and among processes of modernization (or postmodernization), changing value systems, and democracy. In all these works, key explanatory and outcome variables are carefully defined and the relationships between them are demonstrated through comparison of empirical evidence (see Briefing box 1.1.2).

Briefing Box 1.1.2   Hypothesis-Testing

Voting Participation

In *Contemporary Democracies*, Powell (1982) examines a number of key hypotheses concerning voter participation in twenty-nine democratic countries. Participation is measured using voter turnout, or the percentage of the eligible voters who actually voted in national elections. He argues that voting participation ought to be higher in countries with higher levels of economic development (per capita GNP), a representational constitution, electoral laws that facilitate voting, and a party system with strong alignments to groups in society (Powell 1982: 120–121). His statistical analysis of the data from these countries reveals positive effects for all these variables on voter participation, which are depicted graphically in Figure 1.1.3.

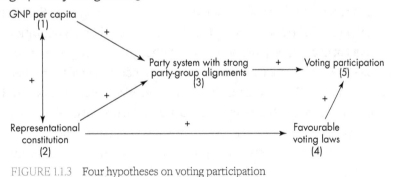

FIGURE 1.1.3   Four hypotheses on voting participation

Sources: Adapted from Powell (1982: 121)

Moreover, his analysis shows that the level of economic development and constitutional structure are not directly related to voter participation, but that they 'lead to or help sustain the development of party systems and the choice of voting laws, which do get the voters to the polls' (ibid.: 120). This causal ordering is depicted in the figure with the arrows and the numbering of each variable.

Prediction

The final and most difficult objective of comparative politics is a logical extension of hypothesis-testing, namely, to make predictions about outcomes in other countries based on the generalizations from the initial comparison, or to make claims about future political outcomes. Prediction in comparative politics tends to be made in probabilistic terms, such as 'countries with systems of proportional representation are more likely to have multiple political parties'. In this example, a political scientist would know the likely effect of a nation switching its electoral system from a plurality or 'first-past-the-post' rule to a proportional one (Hague *et al.* 1992). Another predictive example involves the benefits accrued to political incumbents in contesting future elections. Based on the empirical observations of past electoral contests, political scientists could be reasonably secure in predicting that the incumbent in any given election has a higher probability of winning the election than the non-incumbent (see King *et al.* 1994).

Although prediction is less an aspiration of comparativists today than in the past, there are those who continue to couch their arguments in predictive language. For example, weak predictive arguments are found in Huntington's (1996) *The Clash of Civilizations and the Remaking of the New World Order*, and strong predictive arguments are found in Vanhanen's (1997) *The Prospects of Democracy*. Huntington (1996) identifies nine key cultural groupings which he believes currently characterize the world's population, and predicts that future conflicts will be more likely to appear in the areas where two or more of these cultures meet or 'clash'. Not only does he seek to predict future conflicts in the world, but claims that his 'civilization' approach accounts for more post-Cold War events than rival approaches. His predictions became all the more relevant after the terrorist attacks on the World Trade Center and the Pentagon on September 11, 2001, which many saw as proof of a clash between the 'Western' and 'Islamic' civilizations outlined in his book. Subsequent analysis on pairs of states (or 'dyads') between 1969 and 2003 has shown that Huntington's 'West' civilization has been significantly more targeted than other civilizational groups and that the Islam–West dyad encounters more terrorism, but in contrast to Huntington's prediction, the Islamic group is not more violent *per se*, while overall levels of terrorism did not increase significantly after the Cold War (Neumayer and Plümper 2006).

Similarly, based on observations of the presence of economic resources and the occurrence of democracy in the world from the middle of the nineteenth century until today, Vanhanen (1997:99–154) predicts the degree to which individual countries and regions in the world are likely to become democratic, where his various results invite further research on the dynamics of democratization that moves beyond consideration of his socio-economic variables (see Briefing box 1.1.3). Finally, in the field of human rights, Poe and Tate (1994) find from their analysis of the cross-national variation in the protection of human rights that economic development and democracy have a positive effect on the protection of human rights while involvement in international and civil war have a negative effect. Using these findings, Poe and Tate (1994: 861–866) predict the likely over-time increases in repression (i.e. violations of human rights) due to the loss of democracy, involvement in international war, and experience of civil war, as well as predict the decrease in repression due to the increase in economic standing.

Briefing Box 1.1.3 Making Predictions

Democracy in East and Southeast Asia

Using similar methods as Burkhart and Lewis-Beck (1999), Vanhanen (1997) seeks to predict the expected level of democracy in specific countries and regions of the world based on their distribution of 'power resources'. Democracy is measured by a combination of the smallest parties' share of the vote and the percentage turnout (ibid.: 35). The distribution of power resources is measured by an index that combines the urban population, the non-agricultural population, proportion of students, the size of the literate population, the number of family farms, and the degree of decentralization of non-agricultural economic resources (Vanhanen 1997: 59–60). By examining the relationship between the level of democracy and the distribution of power resources from 1850–1993, Vanhanen compares the actual 1993 values of democracy to those that were predicted using regression analysis. Figure 1.1.4 shows the actual and predicted values of democracy for sixteen countries from East and Southeast Asia. The sixteen countries are listed along the horizontal axis and the values of the index of democratization are listed on the vertical axis. The predicted scores of democracy represent the level of democracy that each country ought to have obtained by 1993, given its corresponding distribution of power resources. The actual level is the score for 1993. The difference between the two values is known as the residual. Japan and South Korea appear to have obtained the levels of democracy that were predicted, while Malaysia, Mongolia, and the Philippines have higher levels of democracy than expected and Brunei, China, and Taiwan have lower scores than were expected. These varied results have several implications. First, the discrepancy between the actual and the predicted values may mean that something other than the distribution of power resources accounts for the level of democracy [...]. Second, the deviant cases whose level of democracy is unexpected for 1993 may be temporary exceptions to the overall pattern. Third, the indicators that were used may not accurately reflect the concepts Vanhanen seeks to measure [...]. Overall, however, the process of making predictions can raise new research questions and identify the need to focus on those cases that do not 'fit' the pattern [...].

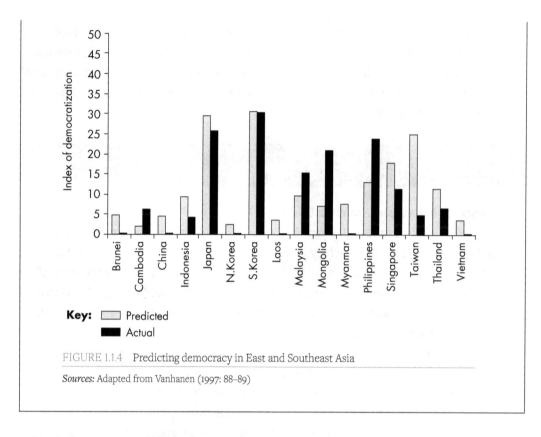

FIGURE 1.1.4   Predicting democracy in East and Southeast Asia

Sources: Adapted from Vanhanen (1997: 88–89)

The Science in Political Science

The preceding section specified the four main objectives of comparison in political science and hinted, through reference to questions of explanation, theory building, and prediction, how the comparison of countries might be considered a science. The key term used throughout the discussion was *inference*. Simply put, making an inference is 'using facts we know to learn something about facts we do not know' (King *et al.* 1994:119 after Mill; see also Couvalis 1997). Gabriel Almond (1996) observes that 'the object of political science ... is the creation of knowledge, defined as inferences or generalizations about politics drawn from evidence'; and Mayer (1989:56) claims that 'comparative analysis ... [is] a method that plays a central role in the explanatory mission of political science itself'. Thus, comparative politics seeks to achieve the goal of inference about politics through comparing countries. This section of the chapter clarifies how the process of making inferences is the underlying principle of comparative politics, and how the methodological assumptions of natural science are important to a science of politics.

For the purposes of this volume, science is defined as the gradual accumulation of knowledge about the empirical world through systematic practices of inquiry, including the collection of evidence, the generation and testing of hypotheses, and the drawing of substantive inferences.[1] But beyond this basic definition, what are the parallels between political science and natural science? What are the main differences between the two? And how does comparison help resolve these differences? The strong case for a science of politics suggests that both (comparative) political science and natural science share the same basic goals, namely, description, classification, hypothesis-testing, and prediction. Both activities require the systematic collection of evidence; an ordering of the evidence and the search for discernible patterns; the formulation and testing of contending explanations for the occurrence of the patterns; and the building of more general theories. Thus, a science of politics always contains this 'evidence-inference methodological core' (Almond 1996:52), or the 'customary pair' of theory and observation (Feyerabend 1993:23; see also Gordon 1991: 589–634).

Two examples from the natural sciences may help make these points clearer. Both the theory of evolution and the theory of gravity are based on the systematic collection of evidence. Charles Darwin sought to document the entirety of the Earth's flora and fauna. Originally in an effort to demonstrate the glory of God's creation, Darwin soon discovered a pattern in what he was observing for which an alternative explanation was possible. The theory of evolution, buttressed later by the theory of natural selection, emerged as the new explanation for the variety of species found in the natural world. Similarly, Isaac Newton formulated the theory of gravity based on the collection of evidence (the falling apple!). Neither scientist had actually seen evolution or gravity but merely observed its effects. In this way, evolution and gravity are mental constructs, whose repeated empirical verification has given them a law-like status.

Political scientists also collect evidence systematically (e.g. archival records, interviews, official statistics, histories, or surveys), search for discernible patterns in the evidence, and formulate theories to account for those patterns. In comparative politics, the political scientist compares countries in an effort to verify the theories that have been formulated. Thus, both the natural and political sciences seek to make inferences based on the empirical world they observe, and both seek to maximize the certainty of these inferences. Despite these general similarities between natural science and political science, there remain two important (albeit not absolute) differences: experimentation and the generation of scientific 'laws'. These differences are discussed in turn.

The first difference between natural science and political science is the role of experimentation. While for some areas of natural scientific research, such as astronomy and seismology, experimentation is not possible, the advances in natural science are generally supported by evidence gathered through experimentation, which involves the controlled manipulation of the subject under study in an effort to isolate causal factors. Evidence in political science, on the other hand, tends not to be gathered through experimentation, even though some political scientists use experiments in their research (e.g. those who work on game theory, focus groups, and 'citizen-juries'). Comparative politics, in particular, cannot use experimentation for both practical and ethical reasons. For example, it would be impossible to re-run the same election in the same country with a different electoral system to observe the differences in the outcome of the two systems. Ethically, it would be impossible to redistribute income intentionally in a developing country to see if civil strife erupts. Both these examples demonstrate the need for using *counterfactuals*, or situations in which the researcher imagines a state of affairs where the antecedent factors to a given event are absent and where an alternative course of events or outcomes is considered (Ferguson 1997b).

Whether it is different electoral systems, different distributions of income, different levels of economic development, or the absence of particular revolutionary groups, political scientists implicitly suggest a counterfactual situation when making claims about important explanatory factors. The claim that 'single-member district electoral systems tend to produce two-party systems' is in effect also claiming that countries *without* such electoral systems will necessarily have different political party systems. While some historians may construct alternative historical scenarios based on 'calculations about the relative probability of plausible outcomes' (ibid.: 85), political scientists compare countries that differ in ways that supply the requisite counterfactual situation. For example, by comparing the political party systems across countries with different electoral systems, the comparativist seeks to demonstrate that the type of electoral system has some bearing on the type of party system. In this way, comparative research 'simulates' experimentation (Lieberson 1987:45; Ferguson 1997b; see also Tetlock and Lebow 2001).

The second difference between natural science and political science involves the law-like status that is given to certain scientific theories. Experimentation and repeated empirical verification give theories in the natural sciences the status of laws (e.g. the law of conservation of energy, Newton's laws of motion, or Boyle's Law of Gases); however, the nature of evidence marshalled in support of theories of political science is such that law-like generalizations are rare. Three famous 'laws' of political science are well known. Michels' 'Iron Law of Oligarchy' suggests that the natural processes observable in the dynamics of organizations and small groups are such that over time, all groups and organizations develop a hierarchical structure of authority with a small elite at their head. In an example from the comparative literature, this law has been tested in the examination of social movement organizations, where evidence suggests that the most successful and long-standing social movement organizations tend to have formal bureaucratic structures and authoritative bodies composed of elites from the movement (see Tarrow 1994). The second law, called 'Duverger's Law', states that electoral systems based on single-member districts tend to produce two parties while systems with proportional representation tend to produce multiple parties. This law has been repeatedly tested in comparative studies on electoral systems and on balance, is supported by the evidence (see Rae 1971; Lijphart 1994a).

The third law on 'the democratic peace' states that democracies do not go to war with other democracies (Babst 1964; see also Chapter 12 in this volume), while a corollary law claims that democracies are less likely to be involved in militarized disputes than non-democracies (see Russett and O'Neal 2001). Repeated comparative studies in international relations of war 'dyads' (i.e. pairs of countries that engage in war with each other), demonstrate that '[t]he number of wars between the democracies during the past two centuries ranges from zero to less than a handful depending on precisely how democracy is defined' (Levy 1989:87–88). Scholars argue that this 'absence of war between democracies comes as close to anything we have to an empirical law in international relations' (ibid.: 88). Moreover, combined with the process of democratization, which has become more pronounced since 1974 [...], the law of democratic peace offers optimism about future conflict in the world, since a larger proportion of democracies in the world means fewer inter-state wars (see Ward and Gleditsch 1998; Przeworski *et al.* 2000; Gelpi and Griesdorf 2001; Russett and O'Neil 2001).

Aside from these three 'laws' of political science, the bulk of comparative research eschews making such strong claims. What then are the main conclusions about comparative politics that can be drawn from this cursory comparison with natural science? First, for practical and ethical reasons, comparative politics relaxes some of the rigours of natural science, but still employs the same logic of inference. Second, comparative politics is a non-experimental (or quasi-experimental) social science that seeks to make generalizations based on the best available evidence (Campbell and Stanley 1963; Lijphart 1975:162; Lieberson 1987). Third, as a substitute for experimentation, comparison allows for *control* (Sartori 1994:16), holding certain things constant while examining and accounting for observed differences [...]. Fourth, while not seeking ironclad laws, comparative politics seeks clarity, understanding, and explanation of political phenomena about which it can be reasonably certain. The goal of this book therefore, is to provide the necessary tools for students of politics to achieve this clarity, understanding, and explanation while avoiding the pitfalls and obstacles that limit such an enterprise.

Scientific Terms and Concepts

Before concluding this chapter, it is necessary to define and clarify terms that have been used thus far, as well as terms that will be encountered throughout the book. These are general terms used throughout the social sciences that all students of politics ought to know if they aspire to a more scientific approach to understanding the political world. These terms include theory and method; ontology, epistemology, and methodology; cases (or countries), units of analysis, variables, and observations; levels of analysis; and quantitative and qualitative methods. Throughout the discussion every effort is made to show how the book uses these terms and concepts of social science.

Theory and Method

There are two basic types of theory in political science, normative and empirical. Normative theory specifies how things in society *ought to be*, given a desired set of outcomes and philosophical position. From the Greeks and Romans to contemporary scholars such as John Rawls, normative political theorists establish frameworks for realizing the common good and address key problems of society through theoretical argumentation. For example, Rawls (1971) carries on the tradition of liberal contract theory found in Locke, Rousseau and Kant, by deriving principles of justice from an idealized thought experiment that involves the key concept of the 'veil of ignorance', behind which individuals are unaware of their age, class, gender, wealth, ethnic identity, etc. In contrast, empirical theory seeks to establish relationships between two or more concepts in an effort to explain the occurrence of observed political phenomena. For example, an empirical theory of social revolution may posit a series of socio-economic factors that account for revolutionary behaviour in certain types of people, which would then be tested using evidence [...]. In addition, theories in political science can be deductive or inductive. Deductive theories arrive at their conclusions by applying reason to a given set of premises (Stoker 1995:17; Lawson 1997:16–19; Couvalis 1997). For example, the rational choice perspective in political science assumes that all political actors maximize their own personal utility, or self-interest, when choosing between alternatives. From that basic assumption, the scholar logically deduces the range of possible outcomes (Ward 1995:79; Levi 1997). Inductive theories, on the other hand, arrive at their conclusions through observation of known facts (Couvalis 1997). For example, a scholar observing higher instances of peasant rebellion in geographical areas with higher levels of land and income inequality will arrive inductively at the conclusion that inequality is related to rebellion. Comparison of evidence from other countries or geographical regions would seek to confirm this generalization.

Method, on the other hand, is the means by which a theory is derived and tested, including the collection of evidence, formulation and testing of hypotheses, and the arrival at substantive conclusions. Evidence can be collected, for example, through the examination of historical records, the collation and analysis of open-ended interviews of political activists, the systematic reporting of the participant observation of social movement activities, or the construction and analysis of mass surveys of a sample of the population. In formulating and testing hypotheses, method makes the decision rules and the rejection of rival hypotheses explicit. Finally, substantive conclusions are drawn from the theories and the evidence. As the preceding discussion in this chapter suggests, this book, although not primarily concerned with different theories of comparative politics, seeks to demonstrate the different ways in which comparative methods can be used to test deductive and inductive empirical theories of politics.

Ontology, Epistemology, and Methodology

Ontology, epistemology, and methodology are terms that occur in the discussion of the philosophy of science and the distinctions between them often become blurred in the comparative literature. Ontology is, quite literally, the study of being, or the metaphysical concern with the essence of things, including the 'nature, constitution, and structure of the objects' of comparative inquiry (Lawson 1997:15). It concerns what can be studied, what can be compared, and what constitutes the political. In other words, for comparative politics, ontology concerns the countries, events, actors, institutions, and processes among other things that are observable and in need of explanation. Epistemology is the study of the nature of knowledge, or how scholars come to know the world, both through a priori means and through a posteriori means of observation, sense impression, and experience. In contrast to ontology, it concerns what knowledge of the political world is possible and what rules of inquiry scholars follow in knowing the political world. In the history and philosophy of science, epistemology has moved from the strong claim made by positivists that a unity of the natural and social sciences is possible to one that recognizes a certain plurality of approaches grounded in the link between evidence and inference of the kind that this book advocates (see Gordon 1991:589–668). In contrast to ontology and epistemology, methodology concerns the ways in which knowledge of the political world is acquired. As its name suggests, methodology is the study of different methods or systems of methods in a given field of inquiry. There are thus rules of inquiry specific to qualitative and quantitative methods, even though both strive to provide explanation and understanding of observed political phenomena. These three concepts also have ordered and 'directional dependence' such that ontology establishes what is knowable, epistemology how it is knowable, and methodology how it is acquired systematically (Hay 2002:61–66).

Having defined these terms, it is helpful for the reader to know how the discussions throughout the rest of this book are grounded in certain ontological, epistemological, and methodological assumptions. Without entering a philosophical debate, this book is grounded in the ontological belief that animate and inanimate objects in the world exist in and of themselves, and by extension observable events exist in and of themselves. The object of political science is to account for and understand these events in terms of why they happened, how they happened, and the likelihood of them happening again in the future, as well as in different parts of the world. While adhering to the notion that history is 'open ended' (Popper 1997), this book accepts that there are certain 'event regularities' (Lawson 1997) in the world that political science seeks to describe, explain, and understand.

Epistemologically, comparative politics inhabits a broad spectrum. One end of the spectrum contends that all things political and social are knowable through the process of deduction based on indisputable assumptions about human nature. Typically labelled 'nomothetic-deductive', such an epistemological position adheres to the positivist quest for law-like generalizations about political behaviour. The other end of the spectrum claims that all knowledge is culturally bound and relative, suggesting that it is impossible to know anything beyond the strict confines of the local cultural context (Kohli *et al.* 1995). Such a position suggests that a science of comparative politics is not possible, since political concepts would not 'travel' across different cultural contexts and there would be fundamental differences in their meaning (see Macintyre 1971).

In an effort to be inclusive of different methods of comparison, this book is located somewhere in between these two extremes. On the one hand, it accepts that certain deductive theories of politics can be tested in the real world and that generalizations about the world of politics are possible given the proper adherence to rules of inquiry. On the other hand, it recognizes that knowledge of the political world cannot be 'value-free' and that the processes of theory generation and observation may not be mutually exclusive (Feyerabend 1993:27; Sanders 1995:67–68; Couvalis 1997). It therefore accepts that certain kinds of cross-cultural comparisons and cross-national comparisons can be made if certain procedures are adopted [...]. Methodologically, the book is concerned with the application of comparative methods to real research problems in comparative politics in an effort to help students make more valid generalizations about the political world they observe. [...]

Cases, Units of Analysis, Variables, and Observations

These four terms are vital aspects of systematic research in comparative politics. Cases are those countries that feature in the comparative analysis. For example, in *States and Social Revolutions* (1979), Theda Skocpol examines the cases of France, Russia, and China. Units of analysis are the objects on which the scholar collects data, such as individual people, countries, electoral systems, social movements, etc. Variables are those concepts whose values change over a given set of units, such as income, political party identification, propensity to join a protest movement, etc. Observations are the values of the variables for each unit, which can be numeric, verbal, or even visual. For example, a hypothetical study of social movements in Britain, France, The Netherlands, and Germany may have a variable entitled 'strategy', which has categories denoted 'political lobbying', 'peaceful demonstration', 'violent direct action', 'grass-roots organizing', and 'consciousness-raising'. In this hypothetical study, the cases are the countries, the units of analysis are the movements, the variable is 'strategy', and the observation is the value of the strategy variable for a given movement in a given country.

In addition to the different values that variables assume, they can either be *dependent* or *independent*. Dependent variables (alternatively referred to as outcome variables, endogenous variables, or the explanandum) are those political outcomes that the research is trying to explain. An independent variable, on the other hand, is that which explains the dependent variable (and is alternatively labelled a causal variable, an explanatory variable, an exogenous variable, or the explicandum). The distinction between dependent and independent variables is derived from the specific research question of a comparative project and the particular theoretical perspective that has been adopted. Since most political events have multiple explanations, it is possible to have more than one independent variable for a given dependent variable. In formal models of politics and in standard notation used for regression equations the dependent variable is often depicted by a y, and the independent variable is often depicted by an x [...].

For example, a dependent variable may include votes for a leftist party, military coups, revolutions, or transitions to democracy. These are all examples of outcomes of interest to political scientists. Independent variables to account for each of these dependent variables may include, respectively, social class, economic crisis, the commercialization of agriculture, or elite bargaining. In his study of guerrillas and revolution in Latin America, Wickham-Crowley (1993) seeks to explain the occurrence of successful social revolutions. In this example, successful social revolution is the dependent variable. The independent variables include the presence of a guerrilla group, the support of workers and peasants, sufficient guerrilla military strength, the presence of a traditional patrimonial regime, and the withdrawal of US military and economic support for the incumbent regime (Wickham-Crowley 1993:312; [...]).

Levels of Analysis

Levels of analysis in political science are divided between the micro, or individual level, and the macro, or system level. Micro-political analysis examines the political activity of individuals, such as respondents in a mass survey, elite members of a political party or government, or activists in a protest movement. Macro-political analysis focuses on groups of individuals, structures of power, social classes, economic processes, and the interaction of nation states. As in other divisions in political science, there are those who believe all of politics can be explained by focusing on micro-level processes, and there are those who believe that all of politics can be explained by a focus on macro-level processes. This is sometimes called the 'structure-agency' problem of politics (see Hay 1995, 2002). Micro-analysts believe that the world of politics is shaped by the actions of 'structureless agents', while macro-analysts believe that that world is shaped by the unstoppable processes of 'agentless-structures'.

The comparative politics literature is rich with examples of these different levels of analysis. In *The Rational Peasant*, Samuel Popkin (1979) argues that revolutionary movements are best understood by focusing on the preferences and actions of individual peasants (a micro-level analysis). Support for this assertion comes from his intense study of peasant activity in Vietnam. In contrast to Popkin, Jeffrey Paige (1975) in *Agrarian Revolution*, demonstrates that revolutions are most likely in countries with a particular structural combination of owners and cultivators. This macro-level analysis is carried out through comparing many countries at once, and then verifying the findings in the three countries of Vietnam, Angola, and Peru [...]. In *Liberalism, Fascism, or Social Democracy*, Gregory Luebbert (1991) claims that the types of regime that emerged in inter-war Europe had nothing to do with 'leadership and meaningful choice' (ibid.: 306), but were determined structurally by mass material interests, social classes, and political parties (a macro-level analysis). Finally, in *The Breakdown of Democratic Regimes*, Stepan (1978) finds the middle ground in accounting for the 1964 breakdown of democracy in Brazil, where he suggests that macro-political conditions at the time of breakdown certainly limited but did not determine the actions of individual leaders. This present book does not privilege one level of analysis over another. Rather, it demonstrates the ways in which different levels of analysis fit into different comparative methods and how different comparative studies have addressed the key tenets of dominant empirical theories in political science [...].

Quantitative and Qualitative Methods

Simply put, quantitative methods seek to show differences in number between certain objects of analysis and qualitative methods seek to show differences in kind. Quantitative analysis answers the simple question, 'How many of them are there?' (Miller 1995:154), where the 'them' represents any object of comparison that can either be counted or assigned a numerical value. There are many such objects in political science, such as protest events, social movement strategies (see above, p. 19), an individual's identification with political parties, democratic transitions [...] and the degree to which human rights are protected [...]. Quantitative data can be official aggregate data published by governments on growth rates, revenues and expenditures, levels of agricultural and industrial production, crime rates and prison populations, or the number of hectares of land devoted to agrarian reform. Quantitative data can also be individual, such as that found in the numerous market research surveys and public opinion polls. Quantitative methods are based on the distributions these data exhibit and the relationships that can be established between numeric variables using simple and advanced statistical methods.

Qualitative methods seek to identify and understand the attributes, characteristics, and traits of the objects of inquiry, and the nature of the method necessarily requires a focus on a small number of countries. In comparative politics, there are three broad types of qualitative methods: macro-historical comparison (and its three subtypes) (Skocpol and Somers 1980; Ragin *et al.* 1996); in-depth interviews and participant observation (Devine 1995); and what is variously called interpretivism, hermeneutics, and 'thick description' (Geertz 1973; Fay 1975). In none of these types of method is there an attempt to give numerical expression to the objects of inquiry, and in all of them, the goal is to provide well-rounded and complete discursive accounts. These more complete accounts are often referred to as 'ideographic' or 'configurative', since they seek to identify all the elements important in accounting for the outcome. Through focus on a small number of countries, comparative macro-history allows for the 'parallel demonstration of theory', the 'contrast of contexts', or 'macrocausal' explanation (Skocpol and Somers 1980). Parallel demonstration of theory tests the fruitfulness of theory across a range of countries. The contrast of contexts helps to identify unique features of countries in an effort to show their effect on social processes, while bringing out the richness of the individual countries and aspiring to 'descriptive holism'. Macro-causal analysis seeks to explain observed political phenomena through the identification and analysis of 'master' variables (Luebbert 1991:5). In-depth interviews and participant observation strive to uncover a deeper level of information in order to capture meaning, process, and context, where explanation 'involves describing and understanding people as conscious and social human beings' (Devine 1995:140). Similarly, interpretivism, hermeneutics, and 'thick description' are concerned with interpretation, understanding, and the deeper structures of meanings associated with the objects of inquiry.

Over the years a division in political science has developed between those who use quantitative methods and those who use qualitative methods; however, it seems that this division is a false one if both methods adhere to the goal of making inferences from available evidence (Foweraker and Landman 1997:48–49). In other words, this book is grounded in the belief that the same logic of inference ought to apply equally to quantitative and qualitative methods (see King *et al.* 1994; see also Brady and Collier 2004). Perhaps more importantly, the qualitative distinction made among categories in comparative classification schemes necessarily precedes the process of quantification (Sartori 1970, 1994). And, as the ensuing chapters will demonstrate, it is clear that the field of comparative politics is richly populated with studies that use quantitative and qualitative methods (or both) at all levels of analysis, as well as across all methods of comparison.

Summary

This chapter has outlined the four main objectives of comparative politics and argued further that these should be seen not as mutually exclusive but as progressively cumulative and necessary for systematic research. Predictions cannot be made without well-founded theories; theories cannot be made without proper classification; and classification cannot be made without good description. The chapter has shown how comparative politics is scientific if it aspires to making inferences about the political world based on the best available evidence and coherent rules of inquiry. Finally, it defined the key terms that will be used throughout the book. The next chapter examines the different methods of comparison that are available to students, all of which can be used to make larger inferences about the political world that we observe.

Note

1. A slightly more cumbersome definition is offered by Goodin and Klingemann (1996a: 9): 'science ... [is] systematic enquiry, building toward an ever more highly differentiated set of ordered propositions about the empirical world.'

References

Almond, G. (1996) 'Political Science: The History of the Discipline', in R.E. Goodin and H. Klingemann (eds) *The New Handbook of Political Science*, Oxford: Oxford University Press.

Apter, D.E. (1996) 'Comparative Politics, Old and New', in R.E. Goodin and H. Klingemann (eds) *The New Handbook of Political Science*, Oxford: Oxford University Press, 372–397.

Aristotle (1958) *The Politics*, trans. E. Barker, Oxford: Clarendon Press.

Babst, D.Y. (1964) 'Elective Governments—A Force for Peace', *The Wisconsin Sociologist*, 3:9–14.

Brady, H. and Collier, D. (eds) (2004) *Rethinking Social Inquiry: Diverse Tools, Shared Standards*, Lanham, MD: Rowman and Littlefield.

Brady, H.E., Collier, D., and Seawright, J. (2006) 'Toward a Pluralistic Vision of Methodology', *Political Analysis*, 14: 353–368.

Burkhart, R.E. and Lewis-Beck, M. (1994) 'Comparative Democracy, the Economic Development Thesis', *American Political Science Review*, 88(4): 903–910.

Campbell, D.T. and Stanley, J.C. (1963) *Experimental and Quasi-experimental Designs for Research*, Chicago: Rand McNally.

Couvalis, G. (1997) *The Philosophy of Science: Science and Objectivity*, London: Sage.

Devine, F. (1995) 'Qualitative Analysis', in D. Marsh and G. Stoker (eds) *Theories and Methods in Political Science*, London: Macmillan, 137–153.

Dogan, M. and Pelassy, D. (1990) *How to Compare Nations: Strategies in Comparative Politics*, 2nd edn, Chatham, NJ: Chatham House.

Dryzek, J.S. and Holmes, L. (2002) *Post-Communist Democratization: Political Discourses across Thirteen Countries*, Cambridge: Cambridge University Press.

Fay, B. (1975) *Social Theory and Political Practice*, London: Allen & Unwin.

Ferguson, N. (1997b) 'Virtual History: Towards a Chaotic Theory of the Past', in N. Ferguson (ed.) *Virtual History: Alternatives and Counterfactuals*, London: Picador, 1–90.

Feyerabend, P. (1993) *Against Method*, London: Verso Press.

Finer, S.E. (1997) *The History of Government*, Vol. I: Ancient Monarchies and Empires, Oxford: Oxford University Press.

Flyvbjerg, B. (2001) *Making Social Science Matter*, Cambridge: Cambridge University Press.

Foweraker, J. and Landman, T. (1997) *Citizenship Rights and Social Movements: A Comparative and Statistical Analysis*, Oxford: Oxford University Press.

Geertz, C. (1973) 'Thick Description: Toward an Interpretative Theory of Culture', in C. Geertz *The Interpretation of Cultures*, New York: Basic Books, 3–30.

Gelpi, C. and Griesdorf, M. (2001) 'Winners or Losers? Democracies in International Crisis, 1918–94', *American Political Science Review*, 95(3): 633–647.

George, A.L. and Bennett, A. (2005) *Case Studies and Theory Development in the Social Sciences*, Cambridge: Cambridge University Press.

Goodin, R.E. and Klingemann, H. (1996a) 'Political Science: The Discipline', in R.E. Goodin and H. Klingemann (eds) *The New Handbook of Political Science*, Oxford: Oxford University Press, 3–49.

Gordon, S. (1991) *The History and Philosophy of Social Science*, London: Routledge.

Hague, R., Harrop, M., and Breslin, S. (1992) *Political Science: A Comparative Introduction*, New York: St Martin's Press.

Hawkins, D. (2002) *International Human Rights and Authoritarian Rule in Chile*, Lincoln, NB: University of Nebraska Press.

Hay, C. (1995) 'Structure and Agency', in D. Marsh and G. Stoker (eds) *Theories and Methods in Political Science*, London: Macmillan, 189–206.

——(2002) *Political Analysis*, London: Palgrave.

Huntington, S.P. (1996) *The Clash of Civilizations and the Remaking of the New World Order*, New York: Simon & Schuster.

Inglehart, R. and Welzel, C. (2005) *Modernization, Cultural Change, and Democracy: The Human Development Sequence*, Cambridge: Cambridge University Press.

King, G., Keohane, R.O., and Verba, S. (1994) *Designing Social Inquiry: Scientific Inference in Qualitative Research*, Princeton, NJ: Princeton University Press.

Kohli, A., Evans, P., Katzenstein, P.J., Przeworski, A., Rudolph, S.H., Scott, J.C., and Skocpol, T. (1995) 'The Role of Theory in Comparative Politics: A Symposium', *World Politics*, 48: 1–49.

Lawson, T. (1997) *Economics and Reality*, London: Routledge.

Levi, M. (1997) 'A Model, a Method, and a Map: Rational Choice in Comparative and Historical Analysis', in M. Lichbach and A. Zuckerman (eds) *Comparative Politics: Rationality, Culture, and Structure*, Cambridge: Cambridge University Press, 19–41.

Levy, J.S. (1989) 'Domestic Politics and War', in R.I. Rothberg and T.K. Rabb (eds), *The Origin and Prevention of Major Wars*, Cambridge: Cambridge University Press.

Lieberson, S. (1987) *Making It Count: The Improvement of Social Research and Theory*, Berkeley: University of California Press.

Lijphart, A. (1975) 'The Comparable Cases Strategy in Comparative Research', *Comparative Political Studies*, 8(2):158–177.

——(1994a) *Electoral Systems and Party Systems: A Study of Twenty-seven Democracies*, 1945–1990, Oxford: Oxford University Press.

Luebbert, G. (1991) *Liberalism, Fascism, or Social Democracy: Social Classes and the Political Origins of Regimes in Inter-war Europe*, New York: Oxford University Press.

Macauley, N. (1967) *The Sandino Affair*, Chicago: Quadrangle Books.

Macintyre, A. (1971) 'Is a Science of Comparative Politics Possible?', *Against the Self-images of the Age*, London: Duckworth, 260–279.

Mackie, T. and Marsh, D. (1995) 'The Comparative Method', in D. Marsh and G. Stoker (eds) *Theory and Methods in Political Science*, London: Macmillan, 173–188.

Mayer, L.C. (1989) *Redefining Comparative Politics: Promise versus Performance*, Newbury Park, CA: Sage.

McClelland, J.S. (1997) *A History of Western Political Thought*, London: Routledge.

Miller, W.L. (1995) 'Quantitative Analysis', *Theories and Methods in Political Science*, London: Macmillan, 154–172.

Neumayer, E. and Plümper, T., 'International Terrorism and the Clash of Civilizations: Was Huntington Right After All?' A SSRN Working Paper (December 17, 2006). Available at SSRN: http://ssrn.com/abstract=952208

Paige, J. (1975) *Agrarian Revolution: Social Movements and Export Agriculture in the Underdeveloped World*, New York: Free Press.

Poe, S.C. and Tate, C.N. (1994) 'Repression of Human Rights to Personal Integrity in the 1980s: A Global Analysis', *American Political Science Review*, 88(4): 853–872.

Popkin, S. (1979) *The Rational Peasant: the Political Economy of Rural Society in Vietnam*, Berkeley: University of California Press.

Popper, K. (1997) *The Lesson of This Century*, London: Routledge.

Powell, G. Bingham (1982) *Contemporary Democracies: Participation, Stability, and Violence*, Cambridge, MA: Harvard University Press.

Przeworski, A., Alvarez, M.E., Cheibub, J.A., and Limongi, F. (2000) *Democracy and Development: Political Institutions and Well-being in the World, 1950–1990*, Cambridge: Cambridge University Press.

Rae, D. (1967) *The Political Consequences of Electoral Laws*, New Haven, CT: Yale University Press.

Ragin, C., Berg-Schlosser, D., and de Meur, G. (1996) 'Political Methodology: Qualitative Methods', in R.E. Goodin and H. Klingemann (eds) *The New Handbook of Political Science*, Oxford: Oxford University Press, 749–768.

Rawls, J. (1971) *A Theory of justice*, Cambridge, MA: Harvard University Press.

Rueschemeyer, D., Stephens, E.H., and Stephens, J. (1992) *Capitalist Development and Democracy*, Cambridge: Polity Press.

Russett, B. and O'Neal, J. (2001) *Triangulating Peace: Democracy, Interdependence and International Organizations*, New York: W. W. Norton

Sanders, D. (1995) 'Behavioural Analysis', in D. Marsh and G. Stoker (eds) *Theories and Methods in Political Science*, London: Macmillan, 58–75.

Sartori, G. (1970) 'Concept Misinformation in Comparative Politics', *American Political Science Review*, 64: 1033–1053.

——(1994) 'Compare Why and How: Comparing, Miscomparing and the Comparative Method', in M. Dogan and A. Kazancigil (eds) *Comparing Nations: Concepts, Strategies, Substance*, London: Basil Blackwell, 14–34.

Skocpol, T. (1979) *States and Social Revolutions: A Comparative Analysis of France, Russia, and China*, Cambridge: Cambridge University Press.

Skocpol, T. and Somers, M. (1980) 'The Uses of Comparative History in Macrosocial Inquiry', *Comparative Studies in Society and History*, 22: 174–197.

Stepan, A. (1978) 'Political Leadership and Regime Breakdown: Brazil', in J.J. Linz and A. Stepan (eds) *The Breakdown of Democratic Regimes: Latin America*, Baltimore, MD: Johns Hopkins University Press, 110–137.

Stoker, G. (1995) 'Introduction', in D. Marsh and G. Stoker (eds) *Theory and Methods in Political Science*, London: Macmillan.

Tarrow, S. (1994) *Power in Movement: Social Movements, Collective Action, and Politics*, Cambridge: Cambridge University Press.

Tetlock, P.E. and Lebow, R.N. (2001) 'Poking Counterfactual Holes in Covering Laws: Cognitive Styles and Historical Reasoning', *American Political Science Review*, 95(4): 829–843.

Vanhanen, T. (1997) *The Prospects of Democracy*, London: Routledge.

Ward, H. (1995) 'Rational Choice Theory', in D. Marsh and G. Stoker (eds) *Theories and Methods in Political Science*, London: Macmillan, 76–93.

Ward, M. and Gleditsch, K. (1998) 'Democratizing for Peace', *American Political Science Review*, 92(1): 51–61.

Wickham-Crowley, T. (1993) *Guerrillas and Revolution in Latin America*, Princeton, NJ: Princeton University Press.

Reading 1.2

Common Themes and Different Comparisons

Todd Landman

Methodological Trade-Offs

Comparing Many Countries

The comparison of many countries provides statistical control and reduces the problem of selection bias; it gives extensive comparative scope and empirical support for general theories, and identifies deviant cases that warrant closer comparative examination. The many-country studies [...] make important generalizations about the key issues identified in each chapter. Those [...] identified important socio-economic correlates of democracy, some of which suggest that economic development actually causes democracy. For political violence ([...]), the studies identify a bundle of explanatory factors, while their different results are more due to their different theoretical conceptualizations and model specifications than to the method they have adopted. The studies [...] identify broad socioeconomic changes and organizational factors as important explanations for social movement origins, while largely ignoring the trajectory, shape, and political impact of movements.

For democratic transition ([...]), Huntington's (1991) qualitative study argues that a crisis of legitimacy in the authoritarian regime, high levels of economic development, the national and international presence of the Catholic Church, other international influences, and the diffusion of democratic ideas all help account for the global spread of democracy since 1974. The quantitative studies either map descriptive attributes of the 'third wave' of democratic transition (Jaggers and Gurr 1995), or identify the importance of key socio-economic variables that lie behind it (Vanhanen 1997; Doorenspleet 2005). The global evidence on institutional design and democratic performance [...] demonstrates that parliamentary systems tend to perform better and break down less frequently than presidential systems. [...], we learn that while economic development and democracy are associated with a greater protection of personal integrity rights, the global comparisons showed that resolving inter- and intra-state conflict is crucial to reducing the violation of such rights. Finally, [...] there is a significant crossover of concerns between the field of comparative politics and international relations, where comparative politics has been slightly more amenable to include international variables than international relations has been in accepting that domestic variables other than material resources and features may also have an impact on state behaviour.

What is clear from these studies is the identification of a parsimonious set of explanatory factors and sufficient degrees of freedom to allow for great variance in the variables, as well as the inclusion of control variables to rule out rival hypotheses. Of the issues [...], the most frequently verified empirical generalization is for the positive relationship between economic development and democracy. The second strongest generalization to emerge from these studies is the superior democratic performance (however measured) of parliamentary systems. There is less academic consensus, however, on the explanation for political violence, a dearth of many-country studies on social movements, few quantitative global comparisons of democratic transition (but see Boix 2003; Boix and Stokes 2003; Doorenspleet 2005), a continued focus on a narrow set of human rights, and a rise in the number of studies looking at the interaction between variables at different levels of analysis.

These problems in the global comparative literature illustrate the key weaknesses of this method. For political violence, many of the theories posit relationships that exist at the individual level, yet the tests for them use the nation state as the unit of analysis. Indicators for social movement activity such as protest event data are difficult to collect for a large number of countries. Similarly, measures of human rights beyond civil and political rights have presented a great challenge, although some advance is being made (see www.humanrightsdata.com; and Hertel *et al.* 2007). Democratic transitions tend to be operationalized in dichotomous terms, while theoretically transition is often thought to be a *longer political process*, which makes its cross-national study more difficult (see Whitehead 1996a). Thus, for the many-country comparisons to provide more valid and reliable inferences, better specification and measurement of the key variables are needed. Given the advances in communication and information technologies, however, the collection and sharing of global data on a variety of social, economic, and political indicators will continue to be easier. Moreover, the establishment of an ethos of replication and data-sharing within the scholarly community will aid in this goal for improving global analysis [...].

Comparing Few Countries

The weaknesses associated with comparing many countries and the discomfort scholars may have in specifying parsimonious models of politics have led many to compare a smaller set of countries. As [...] made clear, this method of comparison also provides control through use of the most similar or most different systems design (or both). It uses concepts and variables that may be more sensitive to the nuances of the particular political contexts under investigation. It allows for historical and intensive examination of cases not possible in studies with a large sample of countries. Together, the strength of few-country studies lies in their lower level of abstraction and their inclusion of historical and cultural factors. While many of these studies do not seek universal aspirations for their inferences, they do seek to extend their generalizations beyond the immediate scope of the countries included in the analysis.

For economic development and democracy, few-country studies introduce a broader set of variables and, using a historical perspective, not only 'unpack' the simple bivariate relationship between development and democracy but also uncover the sequences through which countries have (or have not) become democratic. While the few-country studies do not dispute the generalizations of the global comparative literature, they are keen to point out that there are exceptions to every rule. Thus, the global comparative studies focus on the similarities across the sample, while the few-country comparisons focus on the differences. Both strategies of comparison are equally valid but will necessarily yield different results. Similarly, the studies on political violence introduce a broader set of explanatory variables and historical sequences, as well as the inclusion of full revolution as a dependent variable. These studies focus on the structure of the agricultural sector, capitalist transformation, the cultural and community features of key groups most likely to exhibit violent and revolutionary behaviour, group organization and support, the strength and legitimacy of state power, and the role of international actors. Rather than identifying a mono causal explanation, all these studies seek to demonstrate the configuration of different explanatory factors and their likely association with political violence and revolution. Some of these studies select countries on the basis of having had a revolution (e.g. Wolf 1969), while others select a larger sample of countries to include positive, negative, and mixed cases of revolution (e.g. Paige 1975; Skocpol 1979; Wickham-Crowley 1993). Those that provide greater variance in the dependent variable through this type of selection necessarily can make stronger inferences from their comparisons.

Few-country studies of social movements move beyond explaining their origins to questions of their trajectory, shape, strategies, and political impact. They identify new sectors of the population that support movements, the changing political opportunities that allow for the emergence, shape and impact of movements, the differences between the so-called 'new' and 'old' social movements, as well as the different strategies they employ. The changing political opportunities include the level of repression in a political system, the variable provision of individual rights, and different sets of elite alignments. These studies use both quantitative and qualitative techniques to marshal the comparative evidence on movement activity. Overall, more comparative work on the nature and impact of social movement activity is needed, as this alternative form of politics will continue to be important.

Initially, democratization studies compared few countries and focused on uncertain outcomes of elite manoeuvring at critical moments of crisis during periods of authoritarian rule. More recently, studies have taken into account the nature of the prior regime, fundamental questions of 'stateness' (Linz and Stepan 1996), the political economy of the transition, and important international influences. Like the early studies of political violence and revolution, many of these studies suffer from selection bias as they focus on those countries that have made a democratic transition rather than comparing them to those that have not. While Linz and Stepan (1996) seek to redress this problem by looking at clusters of transitions and non-transitions, they introduce many other explanatory variables that create the problem of indeterminacy. In other words, their study does not quite overcome the problem of 'too many variables not enough countries' [...]. As in the study of political violence and revolution, it is important to compare successful transitions to unsuccessful transitions across a sufficient number of cases to identify the key factors that help explain the process of democratic transition. Clearly, Bratton and van de Walle (1997) adopt just such a strategy within the geographical region of sub-Saharan Africa. By comparing 42 countries that experienced successful, unsuccessful, and flawed democratic transitions, they are able to combine historical analysis with quantitative analysis to draw larger inferences about the domestic political factors that help account for democratic experiments in the region.

The few-country studies on institutional design and democratic performance do not conflict with the global comparisons, but complement their findings with a more intensive examination of the features of presidential systems that may or may not inhibit their overall performance. These comparisons provide a differentiation of presidential systems themselves to demonstrate that both strong presidential systems and those with multiple political party systems tend to have more problems than those with significant limits on presidential power and a small set of strong political parties. Thus, the generalizations made by the many-country comparisons warrant further investigation with a smaller set of countries. In this regard, Jones' (1995) study complements the global comparisons in examining the key differences among the presidential systems of Latin America. His study uses the most similar systems design since he compares countries with similar cultural and historical legacies and similar institutional arrangements. The many- and few-country comparisons of electoral systems complement one another since the general rule that proportional electoral systems tend to have multiparty systems identified by the global comparisons also holds in the comparisons of a smaller sample of countries. Moreover, it is precisely these types of electoral system that produce some of the major problems for the presidential systems examined in the few-country studies.

The comparative study of human rights protection using a smaller selection of countries allows scholars to focus on different topics of research such as transnational influences on state behaviour and the relative successes of truth commissions. Paired comparisons of problematic countries showed to some degree that pressure from above and below can change state behaviour and lead to greater protection of human rights as a rule-consistent culture and a new set of rights-protective institutions become established. Despite the noble impulse for establishing truth, the process of truth-telling is fraught with political complexities involving the negotiated withdrawal from power of military elites in the case of Latin American TCs and ethnic or racial tensions in the African TCs, and more comparative research is needed on why countries adopt truth commissions, and if they do, why particular models of truth commissions are used.

Finally, the few-country comparisons on the market for rebellion and the quest for supranational constraints on state behaviour show that domestic actors frequently look to the international system to provide solutions to their problems. Bob's (2005) study is consistent with the resource mobilization perspective in the literature on social movements, which argues that grievance is everywhere, the key question is to examine how social movements make *their* particular grievance the one that becomes taken up by supporters. Using this logic and applying it at the international level shows that movement entrepreneurs do not need to isolate their strategies within the domestic context. By using strategies of awareness raising and framing that match the aims of objectives of international organizations, social movements and insurgencies can garner much needed international support. Equally, Moravcsik (2000) shows how those domestic actors who worried about the sustainability of their nascent democratic institutions demonstrated a strong set of preferences for a supranational regime of human rights with provisions for enforcement in ways that were different from those actors in more secure democracies or in dictatorships and semi-democracies.

Methodologically, the biggest weakness in few-country comparisons is the problem of selection bias, particularly when the choice of countries relies on the outcome that is to be explained. For example, by including more countries from Europe in their study of capitalist development and democracy, Rueschemeyer *et al.* (1992) find that a violent break with the past is not an important factor for democracy, which contradicts Moore's (1966) findings. In addition, the extension of their study beyond Europe into Latin America and the Caribbean reveals that it is the working class, and not the bourgeoisie as Moore (1966) contends, that is the key agent for democracy. Whether the inclusion of Moore's (1966) cases of China and Japan would have altered the conclusions of Rueschemeyer *et al.* (1992) remains an empirical question; however, it appears that the inclusion of more countries in similar regions provides different substantive conclusions about the relationship between capitalist development and democracy.

Similar selection effects are apparent in the studies on violent political dissent and revolution. Skocpol (1979), Wickham-Crowley (1993), and Parsa (2000) variously include positive, negative, and mixed instances of revolutionary activity at different periods of time in providing more robust accounts of revolution than offered by Wolf (1969). Indeed, the most Wolf does is to identify the presence of a single explanatory factor across six countries that have experienced revolution. In contrast, Wickham-Crowley (1993) and Parsa (2000) demonstrate the key factors for successful revolution as well as account for the failure of many revolutionary attempts in their cases. Thus in both research areas, Moore (1966) and Wolf (1969) select countries based on values of the dependent variable, while Rueschemeyer *et al.* (1992), Skocpol (1979), Wickham-Crowley (1993), and Parsa (2000) select countries based on other criteria. Moore (1966) chooses particular examples of democratic, fascist, and communist outcomes, while Wolf (1969) chooses instances of revolutionary outcomes only. Rueschemeyer *et al.* (1992), Skocpol (1979), Wickham-Crowley (1993), and Parsa (2000) choose countries on regional, cultural, and historical similarity while the outcome they are trying to explain—democracy or revolution—varies. Brockett (2005) adopted a similar strategy in comparing mobilization under repressive conditions in Guatemala and El Salvador. Bob (2005) compares successful and unsuccessful cases of challenger groups and Moravcsik (2000) compares countries that supported the European regime with enforcement provision to those that did not.

Single-Country Studies

By definition, there is great variation in results among the single-country studies. [...] [S]tudies are useful for comparative analysis if they make explicit use of comparative concepts or generate new concepts for application in countries beyond the original study. Such studies can generate hypotheses, infirm and confirm existing theories, allow for the intensive examination of deviant cases identified by larger comparisons, and be a useful way for conducting process tracing and uncovering causal mechanisms implied by the results of studies with a larger number of countries. Single-country studies, however well intentioned and well designed, have serious difficulty in making generalizations that are applicable at the global level. Two of the studies [...] clearly establish a relationship between economic development and democracy (Argentina and South Korea), while three of them (Italy, Botswana, and India) find political culture to be an important intervening explanatory factor for the development of democracy. Thus for Italy, a certain 'civicness' explains good democratic performance. In Botswana, the presence of Tswana political culture inhibits the development of democracy beyond its formal components. The persistence of the caste system in India has meant that modern democracy is still embedded in traditional identities. Thus, closer attention to the historical and cultural specificities of individual countries enriches the understanding of the relationship between economic development and democracy, which may be lost in larger comparisons.

The three case studies on rural rebellion in Mexico show a certain consensus that, among other factors, the historical encroachment on land and lifestyle by outside agents has spurred on rebellious activity from the period of the Mexican Revolution to the latest peasant-based uprising from the Zapatistas in the southern state of Chiapas. Like the studies that compare many countries, the inference from these studies is that the encroachment and displacement of people whose livelihood is derived from land increase the likelihood that they will participate in rebellious and revolutionary activity. This inference is in line with Paige's (1975) comparison of agricultural sectors in 70 countries and it fits well with the types of explanation for rural rebellion offered by Wickham-Crowley (1993). Future single-country studies on rebellion and revolution can test whether the inferences from the Mexican case can be upheld in other contexts.

The single-country studies on social movements demonstrate how changing political opportunities interact with movement activity, as well as how the time-dependent dynamics of social movements can be described as a 'cycle of protest' (Tarrow 1989). The studies of social movements in the United States (Gamson 1975; Costain 1992) both show that protest activity can win concessions from the state. To compensate for some of the limits of the single-country study, both authors, like Tarrow (1989), raise the number of observations to provide greater variance [...]. Gamson (1975) compares the activities and outcomes of over 50 social movement organizations, while Costain (1992) uses time-series indicators of social movement activity, government activity, and shifting patterns of public opinion. This greater variance allows both authors to make important inferences about social movement activity and political impact from a single country.

The quest to understand democratic transition has in large part been driven by studies of individual countries that have undergone such processes since 1974. Two of the studies compared in Part II demonstrate elite and popular struggle perspectives on transition. Colomer and Pascual (1994) develop a game theory model of transition, which is applied to the Polish case. The history of the transition is seen as a series of sequential games 'played' by the key political actors of the period. The strength of the analysis lies in the identification of all the outcomes possible from a combination of 'moves' by the players. Democratic transition is thus seen not as an inevitable outcome, but as one of many outcomes. In the Polish case, the authors demonstrate that democracy was indeed the outcome, yet their model is specified in such a way that it can be applied to other countries. Foweraker (1989) offers a more comprehensive analysis of the democratic transformation of Spanish civil society that preceded the moment of transition. Less attention is paid to elite political actors as the study focuses on the everyday activities of workers as they attempt to contest power through various representative organizations. Like Colomer and Pascual (1994), Foweraker's inferences concerning incremental struggle under conditions of authoritarian rule have application to countries other than Spain, but we saw that the inferences made to the end of the Cold War in the Portuguese study were slightly overdrawn.

Finally, the exclusive focus on the problem of divided government in the United States shows that across a range of conflict and legislative measures, the simultaneous control of the presidency and Congress by different political parties does not appear to make a difference. Even though the post-war period in US political history has seen more years of divided government, the volume of legislation and level of conflict between the executive and legislature have remained unchanged. The global comparison of presidential and parliamentary democracies reveals a certain democratic weakness in presidential democracies and the few-country studies demonstrate that strong presidentialism combined with multiple political parties is particularly problematic. The case of the United States appears to be an outlier to the general rule established by the global comparisons and falls well within the expectations of the few-country comparisons. It is one case where a presidential system does not seem to inhibit democratic performance and it is one case where strong presidentialism combined with a weak two-party system functions.

The single-country studies on human rights [...] reveal many things about the strengths and weaknesses of the various regimes for the protection of human rights. The case of Argentina [...] showed the limits of the UN and Inter-American systems at the time to address the grave concerns over gross human rights violations carried out during the 'dirty war' (1976–1982), while at the same time showing the resilience of civil society within Argentina to bring about significant transformations before and after the democratic transitions. The case of Chile [...] showed that mobilization from global actors aligned with domestic actors brought about a certain capitulation among the hardliners in the regime to begin a process of political liberalization, while the Pinochet case itself illustrates how international actors seized the political opportunity in the late 1990s to invoke the principle of universal jurisdiction to seek extradition of a former head of state to face a foreign court for crimes against humanity. The impact of the arrest, detention, and return of Pinochet to Chile in many ways emboldened his domestic opponents, whose legal actions resulted in a stripping of immunity and his eventual death under house arrest.

Building Theory

The book has throughout intentionally avoided a direct and full discussion of empirical political theory since it has sought to examine how different comparative methods contribute to theory-building. It also takes the view, contrary to some authors, that there is not a distinctive set of comparative theories (see Chilcote 1994). Rather, there is a collection of research problems that is best addressed through some form of comparison, which in turn helps build our theoretical understandings of the world. Cumulatively, the studies in Part II make contributions to theories that span a wide range of different perspectives. In a seminal piece on the contribution of comparative politics to social theory, Mark Lichbach (1997) delimits the following three broad theoretical perspectives and 'research communities' that have emerged in the field of comparative politics: (1) rationalist, (2) structuralist, and (3) culturalist. Each of these approaches has different assumptions about how the world 'works' and which aspects of the world deserve attention in order to understand and explain observed political phenomena. A short outline of each of these approaches is warranted before considering the ways in which the studies [...] have contributed to them.

Rationalist perspectives concentrate on the actions and behaviour of individuals who make reasoned and intentional choices based upon sets of preferences, or interests. Those who adhere to the rationalist perspective are 'concerned with the collective processes and outcomes that follow from intentionality, or the social consequences of individually rational action' (Lichbach 1997:246). Moreover, rationalists in political science believe 'that "bed rock" explanations of social phenomena should build upwards from the beliefs and goals of individuals' (Ward 1995:79). The development of the rationalist perspective followed earlier individual theories that emphasize the non-rational aspects of human behaviour such as grievance and relative deprivation (see the discussion of Gurr 1968 [...]). In contrast to these earlier individual theories, rationalists claim that grievance alone is not enough to explain political action and that real choices at the individual level must be examined. While both perspectives concentrate on individual political behaviour, rationalists look for the intentional and 'means-ends' features of individual choice.

In contrast to the rationalist (and other individual) perspective(s), culturalist perspectives seek an understanding of political phenomena by focusing on the broader holistic and shared aspects of collectivities of individuals. Single individual interests and actions cannot be understood in isolation, but must be placed in the context of the shared understandings, inter-subjective relationships, and mutual orientations that make human communities possible (Lichbach 1997:246–247). These shared meanings and understandings form broader cultures and communities that can be grouped together and analysed as whole units. Such cultures and communities are held together by certain social rules that are emblematic of the identities of both the individuals and the groups themselves (ibid.: 247). Identifying the boundaries of these cultural units and separate identities remains problematic for systematic comparative research; however, scholars have tried to examine the worldviews, rituals, and symbols that provide 'systems of meaning and the structure and intensity of political identity' across different geographical regions of the world (Ross 1997:43–44). Structuralists also focus on the holistic aspects of politics, but unlike the culturalists, they focus on the interdependent relationships among individuals, collectivities, institutions, or organizations. They are interested in the social, political, and economic networks that form between and among individuals. Adherents to this perspective insist that structures that have become reified over time constrain or facilitate political activity so that individual actors are not completely free agents capable of determining particular political outcomes (Lichbach 1997:247–248). Rather, individuals are embedded in relational structures that shape human identities, interests, and interaction. These relational structures have evolved owing to large historical processes such as capitalist development, market rationality, nation state building, political and scientific revolutions, and technological progress (Katznelson 1997:83). These large historical processes, it is argued, provide both possibilities and limits for human action.

Together, these three perspectives have variously sought to account for political phenomena in the world by emphasizing and examining key explanatory factors that adhere to the assumptions of their theories. Thus, rationalists focus on the interests and actions of individuals, culturalists focus on the ideas and norms of human communities, and structuralists focus on the institutions and relationships that constrain and facilitate political activity. These theoretical perspectives are not mutually exclusive, however, since scholars have examined the ways in which the interaction between and among the three perspectives helps explain certain outcomes. There are only very rare instances of work in comparative politics that rely exclusively on one of the three perspectives.[1] The comparative methods in this book have all been used to marshal evidence in support of these perspectives virtually across the range of research topics. With the exception of [...] institutional design and democratic performance, which by definition focuses exclusively on the functions and effects of democratic institutions, the studies in all the other chapters contribute to individual, structural, and cultural theories of politics.

Moreover, the discussions [...] address rational, structural and cultural theories of international relations. The chapter on human rights shows how the normative principles of human rights have been embodied through international law, which uses the inter-state treaty system to govern state–citizens relations at the domestic level, and that the force of the law and the 'power of human rights' (Risse *et al.* 1999) challenges the main tenets of realism, which is in effect a rationalist account of state behaviour in the international arena. Indeed, while rational choice theory has been branded 'methodological individualism' (Przeworski 1985) at the domestic level, realism has been branded 'methodological nationalism' at the international level (Zürn 2002). The democratic peace found in Russett and O'Neal (2001) and liberal republicanism in Moravcsik (2000) focus our attention on democratic institutions and democratic values in ways that demonstrate their impact on inter-state relations. While these variables would be labelled structuralist and culturalist at the domestic level, the international relations literature uses the terms neo-liberal institutionalist and social contructivist, respectively (see e.g. Wendt 1999; Keohane 2001; Carlsnaes, Risse and Simmons 2002; Landman 2005b).

Table 1.2.1 summarizes the studies [...] with reference to their location across individual, structural, and cultural theories of empirical political science and international relations. The first column in the table lists the research topics of each chapter while the remaining columns represent the three theoretical perspectives. Individual theories include the older

TABLE 1.2.1   Empirical Theories of Political Science and International Relations: Topics and Examples From Part II

Topics	Individual/States (interests and actions)	Structuralist (institutions and relationships)	Culturalist (ideas and norms)
	↕	↕	↕
[...]			
Economic development and democracy	Boix (2003) Boix and Stokes (2003)	Lipset (1959) Cutright (1963) Moore (1966) Neubauer (1967) Cutright & Wiley (1969) Dahl (1971) Jackman (1973) Bollen (1979) Waisman (1989) Helliwell (1994) Burkhart & Lewis-Beck (1994) Przeworski et al. (2000) Rueschemeyer et al. (1992) Landman (1999) Mainwaring and Perez-Liñan (2003)	Lerner (1958) De Schweinitz (1964) Putnam (1993a) Holm (1996) Moon & Kim (1996) Kaviraj (1996)
[...]			
Violent political dissent and social revolution	Womack (1969) Gurr (1968) Hibbs (1973) Sigelman & Simpson (1977) Muller & Seligson (1987) Nugent (1993) Parsa (2000) Brockett (2005)	Wolf (1969) Hibbs (1973) Paige (1975) Skocpol (1979) Parsa (2000) Brockett (2005)	Hibbs (1973) Scott (1976) Wickham-Crowley (1993) Nugent (1993) Harvey (1998) Harvey (1998) Parsa (2000)

TABLE 1.2.1 (Continued)

Topics	Individual/States (interests and actions)	Structuralist (institutions and relationships)	Culturalist (ideas and norms)
[...] Non-violent political dissent and social movements	Gamson (1975)	Dalton (1988) Tarrow (1989) Costain (1992) Gurr (1993) Foweraker & Landman (1997) Bashevkin (1998) ↕	Powell (1982) Haas & Stack (1983) Kitschelt (1986) Kriesi et al. (1995)	Gurr (1993) Inglehart (1997) Inglehart and Welzel (2005) ↕
[...] Transitions to democracy	Colomer & Pascual (1994)	O'Donnell et al. (1986a–c) Foweraker (1989) Peeler (1992) Maxwell (1995) Linz & Stepan (1996) Bratton and van de Walle (1997)	Jaggers & Gurr (1995) Linz & Stepan (1996) Vanhanen (1997) Bratton and van de Walle (1997) Doorenspleet (2005)	Huntington (1991) Linz & Stepan (1996) Doorenspleet (2005)
[...] Institutional design and democratic performance		Shugart and Carey (1992) Mayhew (1993) Peterson & Greene (1993) Stepan & Skach (1993) Lijphart (1994a) Lijphart (1994b) Jones (1995) Mainwaring and Scully (1995) Fiorina (1996)	

(continued)

TABLE 1.2.1 *(Continued)*

Topics	Individual/States (interests and actions)		Structuralist (institutions and relationships)		Culturalist (ideas and norms)	
[...]						
Human rights		$\leftrightarrow$	Strouse and Claude (1976) Mitchell and McCormick (1988) Poe and Tate (1994) Poe et al. (1999) Zanger (2000) Hayner (1994, 2002) Risse et al. (1999) De Brito (1997) Guest (1990) Weissbrodt and Bartolomei (1991) Brysk (1994a)	$\leftrightarrow$	Hayner (1994) Risse et al. (1999) De Brito (1997) Brysk (1994a) Keith (1999) Hathaway (2002) Landman (2005b) Hafner-Burton and Tsutsui (2005, 2007) Neumayer (2005)	
					Hayner (1994, 2002) Risse et al. (1999) De Brito (1997) Guest (1990) Weissbrodt and Bartolomei (1991) Brysk (1994a)	
[...]						
International relations and comparative politics	Russet and O'Neal (2001) Bob (2005) Moravcsik (2000) Hawkins (2002)		Li and Reuveny (2003) Russet and O'Neal (2001)		Li and Reuveny (2003) Russet and O'Neal (2001) Bob (2005) Moravcsik (2000) Hawkins (2002) Sands (2005)	

theories that focus on grievances and deprivation as well as the newer rational choice theories that focus on preferences and interests, and also the realist perspective in international relations. The structuralist column refers to the presence of broad socio-economic changes, the development of key institutions, the relational structures in which individuals are embedded, and supranational institutions. The culturalist column concerns the importance of ideas, shared understandings, and accepted norms and rules for behaviour at the domestic and international levels. The arrows between the main columns capture the notion that many studies seek to examine the interplay between these different theories.

The studies on the relationship between economic development and democracy are located in the cells extending from the structuralist to the culturalist approaches. The studies focus on the broad socio-economic changes and processes of modernization that were accompanied by changes in class structure, class alliances, the nature and power of the state, as well as the impact of transnational structures of power. In addition these studies imply, or in some cases state explicitly, that the development of democracy also depends on the formation of a sustainable political culture that emphasizes tolerance and promotes democratic norms. While earlier studies suggested that this political culture would be fomented by an emerging middle class, later studies recognize the importance of the working class in its role as an agent for democratic inclusion. In either case, these studies examine the interaction between broad structural changes and the development of political culture.

The studies on violent political dissent and revolution are located around the middle columns of the table since they seek to explain these political phenomena with a combination of individual and structural theories on the one hand and structural and cultural theories on the other. For example, Wolf's (1969) study shows that capitalist transformation of agriculture is a structural change that produces grievance among a particular set of rural cultivators who then become involved in revolutionary activity. Scott (1976) argues that similar structural changes transformed the moral economy and the culture of reciprocity that had become a key feature of the peasant communities in Burma and Vietnam. Parsa (2000), on the other hand, is quite explicit that structural variables alone cannot account for the differences between social and political revolution that he observes across Iran, Nicaragua, and the Philippines. Hibbs' (1973) comprehensive set of explanatory variables captures a whole range of individual, structural, and cultural concepts. Brockett (2005) relies primarily on the concept of political opportunity structure, which as its name implies, is a structural variable that helped explain the different patterns of peasant mobilization across his two countries.

The comparative studies [...] are equally located in the middle columns as they seek to explain the origins, trajectory, and impact of social movements. All three theoretical perspectives have been used to explain the origin of social movement activity. Rationalists examine the key incentives that may or may not lead individuals to join a social movement. Structuralists look at long-term socio-economic fluctuations and the changing set of opportunities for social protest and political transformation. Culturalists are concerned with the changing nature of collective identities and how these identities provide the shared understanding and common will necessary for sustained political mobilization. The studies that combine these rational and structural theories (column four) look at how individual and collective behaviour in social movements is facilitated or constrained by broader structural changes, while those that combine structural and cultural theories (column five) examine how new values and identities form from broader structural changes.

The initial quest to understand democratic transition centred on the strategic interaction of elites and thus primarily adopted a rationalist perspective. Colomer and Pascual's (1994) application of game theory is a classic example of a strong rationalist effort to explain the democratic transition in Poland. Other elite-centred accounts such as those found in O'Donnell *et al.* (1986a, 1986b) examine the ways in which changing structural conditions lead to opportunities for 'hard-liners' and 'soft-liners' within the authoritarian regime to manoeuvre for political advantage. Popular struggle perspectives, on the other hand, are concerned with the opportunities for social mobilization and democratic transformation that are provided by changing structural conditions. Thus, Bratton and van de Walle's (1997) study of Africa and Foweraker's (1989) study of Spain equally examine the relationship between structure and agency in accounting for democratic transition. Finally, studies that adopt culturalist explanations examine patterns of democratic 'habituation' and the acceptance of rules and democratic norms, as well as the cross-national diffusion of democratic ideas. The global studies on democratic transition identify a variety of structural and cultural variables, including Huntington's (1991) economic development and 'Catholic' effects and Doorenspleet's (2005) economic and democratic diffusion variables.

As mentioned above, the studies on institutional design and democratic performance necessarily ground themselves in structural explanations since they examine the ways in which formal institutions of democracy (e.g. parties, electoral systems, presidential versus parliamentary systems) structure the activities of key political actors. This structuring of action has immediate implications for democratic performance. The studies [...] suggest that the nexus between structure and agency can have direct effects on governance. For example, strong presidents facing multiple parties in the legislature may find it difficult to bring about new legislation or may face recurring governmental gridlock, which can have adverse effects on democratic performance, particularly in new democracies. Indeed, Stepan and Skach (1993) argue that presidents facing such constraints may flout the constitution, seek extra-constitutional means to achieve their objectives, and even encourage military intervention, particularly in countries with a past history of such intervention.

Finally, even though the study of human rights is inspired by normative concerns for human well-being and human dignity, global comparisons in this research area are very similar to the studies on economic development and democracy in identifying broad structural factors that help account for the protection of human rights. While they do control for regional differences and historical legacies such as British colonial influence, the primary focus is on socio-economic variables and differences in political institutions. But as the studies move down the level of abstraction, greater attention is paid to the interaction between structure and agency, as well as the importance of the diffusion of human rights norms transmitted by transnational advocacy networks. Thus the few-country and single-country studies on human rights incorporate a wider range of theoretical concepts from the rationalist and culturalist perspectives while remaining sensitive to the structural and institutional constraints faced by states.

The chapter on human rights crosses over all the theoretical traditions and addresses those at the international level in some degree. The global comparative studies by and large included an array of socio-economic and structural variables to explain the cross-national variation in the protection of human rights, while the latter set of studies on the impact of international law examined the role that international institutions play in constraining the actions of states at the domestic level. The few-country comparisons, in particular the paired comparisons found in Risse *et al.* (1999) address the rational, cultural, and structural dimensions of domestic and international mobilization surrounding violations of human rights. The spiral model itself combines attention to the ways in which the socialization of norms can have an impact on state behaviour, especially when those norms are combined with agency at the domestic and international levels.

Finally, it is clear that the studies [...] illustrate similar kinds of crossover of these theoretical perspectives at the domestic and international levels. The analysis of the impact of globalization on democracy included both the structural aspects of globalization (flows of trade, capital, and finance) as well as its cultural dimension in terms of the diffusion of democracy (see also Doorenspleet 2005). The democratic peace is a proposition informed by structural and cultural theories of politics. As Rosato (2003) aptly points out, the underlying causal logic of the democratic peace proposition involves the normative and institutional constraints on democracies in their ability to wage war, which arguably reduces the probability of democracies fighting one another and other states. The mobilization of challenger groups in search of international support is rational in terms of the market analysis, but also cultural in its attention to raising awareness, framing, and matching the aims and objectives of potential international supporters. Finally, it is clear that the Chilean case in all its complexity reveals the interplay between international norms, political opportunities, and rational calculation at the domestic and international level.

Conclusion: Drawing the Lessons

This review of over 80 comparative studies across a range of different methods, techniques, and substantive topics shows both the trade-offs associated with conducting comparative research as well as the valuable contribution to theory that such studies can make. From this review and analysis, the following four key factors are important for scholars to bear in mind when embarking on comparative research: the research problem, case selection, inferential aspirations, and theorizing. First, since there is no one comparative method that is superior to another, it is important to remember that in most cases, the research problem is intimately linked to the method adopted. Second, case selection significantly affects the answers that are obtained to the research questions that are posed (cf. Geddes 1990). Both the actual countries in the sample and the number of countries that comprise it can lead to different results. In order to make stronger inferences, the rule of thumb for political science method is to raise the number of observations (King *et al.* 1994), which for comparative politics means either a larger sample of countries or more observations within a smaller sample of countries.

Third, the substantive conclusions and inferential aspirations of a particular comparative study should not go too far beyond the scope of its sample. A single-country study of democratic transition may provide some important inferences that can be examined in countries with a similar set of circumstances but it does not provide a universal set of inferences for democratic transition in general. A study of social mobilization under authoritarian rule can make inferences relevant to social mobilization in other countries under similar conditions of authoritarian rule. On the other hand, a study of social movement activity under democratic rule cannot make inferences about such activity under authoritarian rule [...]. Many-country studies may have universal aspirations yet must remain sensitive to the fact that there are exceptions to every rule. In short, comparative scholars must recognize the limits of their own enterprise in making generalizations about the political world they observe.

Finally, comparativists ought to spend more time on careful theorizing and research design. Once the assumptions of a theory are established and the observable implications of that theory are identified, then the research can be designed in such a way to provide the best set of comparisons given the available resources. Careful theorizing about political events and political outcomes will lead scholars to compare similar outcomes in different cases, or different outcomes in similar cases. The differences and similarities that are identified through comparison help provide an explanation for the outcomes themselves. Together, problem specification, case selection, self-limiting inferential aspirations, and careful theorizing provide the foundation for comparative politics. What remains to be examined are the new issues, new methods, and new challenges that are confronting the field. It is to these issues that the final chapter turns.

Note

1. There are exceptions to this rule for each perspective. For the rationalist perspective, see for example Bates' (1989) study of the political economy of Kenya, Tsebelis' (1990) study of European political behaviour, and Geddes' (1991, 1994) work on state reform in Latin America. For the structural perspective, see Luebbert's (1991) study of regime origins in inter-war Europe and Poulantzas' (1976) study of dictatorships in Greece, Spain, and Portugal. For the cultural perspective, see Scott's (1985) study of peasant resistance in Malaysia and his comparison of Burma and Vietnam (Scott 1976) [...].

References

Bashevkin, S. (1998) *Women on the Defensive: Living through Conservative Times*, Chicago: University of Chicago Press.

Bates, G. (1989) *Beyond the Market: The Political Economy of Agrarian Development in Kenya*, Cambridge: Cambridge University Press.

Bob, C. (2005) *The Marketing of Rebellion: Insurgents, Media, and International Activism*, Cambridge: Cambridge University Press.

Boix, C. (2003) *Democracy and Redistribution*, Cambridge: Cambridge University Press.

Boix, C. and Stokes, S. (2003) 'Endogenous Democratization', *World Politics*, 55 (July): 517–49.

Bollen, K. (1979) 'Political Democracy and the Timing of Development', *American Sociological Review*, 44 (August): 572–587.

Bratton, M. and van de Walle, N. (1997) *Democratic Experiments in Africa: Regime Transitions in Comparative Perspective*, Cambridge: Cambridge University Press.

Brockett, C. (2005) *Political Movements and Violence in Central America*, Cambridge: Cambridge University Press.

Brysk, A. (1994a) *The Politics of Human Rights in Argentina: Protest, Change, and Democratization*, Stanford, CA: Stanford University Press.

Burkhart, R.E. and Lewis-Beck, M. (1994) 'Comparative Democracy, the Economic Development Thesis', *American Political Science Review*, 88(4): 903–910.

Carlsnaes, W., Risse, T., and Simmons, B. (2002) *Handbook of International Relations*, London: Sage.

Chilcote, R.H. (1994) *Theories of Comparative Politics: The Search for a Paradigm Reconsidered*, 2nd edn, Boulder, CO: Westview Press.

Colomer, J.M. and Pascual, M. (1994) 'The Polish Games of Transition', *Communist and Post-communist Studies*, 27(3): 275–294.

Costain, A.N. (1992) *Inviting Women's Rebellion: A Political Process Interpretation of the Women's Movement*, Baltimore, MD: Johns Hopkins University Press.

Cutright, P. (1963) 'National Political Development: Its Measurement and Social Correlates', in N. Polsby, R.A. Denther, and P.A. Smith (eds) *Political and Social Life*, Boston, MA: Houghton Mifflin, 569–582.

Cutright, P. and Wiley, J.A. (1969) 'Modernization and Political Representation: 1927–1966', *Studies in Comparative International Development*, 5(2): 23–44.

Dahl, R.A. (1971) *Polyarchy: Participation and Opposition*, New Haven, CT: Yale University Press.

Dalton, R. (1988) *Citizen Politics in Western Democracies*, Chatham, NJ: Chatham House Publishers.

De Brito, A.B. (1997) *Human Rights and Democratization in Latin America: Uruguay and Chile*, Oxford: Oxford University Press.

De Schweinitz, K. (1964) *Industrialization and Democracy: Economic Necessities and Political Possibilities*, New York: Free Press.

Doorenspleet, R. (2005) *Democratic Transitions: Exploring the Structural Sources of the Fourth Wave*, Boulder, CO: Lynne Rienner.

Fiorina, M.P. (1996) *Divided Goverment*, 2nd edn, Needham Heights, MA: Simon & Schuster.

Foweraker, J. (1989) *Making Democracy in Spain: Grassroots Struggle in the South, 1955–1975*, Cambridge: Cambridge University Press.

Foweraker, J. and Landman, T. (1997) *Citizenship Rights and Social Movements: A Comparative and Statistical Analysis*, Oxford: Oxford University Press.

Gamson, W.A. (1975) *The Strategy of Social Protest*, Homewood, IL: Dorsey Press.

Geddes, B. (1990) 'How the Cases You Choose Affect the Answers You Get: Selection Bias in Comparative Politics', *Political Analysis*, 2: 131–150.

——(1991) 'A Game Theoretic Model of Reform in Latin American Democracies', *American Political Science Review*, 85 (June): 371–392.

——(1994) *Politician's Dilemma: Building State Capacity in Latin America*, Berkeley and Los Angeles: University of California Press.

Guest, I. (1990) *Behind the Disappearances: Argentina's Dirty War Against Human Rights and the United Nations*, Philadelphia: The University of Pennsylvania Press.

Gurr, T.R. (1968) 'A Causal Model of Civil Strife', *American Political Science Review*, 62: 1104–1124.

——(1993) 'Why Minorities Rebel: A Global Analysis of Communal Mobilization and Conflict since 1945', *International Political Science Review*, 14(2): 161–201.

Haas, M. and Stack, S. (1983) 'Economic Development and Strikes: A Comparative Analysis', *The Sociological Quarterly*, 24 (Winter): 43–58.

Hafner-Burton, E.M. and Tsutsui, K. (2005) 'Human Rights in a Globalizing World: The Paradox of Empty Promises', *American Journal of Sociology*, 110(5): 1373–1411.

Harvey, N. (1998) *The Chiapas Rebellion: The Struggle for Land and Democracy*, Raleigh, NC: Duke University Press.

Hathaway, O. (2002) 'Do Treaties Make a Difference? Human Rights Treaties and the Problem of Compliance', *Yale Law Journal*, 111: 1932–2042.

Hawkins, D. (2002) *International Human Rights and Authoritarian Rule in Chile*, Lincoln, NB: University of Nebraska Press.

Hayner, P.B. (1994) 'Fifteen Truth Commissions—1974–1994: A Comparative Study', *Human Rights Quarterly*, 16: 597–655.

_____(2002) *Unspeakable Truths: Facing the Challenge of Truth Commissions*, London: Routledge.

Helliwell, J.F. (1994) 'Empirical Linkages between Democracy and Economic Growth', *British Journal of Political Science*, 24: 225–248.

Hertel, S. Minkler, L., and Wilson, R.A. (2007) *Economic Rights: Conceptual, Measurement, and Policy Issues*, Cambridge: Cambridge University Press.

Hibbs, D. (1973) *Mass Political Violence: A Cross-national Causal Analysis*, New York: Wiley.

Holm, J.D. (1996) 'Development, Democracy, and Civil Society in Botswana', in A. Leftwich (ed.) *Democracy and Development*, Cambridge: Polity Press, 97–113.

Huntington, S.P. (1991) *The Third Wave: Democratization in the Late Twentieth Century*, Norman, OK: University of Oklahoma Press.

Inglehart, R. (1997) *Modernization and Postmodernization*, Princeton, NJ: Princeton University Press.

Inglehart, R. and Welzel, C. (2005) *Modernization, Cultural Change, and Democracy: The Human Development Sequence*, Cambridge: Cambridge University Press.

Jackman, R.W. (1973) 'On the Relation of Economic Development to Democratic Performance', *American Journal of Political Science*, 17(3): 611–621.

Jaggers, K. and Gurr, T.R. (1995) 'Tracking Democracy's Third Wave with the Polity III Data', *Journal of Peace Research*, 32(4): 469–482.

Jones, M.P. (1995) *Electoral Laws and the Survival of Presidential Democracies*, Notre Dame, IN: University of Notre Dame Press.

Katznelson, I. (1997) 'Structure and Configuration in Comparative Politics', in M. Lichbach and A. Zuckerman (eds) *Comparative Politics: Rationality, Culture, and Structure*, Cambridge: Cambridge University Press, 81–112.

Kaviraj, S. (1996) 'Dilemmas of Democratic Development in India', in A. Leftwich (ed.) *Democracy and Development*, Cambridge: Polity Press, 114–138.

Keith, L.C. (1999) 'The United Nations International Covenant on Civil and Political Rights: Does it Make a Difference in Human Rights Behavior?' *Journal of Peace Research*, 36(1): 95–118.

Keohane, R. (1984) *After Hegemony: Cooperation and Discord in World Political Economy*, Princeton, NJ: Princeton University Press.

King, G., Keohane, R.O., and Verba, S. (1994) *Designing Social Inquiry: Scientific Inference in Qualitative Research*, Princeton, NJ: Princeton University Press.

Kitschelt, H. (1986) 'Political Opportunity Structures and Political Protest: Anti-nuclear Movements in Four Democracies', *British Journal of Political Science*, 16 (January): 57–85.

Kriesi, H., Koopmans, R., Duyvendak, J.W., and Giugni, M.G. (1995) *New Social Movements in Western Europe*, London: UCL Press.

Landman, T. (1999) 'Economic Development and Democracy: The View from Latin America', *Political Studies*, 47(4): 607–626.

——(2005b) *Protecting Human Rights: A Global Comparative Study*, Washington DC: Georgetown University Press.

Lerner, D. (1958) *The Passing of Traditional Society: Modernizing the Middle East*, Glencoe, IL: The Free Press of Glencoe.

Li, Q. and Reuveny, R. (2003) 'Economic Globalization and Democracy: An Empirical Analysis', *British Journal of Political Science*, 33: 29–54.

Lichbach, M. (1997) 'Social Theory and Comparative Politics', in M. Lichbach and A. Zuckerman (eds) *Comparative Politics: Rationality, Culture, and Structure*, Cambridge: Cambridge University Press, 239–276.

Lijphart, A. (1994a) *Electoral Systems and Party Systems: A Study of Twenty-seven Democracies, 1945–1990*, Oxford: Oxford University Press.

——(1994b) 'Democracies: Forms, Performance, and Constitutional Engineering', *European Journal of Political Research*, 25:1–17.

Linz, J.J. and Stepan, A. (1996) *Problems of Democratic Transition and Consolidation: South America, Southern Europe, and Post-Communist Europe*, Baltimore, MD: Johns Hopkins University Press.

Lipset, S.M. (1959) 'Some Social Requisites for Democracy: Economic Development and Political Legitimacy', *The American Political Science Review*, 53: 69–105.

Luebbert, G. (1991) *Liberalism, Fascism, or Social Democracy: Social Classes and the Political Origins of Regimes in Inter-war Europe*, New York: Oxford University Press.

Mainwaring, S. and Perez-Liñan (2003) 'Level of Development and Democracy: Latin-American Exceptionalism, 1945–1966', *Comparative Political Studies* 36(9): 1031–1067.

Mainwaring, S. and Scully, T.R. (1995) 'Introduction: Party Systems in Latin America', in S. Mainwaring and T.R. Scully (eds) *Building Democratic Institutions: Party Systems in Latin America*, Stanford, CA: Stanford University Press, 1–34.

Maxwell, K. (1995) *The Making of Portuguese Democracy*, Cambridge: Cambridge University Press.

Mayhew, D. (1993) *Divided We Govern: Party Control, Lawmaking, and Investigations, 1946–1990*, New Haven, CT: Yale University Press.

Mitchell, N.J. and McCormick, J.M. (1988) 'Economic and Political Explanations of Human Rights Violations', *World Politics*, 40: 476–498.

Moon, C. and Kim, Y. (1996) 'A Circle of Paradox: Development, Politics and Democracy in South Korea', in A. Leftwich (ed.) *Democracy and Development*, Cambridge: Polity Press, 139–167.

Moore, B. (1966) *The Social Origins of Dictatorship and Democracy: Lord and Peasant in the Making of the Modern World*, Boston, MA: Beacon Press.

Moravcsik, A. (2000) 'The Origins of Human Rights Regimes: Democratic Delegation in Postwar Europe', *International Organization*, 54 (Spring): 217–52.

Muller, E.N. and Seligson, M.A. (1987) 'Inequality and Insurgency', *American Political Science Review*, 81(2): 425–451.

Neubauer, D.E. (1967) 'Some Conditions of Democracy', *American Political Science Review* 61: 1002–1009.

Neumayer, E. (2005) 'Do International Human Rights Treaties Improve Respect for Human Rights?' *Journal of Conflict Resolution*, 49(6): 925–953.

Nugent, D. (1993) *Spent Cartridges of Revolution: An Anthropological History of Namiquipa, Chihuahua*, Chicago: University of Chicago Press.

O'Donnell, G., Schmitter, P.C., and Whitehead, L. (eds) (1986a) *Transitions from Authoritarian Rule: Southern Europe*, Baltimore and London: Johns Hopkins University Press.

———(1986b) *Transitions from Authoritarian Rule: Latin America*, Baltimore and London: Johns Hopkins University Press.

———(1986c) *Transitions from Authoritarian Rule: Comparative Perspectives*, Baltimore and London: Johns Hopkins University Press.

Paige, J. (1975) *Agrarian Revolution: Social Movements and Export Agriculture in the Underdeveloped World*, New York: Free Press.

Parsa, M. (2000) *States, Ideologies, and Social Revolutions: A Comparative Analysis of Iran, Nicaragua, and the Philippines*, Cambridge: Cambridge University Press.

Peeler, J.A. (1992) 'Elite Settlements and Democratic Consolidation: Colombia, Costa Rica, and Venezuela', in J. Higley and R. Gunther (eds) *Elites and Democratic Consolidation in Latin America and Southern Europe*, Cambridge: Cambridge University Press, 81–112.

Peterson, P. and Greene, J.P. (1993) 'Why Executive-Legislative Conflict in the United States Is Dwindling', *British Journal of Political Science*, 24: 33–55.

Poe, S.C. and Tate, C.N. (1994) 'Repression of Human Rights to Personal Integrity in the 1980s: A Global Analysis', *American Political Science Review*, 88(4): 853–872.

Poe, S.C., Tate, C.N. and Keith, L.C. (1999) 'Repression of the Human Right to Personal Integrity Revisited: A Global Cross-national Study Covering the Years 1976–1993', *International Studies Quarterly*, 43: 291–313.

Poulantzas, N. (1976) *The Crisis of the Dictatorships: Portugal, Spain, Greece*, New York: Schocken Books.

Powell, G. Bingham (1982) *Contemporary Democracies: Participation, Stability, and Violence*, Cambridge, MA: Harvard University Press.

Przeworski, A. (1985) 'Marxism and Rational Choice', *Politics and Society* 14(4): 379–409.

Przeworski, A., Alvarez, M.E., Cheibub, J.A., and Limongi, F. (2000) *Democracy and Development: Political Institutions and Well-being in the World, 1950–1990*, Cambridge: Cambridge University Press.

Putnam, R. (1993a) *Making Democracy Work: Civic Traditions in Modern Italy*, Princeton, NJ: Princeton University Press.

Risse, T., Ropp, S.C. and Sikkink, K. (eds) (1999) *The Power of Human Rights: International Norms and Domestic Change*, Cambridge: Cambridge University Press.

Rosato, Sebastian (2003) 'The Flawed Logic of Democratic Peace Theory', *American Political Science Review*, 97(4): 585–602.

Ross, M.H. (1997) 'Culture and Identity in Comparative Political Analysis', in M. Lichbach and A. Zuckerman (eds) *Comparative Politics: Rationality, Culture, and Structure*, Cambridge: Cambridge University Press, 42–80.

Rueschemeyer, D., Stephens, E.H., and Stephens, J. (1992) *Capitalist Development and Democracy*, Cambridge: Polity Press.

Russett, B. and O'Neal, J. (2001) *Triangulating Peace: Democracy, Interdependence and International Organizations*, New York: W. W. Norton

Sands, P. (2005) *Lawless World: America and the Making and Breaking of Global Rules*, London: Allen Lane.

Scott, J. (1976) *The Moral Economy of the Peasant: Rebellion and Subsistence in Southeast Asia*, New Haven and London: Yale University Press.

——(1985) *Weapons of the Weak: Everyday Forms of Peasant Resistance*, New Haven, CT: Yale University Press.

Shugart, M. and Carey, J.M. (1992) *Presidents and Assemblies: Constitutional Design and Electoral Dynamics*, Cambridge: Cambridge University Press.

Sigelman, L. and Simpson, M. (1977) 'A Cross-national Test of the Linkage between Economic Inequality and Political Violence', *Journal of Conflict Resolution*, 21(1): 105–128.

Skocpol, T. (1979) *States and Social Revolutions: A Comparative Analysis of France, Russia, and China*, Cambridge: Cambridge University Press.

Stepan, A. and Skach, C. (1993) 'Constitutional Frameworks and Democratic Consolidation: Parliamentarism and Presidentialism', *World Politics* 46 (October): 1–22.

Strouse, J.C. and Claude, R.P. (1976) 'Empirical Comparative Rights Research: Some Preliminary Tests of Development Hypotheses', in R.P. Claude (ed.) *Comparative Human Rights*, Baltimore and London: Johns Hopkins University Press, 51–67.

Tarrow, S. (1989) *Democracy and Disorder: Protest and Politics in Italy, 1965–1975*, Oxford: Clarendon Press.

Tsebelis, G. (1990) *Nested Games: Rational Choice in Comparative Politics*, Berkeley: University of California Press.

Vanhanen, T. (1997) *The Prospects of Democracy*, London: Routledge.

Waisman, C.H. (1989) 'Argentina: Autarkic Industrialization and Illegitimacy', in L. Diamond, J.J. Linz, and S.M. Lipset (eds) *Democracy in Developing Countries*, Vol. 4: Latin America, London: Adamantine Press, 59–109.

Ward, H. (1995) 'Rational Choice Theory', in D. Marsh and G. Stoker (eds) *Theories and Methods in Political Science*, London: Macmillan, 76–93.

Weissbrodt, D. and Bartolomei, M.L. (1991) 'The Effectiveness of International Human Rights Pressures: The Case of Argentina, 1976–1983', *Minnesota Law Review*, 75: 1009–1035.

Wendt, A. (1999) *Social Theory of International Politics*, Cambridge: Cambridge University Press.

Whitehead, L. (1996a) 'Comparative Politics: Democratization Studies', in R.E. Goodin and H. Klingemann (eds) *The New Handbook of Political Science*, Oxford: Oxford University Press.

Wickham-Crowley, T. (1993) *Guerrillas and Revolution in Latin America*, Princeton, NJ: Princeton University Press.

Wolf, E. (1969) *Peasant Wars of the Twentieth Century*, New York: Harper Torchbooks.

Womack, J. (1969) *Zapata and the Mexican Revolution*, New York: Knopf.

Zanger, S.C. (2000) 'A Global Analysis of the Effect of Regime Changes on Life Integrity Violations, 1977–1993', *Journal of Peace Research*, 37(2): 217–233.

Zürn, M. (2002) 'From Inter-dependence to Globalization', in W. Carlsnaes, T. Risse, and B. Simmons (eds) *Handbook of International Relations*, London: Sage, 235–254.

Chapter 1

1. What are the four goals of comparative studies?
2. What are the two types of theory found in comparative politics?
3. What is the role of method in comparative research?
4. What are the three theoretical perspectives and associated research communities found in the field of comparative politics?
5. What are the four main factors controlling comparative research?

Chapter 2

One Question, Different Answers
Power of Philosophical Methods

T HE AIM OF THE NEXT TWO readings is to argue that comparative analysis needs to pay attention to philosophical assumptions of research, examining and evaluating how meta-theoretical choices shape research questions, research strategies, and findings. The first reading uses Landman's overview of a key issue in comparative politics to raise doubt about the idea that social science is simply concerned with finding correlations between independent and dependent variables. The second reading provides an alternative, more enriching strategy, one that involves acknowledging that social science ultimately depends on the choice of philosophical starting points guiding the research.

Whether democracy depends on free market capitalism is a longstanding topic of investigation and debate. Gabriel Almond points out that "the relation between capitalism and democracy dominates the political theory of the last two centuries." Landman's overview of the literature largely reinforces the existence of a linkage between economic development and democracy, backed by his careful critique of the ways the comparative method had been used and contributed to any variations in findings. Still, a few important research findings question that there is a straightforward positive connection between economics and democracy. In particular, he reports that the studies comparing many countries deviate in their findings from studies comparing only a few or even one country. Landman, nonetheless, remains faithful to the comparative method, claiming that refinements in methods will resolve conflicts in research results.

However, placing research methods in the context of research schools improves analytical control over paradigmatic implications. This view holds that social science depends on philosophical presumptions defining what exists and how it can be known and further that such meta-theory grounds a hypothesis about relationships between variables. In the second reading, Marsh and Furlong emphasize the need to shift the control of research from research design and data collection to their philosophical foundations. These refer to the untestable philosophical presumptions about what constitutes reality (the ontology or what exists) and how we know what exists (epistemology, how to know what we think exists, what is justi-fied belief). Ontology and epistemology identify different philosophical givens, since such assumptions about the nature of the entities making up the world determine what can be looked for and how it can be known. Research methodology then refers to actual methods of data collection and analysis.

Acknowledging that research depends on philosophies of social science leads Marsh and Furlong to explain the characteristics and effects of three fundamental philosophical cur-rents in comparative politics, namely, the *positivist, the realist, and the interpretivist. Positivists* accept that the observable world consists of observable relationships among real things that interact and cause effects. Observation and recording it constitutes data, the ingredients from which regularities are to be identified and verified. Causation, on this view, is simply the correlation among the recorded "facts." The data serves to confirm hypotheses and explanations, thereby facilitating predictions.

The *realist tradition* assumes a foundation of an independent and observable reality but goes beyond what is simply tangible or observable, allowing for the existence of non-observable entities and processes, that is, things that can be only indirectly known. For example, realists explain oligarchy in terms of the organizational processes not directly or completely accessible to observation just as the physicist explains the traits of copper by its atomic composition.

Finally, the *interpretist approach* looks for the role that meanings have in shaping collec-tive action. By studying attitudes, cultures, and how they change, this approach appears in the study of the cultural bases of democracy, of social mobility, potential for conflict among civilizations, and attachments to national identity. The result is insight into motivations for and formation of social organization.

Making clear the ontological (what exists) and epistemological (processes involved in the knowing of what exists) starting points of research (methods appropriate to investigating facts about what exists) is central to all social science. Using all three levels of analysis enables students to have insight into the analyses they encounter, by means of "seeing through" the unspoken influences that predetermine what we can know and how we know it.

Reading 2.1

Economic Development and Democracy

Todd Landman

T HE SCHOLARLY ATTENTION DEVOTED TO THE relationship between economic development and democracy was initially motivated by the search for the 'preconditions' (Karl 1990:2–3) or 'requirements' (Landman 2001) of democracy. Focusing on both the 'old' democracies in the northwest triangle of Europe and North America and the 'new' democracies in the rest of the world, this research seeks to identify the key factors that help explain both the emergence and maintenance of democracy. Among the many factors that have been identified to account for democracy, the level of economic development continues to intrigue comparativists and policy makers in the international development community. This chapter compares the key efforts that examine the link between economic development and democracy to demonstrate whether or not different methods lead to the same result. It examines studies that compare many countries, those that compare few countries, and single-country studies. The discussion of each method of comparison focuses on how different theories specify the dependent and independent variables and nature of the relationship, how the analyses measure the concepts, the different problems that the analyses encounter, and the different results they obtain.

The Research Problem

Are wealthy countries more democratic? If they are, why are they? Does economic development create favourable conditions for the emergence of democracy? Once democracy is established, does continued economic performance help maintain democratic institutions? The model depicted in Figure 2.1.1 is a simple graphical representation of this research problem. It shows that democracy is the dependent variable and economic development is the independent variable. The arrow in the figure has both a plus and minus sign above it to indicate that economic development may have either a positive or negative effect on democracy. Over the years, this model has changed very little in terms of its basic concepts and the relationship between them.

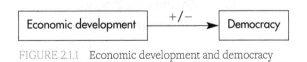

FIGURE 2.1.1   Economic development and democracy

What has changed, however, are the ways in which democracy and economic development are measured, the different forms the relationship takes, the selection of countries used as evidence (Landman 1999),[1] and the methods of comparison employed to support different theories about the relationship (Rueschemeyer *et al.* 1992). In terms of the concepts, some scholars argue that democracy is an all or nothing affair. Either a country is democratic or it is not. Others argue that it is possible to have degrees of democracy (Przeworski and Limongi 1997; Przeworski *et al.* 2000). Similarly, there have been different views on what constitutes economic development. Some authors argue that economic development is best understood as economic growth, while others claim it has more to do with the distribution of income and other economic resources (Todaro 1994:14–20), or overall levels of human development (Ersson and Lane 1996:59; Brohman 1996). The relationship has been specified in different ways, such as linear, curvilinear, and as a 'step' function (see Briefing box 2.1.1). Finally, different methods of comparison focus on different aspects of the relationship. Studies that compare many countries tend to use quantitative techniques to uncover uniform patterns of variation in a small number of variables. Studies that compare few countries and single-country studies use both quantitative and qualitative techniques to uncover the more historically contingent factors that intervene between processes of economic development and democracy, and tend to couch their arguments in more 'path-dependent' language (see Briefing box 2.1.2).

Briefing Box 2.1.1 Possible Relationships Between Economic Development and Democracy

The relationship between economic development and democracy can assume different *functional forms*, the most common of which include linear, curvilinear, and a 'step' function.

Linear Relationship

A positive linear relationship between economic development and democracy suggests that as the level of economic development increases, the likelihood that a country will be democratic also increases. Thus, if a scholar measures both concepts and plots them on a graph, the scatter of points would be around a line that rises from the lower left-hand corner to the upper right-hand corner of the graph, as depicted in Figure 2.1.2. Moving along the line in the figure shows that a rise in one variable is associated with a rise in the other.

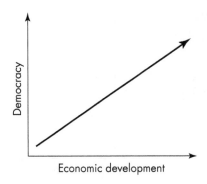

FIGURE 2.1.2   A linear relationship between economic development and democracy

Curvilinear Relationship

A curvilinear relationship between economic development and democracy suggests that a positive change in economic development is accompanied by a positive change in democracy, but unlike a linear relationship, the degree to which democracy increases tapers off with higher levels of economic development. In this case, there is a distinct range of economic development after which the likelihood a country becomes democratic does not change. This relationship is depicted in Figure 2.1.3, where this range, or 'threshold of democracy', is evident. A scatter of data points on this graph would group around the line, but it is clear from the figure that after a certain level of economic development, the level of democracy does not increase.

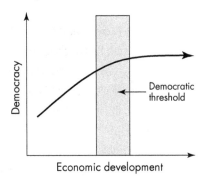

FIGURE 2.1.3   A curvilinear relationship between economic development and democracy

A 'Step' Relationship

A step-function is most different from the first two relationships. In this case, there is a distinct level of economic development after which the likelihood of a country being democratic does not change. Figure 2.1.4 shows that the democratic threshold is not a range of economic development, but a distinct 'take-off' point for democracy (Rostow 1961; Landman 1999)

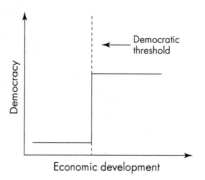

FIGURE 2.1.4   A step relationship between economic development and democracy

Briefing Box 2.1.2 Path-Dependent Arguments

A path-dependent argument focuses on the sequence of events in any given historical account. Its basic assumption is that once a particular event transpires, be it a war, election, revolution, or important decision, the course of events that succeeds it is altered forever. Consider the following two examples: an abstract example called the 'urn problem' (Jackson 1996:723) and one from political science concerning democratic consolidation (Burton *et al.* 1992).

First, consider an urn containing one red ball and one white ball. In the first instance, a ball is selected from the urn, then it and a ball of the same colour are placed back into the urn. If this operation is repeated a second and third time (or infinitely), the urn will develop a distribution of red and white balls that is highly dependent on the first few choices that are made. This situation is illustrated in Figure 2.1.5. The various possible distributions of red and white balls multiply rapidly with each successive round, but it is clear from the figure that each succeeding distribution is highly dependent on the previous round. For example, the left side of the figure shows that if a red ball is chosen on the first round, then two reds and one white are in the urn. If a red is chosen again, the urn will have three reds and a white, and so on. The bottom of the figure shows how many different types of distributions are possible, but what is clear is that the first two choices have a dramatic effect on the subsequent distributions.

In the second example, Burton *et al.* (1992:23) develop a path-dependent argument to account for different types of democratic consolidation in Latin America and Southern Europe, which is illustrated in Figure 2.1.6.

Begin			R	W		
1		RRW			WWR	
2	RRRW	RRRW	WWRR	WWWR	WWWR	WWRR
3	RRRRW	WWWWRR	RRRWW	WWWWWR	WWWRR	RRRWW
	(× 6)	(× 2)	(× 2)	(× 6)	(× 2)	(× 2)

FIGURE 2.1.5   The urn problem and path-dependence

Source: Adapted from Jackson (1996:723)

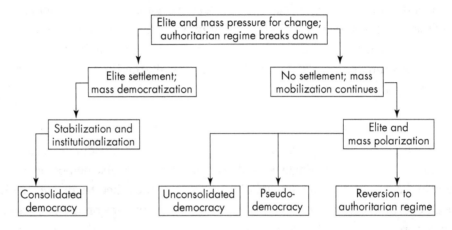

FIGURE 2.1.6   A path-dependent argument about democratic consolidation

Source: Adapted from Burton *et al.* (1992:23)

For countries that experienced democratic transitions accompanied by popular mobilization, the figure shows initially two paths: elite settlement and mass mobilization, or no elite settlement and mass mobilization. The first path leads to stabilization, institutionalization, and consolidated democracy. The second path leads to a state of polarization between elites and masses, which in turn can lead to unconsolidated democracy, pseudo-democracy, or a reversion to authoritarianism. Crucial to their argument is that once a country reaches one of the nodes in the path, certain outcomes are no longer available, suggesting that without an elite settlement and mass democratization, democratic consolidation is not likely. Macro-historical studies on economic development and democracy use path-dependent arguments (Moore 1966; Rueschemeyer *et al.* 1992), and such arguments can be found throughout political science, such as Collier and Collier's (1991) study of labour incorporation and regime formation in Latin America, or the historical analysis of war between countries (e.g. de Mesquita *et al.* 1997:17–19).

Comparing Many Countries

The initial efforts to identify a simple set of democratic preconditions compared many countries at one point in time. Seymour Martin Lipset (1959, 1960) carried out the seminal study on these preconditions by comparing 28 European and English-speaking countries with 20 Latin American countries (Lipset 1959:74). His definition of democracy is as follows:

> a political system which supplies regular constitutional opportunities for changing the governing officials. It is a social mechanism for the resolution of the problem of societal decision-making among conflicting interest groups, which permits the largest possible part of the population to influence these decisions through their ability to choose among alternative contenders for political office.
>
> (ibid.: 71)

Using this definition, Lipset then divides his sample of countries into four different groups. He divides the European and English-speaking countries into stable democracies on the one hand and unstable democracies and dictatorships on the other. He divides the Latin American countries into democracies and unstable dictatorships on the one hand and stable dictatorships on the other. For the first group, those countries that had an 'uninterrupted continuation of political democracy since World War I, and the absence over the past twenty-five years of a major political movement opposed to the democratic "rules of the game"' were considered to be democracies (ibid.: 72, emphasis in original). The Latin American countries were classified as democratic if they 'had a history of more or less free elections for most of the post-World War I period' (ibid.: 72–73).

The comparison provides a range of quantitative indicators of economic development for this sample of countries, including those for wealth, industrialization, education, and urbanization. Wealth is measured by per capita income, thousands of persons per doctor, persons per motor vehicle, telephones per 1,000 people, radios per 1,000 people, and newspaper copies per 1,000 people. Industrialization is measured by the percentage of males employed in agriculture and the per capita consumption of energy. Education is measured by the percentage of the population that is literate and enrolment in primary school, post-primary school, and higher education. Urbanization is measured by the percentage of cities with populations over 20,000, the percentage of cities with populations over 100,000, and the percentage of metropolitan areas (ibid.: 76–77). These various measures are seen as objective indicators of socio-economic development, where higher values indicate higher levels of economic development.

To demonstrate the relationship between the level of economic development and democracy, the study compares the averages of these indicators across both groups of countries. Across all these indicators, the European and English-speaking stable democracies and the Latin American democracies and unstable dictatorships score higher (or better) than their non-democratic counterparts, which means, on average, that democracies tend to have higher levels of socio-economic development than non-democracies. This pattern of results leads Lipset (ibid.: 80) to claim that all the factors 'subsumed under economic development carry with [them] the political correlate of democracy'. He also claims that the 'more well to do a nation, the more likely it will sustain democracy' (ibid.: 75). While not saying that economic development actually *causes* democracy, his study is the first to establish a correlation, or probable association, between the two, and thus paves the way for a succession of studies that seek to build on this original comparison.

Following Lipset, Cutright (1963) compares 77 countries in North America, South America, Asia, and Europe using scales of communications development, economic development, and political development. Unlike Lipset, however, he considers political development (or democracy) to exist on a continuum based on the prolonged presence of viable legislative and freely elected executive branches for the period 1940–1961. The correlation between communications development and political development is higher than that between economic development, yet both are high enough for Cutright (ibid.: 571) to conclude that there is an interdependence between political institutions and the level of social and economic development (see also Rueschemeyer *et al.* 1992:15). The overall confidence in his results leads him to predict the level of political development for the individual countries that comprise his sample based on the individual values of the various independent variables.

In responding to criticism that initial comparative efforts to examine the relationship were 'snapshot analyses', Cutright and Wiley (1969) compare 40 'self-governing' countries using data from before and after the Second World War to examine whether it can be sustained over time. Their dependent variable is political representation, which is defined as 'the extent to which the executive and legislative branches of government are subject to the demands of the non-elite population' (ibid.: 23–24). Annual scores on an index of political representation were compiled for each of four decades: 1927–1936, 1937–1946, 1947–1956, and 1957–1966. They also measure the difference between the scores for the successive decades to capture the change in political representation. Economic development is measured using the amount of energy consumed in any given year. The comparison of the 40 countries over the four decades reveals a significant and stable relationship between the level of economic development and political representation. Moreover, since the analysis uses four different time periods, Cutright and Wiley (ibid.: 29) conclude that the level of political representation is causally dependent on the level of economic development.

In *Polyarchy*, Robert Dahl (1971) seeks to formulate a classification of political forms of which democracy is one type, and then use the typology to examine the conditions that foster democracy. He conceives of democracy as having two critical dimensions: contestation and participation (ibid.: 4–9). Countries that have high levels of contestation (i.e. the degree to which members of a political system are free to contest the conduct of government) and participation (i.e. the proportion of the population entitled to participate in controlling the conduct of government) are considered 'polyarchies', or democracies. Using per capita GNP as a measure of economic development, his comparison of 118 countries and 33 polyarchies and near-polyarchies reveals a weak threshold effect (see Briefing box 2.1.1). In other words, countries that achieve a certain level of economic development (between 700 and 800 1957 US dollars per capita GDP) tend to be polyarchies. Dahl (ibid.: 68–69, 74) is cautious about this finding, since there are many deviant cases that have low levels of development and are polyarchies (e.g. India), or that have high levels of development and are not polyarchies (e.g. the Soviet Union and East Germany).[2] Moreover, history shows that the United States, Australia, New Zealand, Canada, Britain, Norway, and Sweden, among others, were polyarchies long before they achieved high levels of economic development (Dahl 1971:69–70; see also Rueschemeyer *et al.* 1992).

Jackman (1973:611) concentrates his comparison of 60 non-communist countries on the relationship between economic development and democracy, as well as the 'definition of democratic political development itself'. Drawing on the earlier studies conducted by Lipset (1959) and Cutright (1963), Jackman (1973) argues that democracy is best understood as a continuous rather than a dichotomous concept, and that both the linear and curvilinear forms of the relationship ought to be tested. His measure of democracy combines four indicators, including voter turnout, the competitiveness of the party voting system, the degree of electoral irregularity, and relative freedom of the press. Like Cutright and Wiley (1969), his measure of economic development is the level of energy consumption. His statistical analysis reveals that the curvilinear relationship is more significant than the linear relationship, effectively adding comparative evidence to the idea of a democratic threshold in line with Dahl (1971).

Bollen (1979) represents the last study in this earlier sample of comparative efforts that examine the relationship between economic development and democracy. In addition to focusing on the level of economic development, Bollen is also interested in the timing of development. It is possible that the countries that have developed long after those in Europe and North America may have had more difficulty in establishing democratic forms of governance (see below). For example, Britain's model of rapid economic development had profound effects on those countries that developed after it, such as France, Belgium, or the United States (ibid.: 573). When the so-called 'late developers' seek to 'catch up' to other countries in the world economy (Gerschenkron 1962), their efforts to do so may put undue pressure on their burgeoning political systems and thus lead to democratic breakdown. This type of argument suggests that countries that developed early are more likely to be democratic than those countries that developed later.

Thus, Bollen's comparison of 99 countries seeks to examine whether the level of democracy is higher in countries that developed early, whether it is higher in countries that have simply achieved better levels of economic development, or both. His index of democracy includes three indicators of popular sovereignty and three indicators of political liberties (Bollen 1979:580). Like Jackman (1973) and Cutright and Wiley (1969), the level of development is measured using energy consumption. The timing of development is measured by subtracting the starting year of development from 1966 (Bollen 1979:577). His statistical analysis reveals that the timing of development is not significant, but that the level of development has a significant and positive effect on democracy. In other words, for this sample of countries, a country's level of development, regardless of when it actually started developing, has an effect on the degree to which it is democratic.

Since this first phase of comparative work, new studies have been published that use increasingly sophisticated statistical techniques that allow scholars to compare many countries over time, thereby increasing the number of observations [...]. There are three notable studies that use this method of comparison. Helliwell (1994) compares 125 countries over the period 1960–1985 ($n = 1,250$); Burkhart and Lewis-Beck (1994) compare 131 countries from 1972–1989 ($n = 2,358$); and Przeworski and Limongi (1997) and Przeworski *et al.* (2000) compare 135 countries between 1950 and 1990 ($n = 4,126$). The first two studies find significant statistical evidence in support of a relationship between economic development and democracy. The third study casts serious doubt on these findings, and a comparison of all three reveals that their different results depend largely on their conceptualization of democracy and their specification of the relationship.

Helliwell (1994:226) selects a sample of countries for which 'it is possible to obtain comparable measures of per capita income and regular assessments of the extent of political and civil rights'. His index of democracy (or 'probability of political freedom') combines two separate measures of the protection of political and civil liberties[3] and ranges from low (no democracy) to high (full democracy). In addition to his measure of economic development, Helliwell (ibid.: 228–229) controls for different regional effects, including the OECD countries, the oil-producing countries of the Middle East, African countries, and Latin American countries. His statistical analysis reveals a strong positive effect of per capita income on the level of democracy. In addition, his analysis shows positive effects for the OECD countries and Latin America, and negative effects for Africa and the Middle East. Overall, the statistical results confirm the relationship between economic development and democracy established by the comparative studies in the earlier phase.

Burkhart and Lewis-Beck (1994) use a slightly more robust collection of data than Helliwell (1994) and a similar measure of democracy ranging from low (no democracy) to high (full democracy). They use energy consumption to operationalize economic development and control for the effects of 'other social forces' and the 'world position' of the countries in the study. Other social forces are represented by past values of democracy, and the identification of a country's world position (core, semi-periphery, or periphery) is made on the basis of nine other studies (Burkhart and Lewis-Beck 1994:904–995). The results of the statistical analysis show that economic development and other social forces are positively associated with democracy, while both peripheral and semi-peripheral world positions detract from these positive effects. In other words, the effect of economic development on democracy is lower in newly developed and developing countries. By using more advanced statistical techniques than those employed by Helliwell (1994), they are able to claim with confidence that economic development causes democracy (Burkhart and Lewis-Beck 1994:907; see also Foweraker and Landman 2004).

The final studies in this section are those of Przeworski and Limongi (1997) and Przeworski *et al.* (2000), who are sceptical of the findings of earlier comparative work. They do not dispute the fact that the relationship between economic development and democracy has been demonstrated empirically, but they do object to the way in which the results have been interpreted. They classify countries according to strict rules of assessment, which include the election of the executive, the legislature, a competitive party system, and the alternation of power over time (Przeworski and Limongi 1997:178). Simple analysis reveals that the relationship between levels of economic development and democracy is strong. Rather than immediately proclaiming that economic development fosters democracy, however, they argue that 'either democracies may be more likely to emerge as countries develop economically, or they may be established independently of economic development but more likely to survive in developed countries' (ibid.: 156). Further analysis of the data that tests the likelihood of democratic transition, given levels of development, shows that 'democracies are almost certain to survive once they are established in rich countries' (ibid.: 166; Przeworski *et al.* 2000:137). Thus, a slightly different analysis/interpretation of the empirical data avoids the strong causal language of the other two studies.

This review of studies that compare many countries reveals that there is a 'stable positive relationship between socio-economic development and democracy' (Rueschemeyer *et al.* 1992:26). The repeated empirical verification of the relationship, however, leads to two conclusions in the comparative literature. For the majority of studies, robust evidence in support of the relationship has led many to conclude that economic development causes democracy, a finding that has helped develop the 'modernization' perspective in comparative politics (see Briefing box 2.1.3 [...]). In this perspective, it is argued that the development of social institutions enhances the level of education of the population, improves its social and spatial mobility, and promotes the political culture that supports liberal democratic institutions (Lipset 1959; Valenzuela and Valenzuela 1978:538; Karl 1990:3; Inglehart 1997:5). The theory assumes that the process of socio-economic development is 'a progressive accumulation of social changes that ready a society to its culmination, democratization' (Przeworski and Limongi 1997:158). On the other hand, an emerging group of scholars points to the fact that while the relationship appears to hold over time and space, it may be spurious, since rich democracies tend not to collapse. This latter work has opened up a debate between those who support the idea of *endogenous democratization* versus those who support the idea of *exogenous democratization* (see Briefing box 2.1.3).

Briefing Box 2.1.3 Endogenous and Exogenous Democratization

Within the empirical literature on democracy a significant debate has arisen as to the true causal nature of the relationship between economic development and democracy. The debate takes as its starting point the somewhat ambiguous statement made by Seymour Martin Lipset (1959:75) that the 'more well to do a nation, the more likely it will sustain democracy'. The statement is ambiguous since it does not specify whether economic development causes democracy or is a supporting condition for its long-term survival. In a subsequent article published in 1994, Lipset clarified that the correlations he found in the 1959 article and 1960 book, *Political Man* do not necessarily mean that development causes democracy. Nonetheless, scholars have sought to use increasingly sophisticated statistical analysis to uncover the true nature of the relationship.

The studies by Boix (2003) and Boix and Stokes (2003) use a pooled-cross section time-series data set that stretches back into the 19th century to capture the emergence of the so-called first and second wave democracies (see Huntington 1991), as well as the third and fourth wave democracies (see Doorenspleet 2005). The data analysis looks at the probability of a country 'switching' at different levels of economic development and they contend that their data show that economic development is a key causal condition for the emergence of democracy. They argue that these results support the general idea of *endogenous democratization*, which means economic development unleashes a set of social and economic changes that necessarily lead to democratization; a theoretical perspective that is largely in line with modernization theory (see Valenzuela and Valenzuela 1978 [...]).

In contrast, studies by Przeworski and Limongi (1997) and Przeworski *et al.* (2000) use a similar data set that only includes data for the period from 1950 to 1990. They contend that one using a large data set such as theirs will always find a statistically significant relationship between the level of economic and democracy. However, they do not find any evidence of a statistically significant relationship between economic development and the *emergence* of democracy, and argue further that the probability of democratic collapse drops to near zero at high levels of economic development. In other words, for them, once democracy is established within a wealthy country, it tends not to collapse and it is this stability of democracy in rich countries that drives the overall statistical relationship. They label their theoretical perspective *exogenous democratization* since they posit that it is the presence of factors other than economic development that explains the emergence of democracy.

Both perspectives have little say over the political prospects for poor countries. There is an increasing number of 'outlier' countries in which democracy has become established and has become stable despite these countries having relatively low levels of economic development. Like the case of Costa Rica outlined [...], there are other cases in which democracy is flourishing under conditions of economic scarcity. For example, Mongolia has been democratic since the early 1990s when it threw off the Communist regime that had been in power since 1922. Throughout the 1990s, Mongolia privatized its economy while engaging in democratic reforms. It held competitive elections throughout the period in which the former Communists won, were displaced by an alliance of opposition parties, and then formed a grand coalition. This and other cases fit the category of 'least likely' countries since their ability to democratize without substantial progress in economic terms challenges the main tenets of the theories of endogenous and exogenous democratization.

Comparing Few Countries

[...], [S]tudies that compare few countries use both quantitative and qualitative techniques. However, common to both is the intentional selection of countries for comparison based on criteria including theory, regional focus, data availability, and resources. As the review of the comparisons in this section will demonstrate, the choice of countries can affect the inferences that are drawn concerning the relationship between economic development and democracy [...]. This section first examines three studies that use quantitative techniques to compare few countries, namely Lerner's (1958) study of modernization in the Middle East, Neubauer's (1967) comparison of democratic development in 23 countries, and work on economic development and democracy in Latin America (Landman 1999, 2006a; Mainwaring and Perez-Liñan 2003). It then examines three qualitative studies that compare several countries, including de Schweinitz's (1964) study of industrialization and democracy in Britain, the US, Germany, and Russia. Moore's (1966) study of the 'three routes to modernity', and Rueschemeyer *et al.*'s (1992) comparison of developmental paths in advanced capitalist countries, Latin America, and the Caribbean.

Comparing Few Countries Quantitatively

One year before Lipset (1959) provided the first cross-national study of economic development and democracy, Daniel Lerner (1958) published an ambitious study that examined patterns of modernization in the Middle East. His study starts with a comparison of 73 countries which shows a high level of association across a range of indicators of modernity, including urbanization, literacy, media participation, and political participation. This initial evidence leads him to establish such associations across a much smaller sample of countries, including Turkey, Lebanon, Jordan, Egypt, Syria, and Iran using surveys of individuals carried out by a team of country specialists. An initial combined comparison of these six countries is then followed by individual case studies of each country to identify particularities associated with each while remaining sensitive to the overall regularities that exist among them.

For Lerner (1958:89), modernization is a 'secular trend unilateral in direction-from traditional to participant lifeways'. This secular trend is characterized by physical, social, and psychic mobility whose culmination is a modern participant society with high levels of urbanism, literacy, media consumption, and an empathic capacity. While not directly assessing the connection between economic development and democracy, the study implies that democracy is the end-state for modernization and that for two of his most 'modern' societies—Turkey and Lebanon—the control of political power is decided by elections (ibid.: 84–85). History has shown, however, that both countries have had difficulty maintaining democracy as Turkey experienced military intervention in 1971 and 1980 while Lebanon suffered from civil war between 1975 and 1990. Initial comparisons of the six countries using aggregate data lead to the following ranking from low to high levels of modernization: Iran, Jordan, Syria, Egypt, Lebanon, and Turkey. This comparison is then followed by an analysis of the individual-level data from the six national surveys. Among the strongest regularities associated with modernity, Lerner (ibid.: 398–412) finds consistent patterns of happiness among urban dwellers, a decline in traditional forms of rule, increasing opportunities for both genders, and high levels of empathy, or willingness to tolerate the views of others. In the end, Turkey and Lebanon are viewed as having achieved balanced modernization, Egypt and Syria are considered to be 'out of phase', and Jordan and Iran as exhibiting no process of modernization.

The importance of Lerner's study for the comparative method is that he uses aggregate-level data and global comparisons to establish basic associations between important variables.

He then uses individual-level data that measure what he believes are the key characteristics of modernity to allow intensive examination of six countries. This use of data at two levels of analysis seeks to minimize the problem of ecological fallacy [...]. His analysis has not 'proved' the theory of modernization, but has 'only explained and exemplified the regularities it posits', which for him are 'only more plausible hypotheses than they were before' (ibid.: 398). As the comparisons of many countries outlined above have demonstrated, considerable scholarly effort has been devoted to examining more fully the implications of these hypotheses. And as the comparisons of few countries reviewed below will demonstrate, the verification of these hypotheses is by no means a settled matter.

Drawing on the insights of the comparison of many and few countries, Neubauer (1967) compares 23 countries using an index of democratic development and indicators of economic development. The index of democratic development combines four indicators 'which measure the relative amount of *electoral equality* and *competition* present in a given political system' (ibid.: 1004–1005). He uses the same indicators of economic development as those employed by Cutright. The main difference between his study and those that compare many countries is the size of his sample. Neubauer (ibid.: 1006) argues that the 'data necessary for the democratic performance indicator come only from democratic countries', and that the findings of the comparison of many countries ought to hold for his smaller sample. His comparison of the 23 democracies reveals that there is 'simply no relationship between [the] level of democratic performance and measures of socio-economic development' (ibid.: 1007). His only significant correlation is between the level of communication and democratic performance. Overall, he concludes that there may be some threshold effect between economic development and democracy, but that for democratic countries, higher levels of economic development do not lead to improved democratic performance (ibid.: 1007).

Similar work in this area examines the relationship using a smaller sample of countries confined geographically to Latin America (Landman 1999; 2006a; Mainwaring and Perez-Liñan 2003). Seventeen Latin American countries are compared over the period 1972–1995 (Landman 1999), 1976–2000 (Landman 2006a) and for a much longer time series dating back to the 1940s (Mainwaring and Perez-Liñan 2003). Like Neubauer (1967), these three studies argue that the findings of the global comparisons ought to hold for smaller groups of countries, particularly those with great variation in both economic development and democracy. Unlike Neubauer's study, the countries in the sample are geographically proximate and culturally similar, therefore fitting squarely in the most similar systems design [...]. The comparison controls for the cultural commonality of the region (similar Iberian heritage and patterns of economic development), and some of the models specify further controls for sub-regional differences between the Southern Cone and Central America, both of which had somewhat different patterns of development and democracy during the period. The statistical analysis tests for both the linear and non-linear forms of relationship, and finds no significant effects between economic development and democracy.[4] Thus, this smaller sample of most similar countries acts a 'most likely' test that infirms the theoretical propositions that have received strong empirical support at the global level of analysis.

Taken together, these studies use the quantitative techniques of those studies that compare many countries, but confine their comparisons to a smaller selection of countries. It is clear that the comparison over a smaller selection of countries produces different results, but in both examples, selection of the countries was not dependent on the outcome that is to be explained. Lerner (1958) uses his initial extensive comparison as a preliminary guide to his more intensive inquiry into the six case studies, but he maintains a large number of observations by using individual-level data. Neubauer's (1967) comparison across democracies and the time-series comparison of Latin American countries reveal no relationship between economic development and democracy. But are these results simply a product of the sample size, or are there theoretical and historical reasons for raising doubts about the association between economic development and democracy? The review of studies that compare few countries qualitatively seeks to provide some answers to this important question.

Comparing Few Countries Qualitatively

The starting point for this group of qualitative macro-historical studies is to uncover the causal factors inside the 'black box' of the relationship between economic development and democracy (Rueschemeyer *et al.* 1992:29). While accepting some of the theoretical assumptions of the global comparisons, and arguing that at best the positive and significant statistical results they obtain are empirical generalizations (ibid.: 30), these studies seek to identify key intervening variables that help 'unpack' the relationship. These variables include the timing and nature of economic development, the strength and coalitions of different social classes, the strength and nature of the state, and important transnational factors in the form of wars and economic depressions. In this way, these studies emphasize the processes involved in the development of democracy over the *longue durée* (Rustow 1970). As these studies necessarily develop more complex and less parsimonious explanations than the global comparisons, they are discussed at greater length.

In *Industrialization and Democracy*, de Schweinitz (1964:7) argues that 'the rise of the democratic political community has been associated with industrialization and economic growth'; however, these must be seen as 'necessary but not sufficient' conditions for the emergence of democracy. For him democracy is 'a system in which the problems of government are resolved on the basis of an appeal to the preferences of autonomous individuals', through periodic use of a majority voting mechanism open to the adult population (ibid.: 14–15). This democratic system requires rational individuals capable of making appropriate choices and a general consensus on fundamental values in society (ibid.: 23), the cultivation of which depends highly upon high levels of education and income. The key question for de Schweinitz (ibid.: 34) is 'How may economic growth which is a process by which an economy passes from a subsistence to a high-income status economy democratize political systems which initially are nondemocratic?' The answer to this question lies in comparing the historical experiences with economic development and democratization in Britain, the US, Germany, and Russia.

The comparison begins with Britain, since it is seen as the first country to have undergone rapid industrialization and the development of democratic political institutions. Implicit throughout the comparisons is that the British experience somehow radiates out across Europe and North America, effectively offering the countries that comprise these regions a model for growth and governance. The key to explaining British success is the fact that the process of economic development was achieved autonomously, as opposed to being a state-led process. This process of autonomous growth resulted in the rise of the middle class, a well-tamed and well-managed and organized labour force, and the piecemeal installation of democracy, which 'did not have to be sacrificed at the altar of economic growth' (ibid.: 128). What is clear in the British case is that it was not fully democratic before the industrial revolution in the middle of the eighteenth century, but that the process of industrialization unleashed the necessary social forces to realize democracy by the middle of the nineteenth century.

The establishment of democracy in the United States had many factors in its favour that were absent in Britain. It possessed vast amounts of space, a favourable climate, and abundant natural resources, and perhaps most importantly, the American Revolution meant that those pro-democratic forces in this new country did not have the vestiges of a feudal order with which to contend (de Schweinitz 1964:130 after Hartz 1955). In contrast to Britain, where democratization of the political process grew out of industrialization, the political institutions in the United States had to be created to restrain the democratic impulse while unleashing the forces of economic growth (de Schweinitz 1964:142). Like Britain, however, economic growth in the United States was produced autonomously and the period of rapid industrialization did not occur until after the Civil War. For de Schweinitz (ibid.: 148–152), there are several other conditions favourable to the establishment of democracy in the United States, including better working conditions for labourers, lower economic expectations and ethnic differentiation of immigrant groups, a strong political culture of individualism, and the overall size of the continental land mass, all of which helped overcome the 'welfare problem' created by the process of industrialization.

In contrast to the gradual installation of democracy in Britain and the relatively 'easy history' of the United States, de Schweinitz (ibid.: 159) argues that the German experience bore the heavy weight of history, which had created the need for a strong centralized state to unify its diverse political units in the latter half of the nineteenth century. By the First

World War, Germany's rapid industrialization had outpaced that of Britain, but both the war and the subsequent rise to power of Hitler appear to have confounded the hypothesis about autonomous economic growth and democracy (ibid.: 184). This apparently deviant case is explained away with reference to a certain British 'exceptionalism'. At a comparable stage of development, Britain was not fully democratic but had over half a century of peace for democratic practices to flourish. Germany had a different historical legacy than Britain, which had created more formidable obstacles to democratization, and Britain was not as susceptible to political developments and crises on the continent. It is important to note that global comparisons treat deviant cases as a normal occurrence where they simply are outliers to a standard distribution of outcomes. In this comparison, de Schweinitz (1964) is at pains to explain why Germany did not achieve stable democracy by the dawn of the twentieth century. The difference between these two styles of analysis will be addressed further in the summary that follows.

The final case in this study is Russia, which was more underdeveloped and had less access to natural resources than the other cases, did not experience spontaneous and autonomous development, and was more open to foreign invasion. Moreover, the lack of growth of a middle class and the persistence of a system of serfdom further hindered any moves toward democracy. Although Russia achieved rapid industrialization towards the end of the nineteenth century, de Schweinitz (1964) argues that Marxist ideology became an important factor in shaping its subsequent history. Ultimately Russia forms a one-party state with no legitimate opposition. Paradoxically, there is no explanation for the Russian Revolution of 1917. Rather, it becomes a new factor that helps explain its lack of democracy. In the end, Russia and Germany had both late and less autonomous economic development, and either limited or no experience with democracy, while Britain and the US experienced autonomous economic development and the development of fundamental values that fostered the growth of democracy. These comparisons are summarized in Table 2.1.1.

Such qualitative comparison of a few countries allows de Schweinitz to concentrate on historical sequences and factors unique to the individual cases while drawing larger inferences about the more general relationship between development and democracy. He stresses that his research design and method 'raise the possibility that a unique configuration of historical conditions relating to the availability of natural resources, the mobility of the population, ideology, and the locus and sequence of development, accounted for the emergence of the democratic political order' (ibid.: 269). Overall, the key obstacles to successful democratization are late development and state-centred growth. In drawing inferences beyond the confines of his four-country comparison, de Schweinitz (ibid.: 11) argues that the 'Euro-American route to democracy is closed' and that countries developing in the twentieth century must find other means for establishing democratic political institutions.

TABLE 2.1.1   A summary of de Schweinitz's (1964) Industrialization and Democracy

Case	Britain	US	Germany	Russia
Character of economic development	Early autonomous economic development	Autonomous economic development	Late industrialization, partly state-led	Late industrialization, not autonomous
Unique features	Isolated geographically Peaceful half century	Space, climate, natural resources No feudal past	Heavy weight of history Strong centralized state	Limited access to natural resources Centralized state and persistence of serfdom
Social class development	Large middle class Strong labour movement	Large middle class Weak labour movement	Large but alienated middle class Strong labour movement	No large middle class Small working class
Political culture	Liberal individualism	Rugged individualism	Lack of individualism	Marxist ideology
Outcome	Democracy	Democracy	Unstable democracy	No democracy

In *The Social Origins of Dictatorship and Democracy*, Barrington Moore (1966) extends the comparison of democratic and non-democratic outcomes found in de Schweinitz (1964) to a larger group of countries, including Britain, France, the United States, Japan, India, and China; he also makes implicit comparisons with Germany and Russia. Like de Schweinitz, Moore seeks to understand the relationship between processes of economic development and political form through comparing few countries. These comparisons 'serve as a rough negative check on accepted historical explanations. And a comparative approach may lead to new historical generalizations' (Moore 1966: xiii). Like de Schweinitz (1964), he believes that certain political outcomes are the product of discrete historical configurations, which may not be repeated. His comparisons reveal three 'routes to the modern world': (1) bourgeois revolutions and democracy, (2) revolution from above and fascism, and (3) revolution from below and communism. The central categories of comparison include economic development, state structures, and social classes.

The democratic route to modern society was achieved in Britain, France, and the United States. The Puritan Revolution (English Civil War), the French Revolution, and the American Civil War are seen as events that altered dramatically the developmental paths these three countries would take. The process of economic development was accompanied by a balance of power between the crown and the landed nobility. The development of commercial agriculture weakened the role of the landed upper classes, while building the ranks of the bourgeoisie, which for Moore (1966:418) was critical for the development of democracy: 'No bourgeois, no democracy.' There was no coalition between the landed upper classes and the bourgeoisie against the interests of peasants and workers. Finally, all three cases had a *revolutionary break with the past* (ibid.: 431). The Puritan Revolution altered forever the role of the monarchy in Britain, while the French Revolution abolished royal absolutism and established the political rights of modern citizenship.[5] While the American Revolution initially removed the role of the British crown, the American Civil War broke the landed upper classes and so paved the way for the continued growth of industrial capitalism. In this way, Moore (1966) argues that all three historical events were bourgeois revolutions, the conditions of which were made possible by economic development, and the resolution of which ultimately led to the establishment of liberal democracy.

The fascist and 'top-down' route to modern society is illustrated through a detailed analysis of Japanese history that is compared implicitly to that of Germany. In both countries, Moore (ibid.: 437) argues that the development of the commercial and industrial class was too weak and dependent to take power on its own and it therefore forged coalitions with the landed upper classes and royal bureaucracy, 'exchanging the right to rule for the right to make money'. This coalition against the interests of peasants and workers was supported by a strong state that provides trade protection and labour control. Any experiments with democracy soon disappeared as they were ultimately not to the liking of the landed upper classes and 'fascist repression is the final outcome' (Rueschemeyer *et al.* 1992:24).

The communist route in both Russia and China has four main causal factors. Both countries had a highly centralized state and a landed upper class, both of which repressed the labour force, which was the essential means of economic development at that time. The lack of commercial agriculture meant that only a weak bourgeoisie developed, which was not strong enough either to confront the strong land-owning class or the crown (as in Britain and France). Both societies had a mass peasantry that showed great potential for collective action. Thus, the 'absence of a commercial revolution in agriculture led by the upper classes and the concomitant survival of peasant social institutions' provided the social and political backdrop for communist revolution (Moore 1966:477). The failure of the landed upper classes to maintain institutional links with the peasantry and their continued exploitation of the peasants created the conditions by which the agrarian bureaucracies in Russia and China were ultimately overthrown.

Table 2.1.2 summarizes Moore's (1966) three routes to modernity, including the character of economic development, the nature of the emergent class coalitions, the role of the state, and the different political outcomes. Most striking is the fact that democracy is seen to be

TABLE 2.1.2 Moore's (1966) Three Routes to Modern Society

	I Britain, France, United States (India)	II Germany, Italy, Japan	III Russia, China
Character of economic development	Development of commercial agriculture	Development of commercial agriculture	No development of commercial agriculture
Class development and coalitions	Weakening of landed aristocracy Balance of power between crown and landed aristocracy (in Britain, France, and India) Absence of aristocratic–bourgeois coalition against peasants and workers	Strong land-owning class Coalition of powerful land-owning class and weak, dependent bourgeoisie	Strong land-owning class Weak bourgeoisie Mass peasantry with capacity for collective action
Role of the state	Revolutionary and violent break with the past	Strong state that provides trade protection, manages industrialization, and controls labour	Centralized state and labour repression
Outcome	Capitalist parliamentary democracy	Capitalist fascism	Communism

Source: Adapted from Moore (1966)

the product of a violent break with the past, not a gradual installation of a political form as the result of incremental advances in the process of economic development. The beheading of Charles I in Britain, the execution of Louis XVI in France, and the Union Army's defeat of the Confederates in the United States all serve as radical events that altered fundamentally the social, economic, and political conditions that made democracy possible. Like de Schweinitz (1964), Moore (1966) is keen to point out that the constellation of events that led to these democratic outcomes was by no means inevitable, and that any one of these three societies (given a slightly different set of events), could have ended up taking one of the other two routes to the modern world.

In response to some of the limitations of both these two key qualitative studies and the quantitative global comparisons, Rueschemeyer *et al.* (1992) extend the analysis of the relationship between economic development and democracy. They accept that the global comparisons yield empirical generalizations, but like de Schweinitz (1964) and Moore (1966), they seek to examine the historical sequences that comprise the links between development and democracy. In contrast to de Schweinitz and Moore, they expand the number of countries to include smaller advanced countries of Europe, Britain's settler colonies, and countries in Latin America and the Caribbean. In contrast to Moore (1966), they emphasize the role of the working class and the importance of international factors, which they claim are lacking from his analysis. They thus focus on the meaning of democracy and its relation to social inequality, social class divisions, the role of the state, and transnational power constellations (Rueschemeyer *et al.* 1992:40). Due to the length and complexity of their study, the following review will sketch out in skeletal fashion the main points of the comparative analysis and subsequent argument.

The first part of the study compares the experiences with development and democracy in seventeen advanced countries, including Sweden, Denmark, Norway, Switzerland, Belgium, The Netherlands, France, Britain, the United States, Australia, Canada, New Zealand, Austria-Hungary, Spain, Italy, and Germany. The goal of the comparison is to identify the key variables that help explain prolonged periods of democracy, unstable periods of democracy, and authoritarianism in all these countries. All of them underwent some form of capitalist development, and most experienced the rapid development of industrial capitalism in the latter half of the nineteenth century.

Despite this similar set of starting conditions, some countries (Austria-Hungary, Spain, Italy, and Germany) were unable to sustain democracy through the inter-war years. Thus, the comparisons seek to explain these differences in outcome.

Like Moore (1966), the analysis stresses the importance of the strength of different social classes, including the agrarian elite, the bourgeoisie, and the working class. Except for Britain, the United States, and Australia, a strong *agrarian* elite stood as a key obstacle to democratization. In these exceptional cases, other important factors such as an autonomous state, a strong working class, and the legacy of British institutional practices in its former colonies helped attenuate this antidemocratic tendency within the agrarian elite. Elsewhere, a weak agrarian elite coupled with the presence of a strong bourgeoisie meant that the chances for sustaining democracy remained very high. The comparisons also reveal that historically it has been the working class that has been the main agent of democratization in the advanced countries. While certain elements in the middle class have supported democratic ideals, it has been the push for inclusion through the extension of rights by the working class that has made the key difference to the realization of liberal democracy in these countries (Rueschemeyer *et al.* 1992:97–98). Moreover, the inclusion in the comparison of the smaller democracies demonstrated that democracy is not dependent on a revolutionary break with the past as Moore (1966) maintained.

The authoritarian countries had a different set of experiences. They industrialized later than the democratic countries and had a strong agrarian elite. This elite formed a coalition with the bourgeoisie and the state that oversaw labour-repressive agricultural practices and the establishment of a certain authoritarian ideological hegemony, which manifested itself in fascist tendencies inimical to the development of democracy. Like Moore (1966), Rueschemeyer *et al.* (1992) suggest that the conditions for authoritarianism existed in countries that managed to avoid it. They insist that the United States was not fully democratic until the passage of the 1965 Voting Rights Act, which extended suffrage to African-Americans in the former Confederate states. In contrast to Moore (1966), they argue that the Civil War helped establish democracy in the north and the west, but the south was characterized by the re-institution of authoritarian practices dominated by a strong agrarian elite (Rueschemeyer *et al.* 1992:122–132, 148). These different historical trajectories are summarized in Table 2.1.3, including the nature of development, the strength of classes and class alliances, and the role of the state.

The comparison of the Latin American countries begins with the basic premise that they developed differently than the advanced countries in two major respects. The process of development was initiated much later than in the advanced countries and succeeded a period of growth that was highly dependent on the export of primary products particularly vulnerable to changing market conditions. The key determinants for the emergence of democracy in the first half of the twentieth century include the consolidation of state power, the nature of the export economy (mineral vs. agricultural), the strength and timing of the process of industrialization, and the agent of political articulation of the subordinate classes. Early consolidation of state power institutionalizes contestation among competing groups and ends overt challenges to the authority of the state. Mineral and agricultural export expansion developed different sets of social classes, which articulated their demands in different types of political party organizations; clientelistic parties developed in the agricultural countries while mass radical parties developed in the mineral countries. An early initialization of the process of industrialization breaks the landed classes and produces an active and strong subordinate class that can attract some middleclass support. The presence of two powerful political parties that seek to mediate competing interests in society helps foster democracy (Rueschemeyer *et al.* 1992: 197–199). Clientelistic parties that help channel the demands of the subordinate classes are seen as less threatening to elites. Taken together (see Table 2.1.4), these factors greatly enhance the chances of democratization in the region.

TABLE 2.1.3 Conditions for Democracy and Authoritarianism in Advanced Countries

	Sweden, Denmark, Norway, Switzerland, Belgium, The Netherlands, France	Britain	United States, Australia	Canada, New Zealand	Austria–Hungary Spain Italy Germany
Development	Rapid development of industrial capitalism in latter half of 19th cent.	Rapid development of industrial capitalism in latter half of 19th cent.	Rapid development of industrial capitalism in latter half of 19th cent. in US only		Late industrialization
Classes	Weak agrarian elite Strong bourgeoisie	Strong agrarian elite Strong bourgeoisie	Strong agrarian elite Strong bourgeoisie	Weak agrarian elite Strong bourgeoisie	Strong agrarian elite Strong bourgeoisie (except Germany)
	Strong working class No labour-repressive agriculture	Strong working class No labour-repressive agriculture	Weak working class Autonomous state Labour-repressive agriculture	Autonomous state No labour-repressive agriculture	Agrarian elite–bourgeoisie–state alliance Labour-repressive agriculture
History			Vast supplies of cheap land British colonial influence: representative government & suffrage	Vast supplies of cheap land British colonial influence: representative government & suffrage	Authoritarian ideological hegemony
	Revolutionary break from the past only in France	Revolutionary break from the past	Revolutionary break from the past (except Australia)	No revolutionary break from the past	No revolutionary break from the past
Outcome	Democracy	Democracy	Democracy	Democracy	Authoritarianism

Source: Rueschemeyer et al. (1992: 79–154)

TABLE 2.1.4 Development and Initial Democratization in Latin America

	Uruguay, Argentina	Colombia, Ecuador	Brazil	Bolivia, Venezuela	Chile, Peru	Mexico	Paraguay
Development	Export expansion	Export expansion	Export expansion	Export expansion	Export expansion	Export expansion	No export expansion
	Agriculture Non-labour-intensive	Agriculture Labour-intensive	Agriculture Labour-intensive	Mineral	Mineral	Mineral	Agriculture Labour-intensive
Mobilizing agent	Clientelistic parties	Clientelistic parties	State	Radical mass parties	Radical mass parties	Revolution	State
Industrialization	Before 1930	After 1945	1930–1945	After 1945	After 1945	Before 1930	After 1945
Initial democracy	Before 1930	1930–1945 Ecuador after 1945	1945–1964	1930–1945 Bolivia after 1945	1930; 1930–1945 for Peru		
Outcome	Full stable democracy > 12 yrs	Restricted stable democracy > 12 yrs	Restricted stable democracy > 12 yrs	Full unstable democracy < 12 yrs	Restricted unstable democracy < 12 yrs	Authoritarianism	Authoritarianism

Source: Rueschemeyer et al. (1992: 159–199)

After the period of initial democratization, all of the countries in the comparison experienced breakdowns of democracy in one form or another. Some saw a collapse into civil war (Colombia and Venezuela), while others saw the rise of military authoritarianism (e.g. Brazil 1964–1985; Argentina 1966–1973, 1976–1983; Uruguay 1973–1984; and Chile 1973–1990). For Rueschemeyer *et al.* (1992: 216) the key to maintaining democracy and political stability is an institutionalized party system that protects the interests of elites (see Chapter 10). In addition to the weakness of party systems and the breakdown of democracy, they also stress the fact that the nature of the military and its relationship to the civilian world are different for Latin America, leading to frequent, and in some cases, long interventions into the political sphere. In sum, if the social and political forces unleashed by economic development are not channelled in such a way that the threat to elites is sufficiently minimized, the likelihood of democracy surviving during this period is very limited indeed.

This basic explanation for democracy holds in the comparisons of Central America and the Caribbean, with the added effects of the British colonial experience. Except for Costa Rica, the Central American cases have had difficulty in establishing organizations within civil society and representatives of the subordinate classes that are strong enough to counter an elite-dominated state, leading to a history of civil war, political instability, and repression (Rueschemeyer *et al.* 1992:259). Moreover, the heavy presence of US intervention has tended to strengthen the repressive apparatus of the state in these countries. In the Caribbean countries, the agrarian elite did not control the state during the period in which groups in civil society were forming, and by the time these countries achieved independence, both political parties and unions were well established (ibid.: 260).

It is clear from the examination of these various studies that the comparison of few countries offers different analytical opportunities for scholars. This method of comparison allows the intensive examination of individual countries and more focus on the differences between countries in order to explain the ways in which economic development may or may not foster democracy. A small number of countries allows the comparison to highlight historical sequences, and the importance of specific historical events on the subsequent chances of establishing democracy, including wars, revolutions, and economic crises. The difference in results between these studies and those that compare many countries regarding the relationship between economic development and democracy awaits final discussion, as it is important to consider a few single-country studies on this topic from the field.

Single-Country Studies

Clearly, there are likely to be as many (if not more) single-country studies as there are countries in the world that seek to explain paths of development and their relationship to democracy. From Tocqueville's classic study of democracy in the United States to the latest single-country studies of democratization, the field of comparative politics is replete with examples of such studies. As outlined in the previous chapter, among their many different functions single-country studies can confirm existing theories, infirm existing theories, or generate new hypotheses. Thus, this section presents some recent efforts to relate economic development and democracy at the single-country level that serve any or all of these comparative purposes. Moreover, they all in some way use the comparative categories and explanation found in the preceding studies. The studies in this section include Putnam's (1993) study of democratic institutional performance in Italy, Waisman's (1989) study of Argentina, and three case studies on Botswana, South Korea, and India found in Leftwich's (1996) *Democracy and Development.*

In *Making Democracy Work*, Putnam (1993a) offers a single-country study of Italy that compares democratic institutional performance across its twenty administrative regions using quantitative and qualitative research techniques. Putnam (1993a:63–82) establishes a measure of democratic institutional performance, which is an index at the regional level that combines twelve indicators of policy processes, policy pronouncements, and policy implementation. These indicators include cabinet stability, budget promptness, statistical and informational services, reform legislation, legislative innovation, the provision of daycare centres, the number of family clinics, industrial policy instruments, agricultural spending capacity, local health unit expenditures, housing and urban development, and bureaucratic responsiveness (ibid.: 65–73). This combined index then serves as the key dependent variable for the remainder of the study.

Geographically, the level of democratic institutional performance is higher in the northern regions of Italy than in the southern regions. Drawing on many of the same studies reviewed in this chapter, Putnam (ibid.: 83–86) initially posits that the level of socio-economic modernization accounts for the differences in institutional performance that he observes. A simple analysis that compares measures of economic development (per capita income, gross regional product, and agricultural and industrial shares of the workforce and value added) and institutional performance reveals that those regions with higher levels of economic development have higher levels of institutional performance (ibid.: 85). Moreover, these levels of economic development are higher in the north than in the south. Closer inspection of the figures, however, reveals that within either the north or the south, the relationship drops out. In other words, economic development goes some way towards explaining differences in institutional performance *between* regions, but it cannot account for differences *within* the north or the south.

Putnam suspects that the simple relationship between economic development and institutional performance is spurious, and the paradox identified for the north–south divide leads him to look for some other factor that may help explain institutional performance in

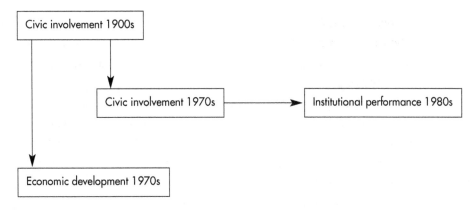

FIGURE 2.1.7   Explaining democratic institutional performance in Italy

Source: Adapted from Putnam (1993:157)

Italy. The answer for Putnam lies in the history of civic involvement in Italy: a slow process of accumulation that begins in medieval times and extends to modern-day Italy (ibid.: 121–162). Civic involvement consists in active participation in public affairs, the development of ideas of political equality, solidarity, trust, tolerance, and the formation of voluntary associations (ibid.: 86–91). When the effects of this additional factor are analysed, the direct relationship between economic development and institutional performance disappears. In its place, Putnam (ibid.: 157) specifies a model (see Figure 2.1.7) that establishes a link between past civic involvement (1900s) to civic involvement and socio-economic development in the 1970s. The level of civic involvement in the 1970s is related to democratic institutional performance in the 1980s.

Waisman's (1989:59) study of Argentina opens with a key question: 'Why did this country fail to become an industrial democracy?' He shows that between 1900 and the Great Depression, Argentina experienced growth rates in per capita GNP that were higher than growth rates in Sweden and France. On the eve of the Great Depression, per capita GNP was higher than that in Austria and Italy. And by the mid-1940s, the country had higher levels of urbanization than the United States and most of Europe (ibid.: 61–63). Throughout this period, Argentina saw the emergence of restricted liberal democracy with the beginnings of an institutionalized political party system, but by 1930 democracy collapsed and would only make fleeting returns from this year until its full re-emergence in 1983 (see also Chapter 9 in this volume). Between 1930 and 1983, the country saw six major military coups, 22 years of military rule, and 25 presidents, eighteen of whom were elected and subsequently overthrown between 1955 and 1983. The country's spectacular economic performance also collapsed by the middle of the century. Growth rates fell to 0.9 per cent in the 1950s, 2.8 per cent in the 1960s, 2.3 per cent in the 1970s, and negative levels in the 1980s, so that between 1950 and 1983, the country experienced only an average of 1 per cent growth (ibid.: 62).

To explain the fluctuations in the experience of democracy in Argentina, Waisman (1989) uses similar analytical categories to those found in Rueschemeyer *et al.* (1992). He argues that the emergence and stability of democracy in the first period (1900–1930) were due first to a high and sustained rate of economic growth. The expansion during this period allowed for the 'absorption of mass immigration, rapid urbanization and industrialization, expansion of education, and high standards of living for the lower classes'. Second, middle-class demands for participation and intense labour mobilization were absorbed by elites through inclusionary strategies (Waisman 1989:84). He argues that the subsequent periods of authoritarianism were largely due to the emergence of an autonomous developmental state and the presence of entrenched economic elites who opposed the interests of the subordinate classes as well as the representation of all interests through democratic political institutions (ibid.: 85–97). This study can be read alongside Hawkins' (2001) study of Cuba, since it too is a case of failure to make a transition to democracy given the presence of favourable economic conditions [...].

The three separate case studies of Botswana (Holm 1996), India (Kaviraj 1996), and South Korea (Moon and Kim 1996) show great variation in both economic development and experiences with democracy. Holm (1996) argues that Botswana has had a developing economy and an emerging democracy for over thirty years. From 1965 onwards, the country has seen 10 per cent annual growth rates based on a mineral economy that has diversified into producing coal, soda ash, and manufactured products. It has a hybrid presidential-parliamentary democracy and well-developed bureaucracy (due to the British colonial experience 1885–1965). In terms of free elections and the protection of political liberties, Botswana meets the criteria of a democracy as found in the global comparisons reviewed above (ibid.: 103). Despite this seeming association between economic development and democracy, Holm is keen to point out that Botswana still only has formal democracy, and that the society remains characterized by government secrecy and low accountability, weak opposition parties, and an underdeveloped civil society. For Holm (ibid.: 98, 107) the key intervening variable that lies between economic development and democracy is Tswana political culture, which maintains authoritarian and hierarchical patterns of organization, and tends to separate the activities of civil society and politics.

Like Moore (1966), Kaviraj (1996) argues that the temporal sequence of the relation between economic development and democracy is different for India than for the patterns observed in Europe. The secularization of politics, the individuation of civil society, and the development of a modern capitalist economy preceded the development of democracy in the West. In India these processes all happened at the same time. Thus, the development of democracy has altered but not displaced traditional identities based on the caste system and religious divisions. A formalized and 'modern' redefinition of the caste system has profound implications for the distribution of the economic goods of development as well as the definition of the proper activities for political and economic actors in society (ibid.: 132–133). Moreover, the case of India illustrates that both the process of economic development and democracy can raise expectations within a society as well as threaten political stability (ibid.: 133–134).

The final case of South Korea appears as the model of successful modernization. As in Botswana, it has maintained 10 per cent growth rates since 1965, a process of development which has also been accompanied by a reasonably equitable distribution of economic resources (Moon and Kim 1996:139). Politically, however, the country has seen the repressive Yushin regime in the 1970s, the quasi-military rule of Chun Doo Hwan in the 1980s, a period of democratic transition between 1988 and 1992, and its first free and fair elections only in 1992 (ibid.: 140). Thus, the successful model of economic growth has been accompanied by a long period of non-democratic rule. Moon and Kim (ibid.: 148) attribute the transition to democracy and the subsequent period of democratic consolidation to sustained economic growth, which has been mediated by two further important factors. Economic development has altered the distribution of power in society and this has favoured the emergence of democracy. Following Inglehart (1990), they argue that economic development has changed Korean political culture by replacing traditional conservative and authoritarian values with modern and participant values.

Summary

Table 2.1.5 summarizes the 'comparison of comparisons' on the relationship between economic development and democracy presented in this chapter. There appears to be a contradiction between the main findings of those studies that compare many countries and those that either compare a few countries or those that study one country. On balance, the comparison of many countries at one time or over time reveals a strong positive effect between the level of economic development and democracy. Some of these comparisons claim that the two phenomena are associated with each other, others argue that they are causally related, while others contend that the positive relationship is due to the fact that once established, wealthy democracies tend not to collapse. In contrast, the comparison of few countries and single-country studies claim that the relationship between economic development and democracy is mediated by other important factors, such as class structures, the nature of economic development, the role of the state, important historical events, political culture, and international factors.

The different conclusions reached by different methods raise an important question. Is there something wrong methodologically with each major type of comparison? The short answer is no. [...], [E]ach method of comparison is useful for drawing inferences, and as the review of comparisons here demonstrated, scholars interested in this research question have used different methods precisely to redress problems of earlier studies, draw stronger inferences, and test different theories. A longer answer suggests that there

TABLE 2.1.5 Economic Development and Democracy in Comparative Perspective

Method of Comparison	Number of Countries	Exemplars	Result
Many countries	Between 48 and 135 either at one point in time or over time	Lipset 1959; Cutright 1963; Cutright and Wiley 1969; Dahl 1971; Jackman 1973; Bollen 1979; Helliwell 1994; Burkhart and Lewis-Beck 1994; Boix 2003; Boix and Stokes 2003 Przeworski and Limongi 1997; Przeworski *et al.*, 2000	Weak version: democracy is associated with development; Strong version: development causes democracy Once established, wealthy democracies tend not to collapse
Few countries (quantitative)	Between 6 and 23 either at one point in time or over time	Lerner 1958; Neubauer 1967; Landman 1999, 2006; Mainwaring and Perez-Liñan 2002	For Lerner, modernity associated with democracy; for Neubauer, Landman, Mainwaring and Perez-Liñan no relationship exists
Few countries qualitative)	Between 4 and 37 countries over time	De Schweinitz 1964; Moore 1966; Rueschemeyer *et al.* 1992	Democracy is a product of discrete historical events that are not likely to be repeated in the future
Single-country studies	One country over time	Waisman 1989a; Putnam 1993a; Holm 1996; Kaviraj 1996; Moon and Kim 1996	Country-specific factors, particularly political culture, condition the relationship

are three factors inherent in these comparisons that account for the difference in result, including the role of historical time, the selection of cases, and the different emphasis put on similarities and differences between countries. This concluding section will discuss these in turn.

The global comparisons assume that all countries are on a common trajectory that extends from a 'traditional' end to a 'modern' one, which suggests that sooner or later, any country at any time will necessarily make this transition. Comparisons of many countries at one point in time imply this trajectory, since each country in their sample is located at a different point along this trajectory. Later global comparisons reacted to this criticism by comparing over time and space, and Bollen (1979) controlled for the effects of the timing of development. Studies that compare few countries argue that the inclusion of both time and the timing of development are not enough, since these factors still ignore the importance of history. These studies argue that specific historical events and the contingent concatenation of these events affect the nature of the traditional–modern trajectory implied by the global comparisons. In the 1960s, countries were undergoing the process of development after the Russian, Mexican, Chinese, and Cuban revolutions, all of which demonstrated different developmental trajectories than those assumed by the global comparisons.

The importance of historical time and the emphasis on historical sequences are necessarily related to the selection of cases, which is in turn related to the difference in results for the comparisons examined in this chapter. Thus, Neubauer (1967) compares only democracies, since he seeks to measure democratic development. Lerner (1958), Landman (1999, 2006a), and Mainwaring and Perez-Liñan (2003) compare countries that share geographical proximity and cultural similarities. Both de Schweinitz (1964) and Moore (1966) choose countries based on the key outcomes of democracy, fascism, and communism. Neubauer (1967), de Schweinitz (1964), and Moore (1966) all have problems with selection bias since the choice of cases is determined by the dependent variable (see Chapter 3). Lerner's (1958) study of the Middle East and the studies on Latin America do not have problems with selection bias since their choice of countries is not related to the dependent variable. In similar fashion, Rueschemeyer *et al.* (1992) avoid selection bias by comparing all the countries in each of their clusters (i.e. advanced countries, Latin America, Central America and the Caribbean). Indeed, by looking at the smaller democracies of the advanced world, they rule out a revolutionary break with the past as a significant explanatory variable for democracy. Even when selection bias is avoided, the selection of cases still helps explain the difference in results between the global comparisons and those that examine a smaller number of countries. The global comparisons concentrate their efforts on the regularities that hold across a large sample. Deviant cases are a natural occurrence in large samples, while the goal of the analysis is to demonstrate the commonality across the countries.

In contrast, studies that compare few countries place more emphasis on the differences across the countries. These studies demonstrate that the relationship between economic development and democracy does not hold for all countries. The global comparativists would not disagree; they would merely reply that the relationship does hold more often than not. Thus, the differences in results lie as much in the nature of the comparison as in the interpretation of the evidence. In sum, the different comparative methods should be seen as complements to one another. Global comparisons establish general patterns of co-variation, which can be examined further through the analysis of a smaller number of countries. Global comparisons allow for the specification of parsimonious explanations that are based on a small set of variables, while additional variables can be specified in studies that compare a few countries. Finally, both methods of comparison may identify deviant cases that can be examined further with a more intensive single-country study. In the case of the relationship between economic development and democracy, the evidence suggests that there is a stable positive association between the two, but as in many things, there are exceptions to the rule. The lesson for comparative politics is to determine whether these exceptions are important for the overall inferences that are drawn about the political world.

Notes

1. A corollary branch of comparative research inverts the relationship to examine whether democracies achieve better levels of economic development. See Helliwell (1994).
2. The comparison was made in 1971 with 1957 GNP per capita figures, when both the USSR and GDR existed.
3. The separate scales were originally developed by Raymond D. Gastil and since then have been maintained on an annual basis by Freedom House (see Foweraker and Landman 1997:55–56).
4. A similar style of analysis was carried out for Central America and arrived at similar results (see Seligson 1987).
5. Moore concedes that there were some conservative reversals with the Bourbon Restoration (1815–1848), but by 1830 the power of the old aristocracy had been effectively eliminated (Moore 1966:106).

References

Boix, C. (2003) *Democracy and Redistribution*, Cambridge: Cambridge University Press.

Boix, C. and Stokes, S. (2003) 'Endogenous Democratization', *World Politics*, 55 (July): 517–49.

Bollen, K. (1979) 'Political Democracy and the Timing of Development', *American Sociological Review*, 44 (August): 572–587.

Brohman, J. (1996) *Popular Development*, Oxford: Blackwell.

Burkhart, R.E. and Lewis-Beck, M. (1994) 'Comparative Democracy, the Economic Development Thesis', *American Political Science Review*, 88(4): 903–910.

Burton, M., Gunther, R., and Higley, J. (1992) 'Introduction: Elite Transformation and Democratic Regimes', in John Higley and Richard Gunther (eds), *Elites and Democratic Consolidation in Latin America and Southern Europe*, Cambridge: Cambridge University Press, 1–37.

Collier, D. and Collier, R.B. (1991) *Shaping the Political Arena: Critical Junctures, the Labor Movement, and Regime Dynamics*, Princeton, NJ: Princeton University Press.

Cutright, P. (1963) 'National Political Development: Its Measurement and Social Correlates', in N. Polsby, R.A. Denther, and P.A. Smith (eds) *Political and Social Life*, Boston, MA: Houghton Mifflin, 569–582.

Cutright, P. and Wiley, J.A. (1969) 'Modernization and Political Representation: 1927–1966', *Studies in Comparative International Development*, 5(2): 23–44.

Dahl, R.A. (1971) *Polyarchy: Participation and Opposition*, New Haven, CT: Yale University Press.

De Mesquita, B., Morrow, J.D., and Zorick, E.R. (1997) 'Capabilities, Perception, and Escalation', *American Political Science Review*, 91 (March): 15–27.

De Schweinitz, K. (1964) *Industrialization and Democracy: Economic Necessities and Political Possibilities*, New York: Free Press.

Doorenspleet, R. (2005) *Democratic Transitions: Exploring the Structural Sources of the Fourth Wave*, Boulder, CO: Lynne Rienner.

Ersson, S. and Lane, J.E. (1996) 'Democracy and Development: A Statistical Exploration', in A. Leftwich (ed.) *Democracy and Development*, Cambridge: Polity, 45–73.

Foweraker, J. and Landman, T. (1997) *Citizenship Rights and Social Movements: A Comparative and Statistical Analysis*, Oxford: Oxford University Press.

———(2004) 'Economic development and Democracy Revisited: Why Dependency Theory is Not Yet Dead', *Democratization*, 11(1): 1–21.

Gerschenkron, A. (1962) *Economic Backwardness in Historical Perspective*, Cambridge, MA: Belknap Press of Harvard University Press.

Hartz, L. (1955) *The Liberal Tradition in America; An Interpretation of American Political Thought since the Revolution*, New York: Harcourt Brace.

Hawkins, D. (2001) 'Democratization Theory and Non-Transitions: Insights from Cuba', *Comparative Politics*, 33(4): 441–461.

Helliwell, J.F. (1994) 'Empirical Linkages between Democracy and Economic Growth', *British Journal of Political Science*, 24: 225–248.

Holm, J.D. (1996) 'Development, Democracy, and Civil Society in Botswana', in A. Leftwich (ed.) *Democracy and Development*, Cambridge: Polity Press, 97–113.

Huntington, S.P. (1991) *The Third Wave: Democratization in the Late Twentieth Century*, Norman, OK: University of Oklahoma Press.

Inglehart, R. (1990) *Culture Shift in Advanced Industrial Societies*, Princeton, NJ: Princeton University Press.

———(1997) *Modernization and Postmodernization*, Princeton, NJ: Princeton University Press.

Jackman, R.W. (1973) 'On the Relation of Economic Development to Democratic Performance', *American Journal of Political Science*, 17(3): 611–621.

Jackson, J.E. (1996) 'Political Methodology: An Overview', in R.E. Goodin and H. Klingemann (eds) *The New Handbook of Political Science*, Oxford: Oxford University Press, 717–748.

Karl, T.L. (1990) 'Dilemmas of Democratization in Latin America', *Comparative Politics*, 23: 1–21.

Kaviraj, S. (1996) 'Dilemmas of Democratic Development in India', in A. Leftwich (ed.) *Democracy and Development*, Cambridge: Polity Press, 114–138.

Landman, T. (1999) 'Economic Development and Democracy: The View from Latin America', *Political Studies*, 47(4): 607–626.

———(2001) 'The Economic Requirements of Democracy', in J. Foweraker and P.B. Clarke (eds) *Encyclopaedia of Democratic Thought*, London: Routledge, 235–239.

———(2006a) 'Development, Democracy, and Human Rights in Latin America' in Janet Dine and Andrew Fagan (eds) *Capitalism and Human Rights*, Cheltenham: Edward Elgar Publishers, 330–357.

Leftwich, A. (ed.) (1996) *Democracy and Development*, Cambridge: Polity Press.

Lerner, D. (1958) *The Passing of Traditional Society: Modernizing the Middle East*, Glencoe, IL: The Free Press of Glencoe.

Lipset, S.M. (1959) 'Some Social Requisites for Democracy: Economic Development and Political Legitimacy', *The American Political Science Review*, 53: 69–105.

———(1960) *Political Man*, London: Heinemann.

Mainwaring, S. and Perez-Liñan (2003) 'Level of Development and Democracy: Latin-American Exceptionalism, 1945–1966', *Comparative Political Studies* 36(9): 1031–1067.

Moon, C. and Kim, Y. (1996) 'A Circle of Paradox: Development, Politics and Democracy in South Korea', in A. Leftwich (ed.) *Democracy and Development*, Cambridge: Polity Press, 139–167.

Moore, B. (1966) *The Social Origins of Dictatorship and Democracy: Lord and Peasant in the Making of the Modern World*, Boston, MA: Beacon Press.

Neubauer, D.E. (1967) 'Some Conditions of Democracy', *American Political Science Review* 61: 1002–1009.

Przeworski, A. and Limongi, F. (1997) 'Modernization: Theories and Facts', *World Politics*, 49 (January): 155–183.

Przeworski, A., Alvarez, M.E., Cheibub, J.A., and Limongi, F. (2000) *Democracy and Development: Political Institutions and Well-being in the World, 1950–1990*, Cambridge: Cambridge University Press.

Putnam, R. (1993a) *Making Democracy Work: Civic Traditions in Modern Italy*, Princeton, NJ: Princeton University Press.

Putnam, R. (1993b) 'Diplomacy and Domestic Politics: the Logic of Two-Level Games', in P.B. Evans, H.K. Jacobson, and R.D. Putnam (eds) *Double-Edged Diplomacy: International Bargaining and Domestic Politics*, Los Angeles: University of California Press, 431–468.

Rostow, W.W. (1961) *The Stages of Economic Growth: A Non-communist Manifesto*, Cambridge: Cambridge University Press.

Rueschemeyer, D., Stephens, E.H., and Stephens, J. (1992) *Capitalist Development and Democracy*, Cambridge: Polity Press.

Rustow, D.A. (1970) 'Transitions to Democracy: Toward a Dynamic Model', *Comparative Politics*, 2: 337–363.

Seligson, M. (1987) 'Development, Democratization, and Decay: Central America at the Crossroads', in J. Malloy and M. Seligson (eds) *Authoritarians and Democrats: Regime Transition in Latin America*, Pittsburgh, PA: University of Pittsburgh Press.

Todaro, M.P. (1994) *Economic Development*, 5th edn, London: Longman.

Valenzuela, J.S. and Valenzuela, A. (1978) 'Modernization and Dependency: Alternative Perspectives in the Study of Latin American Underdevelopment', *Comparative Politics*, 10, 535–557.

Waisman, C.H. (1989) 'Argentina: Autarkic Industrialization and Illegitimacy', in L. Diamond, J.J. Linz, and S.M. Lipset (eds) *Democracy in Developing Countries*, Vol. 4: Latin America, London: Adamantine Press, 59–109.

Reading 2.2

A Skin, Not a Sweater: Ontology and Epistemology in Political Science

Paul Furlong and David Marsh

THIS CHAPTER INTRODUCES THE READER TO the key issues that underpin what we do as social or political scientists. Each social scientist's orientation to their subject is shaped by their ontological and epistemological position. Most often those positions are implicit rather than explicit, but, regardless of whether they are acknowledged, they shape the approach to theory and the methods which the social scientist utilises. At first these issues seem difficult but our major point is that they are not issues that can be avoided. They are like a skin not a sweater: they cannot be put on and taken off whenever the researcher sees fit. In our view, all students of political science should recognise and acknowledge their own ontological and epistemological positions and be able to defend these positions against critiques from other positions. This means they need to understand the alternative positions on these fundamental questions. As such, this chapter has two key aims. First, we will introduce these ontological and epistemological questions in as accessible a way as possible in order to allow the reader who is new to these issues to reflect on their own position. Second, this introduction is crucial to the readers of this book [...] who want fully to appreciate the substantive content of this book.

The chapter is divided into three major sections. The first section describes what we mean by these two terms 'ontology' and 'epistemology' and considers briefly why these questions are important. The second section then outlines the different positions on ontology and epistemology and the arguments which have been put forward for and against these positions. Finally, we shall illustrate how these different positions shape the approaches that researchers take to their research by focusing on research in two broad areas: globalisation and multilevel governance.

Ontology and Epistemology

Ontological and epistemological positions are related, but need to be separated. To put it crudely, one's ontological position affects, but far from determines, one's epistemological position.

Ontology

Ontological questions are prior because they deal with the very nature of 'being'; literally, an ontology is a theory of 'being' (the word derives from the Greek for 'existence'). This sounds difficult, but really it is not. The key question is whether there is a 'real' world 'out there' that is independent of our knowledge of it. For example, are there essential differences between genders, classes or races that exist in all contexts and at all times?

A simple illustration easily makes the point. Over the last ten years John Gray's book *Men are from Mars and Women are from Venus* (1992) has sold seven million copies in the USA and millions more in forty countries worldwide. He argues that men and women are very different and that men and women can only understand and deal with one another better if they recognise this fact of life. This book takes a clear ontological position; there are fundamental differences between men and women that are features of their very existence. These differences persist over time and are common across cultures. This is an essentialist or a foundationalist ontological position. So, its proponents argue that there are essential differences of 'being' that provide the foundations upon which social life is built.

Of course, this is a contentious position; one which is strongly attacked by many, if not most, feminists. They believe that the differences between men and women are socially constructed. As such, they are not essential differences but are particular to a given culture and time. They are the product of patriarchy, in which male dominance shapes the culture and values of society, affects patterns of socialisation and perpetuates gender inequality. This argument reflects a different ontological position that is anti-foundationalist and emphasises the social construction of social phenomena.

Epistemology

If an ontological position reflects the researcher's view about the nature of the world, their epistemological position reflects their view of what we can know about the world and how we can know it; literally an epistemology is a theory of knowledge. Again, this sounds difficult, but the basic concerns are not too difficult. There are two key questions. Can an observer identify 'real' or 'objective' relations between social phenomena? If so, how? The first question itself subsumes two issues. Initially, it takes us back to ontology; if one is an anti-foundationalist, then one argues that there is not a 'real' world, which exists independently of the meaning which actors attach to their action, to discover. At the same time, such an anti-foundationalist would also suggest that no observer can be 'objective' because they live in the social world and are affected by the social constructions of 'reality'. This is sometimes called the double hermeneutic; the world is interpreted by the actors (one hermeneutic level) and their interpretation is interpreted by the observer (a second hermeneutic level).

The second question raises another important, and clearly related, issue. To the extent that we can establish 'real' relationships between social phenomena, can we do this simply through direct observation, or are there some relationships which 'exist' but are not directly observable? The answers one gives to these questions shapes one's epistemological position.

Of course, there are different ways of classifying epistemological positions and there is no agreement as to the best way. Probably the most common classification distinguishes between scientific (sometimes positivist) and hermeneutic (or interpretist) positions. We shall begin with a brief review of that distinction, before proposing an alternative, which distinguishes between positivist, realist and interpretist positions.

Scientific versus Hermeneutic Approaches

Social science was influenced by the ideas of science as the nomenclature clearly indicates. In particular, the *empiricist* tradition played a crucial role in the development of social science. David Hume argued that knowledge starts from our senses. On the basis of such direct experience we could develop generalisations about the relationships between physical phenomena. The aim was to develop causal statements which specified that, under a given set of conditions, there would be regular and predictable outcomes (on this see Hollis and Smith 1990: ch. 3). The adherents of the scientific tradition saw social science as analogous to science. In ontological terms they were foundationalists; they thought there was a real world 'out there' which was external to agents. Their focus was upon identifying the *causes* of social behaviour. The emphasis was upon *explanation* and many felt that the use of rigorous 'scientific' methods would allow social scientists to develop laws, similar in status to scientific laws, which would hold across time and space.

In methodological terms, the scientific tradition was greatly influenced by logical positivism that posited a very straightforward characterisation of the form of scientific investigation. As Hollis and Smith put it (1990: 50):

> To detect the regularities in nature, propose a generalisation, deduce what it implies for the next case and observe whether the prediction succeeds. If it does, no consequent action is needed; if it does not, then either discard the generalisation or amend it and [test the] fresh [predictions].

In contrast, there is an alternative hermeneutic (the word derives from the Greek for 'to interpret') or interpretist tradition. The adherents of this position are anti-foundationalists, believing that the world is socially constructed. They focus upon the *meaning* of behaviour. The emphasis is upon *understanding*, rather than *explanation*. As such, in the interpretist tradition it is not possible to establish causal relationships between phenomena that hold across time and space.

We prefer this classification because the scientific tradition identified by Hollis and Smith conflates two distinct positions, positivism and realism. Positivists adhere to a foundationalist ontology and are concerned to establish causal relationships between social phenomema, thus developing explanatory, and indeed predictive, models. The realist is also foundationalist in ontological terms. However, realists, unlike positivists, do not privilege direct observation. The realist believes that there are deep structural relationships between social phenomena which cannot be directly observed, but which are crucial for any explanation of behaviour. So, as an example, a realist might argue that patriarchy as a structure cannot be directly observed, although we can see many of the consequences of it; we return to this example later.

The distinction between positivist, realist and interpretist approaches is examined in much more depth in the next section. However, the key point here is that any classification that we adopt would annoy some social scientists. We use this particular distinction because we are realists and, as such, do not like the conflation between positivism and realism involved in the first distinction. However, many other authors would question our distinction. In particular, many, like Bevir and Rhodes (see below) would want to make further distinctions within the tradition of interpretive theory. The point is that any way of classifying epistemological positions can be contested; we choose one, but are aware of the criticism of it. In addition, we shall deal with many of those criticisms when we look at the variants within the three positions we identify.

Why are Such Distinctions Important?

In our view, ontological and epistemological concerns cannot, and should not, be ignored or downgraded. Three points are important here:

1. First, these concerns should not be put in what the Australians, with typical directness, call the 'too hard basket'. Certainly, the issues involved are not easy, but neither are they difficult, if they are explained simply and with appropriate examples.

2. Second, ontological and epistemological positions should not be treated like a sweater that can be 'put on' when we are addressing such philosophical issues and 'taken off' when we are doing research. In our view, the dominance of a fairly crude positivist epistemology throughout much of the postwar period encouraged many social scientists to dismiss ontological questions and regard epistemological issues as more or less resolved, with only the details left to be decided by those interested in such matters. Such social scientists have tended to acknowledge the importance of epistemology without considering it necessary to deal with it in detail; positivism has

been regarded as a comforting sweater that can be put on where necessary. In contrast, we would argue that epistemology, to say nothing of ontology, is far from being a closed debate.

3. Third, researchers cannot adopt one position at one time for one project and another on another occasion for a different project. These positions are not interchangeable because they reflect fundamental different approaches to what social science is and how we do it. This is the key point. As we pointed out in the introduction, a researcher's epistemological position is reflected in what is studied, how it is studied and the status the researcher gives to their findings. So, a positivist looks for causal relationships, tends to prefer quantitative analysis [...] and wants to produce 'objective' and generalisable findings. A researcher from within the interpretist tradition is concerned with understanding, not explanation, focuses on the meaning that actions have for agents, tends to use qualitative evidence and offers their results as one interpretation of the relationship between the social phenomena studied. Realism is less easy to classify in this way. The realists are looking for causal relationships, but think that many important relationships between social phenomena cannot be observed. This means they may use quantitative and qualitative data. The quantitative data will only be appropriate for those relationships that are directly observable. In contrast, the unobservable relationships can only be established indirectly; we can observe other relationships which, our theory tells us, are the result of those unobservable prelationships. We return to these issues in the next section.

Different Approaches to Ontology and Epistemology

Here we outline the positivist, the interpretist and the realist positions in more detail. We shall focus on: the major criticisms of the positions; the variations within these positions; and the way the positions have changed over time. At the outset, however, it is important to emphasise that the distinctions between the positions, and more specifically that between interpretism and realism, are not clear-cut.

Positivism

The core of positivism is fairly straightforward, although of course there are variants within it:

- Positivism is based upon a foundationalist ontology. So, to the positivist, like the realist, but unlike those from the interpretist position, the world exists independently of our knowledge of it.

- To the positivist, natural science and social science are broadly analogous. We can establish regular relationships between social phenomena, using theory to generate hypotheses which can be tested by direct observation. In this view, and in clear contrast to the realist, there are no deep structures that cannot be observed. Traditionally, positivism contended that there is no appearance/reality dichotomy and that the world is real and not socially constructed. So, direct observation can serve as an independent test of the validity of a theory. Crucially, an observer can be objective in the way they undertake such observations. Researchers from the interpretist tradition rarely accept any notion of objectivity. Realists accept that all observation is mediated by theory (to the realist, theory plays the crucial role in allowing the researcher to distinguish between those social phenomena which are directly observable and those which are not).

- To positivists the aim of social science is to make causal statements; in their view it is possible to, and we should attempt to, establish causal relationships between social phenomena. They share this aim with realists, while interpretists deny the possibility of such statements.

- Positivists also argue that it is possible to separate empirical questions—that is, questions about what is—from normative questions—that is, questions about what should be. Traditionally, positivists thought that the goal of social science was to pursue empirical questions, while philosophy, metaphysics or religion pursued the normative questions. Because we can separate empirical and normative questions, it is possible for social science to be objective and value-free. Realists and, especially, those from within the interpretist tradition would reject that proposition.

Many social scientists are positivists, although much of the positivism is implicit rather than explicit. The behavioural revolution in the social sciences in the 1960s [...] was an attempt to introduce scientific method into the study of society. It was an explicit reaction to political theory, which it saw as concerned with normative questions, and institutionalism, which it saw as lacking theoretical and methodological rigour. In contrast, it was based upon a foundationalist ontology and, most often, a quantitative methodology (but see below [...]). The view was that a social 'science' was possible if we followed the scientific method; deriving hypotheses from theory and then testing them in an attempt to falsify them. We needed 'objective' measures of our social phenomena, our variables; as such, we would focus upon 'hard' data—from government statistics, election results and so on—rather than soft data—from interviews or participant observation. So, for example, if a positivist was studying political participation, they would be interested in measuring the level of voting, party or pressure group membership, direct action or whatever, and relating it to demographic variables such as class, gender, race and education. The aim would be to establish the precise nature of the relationship between these variables and participation in order to produce causal models. We shall return to this example later. The key point here is that, as always, the ontological and epistemological position adopted had clear methodological implications.

The criticism of positivism takes two broad forms. The first line of criticism broadly argues that, in following the methods of science, positivists misinterpret how science really proceeds. Two lines of argument have been particularly important here. First, there is the pragmatist position of Quine (1961) who develops two crucial critiques of positivism (for a fuller exposition see Hollis and Smith 1990: 55–7; they deal with a third, less important, criticism):

(i)   Quine argues that any knowledge we derive from the five senses is mediated by the concepts we use to analyse it, so there is no way of classifying, or even describing, experience without interpreting it.

(ii) This means that theory and experiment are not simply separable, rather theory affects both the facts we focus on and how we interpret them. This, in turn, may affect the conclusions we draw if the facts appear to falsify the theory. As such, if we observe 'facts' which are inconsistent with the theory, we might decide that the facts are wrong rather than that the theory is wrong. Of course, this undermines the notion that observation alone can serve to falsify a theory.

Second, there is Kuhn's view (1970) that, at any given time, science tends to be dominated by a particular paradigm that is unquestioned and which affects the questions scientists ask and how they interpret what they observe (for a fuller discussion, see Hollis and Smith 1990: 57–61). Consequently, scientific investigation is not 'open', as positivism implies, rather certain conclusions are almost unthinkable. There is a 'paradigm shift' when a lot of empirical observation leads certain, brave, scientists to question the dominant paradigm, but until that time, and for the most part, scientists discard observations which do not fit (obviously this fits well with the second of Quine's criticisms above) and embrace the results which confirm the paradigm.

The second main line of criticism of positivism is more particular to social science. It argues that there are obvious differences between social and physical or natural phenomena that make social 'science' impossible. Three differences are particularly important. First, social structures, unlike natural structures, do not exist independently of the activities they shape. So, for example, marriage is a social institution or structure, but it is also a lived experience, particularly, although not exclusively, for those who are married. This lived experience affects agents' understanding of the institution and also helps change it. Second, and related, social structures, unlike natural structures, do not exist independently of agents' views of what they are doing in the activity. People are reflexive; they reflect on what they are doing and often change their actions in the light of that reflection. This leads us to the third difference. Social structures, unlike natural structures, change as a result of the actions of agents; in most senses the social world varies across time and space. Some positivist social scientists minimise these differences, but, to the extent they are accepted, they point towards a more interpretist epistemological position.

Many positivists avoid these critiques which are put in the 'too hard basket'. However, the more sophisticated positivists are aware of these criticisms and the position has changed significantly as a result. Fortunately, this volume boasts two sophisticated behaviouralists who are positivists, Sanders and John. It is particularly worth examining David Sanders' view in a little more detail because it represents an excellent example of the modern, more sophisticated, positivist position. Sanders [...] accepts he has been strongly influenced by the positivist position, but acknowledges the 'ferocious philosophical criticism' to which it was subjected. He argues that 'post-behaviouralists', who might also be called 'post-positivists': acknowledge the interdependence of theory and observation; recognise that normative questions are important and not always easy to separate from empirical questions; and accept that other traditions have a key role to play in political and social analysis. As such, this post-positivism has moved a significant way from more traditional positivism, largely as a result of the type of criticisms outlined here.

However, the ontological and epistemological problems have not gone away, rather they have been elided. Two quotes from Sanders illustrate the point. First, he argues [...]:

> Modern behaviouralists—'post-behaviouralists'—simply prefer to subject their own theoretical claims to empirical tests. They also suspect that scholars working in non-empirical traditions are never able to provide a satisfactory answer to the crucial question: 'How would you know if you were wrong?'

Later he continues [...]:

> For modern behaviouralists, the ultimate test of a good theory is still whether or not it is consistent with observation—with the available empirical evidence. Modern behaviouralists are perfectly prepared to accept that different theoretical positions are likely to produce different observations. They insist however, that, whatever 'observations' are implied by a particular theoretical perspective, those observations must be used in order to conduct a systematic empirical test of the theory that is being posited.

This is a sophisticated statement of a positivist epistemological position, but it is still essentially positivist. The aim is to use observation (of whatever type) to test hypothesised relationships between the social phenomena studied. Research from within other traditions must still be judged against the positivists' criteria: 'observation must be used in order to conduct a systematic empirical test of the theory that is being posited'. Yet, that is not a standard most researchers from within an interpretist tradition could accept (even Bevir and Rhodes 1999 could only do so with major qualifications), because they do not believe that direct observation can be objective and used as a test of 'reality'. Most realists would also have a problem with Sanders' position because they would see many of the key relationships as unobservable.

One other aspect of Sanders' position is important here. He accepts that interpretation and meaning are important, which might suggest that the differences between positivist and interpretist traditions are beginning to dissolve. So, Sanders argues [...] in criticising prior studies of voting behaviour: 'There are other areas—relating to the way in which individuals reflect, to a greater or lesser degree, upon themselves—where behavioural research has simply not dared to tread.' He recognises that such factors might, or might not, be important, but emphasises that they would be difficult to study empirically. However, the crucial point is that Sanders wants to treat interpretation and meaning as intervening variables. In this view, how a voter understands the parties and their own position may affect their voting behaviour. At best, this acknowledges only one aspect of the double hermeneutic; the interpretist tradition would argue that we also need to acknowledge the subjectivity of the observer.

So, positivism has changed in response to criticism. Post-positivism is much less assertive that there is only one way of doing social science. However, it still emphasises explanation, rather than understanding, and the primacy of direct observation. In our terms, it is still foundationalist and firmly located in the scientific tradition.

The Interpretist Position

The interpretist tradition is the obvious 'other' of positivism. However, it is a much broader church than positivism and much of this subsection will deal with its variants. Nevertheless, it is useful to begin with an outline of the core of the position.

- In the interpretist tradition researchers reject the notion that the world exists independently of our knowledge of it. Rather, they contend that the world is socially or discursively constructed. This view is diametrically opposed to positivism, but shares certain features with some modern variants of realism. In ontological terms, then, this position is anti-foundationalist.

- This means that for researchers working within this tradition social phenomena do not exist independently of our interpretation of them; rather it is this interpretation/understanding of social phenomena which affects outcomes. As such, it is the interpretations/meanings of social phenomena that are crucial; interpretations/meanings which can only be established and understood within discourses or traditions.

Consequently, we should focus on identifying those discourses or traditions and establishing the interpretations and meanings they attach to social phenomena.

- However, we must also acknowledge that 'objective' analysis is impossible. Social 'scientists' (of course interpretists would not use this term) are not privileged, but themselves operate within discourses or traditions. Consequently, knowledge is theoretically or discursively laden. As such, this position acknowledges the double hermeneutic.

This position has clear methodological implications. It argues that there is no objective truth, that the world is socially constructed and that the role of social 'scientists' [sic] is to study those social constructions. Quantitative methods can be blunt instruments and may produce misleading data. In contrast, we need to utilise qualitative methods—interviews, focus groups, vignettes and so on—to help us establish how people understand their world. So, for example, someone operating from within this tradition studying political participation would start by trying to establish how people understand 'the political' and 'political' participation

The major criticism of the interpretist tradition comes, unsurprisingly, from positivists, though some realists would agree with elements of that critique. To positivists, the interpretist tradition merely offers opinions or subjective judgements about the world. As such, there is no basis on which to judge the validity of their knowledge claims. One person's view of the world, and of the relationship between social phenomena within it, is as good as another's view. To many positivists, this means that such research is akin to history, or even fiction, whereas they aspire to a science of society. It is difficult for someone in the interpretist tradition to answer this accusation, because it is based on a totally different ontological view and reflects a different epistemology and, thus, a different view of what social science is about. However, as we shall see, most researchers do believe that it is possible to generalise, if only in a limited sense. Perhaps more interestingly, Bevir and Rhodes (forthcoming) attempt to defend their approach against this positivist critique by establishing a basis on which they can make knowledge claims; on which they can claim that one interpretation, or narrative, is superior to another. We shall return to their argument below.

Bevir and Rhodes (forthcoming: ch. 2) distinguish between the hermeneutic and postmodern, or post-structuralist, strands in the interpretist position. In essence, the hermeneutic tradition is idealist; it argues that we need to understand the meanings people attach to social behaviour. So, hermeneutics is concerned with the interpretation of texts and actions. This involves the use of ethnographic techniques (participant observation, transcribing texts, keeping diaries and so on) to produce what Geertz (1973) calls 'thick description'. As Bevir and Rhodes put it, quoting Geertz, the aim is to establish 'our own constructions of other people's constructions of what they and their compatriots are up to'. However, ethnographers do generalise. They develop a narrative about the past based upon the meanings which the actions had for social actors. Then, on the basis of this 'thick description', they offer an interpretation of what this tells us about the society. The point is that these interpretations are always partial, in both senses of the world, and provisional; they are not 'true'.

More recently, as Bevir and Rhodes (forthcoming) emphasise, post-structuralism and postmodernism have provided a powerful challenge to foundationalism in both philosophy and social science. Yet, as Bevir and Rhodes also point out, this variant of the interpretist tradition is itself so diverse that it is difficult, if not impossible, to characterise. They overcome this problem by focusing on the work of Michel Foucault, who is perhaps the best-known writer in this broad tradition. He, like most post-structuralists and postmodernists, is a strong opponent of foundationalism and the modernisation project associated with the Enlightenment. This project argues that: the basis of human knowledge is direct experience; as such, it is possible to develop an 'objective' view of the 'real' world (thus, it denies both elements of the double hermeneutic); language is transparent or neutral; and that human history is inevitably progressive, with present knowledge building on past knowledge to improve our information about the world and our ability to control it.

In contrast, Foucault argues that experience is acquired within a prior discourse. As such, language is crucial because institutions and actions only acquire a meaning through language. Thus, as Bevir and Rhodes (forthcoming) argue, for Foucault: 'to understand an object or action, political scientists have to interpret it in the wider discourse of which it is part'. This means that, as Bevir and Rhodes stress, it is the social discourse, rather than the beliefs of individuals, which are crucial to Foucault's version of the interpretist position. The identification of that discourse, and the role it plays in structuring meanings, is thus the key concern of those adopting this approach (for an example of this broad approach in use see Howarth (1995).

Bevir and Rhodes (forthcoming) develop their own take on the interpretist tradition. It is particularly interesting because it directly addresses the key issue raised in the positivist critique of this tradition. They argue that social science is about the development of narratives, not theories. As such, they stress the importance of understanding and the impossibility of absolute knowledge claims, but they want to explain and they defend a limited notion of objectivity.

Broadly, Bevir and Rhodes are within the hermeneutic, rather than the postmodern, or post-structuralist, stream of the interpretist tradition. As such, they follow Geertz and others in arguing that it is possible to produce explanations within the interpretist tradition. However, their understanding of explanation is very different from that of a positivist. In their view, the researcher can produce an explanation of an event or of the relationships between social phenomena. But, this explanation is built upon their interpretation of the meanings the actors involved gave to their actions. What is produced is a narrative which is particular, to that time and space, and partial, being based on a subjective interpretation of the views of, most likely, only some of the actors involved. Consequently, any such narrative must be provisional; there are no absolute truth claims.

However, Bevir and Rhodes do wish to make some, more limited, knowledge claims. They argue (forthcoming): 'Although we do not have access to pure facts that we can use to declare particular interpretations to be true or false, we can still hang on to the idea of objectivity.' They suggest that a field of study 'is a co-operative intellectual *practice*, with a *tradition* of historically produced norms, rules, conventions and standards of excellence that remain subject to critical debate, and with a *narrative* content that gives meaning to it' (original emphasis).

They continue:

> [Practice, tradition and narrative provide] for a negotiated and dynamic set of standards through which rational debate and argumentation between proponents of rival perspectives or approaches is possible [where] these standards are historically embedded within social practices, traditions and narratives which provide 'embedded reasons' … for judging an argument true or false or an action right or wrong.

Such criteria are not universal or objective; rather, they are 'shared criteria for assessing … knowledge claims'. To Bevir and Rhodes, postmodernism errs in failing to acknowledge 'significant, grounded rationality' that is to be found in these practices and traditions.

In Bevir and Rhodes' view, such knowledge claims are not self-referential because they can be 'reconfirmed' at three distinct points:

> The first is when we translate our concepts for fieldwork: that is, are they meaningful to practitioners and users and if not, why not? The second is when we reconstruct narratives from the conversations: that is, is the story logical and consistent with the data? And the third is when we redefine and translate our concepts because of the academic community's judgement on the narratives: that is, does the story meet the agreed knowledge criteria?

Overall, they argue:

> To overcome this difficulty, we should conceive of objective knowledge, less as what our community happens to agree on, and more as a normative standard embedded in a practice of criticising and comparing rival accounts of 'agreed facts'. The anti-foundational nature of this practice lies in its appeal, not to given facts, but to those agreed in a particular community or conversation. In addition, and of key importance, the normative, critical bite of our approach

lies in conducting the comparison by the rules of intellectual honesty. These rules originate in anti-foundationalism and not in a straightforward acceptance of the norms of the relevant community or conversation.

As we can see then, there are a number of variants within the interpretist tradition. However, they are all anti-foundationalist and critical of positivism. These approaches have become much more common in political science since the 1970s for a number of reasons. First, increasingly philosophical critiques have led to the questioning of positivism. Second, the postmodern turn in social science has had an affect on political science, although much less so than in sociology. Third, normative political theory has changed fundamentally. Historically, it was foundationalist; the aim was to establish some absolute notion of the good or of justice. [...] [T]hat is no longer the case. Some normative political theorists have been influenced by postmodernism, again variously defined, and more by the work of Quine and others. Now, most political theorists are anti-foundationalists or, at the very least, have a very limited conception of any universal foundations. Fourth, [...] much, but by no means all, feminist thought has been strongly influenced by postmodernism; it is anti-foundationalist and operates within the interpretist tradition. As such, we can see the influence of this interpretist tradition very broadly across political science.

Realism

Realism shares an ontological position with positivism, but, in epistemological terms, modern realism has more in common with relativism. The core views of classical realism are again fairly clear and owe much to Marx's work:

- To realists, the world exists independently of our knowledge of it. In ontological terms they, like positivists, are foundationalists.

- Again like positivists, realists contend that social phenomena/structures do have causal powers, so we can make causal statements.

- However, unlike positivists, realists contend that not all social phenomena, and the relationships between them, are directly observable. There are deep structures that cannot be observed and what can be observed may offer a false picture of those phenomena/structures and their effects (for an excellent exposition of this position see Smith, in Hollis and Smith 1990: 205–8). But, as Smith puts it, although we cannot observe those structures, 'positing their existence gives us the best explanation of social action. To use a phrase familiar to the philosophy of science, we are involved in "inference to the best explanation" (Hollis and Smith 1990: 207). As such, to a realist there is often a dichotomy between reality and appearance. This is a very important issue because it has clear methodological implications. It means that realists do not accept that what appears to be so, or, perhaps more significantly, what actors say is so, is necessarily so. As an example, classical Marxism, and Marxism is the archetypal classical realism, argued that there was a difference between 'real' interests, which reflect material reality, and perceived interests, which might be manipulated by the powerful forces in society. Given this view, we cannot just ask people what their interests are, because we would merely be identifying their manipulated interests, not their 'real' interests.

The criticisms of classical realism were of two sorts, which reflect different epistemological positions. The positivists denied the existence of unobservable structures. More importantly, they argued that positing them makes the knowledge claims of realism untestable and, thus, unfalsifiable. As such, realist claims that rely on the effect of unobservable structures have the same status to positivists as the claims of scholars from within the interpretist tradition. In contrast, authors from the interpretist tradition criticise the foundational claims of realism. In their view, there are no structures that are independent of social action and no 'objective' basis on which to observe the actions or infer the deep structures. So, the realist claim that structures cause social action are rejected on ontological and epistemological grounds.

In our view, contemporary realism has been significantly influenced by the interpretist critique. In particular, this modern critical realism acknowledges two points. First, while social phenomena exist independently of our interpretation of them, our interpretation/ understanding of them affects outcomes. So, structures do not determine; rather they constrain and facilitate. Social science involves the study of reflexive agents who interpret and change structures. Second, our knowledge of the world is fallible; it is theory-laden. We need to identify and understand both the external 'reality' and the social construction of that 'reality' if we are to explain the relationships between social phenomena.

Realism also has clear methodological implications. It suggests that there is a real world 'out there', but emphasises that outcomes are shaped by the way in which that world is socially constructed. As such, it would acknowledge the utility of both quantitative and qualitative data. So, for example, realists might use quantitative methods to identify the extent to which financial markets are 'globalised'. However, they would also want to analyse qualitatively how globalisation is perceived, or discursively constructed, by governments, because the realist argument would be that both the 'reality' and the discursive construction affect what government does in response to global pressures. We shall return to this example later.

Modern realism then attempts to acknowledge much of the interpretist critique, while retaining a commitment to causal explanation. The key problem here of course is that it is not easy, indeed many would see it as impossible, to combine scientific and interpretist positions because they have such fundamentally different ontological and epistemological underpinnings, one focusing on explanation and the other on understanding (on this point, see Hollis and Smith 1990: 212).

One of the main criticisms of realists has been that they often treat concepts as if they related to some fixed, or at least more or less given, 'essences' or cores. It should be noted first that this is not a necessary tenet for realists; it reflects rather the philosophical traditions from which they derive. Nevertheless, the question of what a concept is for is an important one, and it affects ontology directly. If a concept cannot be tied firmly to an underlying reality, as traditional philosophy seems to imply, the concept of 'being' itself may be detached from the real world of experience. This is one of the reasons why modern philosophy has considerable difficulty even recognising that there may be a subject of ontology. It should also be noted that this is one of those issues on which positivists and interpretists can find themselves temporarily in agreement, even though, as we have seen, they have fundamentally different views about knowledge and being. Any apparent agreement between them, however, has limited scope, as they have different origins and are heading for different destinations. Having considered how these categories relate to some important issues in the social sciences, we can now move on to apply the arguments to particular cases so as to illustrate their use and their limits.

Ontology and Epistemology in Political Science: Two Cases

The aim in this section is to examine how a researcher's ontological and epistemological position affects the way they approach empirical questions in political science. We shall focus on two areas: globalisation and multilevel governance. These areas have been chosen because they reflect a broad spread of the concerns, but, in our view, similar arguments could be made in relation to other substantive areas.

Case 1: Globalisation

The literature on globalisation mushroomed in the 1990s. It has been common to distinguish between processes or aspects of globalisation: so many authors have distinguished between economic, political and cultural processes, while acknowledging that they are interrelated. In this vein, many have argued that economic globalisation has grown apace and that this process has significantly restricted the autonomy of the nation state. Indeed, Ohmae (1990) goes as far as to argue that only two economic forces, global financial markets and transnational corporations, will play any role in the politics of the future. In his view, the future role of states will be analogous to the current role of local councils. At the same time, other authors have focused on cultural globalisation, suggesting that world culture is becoming increasingly homogeneous: in the view of most, reflecting a growing US hegemony. Certainly, there is little doubt that the issue of globalisation in a crucial one for those interested in questions of contemporary political economy and governance.

Political scientists have probably been most concerned with economic globalisation and the way in which it restricts the autonomy of the state, and have utilised a foundationalist ontology and a positivist epistemology, although, as we shall see below, some more recent work is realist. In contrast, sociologists, particularly those who focus on cultural studies, concentrate upon cultural globalisation, operating from an anti-foundationalist and interpretist position.

The main debate about economic globalisation has concerned the extent to which it has increased. There are two main positions. Some authors, like Ohmae (1990), who are christened hyperglobalists by Held *et al.* (1999) and seen as first-wave theorists by Hay and Marsh (2000), argue that there has been a massive increase in various indicators of economic globalisation: direct foreign investment; international bank lending; transnational production; international trade and so on. In contrast, authors such as Hirst and Thompson (1999), christened sceptics by Held *et al.* (1999) and seen by Hay and Marsh (2000) as second-wave theorists, argue that the process is more limited. More specifically, they suggest that: globalisation is not a new phenomenon; regionalisation, rather than globalisation, is a better description of the changes that have occurred; and the only area in which there has been significant globalisation is in relation to financial markets. We are not concerned here with the detail of this argument. Our point is that both sets of authors agree about what constitutes evidence of globalisation and how we can go about studying that evidence. Globalisation is an economic process that can be measured quantitatively, indeed there is large agreement as to the appropriate measures, and which, to the extent that it exists, has an effect on patterns of governance.

More recently, other authors have been, in most cases implicitly rather than explicitly, critical of this ontological and epistemological approach. The point is easily made if we return to two ways of classifying the literature on globalisation to which we have already referred. Held *et al.* (1999) contrast hyperglobalist and sceptical approaches to globalisation with a third approach to which they adhere: the transformationalist thesis. In contrast, Hay and Marsh (2000) identify a third wave of the globalisation literature that builds upon a critique of the first two waves. These two 'third ways' share something in common, but do differ significantly in a manner that reflects ontological and epistemological debates.

The transformationalists differ significantly from the sceptics in that they share:

> a conviction that, at the dawn of a new millennium, globalisation is a central
> driving force behind the rapid social, political and economic changes that are
> reshaping modern societies and world order ... In this respect, globalisation is
> conceived as a powerful transformative force which is responsible for a mas-
> sive shake out of societies, economies, institutions of governance and world
> order. (Held *et al.* 1999: 7)

Held *et al.* also emphasise the major way in which the transformationalist account parts company with both the other two positions (1999: 7):

> The transformationalists make no claims about the future trajectory of globalisation ... Rather [they] emphasise globalisation as a long-term historical process which is inscribed with contradictions and which is significantly shaped by conjunctural factors.

So, they argue that: there are 'real' social, political and economic changes occurring in the world; globalisation is a cause of these changes, a transformative force; but there is no inevitable process of globalisation which, as social scientists, we can identify. This last point is especially important here. The putative development of globalisation is dependent on the actions of agents, whether individuals, companies, institutions or states; as such it is a socially constructed process. It seems clear then that the transformative position is a realist one.

This position has methodological consequences. It points strongly to comparative analysis, because the emphasis is upon how different countries, and indeed different companies and markets, are affected by, and respond to, this process of globalisation in different ways. If globalisation is not an inevitable or universal process, then we need to focus on how it is differently experienced in different contexts.

This point is even clearer if we turn to what Hay and Marsh call the third-wave literature on globalisation. Hay and Marsh (2000: 6) follow Held *et al.* in arguing that we: 'shouldn't make essentialising and reifying assumptions about the effects, consequences, or even the very existence, of globalisation'. Rather, globalisation is a series of contradictory and contingent processes. More specifically, they suggest that, for many authors, especially the hyperglobalists, globalisation is a process without a subject. In contrast, they argue that it is agents who construct globalisation and, as such, the researcher should identify the actors involved and how they perceive and discursively construct globalising tendencies.

However, Hay and Marsh go further to contend that these discursive constructions have significant effects on outcomes. So, they suggest that it is the discursive construction of globalisation that affects government economic policies, rather than the 'real' processes of globalisation. As such, and taking the UK as an example, their argument would run along the following lines:

- While there has been a significant increase in regionalism in patterns of trading and a globalisation of financial markets, there is limited evidence that Britain is locked into a globalised political economy which determines the economic policy which the British Government can adopt.

- However, British governments, and especially the Blair Government, have argued that it is constrained in that way. It suggests that the extent of globalisation is such that the pursuit of neo-liberal policies is inevitable: there is no alternative.

- As such, it is not the 'reality' of globalisation that is shaping British economic policy, but the dominant discursive construction of that reality.

We are not concerned here about the validity or otherwise of this argument. The crucial point for us is that this view clearly marks a break with the positivism that underpins most work on globalisation. To Hay and Marsh, there may be 'real' processes at work, but the way they affect outcomes is mediated by the discursive construction(s) of these processes. This argument has both realist and interpretist elements. There is an appeal to a real world, but the emphasis is on the discursive construction of that world. This position illustrates how realist and interpretist positions interface. In our view, this position is a realist one if it recognises that there is an interactive or dialectical relationship between the 'real' world and the discourses. A realist would acknowledge not only that discourses have real effects, in this case that the dominant discourse of globalisation shapes economic policy, but also that the 'real' processes of globalisation constrain the resonance of different discourses. So, if the dominant discourse is at odds with the 'reality', alternative discourses can appeal to that 'reality deficit'. However, if it is merely the discourses that have the causal power, then, in our view, it is an interpretist position.

There are other approaches to globalisation which are clearly located in an interpretist tradition. As we emphasised above, most of these approaches stress cultural globalisation. Of course, as Held *et al.* point out (1999: 328), the concept of culture has a long and complex history but 'normally refers to the social construction, articulation and reception of meaning'. This definition immediately suggests an anti-foundationalist ontology and, most often, an interpretist epistemology.

It is possible to approach the issue of cultural globalisation utilising a positivist epistemology. So, one could focus empirically on the extent to which certain cultural icons, such as Coca-Cola, McDonald's or Madonna, have become universal, or whether colonialism was associated with a similar global culture. However, the focus of a cultural studies approach to globalisation is much more likely to be on difference. Two points are important here. First, the argument would be that there are various discourses about globalisation, none of which is 'true', although at any time one discourse may be dominant. Second, while one discourse may dominate, it can be, and will always be, resisted: different agents—citizens and researchers—will offer different narrations of globalisation and its effects. In this way, this alternative 'cultural studies' approach reflects an anti-foundationalist and an interpretist position.

Case 2: Multilevel Governance

Multilevel Governance and Intergovernmentalism: Realism versus Positivism

The term 'multilevel governance' covers a variety of familiar phenomena that are normally located in the areas of regional policy and European integration. Though 'multilevel governance' (MLG) is rapidly acquiring the status of a fashionable mainstream concept, it is not as established as 'globalisation' in the vocabulary of politicians and commentators. Here again, the contemporary debates in large part reflect different ontological and epistemological positions. In this case study, we concentrate not on the different uses of the term, although these can be significant, but rather on the contrast between MLG and its main opponent, which is liberal intergovernmentalism.

A useful definition of MLG is provided by Hunt (1999): '[According to multilevel governance theories] the policy process involves the interaction between a constellation of public and private actors located at the supranational, national and sub-national level.' This interaction is usually understood as non-hierarchical and as lacking a central, predominant authority, and similar usages can be found in Marks *et al.* (1996) and Armstrong and Bulmer (1998). These theorists argue against the view of the EU as an international organisation whose decision-making is based predominantly on national interests determined by member states, a view known as intergovernmentalism.

The intergovernmentalist perspective is closely associated with international lawyers, but an influential political analysis is provided by Andrew Moravscik (1993), who argues that the European policy process can be understood as a nested game played out both in the domestic politics of member states and in the international arena of the EU's institutions. While the MLG theorists derive their frameworks from institutionalist perspectives, arguing that 'institutions matter' in shaping interaction, analysts such as Moravscik generally utilise rational choice perspectives. Both approaches would claim to be empirically grounded, but the nature of the empirical grounding differs.

Most MLG theorists are realists in epistemological terms, emphasising how the continuity of rules, norms and operating procedures, and sometimes of 'deep, non-observable structures', can, and does, determine the outcomes of decision-making in the long term. As such, their logic is inductive rather than deductive. Overall, MLG is not so much concerned with the debate between neo-federalists and intergovernmentalists as with the consequences of different possible forms of integration for normative issues such as democratic participation, effective government and distributive justice.

In contrast, liberal intergovernmentalists seek to identify the preferences and the parameters of the individual actors (usually member states) and show how, after the event, the outcomes can be understood as the result of rational calculated behaviour. Their logic is therefore deductive: they argue from the general to the particular. Liberal intergovernmentalism is foundationalist in ontological terms and operates with a positivist epistemology. In its treatment of European integration it is clearly unsympathetic to neo-federalism and to supranationalism.

The Normative Underpinnings of Multilevel Governance and Intergovermentalism

MLG theorists argue that, rather than conceptualising regional policy as a national issue in which the lead role is taken by the national state institutions, it should be identified as an arena in which the European Union plays an integral role in policy-making, together with the separate regional authorities and the central national institutions. In this sense, theories of multilevel governance make a distinction between 'government' and 'governance'. 'Government', it is argued, is too narrowly concerned with the formal structures of state authority, and with the associated processes and issues, whereas 'governance' is concerned with much wider notions of politics, encompassing the production, accumulation and regulation of collective goods at all levels including the international. Power relations in multilevel governance are structured by reciprocal interdependence on each other's resources, rather than on conflict over either scarcity or fundamental values. Typically, these theories argue that relations of decision-making between the various levels should be seen as loosely interconnected rather than as tightly nested; that is, characterised by multilateral links, and non-hierarchical in form, rather than by a hierarchical chain of bilateral links in which the national state authority has a predominant role, as is the case with intergovernmental approaches.

There is thus a strong normative element in multilevel governance. From describing the increased evidence of the multiplicity of decision-making forms and levels in European integration, proponents move to arguments about the value of multilevel governance in enhancing democratic legitimacy and effective decision-making under conditions of globalised political economy. In comparison with state-centred accounts, multilevel governance is said to be 'closer to the people', and therefore more acceptable, and more flexible and adaptable, so better able to respond to the rapidly changing economic climate (Marks *et al.* 1996).

The arguments against multilevel governance, if it is regarded as a policy prescription as well as empirical analysis, concentrate on two main issues (Moravscik 1993; Scharpf 1988). The first is what is known as the 'joint decision trap'. This focuses upon the danger of deadlock in decision-making where there are many participants, interdependent arenas and a variety of possible combinations of policy-making processes. Though multilevel governance may offer the prospect of policy-making close to the people and greater legitimacy, it risks sacrificing efficiency in decision-making if there is no authoritative procedure for resolving disagreements among equal participants. A second criticism denies even that multilevel governance provides greater legitimacy and argues that, when the smaller units and more local levels of decision-making are included, the greater complexity of procedures results in opacity of decision-making and, therefore, in less accountability. In practice, multilevel governance can mean obscure elite-led agreements and public incomprehension. Neoliberal arguments try to resolve these problems by emphasising how the member states in the EU remain both the focus of popular legitimacy, albeit with some rebalancing towards regional authorities, and the main guarantors of effective governmental decision-making.

In response to this, Marks *et al.* (1996) have three main criticisms of the intergovernmental approach. Underlying these disagreements is a fundamental dispute about the nature of social reality. First, positivist explanations of societal phenomena neglect the structural constraints within which individuals operate. These are varied in kind, but the most important are generally the impact of differential allocation of resources, the culturally-given nature of the value framework within which individuals choose and the unpredictability of external factors, such as the international economic and security climate.

Second, the realist perspective emphasises how the institutional frameworks have a primary effect in shaping decision-making through their formal rules, their informal procedures, their value structures and their effect on office-holding and internal role-oriented behaviour. In one sense, the institutions are no more than the sum of countless individual choices, but merely to state this does not get us very far. Realists seek to find ways of characterising different institutional frameworks so as to move beyond this and to introduce other levels of analysis and explanation which recognise the weight of the long-term structural and institutional context.

Third, it is argued that intergovernmentalists are insufficiently critical about what timeframes are relevant and why. The term 'path dependency' used in this context (Pierson 1996) does not just refer to the given nature of resource allocations at 'point zero' which the researcher takes as the start. It also directs our attention to the impact of decisions prior to point zero, and of the ways in which the institutional frameworks lock actors into particular sets of choices. This implicitly asks positivists to justify why they adopt diachronic modes of explanation, which imply social understanding as a set of discrete operations in fixed points in time, as opposed to synchronic explanations, which emphasise a more continuous and context-led understanding of the social nature of time.

Despite these epistemological and methodological differences, writers such as Moravscik and Scharpf (Scharpf 1988, 1997) appear to be able to integrate some of the concerns of multilevel governance into their own perspective, so that, despite the methodological differences between the positivists and realists, we can identify these as distinct strands in the study of the European policy process, marked by an attentiveness to similar policy problems and with some of the same language.

The Constructivist Approach

This is not true of the social constructivist approach (see, for example, Jørgensen 1998; Weldes 1996; Wendt 1994). This rejects the language of causality, with which positivists and realists are content in their different ways, and in contrast, is based upon an interpretist epistemological position. Constructivists argue that, if there is a problem of increasing complexity of decision-making associated with the decline of the nation state, this complexity must be understood as an intentional social construct on the part of decision-makers, part of a set of political projects associated with responses to perceptions of external and internal constraints. The questions which arise are concerned with political decision-making as a series of attempts to resolve conflicts over meaning and identity, understood in the broadest sense. Constructivists take issue with the positivist understanding of the nature of political choice. They argue against the acceptance of individual preference as a given and instead interrogate specifically why and how preferences come to be formed and how these preferences and choices relate to the strategic aims of powerful interests in society. Multilevel governance then would not be seen as a set of objectively perceived phenomena, but as a normative framework which is itself part of the political conflict between the interests associated with neo-liberal economic restructuring and those seeking a more social democratic accommodation with technological change.

This locates the arguments about multilevel governance within the discussion about the nature of globalisation, which we dealt with above, and in which one of the main disputes is about the underlying realities of technological economic and social change and their relationship with the discursively constructed political uses made of them within specific political projects.

Conclusion

The point here is not to attempt to resolve these disputes. Rather, what we have sought to do is to show how the different approaches in different issues relate to epistemological and methodological assumptions, and to one another. The terms introduced here can be used as signposts, suggesting how we can come to terms with the deeper implications of the theories and groups of concerns [...]. One of the temptations in so doing is to attempt to find a synthesis of all the available positions, in the hope that, at some level of analysis, agreement is possible over fundamental issues. Unfortunately, experience and logic combine to warn against this temptation. These debates have been part of the intellectual and moral climate of Western thought for centuries and continue because they reflect disagreements not just about logic or technicalities but also about the proper scope of human action in society. In other words, they are questions which relate to deep-rooted moral positions that may be internally coherent, but are incompatible with one another, except in so far as they all include some appeal to intellectual and ethical tolerance of diversity. In the face of these difficulties, another strategy, alluring at least to risk-averse researchers, is to avoid the issue. Far from being safe, this position is actually rather unsafe, since it does not enable one to distinguish between good and bad research and between good and bad arguments. The least one can say about these issues is that they are of sufficient importance to warrant a genuine commitment to coming to terms with them. Coming to terms with the issues requires one to think through the different arguments separately, to compare them and to evaluate them. As we argued at the beginning of this chapter, this means identifying, as far as possible, what are the epistemological and ontological underpinnings and what these imply in terms of argumentation, practical research method, explanatory logic and research construction. The purpose of this chapter has been to encourage this and to attempt to provide an introduction to some of the main ideas and methods involved.

Further Reading

- The best introductions to the philosophy of science and social science are Chalmers (1985, 1990) and Winch (1958).
- For an accessible overview of ontology and epistemology, see Hay (2002).
- On the positivist approach, see Kuhn (1970), Hempel (1965, 1966) or Halfpenny (1982).
- On the interpretive approach, see Bevir and Rhodes (1999).
- On realism, see Sayer (1992).

Bibliography

Armstrong, K. and Bulmer, S. (1998) *The Governance of the Single European Market* (Manchester, Manchester University Press).

Bevir, M. and Rhodes, R. (1999) 'Studying British Government: Reconstructing the Research Agenda', *British Journal of Politics and International Studies*, 1: 215–39.

Bevir, M. and Rhodes, R. A. W (forthcoming) *Interpretive Theory* (Basingstoke, Palgrave).

Chalmers, A. (1985) *What is this Thing called Science?* (Milton Keynes, Open University Press).

Chalmers, A. F. (1990) *Science and its Fabrication* (Milton Keynes, Open University Press).

Geertz, C. (1973) *The Interpretation of Cultures* (New York, Basic Books).

Gray, J. (1992) *Men Are from Mars and Women are from Venus* (New York, HarperCollins).

Halfpenny, P. (1982) *Positivism and Sociology: Explaining Social Life* (London, Allen & Unwin).

Hay, C. (2002) *Political Analysis* (Basingstoke, Palgrave).

Hay, C. and Marsh, D. (2000) 'Introduction: Demystifying Globalisation', in C. Hay and D. Marsh (eds), *Demystifying Globalisation* (Basingstoke, Macmillan).

Held, D. *et al.* (eds) (1999) *Global Transformations: Politics, Economics and Culture* (Cambridge, Polity Press).

Hempel, C. (1965) *Aspects of Scientific Explanation and Other Essays in the Philosophy of Science* (New York, Free Press).

Hempel, C. (1966) *Philosophy of Natural Science* (Englewood Cliffs, NJ, Prentice-Hall).

Hirst, P. and Thompson, G. (1999) *Globalisation in Question* (Cambridge, Polity Press).

Hollis, M. and Smith, S. (1990) *Explaining and Understanding in International Relations* (Oxford, Clarendon Press).

Howarth, D. (1995) 'Discourse Theory', in D. Marsh and G. Stoker (eds), *Theory and Methods in Political Science* (Basingstoke: Macmillan).

Hunt J. (1999) 'Inter-disciplinary Approaches to EU Decision-Making: Law, Politics and the Multi-Levelled Governance Regime', Working Paper 4/99 (Centre for the Study of Law in Europe, University of Leeds).

Jørgensen K.E. (ed.) (1998), *Constructivism, International Relations and European Studies* (Department of Political Science, University of Aarhus).

Kuhn, T. (1970) *The Structure of Scientific Revolutions* (Chicago, Ill., University of Chicago Press).

Marks, G., Hooghe, E. and Blank, K. (1996) 'European Integration and the state', *Journal of Common Market Studies*, 34: 341–78.

Moravscik, A. (1993) 'Preferences and Power in the European Community: A Liberal Intergovernmentalist Approach', *Journal of Common Market Studies*, 31: 473–524.

Ohmae, K. (1990) *The Borderless World* (London, Collins).

Pierson, P. (1996) 'The Path to European Integration: A Historical Institutionalist Analysis', *Comparative Political Studies*, 23: 122–63.

Quine, W. (1961) *From a Logical Point of View* (New York, Harper & Row).

Sanders, D. (1990) *Losing an Empire, Finding a Role: British Foreign Policy Since 1945* (London, Macmillan).

Sanders, D. (1999) 'The Impact of Left-Right Ideology', in G. Evans and P. Norris (eds), *Critical Elections: British Parties arid Voters in Long-term Perspective* (London, Sage).

Sayer, A. (1992) *Method in Social Science: A Realist Approach* (London, Routledge).

Scharpf, W. (1988), 'The Joint-Decision Trap: Lessons from German Federalism and European Integration' *Public Administration*, 66: 239–78.

Scharpf, W. (1997), *Games Real Actors Play: Actor-centred Institutionalism in Policy Research* (Boulder, Colo, Westview Press).

Weldes, J. (1996) 'Constructing National Interests', *European Journal of International Relations*, 2(3).

Wendt, A. (1994), 'Collective Identity Formation and the International state', *American Political Science Review*, 88(2).

Winch, P. (1958) *The Idea of a Social Science and its Relation to Philosophy* (London, Routledge & Kegan Paul).

Chapter 2

1. How do different theories lead to the same result?
2. How does Moore's comparison of three routes to modern society lead to similar outcomes?
3. What are the differences between the ontological positions of realism and positivism?
4. What are three positions of realism that set it apart from positivists and interpretivists?
5. Characterize the main elements of constructivism.

Chapter 3

The State
Power, Supremacy, Forms

T HUS FAR THIS READER HAS INTRODUCED concepts and analytical tools used in comparative politics. The foundational role of philosophical tools stands out since it frames all research, producing different benefits and limitations for various modes of research. All comparativists aim to achieve insight into the various ways politics operate around the world, but their results can be seen to divide into different schools of interpretation. Understandings of different cultures and political systems depend, in short, on the political theories and their associated ontological, epistemological, and methodological choices used in research.

With this chapter, the focus turns to the modern state. The four readings outline concepts of power, the unique nature of state power, types of democracy, and varieties of authoritarianism.

The first reading identifies types of powers exercised by states. The first group categorizes operations for making differences in the actions of others: coercion, authority, influence, and manipulation. The second group identifies what Steven Lukes characterizes as the "three faces" of power. These incorporate the first group since all are types of either "power over" or "power to," which identifies a capacity to exert "power over." They also identify power with types of interaction between different agents. The "first face" is direct power where one party possesses the capacity to impose on another by coercion or the assertion of authority. This is often stated as the ability of agent A to get agent B to do what B would not otherwise do. The "second face" identifies instances when agent A controls situations, such as the issues on the agenda of a town meeting, to prevent opponents' demands unwanted by A from ever becoming a public issue. The "third face" involves using societal pressure, with agent A drawing on institutional norms, such as opposition to tax increases, to influence or even compel B's acceptance of A's objective.

The second selection focuses on factors distinguishing state power, namely, political authority empowered by its legitimation. State power is the capacity to decide issues affecting the polity, to exercise force or enforce law imposing a decision on issues in dispute between various groups in society. Authority of the state is the special rights to ultimate decision-making and the use of force if needed. This capacity to impose order within the collectivity is unique to states. However, a state's authority itself depends on its acceptance, on the approval of citizens. The public sentiment "authorizing" state officials is called legitimacy.

The third chapter explores democracy, its meanings, types, and proliferation in the twentieth century. The concept of Democracy refers to political systems with pluralist and competitive patterns of power, that is, systems of checks and balances in which citizens mobilize to articulate their views and hold government officers accountable through political activities, such as supporting political parties, voting in elections, or membership in interest groups. The chapter describes how competition for office works in both presidential and parliamentary models. In their own ways, both presidential and parliamentary systems succeed by ensuring citizens' participation, contestation for office and over policies, and the twin functions of empowering office holders and holding them accountable.

The final article on authoritarianism analyses systems that limit or totally suppress the ability of citizens to check state power. Authoritarian political systems generally function to facilitate the rule of an elite while denying public interests. The composition of authoritarian formations varies considerably. Notably, the authors report on the recent resurgence of authoritarianism, a reversal of the "third wave" of democratization that followed the collapse of the Soviet Union in 1990. This reading from *Authoritarianism Goes Global* usefully outlines the different patterns of elite domination in leading authoritarian states (China, Russia, Iran, Venezuela, and Saudi Arabia). Finally, the article encourages further study of the causes of this turn toward authoritarianism and the attrition of democratic politics.

Reading 3.1

Political Power

Anthony H. Birch

Problems of Definition

The *OED* defines power as 'the ability to do or act' and 'control, influence, ascendancy', while *Webster's Dictionary* defines it as the 'possession of control, authority, or influence over others'. Power can be possessed and exercised in all kinds of social contexts, from an office or factory to national or international society. Political power is power within a political system and in this book we are concerned not with the international system or the tribes of the Amazon rainforest but with the political system of the modern state.

Unfortunately, it is not feasible to begin with an operational definition of political power, even when the context is limited to the modern state, because different scholars operate with different definitions and there is no agreement between them. This raises the question of whether political power is an inevitably contestable concept in the modern world, and on this question too, more than one view is possible. At first sight, it would seem that it ought not to be contestable, because, except perhaps to anarchists, power appears to be a value-neutral concept. Power can be exercised in good or bad ways but it is not a capacity that all groups wish to claim they possess, varying the definition to make their claims more plausible. It is not, that is, an obviously contestable concept like freedom or democracy. However, in practice, the meaning of the concept is contested, and the literature is full of controversies about it. It therefore seems wise to leave open the question of whether this contestability is unavoidable, and to proceed instead to examine the difficulties of handling the concept.

One difficulty arises from the complexity of the political system in the modern state. Political power is wielded through numerous channels, by a great variety of political actors, in a large number of direct or indirect ways. Some forms of power can be readily identified, as when the police carry out an arrest or a judge pronounces sentence. However, the most interesting form of political power, which is the main concern of this chapter, is the power to influence decisions taken by government agencies, and this is often more difficult to identify.

Another problem is that of identifying political actors. Voters are political actors when they go to the polls, but are non-voters to be regarded as actors? Since their abstention may determine the result of the election, presumably they are. In between elections, political leaders will frequently be influenced by their expectations about the likely effects of proposed policy decisions on voting behaviour at the next election. Does that mean that electors are exerting influence,

Anthony H. Birch, "Political Power," *The Concepts and Theories of Modern Democracy*, pp. 199–216, 293–303. Copyright © 2007 by Taylor & Francis Group. Reprinted with permission.

and therefore a degree of power, all the time? Are we to say that electors who are completely passive and uninterested in politics are nevertheless political actors because their possession of the right to vote may influence decision makers? Should we say that school children are political actors because, while lacking the right to vote, they have the ability to disrupt classes or boycott the schools if they object to certain decisions on educational policy? Should we say that financial institutions exercise political power because governments moderate their economic policies for fear of a flight of capital out of the country, even if the institutions in question make no political move? Would this be the case even if the fear of a flight of capital were quite unfounded? If we answer all these questions in the affirmative, and some do, this means that political power can be a very tricky thing to identify, let alone measure.

A further problem about the concept of political power is that of assigning causality in a chain of political events and responsibility for political outcomes. Let us suppose that a convict with a record of violent crimes is released on parole, buys a gun, and kills his former wife. There is more than one way of assigning responsibility for this death, beyond the simple answer that the murderer is responsible. Some would say that the members of the parole board are responsible, for they took the decision to release the convict. Others would say that the psychiatrist who advised the board is responsible, for the precedents and conventions that govern the behaviour of parole boards make it very difficult for a board to reject a psychiatrist's recommendation. Others again would criticize the whole system of parole and parole boards, saying that a sentence of ten years' imprisonment should mean just that. Yet another group would argue that the real trouble is the absence of effective controls on the sale of guns. None of these ways of assigning responsibility for the death can be dismissed as wrong. They differ because each of them reflects the perspective of the person or group making the judgement.

This simple example illustrates the problem of multi-causality, which affects the analysis of most political decisions in the government of modern states. It is only in relatively rare circumstances that one can say: 'X exercised power; he or she had a free choice and decided that Y should be done'. In the real world of politics X rarely has a free choice, but is constrained by many pressures and considerations. Nor can a decision normally be taken without consulting others or working through committees. There is always a procedure to be followed, and the final decision depends on the nature of the procedure, the behaviour of all the political actors who can exercise direct or indirect influence through it, the values prevalent in the society, and the external constraints that in practice limit the freedom of choice. This means that assessing the distribution of political power is an inherently difficult operation, liable to be affected by the preconceptions, perspectives and values of the analyst. However, the operation can be made somewhat easier if it is preceded by a process of conceptual clarification.

Four Types of Political Power

If we start with the most obvious manifestations of political power and move to the least obvious, it is possible to outline a four-fold typology.

First, there is political coercion, defined as the control of citizens by agents of the government using force or the immediate threat of force, leaving the citizens with no real choice about their behaviour. Examples include the power of a riot squad breaking up a demonstration, of the police carrying out an arrest, of prison guards controlling convicts, of a municipality using bulldozers on a gypsy encampment, of an army enforcing a curfew. This type of power rarely raises conceptual problems. Its exercise often raises legal or moral problems, but there is no real difficulty about defining coercion or recognizing it when it is used.

Second, there is political authority, defined as the exercise by certain designated persons and institutions of the right, generally regarded as legitimate, to make and implement decisions that are binding within a prescribed area of jurisdiction. Examples include the power of legislative assemblies to pass laws, of judges to interpret the laws, of ministers to take executive decisions, of civil servants to implement these decisions, of municipalities to make zoning regulations, of regulatory agencies to control pollution or license new medications, of the police to direct traffic or investigate breaches of the law. This type of political power involves a number of interesting conceptual and practical [...].

Third, there is political influence, defined as the exercise of indirect or direct influence over the personnel or decisions of governmental institutions and agencies. This sounds clear and simple, but it has to be added that there is a wide spectrum of political influence ranging from the most diffuse influence over political opinions to the most specific influence over appointments to political office or the decisions of political agencies. It is not easy to draw a hard and fast line between diffuse and specific forms of influence as if they were watertight categories, but an example may illustrate the difference.

If I persuade a group of friends or acquaintances that the government ought to spend more money on preventive medicine I am exercising a degree of political influence as an opinion leader, but the probable impact of this influence on future governmental actions is so small that it can hardly be counted as an example of political power. On the other hand, it would certainly be an example of power if I were to persuade the members of a decision-making committee on health service expenditure that their priorities should be changed in the way I preferred. In between these extremes of diffuse and specific influence, there is an example of a person who might use argumentative skills to persuade delegates at a party conference that a certain policy should be added to the party's list of long-term objectives. To cut through this maze, it might be sensible to stipulate that persuading other people about the merits of a proposed policy should be regarded as a form of political power if, but only if, the people persuaded have the ability and desire to take decisions binding on a wider category of people who have no say in the matter.

The definition and identification of political influence raises a number of conceptual and empirical problems that will be discussed below. Much of the controversy about political power in the recent literature of political science has in fact been about whether political influence has one, two, or three dimensions, and how these should be defined, recognized and measured.

The fourth and least tangible type of political power is political manipulation, defined as the activity of shaping the political opinions, values and behaviour of others without the latter realizing that this is happening. Examples include teachers teaching history or civics in a biased way, journalists disseminating partial or slanted information about a political event or issue, opinion leaders acting and speaking as if a certain set of preferred values are the only ones open to reasonable people, the mass media presenting a political or social situation as inevitable when it is actually open to change.

This type of power is inherently controversial, since it can rarely be identified, let alone measured, in a way that will be accepted by other scholars as objective. The writing or teaching of history provides an obvious example. In history the truth is everything that happened, so that every book, article or lecture on a historical topic contains a small sample of the truth chosen to form a coherent pattern. Some presentations are more partial and biased than others, but since every account is selective there is no clear way of establishing what would be truly objective. A similar comment could be made about journalistic summaries of current (meaning very recent) events, or about presentations of belief systems and social values. In these circumstances the identification of political manipulation is an inevitably tricky business that is difficult to separate from the political values of the identifier.

If we consider the work that has been done by political scientists on the distribution and exercise of political power, it is immediately apparent that scholars have nearly always concentrated on one or the other of these types of power, choosing one that fits their preferred research methods, without much effort to put their studies into perspective by discussing the relationship of their findings to work on the other types of power. Up until the 1950s, political scientists writing about the government of the modern state were concerned with political authority rather than with political coercion, political influence, or political manipulation. They wrote about constitutions and institutions; about the sovereignty of Parliament, the rule of law, the separation of powers, the structure of the administration, and the authority granted to the president, prime minister, legislative assemblies, government departments and courts. The only important exception to this generalization was research done in the United States, but not elsewhere, into the influence exerted on the legislative process by certain national pressure groups chosen for case studies.

In the 1950s two different kinds of study were made as a result of the development of new research techniques, coupled with a new emphasis on the desirability of turning the study of politics into a truly scientific activity. The object was to supplement (and in the ambitions of some to replace) the delineation of legal powers and institutional structures by the production of causal generalizations about political behaviour. One consequence was that scholars turned their attention to the attempt to assess the distribution of political influence within systems of government.

The Assessment of Political Influence

The first wave of this new type of research focused on opinion formation and electoral behaviour among the general body of citizens. Sample surveys of electors yielded generalizations about the relationship between demographic variables like age, sex and class, political attitudes, and political participation. They also yielded, though not so clearly, some suggestive evidence about the impact of election campaigns, the mass media and opinion leaders on the attitudes and behaviour of the ordinary citizen, which constituted political influence of a rather diffuse kind.

A second wave of behavioural research focused on the distribution of political influence on municipal government within particular communities selected for study. Several studies by sociologists reached the conclusion that political influence, which they called by the generic term political power, was concentrated in the hands of a social and economic elite. The most influential of these was a book by Floyd Hunter entitled *Community Power Structure*, which analysed the distribution of power in Atlanta, Georgia. This book can easily be criticized. In it, Hunter seemed to assume from the beginning what he claimed to have proved, namely that power in Atlanta was concentrated in the hands of a business elite. In his opening pages he stated it as a 'self-evident proposition' that 'power is a relatively constant factor in social relationships with policies as variables' (Hunter 1953: 6), thus excluding the possibility that power might vary from one issue-area to another. His method of inquiry was to ask a panel of people whom he selected to say whom they thought had most power in the city, permitting them to choose forty, but only forty, persons. The fact that most of the forty chosen were members of the business elite was taken to be evidence that this elite dominated the local political system, without it being thought necessary to investigate particular areas of policy or particular decisions.

The influence of electors was discounted on the ground that relatively few of them were politically active, while the inactivity of the majority was taken as evidence that the power structure prevented them from participating. No consideration was given to the possibility that they might not have participated because they were reasonably content with the system, or because they preferred to spend their time working in the garden or playing baseball. It was simply assumed that they would have liked to participate but were somehow prevented from doing so. In short, the analysis presented was unconvincing. It may conceivably have been true that Atlanta was dominated by a business elite—the city certainly had one very large and wealthy industrial concern in the shape of the Coca-Cola Company—but Hunter's book fell a long way short of demonstrating this to be the case. It is instructive to note that, despite its obvious shortcomings, Hunter's book received favourable reviews in the *American Political Science Review* (vol. 48, 1954, pp. 235–7), the *Journal of Politics* (vol. 16, 1954, pp. 146–50), and the *American Journal of Sociology* (vol. 60, 1955, pp. 522–3). It was in this climate of opinion that Robert Dahl and his colleagues at Yale launched their elaborate inquiry into the structure of power in New Haven, Connecticut, which was subsequently to play a central role in academic controversies about the forms or dimensions of political influence.

Dahl defined political power as a relationship in which A (being an individual or group) induces B to behave in a way that B would not have chosen without A's pressure. This was a fairly conventional definition, very similar to those that had previously been adopted in books by Harold Lasswell and Abraham Kaplan (see Lasswell and Kaplan 1950: 75) and Herbert Simon (see Simon 1957: 65–6). As Terence Ball has pointed out, in its origins this definition was three centuries old, having been first advanced by Hobbes and copied by Locke (see Ball 1988: 83–7). The assumption is that power, properly defined, is exercised only in situations where there is an overt disagreement or conflict between parties about what should be done and one side comes out on top. Dahl acknowledged that in the modern state, at either the national or local level, only a small minority of citizens actually participate in power struggles about the policies to be followed. His approach in the New Haven study was to choose three key issue areas and to discover who actually took part in the struggles in these areas.

The research carried out by Dahl and his team revealed that the active minority differed from one issue area to another and that the citizens classified as 'economic and social notables' did not play a leading role, or anything approaching a leading role, in any of the three areas. It was therefore concluded that in New Haven there was no 'power elite' (to use the term popularized by C. Wright Mills) but a distribution of political influence that Dahl described as pluralist. There were undoubtedly inequalities between citizens in the degree of power they exercised in the system, but these inequalities were dispersed rather than cumulative. The 1,066 positions identified as influential in the three issue areas were occupied by 1,029 persons, so that fewer than 40 persons had exercised influence in more than one area. The government of New Haven was said to be an example of pluralist democracy (see Dahl 1961: Chapters 6, 7, 19–24).

There was much more to Dahl's study than this bare sketch suggests [...]. In this chapter what is important is the operational definition of power that was adopted, which has been criticized and has led to a prolonged debate among scholars. In a seminal article, Bachrach and Baratz (1962) disputed Dahl's assumption that political power is exercised only when an overt disagreement over an issue is argued about and subsequently resolved by the victory of one side or the other. They pointed out that power may also be exercised by preventing an issue from being brought up for decision:

> Of course power is exercised when A participates in the making of decisions that affect B. But power is also exercised when A devotes his energies to creating or reinforcing social and political values and institutional practices that limit the scope of the political process to public consideration of only those issues which are comparatively innocuous to A.
>
> (Bachrach and Baratz 1962: 149)

They described this second face of power as 'non-decision-making' and described the process by which issues are kept off the agenda as 'the mobilization of bias', using a term that had first been coined by Schattschneider (see Schattschneider 1960: 71; Bachrach and Baratz 1962: 150).

There can be no doubt that these writers drew attention to a significant aspect, or more precisely two significant aspects, of the process by which communities are governed. A minority wishing to get an issue considered by decision-making bodies may indeed find itself frustrated in this aim, either by the strength of prevailing opinion in favour of the status quo or by procedural rules and conventions. However, there can be practical problems about identifying the political actors in such situations. A prevailing consensus of political values may make things difficult for reformers, but it is rarely easy to say who created the consensus. A consensus is apt to be the product of many factors, operating over a period. The problem of multi-causality always arises. Institutional practices may also hinder reformers, but these practices may have been developed over the years for the convenient conduct of business, without any reference to the issue that reformers now wish to get on the agenda and possibly without any intention of hindering reformers in general. In an important article, Nelson Polsby has argued forcibly that it is difficult to make empirical investigations of the mobilization of bias (Polsby 1979).

Notwithstanding these difficulties, it is certainly true that political scientists studying decision making should take note of the prevailing social and political values in that community or society relevant to the issue and of the institutional channels through which would-be reformers have to work. If individuals can be identified as overtly reinforcing the values and procedures that favour the status quo, as is suggested by the passage quoted from Bachrach and Baratz's (1962) article, then they are exercising political influence that is rather different from the influence exerted by the people who actually participate in controversies over particular issues of policy. It is an open question whether this more general kind of influence on the political system is more significant than the specific influence exerted by those who argue about education, housing or defence policies. It is inherently difficult to compare different kinds of influence and it is best to leave this question unanswered and simply acknowledge that Bachrach and Baratz made a valuable contribution by indicating that political power takes more than one form, or has more than one dimension.

A Third Possible Dimension

Other scholars have suggested that there is also a third dimension of political influence, whose exercise prevents potential issues from even emerging as actual issues. The lead in this was taken by Steven Lukes (1974), arguing from a Marxist or neo-Marxist perspective. Lukes observed that in many capitalist societies workers accept the system even though their real interests should lead them to favour radical change. They do this because they have been socialized into acceptance by dominant groups who control the processes of socialization, such as the educational system and the mass media. The ability to influence the way people think, to induce them to accept false values, and/or to make them feel powerless should be regarded as a highly important form of political power (see Lukes 1974). While Lukes agrees that both the first and second dimensions of political influence are significant, he believes that this third dimension, by means of which the whole economic and social system is protected, may be the most significant of the three.

The great problem about this view, of course, is that it assumes people have 'real interests' that can be identified by the observer even though the people themselves are unaware of them or would reject them. How can an observer claim to know better than the people where their real interests lie? To Marxists this is not a serious problem, because Marxists believe that their understanding of the economic and social system and the way it is developing enables them to recognize that in capitalist societies the workers are inevitably exploited, and would serve their interests best by working to replace the capitalist system by a socialist system. Workers who do not realize this are suffering from 'false consciousness' and need to be re-educated. If they accept the ideas of Antonio Gramsci, Marxists will accept that western capitalist societies in the twentieth century suffer from a hegemony of bourgeois values, so that the re-education of the masses can only be a long and difficult process. But the fact that bourgeois values are generally dominant might be said only to emphasize the power of those groups who have promoted these values and inculcated them into the minds of their contemporaries.

Empiricists such as Dahl and Polsby reject this whole line of argument as impossible to verify by empirical methods and therefore worthless. Whether the masses suffer from false consciousness can only be a matter of faith or ideology, not a proposition that social scientists can establish or refute. That the proposition cannot be proved empirically is accepted by Lukes, who says, very honestly, that only scholars with a Marxist perspective can be expected to agree with his contention about the significance of what he calls 'the third dimension of power'.

However, if his contention cannot be proved, it can be illustrated, and Lukes encouraged one of his research students to make a study of a community in the Appalachian hills where the workers acquiesced in a situation of obvious exploitation and poverty. The resulting book provided an interesting case study of a coal-mining community dominated by a single foreign (actually British) company, with workers enduring low wages, poor housing and a miserable environment (Gaventa 1980). The workers did not protest or struggle to improve their conditions, as workers in other mining communities had done, and their union was remarkably passive. It was concluded by the author that the workers had been socialized into feelings of powerlessness, which led them to acquiesce in their poverty. However, it was not possible to produce evidence of the socialization process or to show that the company had controlled it, so in the end the study, though suggestive, was inconclusive in its attempt to reveal an example of what Lukes called the third dimension of political power and I prefer to call political manipulation.

At this point I should like to introduce a helpful suggestion bearing on the second and third dimensions of political influence made by Bob Jessop. He says that analysts should distinguish between the structural elements in a situation and what he calls the 'conjunctural' elements and I prefer to call the modifiable elements. The structural elements are 'those elements in a social function that cannot be altered by a given agent (or set of agents) during a given time period' (Jessop 1982: 253), while the modifiable elements are those that can be altered. The structural elements constitute a restraint on potential reformers. In some situations 'the same element can function as a "structural restraint" for one agent (or set of agents) at the same time as it appears as a modifiable element to other agents' (Jessop 1982: 253).

In the light of this, I would argue that it is helpful to distinguish four situations, rather than three, in which the exercise of power, in the form of political influence, may possibly be identified. If we assume the existence of a potential political actor called Smith, the four situations can be summarized as follows:

1. Smith takes the opportunity to intervene in a debate or vote so as to influence the policy adopted by a group, party or authority regarding a given issue. This is an example of the first dimension of political influence, the dimension studied by Dahl.
2. Smith would like to influence policy regarding a given issue, but cannot do so because she/he cannot get the issue on the agenda, either because (a) another actor called Jones is able to keep the issue off the agenda or (b) the procedural rules and conventions

operate as a structural constraint preventing Smith from raising the issue. In case (a) this would be an example of the second dimension of influence being exercised by Jones. Case (b) might be regarded as an example of the second dimension of influence exercised by those who, in an earlier time period, framed the rules or helped to form the conventions. If there are people or groups in society who have the capacity to modify the rules or conventions, then it could be said that the rules and conventions operate as a structural constraint on Smith but afford an opportunity for the exercise of power by these other people or groups.

3. Smith would like to change the system, whether this be the system of industrial relations, the system of government, or (the favourite example) the capitalist system. However, she/he does not think it is feasible to do this, does not think it is worthwhile to try, decides instead to work for small improvements within the system, and after a time comes to accept the system and take it for granted. The complexity and entrenched nature of the system would in this case be a structural constraint for Smith. If his/her perception of the near-impossibility of changing the system had been developed by a conscious campaign of socialization by teachers, journalists and groups who had an interest in maintaining the system, then the behaviour of the latter could probably be regarded as an example of the exercise of the third dimension of influence.

4. Smith is quite content with the system, even though, in the opinion of a radical critic called Robertson, the system is oppressive and has provided Smith with a poorer lifestyle than he deserves, and could probably secure under a different system. Steven Lukes's position is that Smith's complacency can be regarded as the result of the exercise of the third dimension of influence by all those groups in society who manipulate the minds of citizens like Smith so as to make the latter content with a system that is oppressive and unfair, the contentment being a form of 'false consciousness' in the heart of Smith and others. However, most social scientists, including me, reject this position on the ground that the characterization of the system as oppressive is a value judgement by Robertson, who has no right to say that Smith is mistaken in having reached a different value judgement. The concept of false consciousness seems, to almost everyone except Marxists, to involve a degree of certainty about highly controversial questions that is inappropriate.

Four Additional Concepts

At this stage in the argument it will be helpful to add a word about four additional concepts that are relevant to the study of political power. One of these is the 'raising of consciousness'; another is 'real interest' (as distinct from apparent interest); a third is 'cultural and ideological hegemony'; and the fourth is 'political socialization'.

The term 'raising of consciousness' did not come into popular usage until the 1970s, although the process has existed for centuries and was known earlier as (according to taste) enlightenment, education or agitation. It is very relevant to situations 3 and 4, as outlined in the previous paragraphs. In situation 3, radical reformers might be able to persuade Smith that, although he or she could not hope to change the system alone, Smith might be able to do so if he or she joined with others and took part in a long-term campaign of propaganda and political activity. If radicals were successful in changing Smith's mind, they would have raised Smith's consciousness about the possibilities of collective political action. In situation 4, radicals might be able to change Smith's evaluation of the system, so as to lead him or her to regard it as oppressive rather than benign. This also could be described as the raising of consciousness.

This concept has become relevant in recent years to the feminist movement, whose leaders have been able in most advanced industrial countries to raise the consciousness of women in situation 3, who were discontented with the opportunities open to women but did not previously think much could be done about the matter. In North America, and to a smaller extent in Europe and Australasia, feminists have also raised the consciousness of women in situation 4, who were previously content with the position of women in society but have now changed their minds about this.

The concept is also relevant to campaigns by homosexual and lesbian groups to increase public tolerance of differing forms of sexual preference and behaviour. When municipal authorities in Greater London established lesbian workshops in the 1980s, the object was not only to provide meeting places but also to raise the consciousness of lesbians about their position, the need to educate the general public about it, and the desirability of changes in law and custom that would make it possible for lesbian couples to adopt children.

The concept of 'real interests' is commonly used in connection with the assertion that the real interest of workers in a capitalist system is to bring about the transformation of that system to socialism or communism. However, it may be a mistake to identify the concept solely with this assertion, on which the gap between the two sides is unbridgeable, for there are other issue areas in which the idea of real interests, though hardly scientific, may spark off useful pieces of research.

As an example, British social scientists visiting the United States often come away with the belief that the real interest of Americans would be served by the creation of a national health insurance scheme, though only a minority of Americans have seemed to want this and it has only recently got on to the political agenda. This issue is one that can fruitfully be studied by scholars interested in political power. When the question of national health insurance was put on the agenda in the late 1940s under Truman's presidency, a lively debate was won by the American Medical Association, which scored a brilliant propaganda victory by the tactic of dubbing national health insurance with the name of 'socialized medicine' and thus mobilizing the strong bias that Americans have against socialism. This controversy can be studied by empirical methods as an example of pressure-group politics. Since that debate, it could be argued that all the publicists who use the term 'socialized medicine' are continuing to mobilize bias against the idea, with the aim of keeping the issue off the agenda. While the debate in 1948 was an example of the first dimension of political power, with the Medical Association coming out on top, the intermittent propaganda on the question since that time can be regarded as an example of the second dimension of power.

It would be quite a different matter to investigate why the American people have not embraced socialism. Numerous scholars have attempted an explanation, in terms of such factors as the opportunities offered to immigrants, the expanding frontier, the rapid growth of the American economy, the degree of social mobility, and the existence of ethnic divisions that led to conflict between ethnic groups rather than between social classes. However, it is doubtful whether it would be useful to employ the concept of political power when making an inquiry into this question. People were not prevented from adopting socialist ideas by censorship or controls over political association or institutional hurdles. Socialist ideas were floated, but they did not catch on.

[...] [T]he concept of cultural and ideological hegemony [...] was developed by Gramsci in the 1930s. It seems to me to be clearly true that in most advanced capitalist societies there exists a dominant set of values that is compatible with capitalism and supports the operation of the capitalist system. It is not the only set of values present, for there is also a quite widely held set of trade-union values that are rather different, though they are not normally incompatible with capitalism, together with a set of revolutionary values held by a small minority of citizens. It is fair to say that the dominant values are generally upheld by schools, churches, the mass media and other opinion-formers as well as by politicians. The process of upholding social values and passing them on to the next generation is commonly known as socialization, and in the opinion of Marxists and neo-Marxists the result of the socialization process in western societies has been the development and maintenance of an ideological and cultural hegemony of bourgeois values.

If the development and maintenance of this hegemony is to be regarded as the exercise of political power, in the third dimension of power suggested by Lukes (1974), it is important to ask how this can be studied empirically. The concept of power involves the idea of a political actor with certain intentions, who communicates a message and is able to make some difference to the political behaviour of others. If it can be shown that people who control the dissemination of ideas, be they teachers, journalists or newspaper proprietors, have deliberately presented slanted information that has had a measurable impact on the attitudes and values of their audience, then this should be regarded as a form of political power, of the type that I have called political manipulation. The audience may not have the resources of time and knowledge required to check the validity of the messages presented to them, and in the long run beliefs instilled in this way are likely to affect political behaviour. However the problems of analysing this hypothetical power to shape ideas are very great indeed. Much political communication takes the form of private conversation or classroom dialogue that is simply not on record. When communications are on record their content can be analysed, but one can rarely do more than infer the intentions of the author and it is not easy to assess the impact of the message.

A good deal of research has been carried out, but the results of it have been highly inconclusive. People are socialized throughout life, the main sources of influence being parents, schools, peer groups, colleagues at work, life experiences and the mass media. Of these, the only sources amenable to empirical research are school curricula with a political content and the mass media. However, it has been reported that 'most of the survey type research ... on the impact of various types of political education curricula seems to confirm that their influence on children is minimal' (Dowse 1978: 408). The results of research on the influence of the mass media have also been largely negative. The public seem to take what they want from the mass media rather than be educated by the messages presented, with the consequence that 'on the whole, the mass media serve to reinforce existing orientations rather than to alter old ones or create new ones' (Dawson and Prewitt 1969: 198).

People certainly acquire and develop political attitudes as they go through life, and it may be appropriate to call this a process of political socialization, but in modern industrial societies citizens are exposed to such a multitude of communications and experiences from which they may acquire a political message that it is almost impossible to assess the impact of any one of them. After surveying the literature, Dowse and Hughes report that 'in recent years the interest political sociologists have shown in the process of socialization has waned, due in no small part to the inconclusiveness of much of the research' (Dowse and Hughes 1986: 217).

Even in closed societies the evidence suggests that people are markedly resistant to indoctrination by political propaganda. The citizens of the Communist Party states of eastern Europe were supposedly brain-washed for forty years after the Second World War about the advantages of a socialist economic system and a single-party state. The dramatic events of 1989–90 showed that most people did not believe the propaganda. In view of these revelations, it behoves political scientists to think very carefully before using phrases like 'the power of the capitalist press'. The evidence suggests that life experiences have much more influence on people's attitudes than the mass media can exert, even when the media are substantially in unison.

Some Concluding Reflections

It sometimes happens that the discussion of a political concept comes to be dominated by the terminology used in a particular dispute, even though that dispute focuses on only one aspect of the process or activity or pattern of behaviour covered by the concept. This has happened to the concept of political power. The article by Bachrach and Baratz (1962) discussed above referred to a 'second face of power', while the book by Lukes (1974) referred to the 'three dimensions of power'. In fact these contributions dealt only with forms of political influence, or in Lukes' case with two forms of influence and one form of what I prefer to call political manipulation. They said nothing whatever about political coercion or political authority. In consequence there is some danger that the lively and useful controversy about whether 'power' has one, two, or three dimensions will divert attention from the fact that political coercion and political authority are just as important as political influence and logically distinct from it.

It is important to recognize that these types of political power are logically distinct, just as it is important [...] to recognize that there are four logically distinct types of representation. This recognition promotes clarity of analysis and enables the scholar to put particular empirical or historical studies into proper perspective. Let us therefore conclude with some thoughts on each of the four types of power.

In the literature of political science, *political coercion* features mainly in case studies of particular examples of political violence. In recent years terrorism has been extensively studied and an excellent literature on that topic now exists, including a specialized journal. The literature on the coercion exerted by the police and allied security agencies, such as the US National Guard, is more patchy. Since the late 1970s half a dozen good books on the British police have appeared, but other countries have not been so well served. Since the police constitute the sharp end of the power of the modern state, it could be expected that every textbook on a national system of government would include a chapter on the powers, organization and behaviour of the police. These matters are important, both because contacts (even if usually only visual contacts) with the police are the most frequent contacts that the average citizen has with agencies wielding state power and because the police have enormous discretion in deciding on the priority they will give to different types of law enforcement and on the methods they will use. It therefore seems unfortunate that only a small minority of textbooks include a chapter on the police.

The exercise of *political authority* in the modern state has been much more thoroughly covered by the literature. Accounts of the structure, powers and work of the executive, legislative and judicial organs of government have always been at the heart of the discipline and it can be expected that this will be so for the foreseeable future.

The study of *political influence* has, as already suggested, tended to follow fashions. An emphasis on the legislative influence of economic pressure groups was followed and accompanied in the 1950s by an emphasis on the nature and influence of public opinion, through elections, political parties and promotional groups for various good causes. This emphasis was followed in the 1960s by an enthusiasm for analysing the patterns of influence within municipal government. That decade saw the completion of over thirty substantial studies of community power structure in American cities and about eight studies in British cities.

In the 1970s and 1980s the emphasis shifted again. On the one hand, as noted in Chapter 3, a revival in support for minority nationalist movements within several democratic states led to a new focus on the political significance of non-economic cleavages within society. On the other hand, a new generation of Marxist or neo-Marxist scholars stressed the influence, amounting to dominance, that Marxists believe the capitalist class to exercise over government policy in all societies where the economic system is one of capitalism.

[...]

Political manipulation is inherently more difficult to study by empirical methods. The enthusiasm for studying political socialization that was evident in the 1960s has largely faded away in recent years, because the many studies yielded results that were, on the whole, disappointing. Since the early 1980s, thought about political manipulation has been dominated not by empirical research but by the theoretical suggestions of Michel Foucault, the French social philosopher and, through his writings, by reflections about the ways in which we are all manipulated in our daily lives. Foucault's explorations of power relationships focused not on the power of people at the top of the political system, the decision makers and the groups that influence decision makers, but on the power relationships in the system itself, as seen in the numerous forms of local power applied to citizens so as to induce conformity in their behaviour. Some of these forms are explicit and brutal, such as the powers exercised by police officers and magistrates, while others are subtle and exercised without the subject being conscious of the fact, so that they can be regarded as manipulative power. In any area of human activity there is a multiplicity of customs and pressures that collectively limit freedom of action, pushing people to do what is thought proper and appropriate, and in the second half of the twentieth century it has been evident that one of the instruments of this kind of power is the accumulation and dissemination of various types of specialized knowledge; particularly knowledge of the human sciences. This line of reasoning led Foucault to his assertion that in modern society knowledge is itself an important form of power, giving experts a way of shaping the behaviour of others.

Foucault, himself a radical, maintained that the cumulative impact of the power of experts is conservative in its nature. Psychiatrists, by defining what is normal or abnormal, have the long-term effect of inducing conformity in behaviour. It could be added that sociologists give us generalizations about the normal family, sexologists tell us how to conduct our sex lives, and dieticians tell us what to eat. University professors, by defining what research methods are appropriate or inappropriate, may limit the new knowledge that becomes available. Art and dramatic critics may influence what kinds of painting or drama are produced. It is not difficult to find examples of the kind of power that Foucault had in mind, though it is not necessary to follow him in his apparent assumption that expert knowledge is always conservative in its impact on society. Some forms of knowledge have this kind of impact whereas other forms have a liberating or reforming impact. Anyone familiar with the outlines of history in the past two centuries knows that intellectuals have often taken the lead in promoting social and political change. A clear contemporary example of the reforming impact of intellectuals is the impact of educational theorists on school education in Britain and North America since the 1960s. However, Foucault, though in some sense a political theorist, was not interested in broad movements leading to change at the top. His concern was with the local mechanisms of social control found everywhere in modern society. The kind of power that interested him is only indirectly political, and is not state-centred but diffuse; as Ball puts it, this knowledge/power consists of 'a highly decentralised array of ... practices operating in unsuspected and subtle ways in everyday life to produce "normal" subjects' (Ball 1988: 101). Moreover, it is central to Foucault's thinking that people may themselves assist in the process that leads to what he calls their subjugation, as in the case, presumably, of people who willingly provide data for computerized data-banks that may subsequently be used to their disadvantage.

Another general point, however, is that this kind of power is far from being absolute. Human beings are constantly influenced by it, but they can escape from it if they have the mind to do so. There are 'points of insubordination which, by definition, are means of escape' (Foucault 1983: 225). One task of the theorist, Foucault maintained, is to clarify the nature of this kind of power, 'thereby disclosing points of possible intervention and resistance and thus helping to empower others to take advantage of them' (Ball 1988: 103). When there is resistance 'the relationship of power may become a confrontation between two adversaries' (Foucault 1983: 226) which may modify the structure of dominance.

One source of resistance to the power of organized knowledge, that is, to knowledge as science which commands respect and conformity, lies in the local and 'minor knowledges' that also exist in society. An example is the knowledge of psychiatric patients and nurses, as contrasted to the knowledge embodied and formalized in medical science (see Foucault 1980: 82). Foucault explained that his research into the history of sexuality, the history of psychiatric illness and the emergence of the prison system had been intended to rediscover the 'historical knowledge of struggles' that had been 'confined to the margins of knowledge'

(Foucault 1980: 83). He called these rediscoveries 'genealogies'; he described them as 'anti-sciences'; and he did not claim that in any objective way they were more correct than normal scientific knowledge. What he claimed is that knowing them would be a weapon opposed not to the contents or methods of science but to 'the effects of the centralizing powers which are linked to the institution and functioning of an organized scientific discourse within a society such as ours' (Foucault 1980: 84).

Foucault's dislike of the society in which he lived was not explained or justified in an explicit manner, but it seems to have been quite intense. He said, for instance, that 'what is at stake in all these genealogies is the nature of this power that has surged into view in all its violence, aggression and absurdity in the course of the last forty years' (Foucault 1980: 87). The overall impression left by his writings is not that of a scholar who had a coherent theory about political power to put alongside other theories, but rather that of an individualistic scholar who distrusted coherent theories, disliked the organization and discipline of contemporary society, and linked this to the dominance of orthodoxies in the human sciences. His objects in acting as an intellectual archaeologist, digging out examples of past social thought and practice for current inspection, were to open windows for speculation, to shock people out of complacency, to liberate thought from its conventional limits, and to encourage society's rebels and critics. In one of his several revealing interviews, he said that all his books were 'if you like, little tool-boxes. If people want to open them, use a sentence, an idea, an analysis as a screwdriver or a spanner in order to short-circuit, disqualify and break systems of power ... well, so much the better' (quoted O'Farrell 1989: 110). Taken as a whole, Foucault's writings have the bracing effect of leading readers to regard familiar situations and relationships in an entirely fresh light.

References

Bachrach, P. and Baratz, M. S. (1962) 'The two faces of power', *American Political Science Review*, 56: 947–52.

Ball, T. (1988) *Transforming Political Discourse*, Oxford: Blackwell.

Dahl, R. A. (1961) *Who Governs?*, New Haven, CT: Yale University Press.

Dawson, R. E. and Prewitt, K. (1969) *Political Socialisation*, Boston, MA: Little, Brown.

Dowse, R. E. (1978) 'Some doubts concerning the study of political socialisation', *Political Studies*, 26: 403–10.

Dowse, R. E. and Hughes, J. A. (1986) *Political Sociology*, 2nd edn, New York: Wiley.

Foucault, M. (1980) *Power/Knowledge*, ed. C. Gordon, New York: Pantheon.

——(1983) 'The subject and power', Afterword to H. L. Dreyfus and P. Rabinow (eds) *Michel Foucault: Beyond Structuralism and Hermeneutics*, 2nd edn, Chicago, IL: University of Chicago Press.

Gaventa, J. (1980) *Power and Powerlessness*, Urbana, IL: University of Illinois Press.

Hunter, F. (1953) *Community Power Structure*, Chapel Hill, NC: University of North Carolina Press.

Jessop, B. (1982) *The Capitalist State*, Oxford: Blackwell.

Lasswell, H. D. and Kaplan, A. (1950) *Power and Society*, New Haven, CT: Yale University Press.

Lukes, S. (1974) *Power: a Radical View*, London: Macmillan.

O'Farrell, C. (1989) *Foucault: Historian or Philosopher?*, London: Macmillan.

Parry, G. (1969) *Political Elites*, London: Allen & Unwin.

Polsby, N. (1979) 'Empirical investigations of mobilization of bias in community power research', *Political Studies*, 27: 527–41.

Schattschneider, E. E. (1960) *The Semisovereign People*, New York: Holt, Rinehart & Winston.

Simon, H. A. (1957) *Models of Man*, New York: Wiley.

Reading 3.2

Political Authority and Legitimacy

Anthony H. Birch

The Definition of Political Authority

For the ordinary citizen of a modern democratic state in times of peace, the nature of political authority is not problematical. It is embodied in a complex system of laws and administrative regulations that most citizens accept without question and that the questioning or recalcitrant minority are forced to comply with by the actions of tax inspectors, police officers and other public officials holding what are commonly called positions of authority. It has to be recognized, however, that the very notion of authority has caused difficulty to philosophers, who have argued among themselves about its meaning and nature.

In part, this difficulty flows from the fact that there are significant differences between political authority, moral authority, divine authority, parental authority and so forth, so that it is a good deal more difficult to define the single term 'authority' than it is to define each of the various types of authority. In part, the difficulty flows from the fact that philosophers commonly concern themselves with the meanings given to concepts from the time of the Greek city-states onwards, during which period the meaning of each concept has often been modified. In this book our task is simpler, as we are concerned only with the meaning, nature and basis of political authority, not with other types of authority, and only with the period of the modern democratic state, that is to say from the late eighteenth century onwards.

On the question of definition, it is perhaps best to start with a dictionary, as the word authority clearly has more than one meaning in contemporary English usage. The first, and politically most important, meaning of authority is defined in the *Oxford English Dictionary* (OED) as 'the right to command, or give an ultimate decision'. This is the type of authority wielded by presidents and prime ministers and parliaments, by generals in charge of armies, by judges and police officers, by managing directors of business firms, or (in a weaker form) by school principals and teachers. This meaning of the term implies a community or group with some kind of hierarchy, a widespread acceptance within the community of the right of certain persons or institutions to take decisions and issue commands, and probably some kind of sanction against individuals who might wish to ignore particular decisions or commands.

A second meaning, invoked in both political and non-political situations, relates to the possession by one person of a conferred right or title to speak or act on behalf of others. A lawyer might say that she has 'the authority of her client' to reject offers made by another

Anthony H. Birch, "Political Authority and Legitimacy," *The Concepts and Theories of Modern Democracy*, pp. 91–105, 293–303. Copyright © 2007 by Taylor & Francis Group. Reprinted with permission.

party. An ambassador to the United Nations has this kind of authority when he speaks on behalf of his country's government. This is the authority enjoyed by representatives, be they politicians, lawyers, or union negotiators in wage disputes, who have been appointed to carry out certain duties.

A third meaning relates to expertise. A literary critic might be described as an authority on Shakespeare, an historian as an authority on the French Revolution, or a House of Commons clerk as an authority on parliamentary procedure. None of these persons wields power as a consequence of his expertise, but they might well exercise a good deal of influence over the opinions and in some circumstances the actions of others.

Students of politics are mainly concerned with authority in the first of these three senses, namely with the power to take decisions that are binding on others and to induce or force others to abide by these decisions. As noted, this kind of authority is exercised in non-political as well as political situations, but in modern industrial societies the state is so thoroughly enmeshed in societal relationships that the exercise of authority by some people over others nearly always depends ultimately upon the existence of state authority. It is the state that provides the legal framework within which social and economic relationships are defined, and it would now be somewhat unrealistic to draw the clear distinction between the state and civil society that was often drawn by political theorists in earlier periods. It follows that a clear understanding of the nature of political authority is helpful to all students of modern government and society.

In practice, the exercise of authority, in the first of the senses itemized above, depends upon the readiness of the people over whom it is exercised to accept the decisions and orders that are given. If players in a football match refuse to accept a referee's decision and hold up the game, or if school children take no notice of their teacher's instructions, it could properly be said that the referee or teacher in question have temporarily lost their authority. Having formal authority over a situation or a group of people does not necessarily mean that the person having the right to issue orders will always be obeyed. It may be that other qualities are necessary to ensure compliance, such as a certain amount of authority in the sense of expertise. A referee is likely to lose control of the game if he or she repeatedly misinterprets the rules. A teacher who displays ignorance of child psychology or ignorance of the subject he or she is supposed to be teaching may lose control of the class. It helps to ensure compliance if the person nominally in charge not only is *in* authority, in a formal sense, but also is *an* authority on the activity being engaged in by the group. It may help even more if they have personal qualities that inspire respect. A sociologist has listed the qualities of an authority as 'assurance, superior judgment, the ability to impose discipline, the capacity to inspire fear' (Sennett 1980: 17–18).

This kind of consideration has led R. S. Peters to suggest that there is a continuum between three senses of authority: namely, being appointed to be in authority; having special knowledge or qualities that make the person an authority; and the ability to exercise authority in practice (see Peters 1958). It is undoubtedly the case that authority relationships work most smoothly when the leader enjoys authority in both the first and second of these senses of the term; when, for instance, a minister appointed to control a department possesses an incisive understanding of the problems and work of the department that commands the respect of his or her staff. However, there are two reasons why it is important not to overemphasize the importance of expertise and related personal qualities in the exercise of authority.

The first reason is that these qualities by themselves are not all that much of an asset. Spectators or team managers at a game might possibly have a better understanding of the rules than the referee does and might indicate this in shouted comments, but they never get to take charge of the game themselves. A senior civil servant often understands departmental problems better than the minister in charge does, but this does not enable the civil servant to replace the minister. It may enable the civil servant to persuade the minister to modify his or her policies and may sometimes enable the civil servant to frustrate a minister who persists in issuing instructions that the civil servant regards as unwise, but if there is a direct clash the minister always has the power to come out on top. In the highly organized and bureaucratized societies of the advanced industrial countries, having the official right to exercise authority is four-fifths of the battle.

The other reason is that most people who are legally in charge have a weapon not available to others, namely the threat of coercion. Sergeant-majors can nearly always get their orders obeyed, even if they are ignorant people, because the expected consequences of disobedience are too serious for those under them to think disobedience is worth the candle. This raises the whole question of the relationship between coercion and authority (in the first sense of the term), on which the views of political theorists differ markedly. Robert Michels, writing in 1930, said that 'one of the principal means of exercising authority is the dispensation of rewards and punishments' (Michels 1930: 319). The acceptance of authority, he declared, 'may be due to a fear of force' and 'submission to authority may result either from a deliberate recognition of it as a good or from an acquiescence in it as inevitable, to be endured permanently or temporarily with scepticism, indifference or scorn, with fists clenched but in the pockets' (Michels 1930: 319). On the other hand, Hannah Arendt has said that 'if authority is to be defined at all … it must be in contradistinction to both coercion by force and persuasion through arguments' (Arendt 1968: 93). April Carter has followed Arendt in this view, saying also that authority excludes 'appeals to self-interest through promises, incentives and bribes' (Carter 1979: 14). Authority, she says, 'entails a belief in the right of the authority figure to issue commands or judgments' and 'to recognize authority is to be persuaded in advance that whatever is advocated will be worthy of respect and compliance' (Carter 1979: 14). C. W. Cassinelli has also gone some way towards this kind of view, saying that 'fear of … legal sanctions is a fear normally held incompatible with the exercise of political authority' (Cassinelli 1961: 639).

Between the views of Michels on the one hand and Arendt and her followers on the other, there is clearly a large gulf. Which view is more appropriate for the student of politics in the modern democratic state? My belief is that Michels' view is the more realistic and thus more helpful. The Arendt/Carter view is appropriate for students of moral authority, but political authority differs from moral authority. When we discuss authority in modern systems of government we are not discussing the kind of authority that priests enjoy over their parishioners. Relatively few citizens in modern democratic states now believe in the laws of God, the laws of nature, the divine right of kings, or similar concepts that bolstered political authority in times past. Political authority in the modern state is seen to be wielded by identifiable and fallible human beings over their fellow citizens, and is therefore always open to question. That it is usually accepted by most citizens clearly owes something to the fact that non-compliance is likely to lead to penalties of one kind or another. It seems to me that to deny this is to be unrealistic.

Having said this, the proviso should be added that the actual use of force, as distinct from the implied threat of force, usually indicates a partial loss of authority. A government that is regarded as legitimate should not have to use force over more than a very small minority of its citizens, just as army officers should not have constantly to put their subordinates on disciplinary charges and police officers should not often have to use their batons. Ideally, authority should be exercised by word of mouth or by the pen, without any need to use force.

In the real world of politics, however, it must be accepted that the threat of coercion is always present. Thomas Hobbes likened life to a game of cards in which the player who has a trump has authority. But 'in matters of government', he added, 'when nothing else is turned up, clubs are trumps'. This is undoubtedly true, and it is not just that the breakdown of political authority can be expected to lead to violence, it is also true that most kinds of political authority are backed by the threat, open or veiled, of coercion in cases of non-compliance. When a motorist pulls over and stops in response to flashing lights and sirens on a police car just behind him, he may be doing so out of inherent respect for the authority of the police. On the other hand, he may be stopping because he knows that a refusal to stop will eventually result in his arrest and punishment. The observer cannot tell which reason is predominant, and the two reasons may be so intermingled in the mind of the motorist that responses to questions on the subject would not be very meaningful. It is best to recognize that political authority is usually backed by the possibility of coercion, even in circumstances where the actual use of coercion is rare.

In view of this, political authority is best defined as a combination of political power and legitimacy, where power is the ability to get things done and legitimacy is the quality of ascribed entitlement to exercise that power. The appropriateness of this definition can be seen most clearly in circumstances where authority breaks down. In normal circumstances, for instance, the captain of an aircraft has both the legitimate right to control the movements of the aircraft and the actual power to do so, but if the aircraft is hijacked she loses this power and therefore loses her authority. In a hijacked aircraft nobody has authority, as the hijackers possess power without legitimacy and the captain possesses legitimacy without power. It could equally be said that nobody has authority in a riot where the police lose control or a classroom where pupils pelt the teacher with chalk. Power is an essential ingredient of authority and those theorists who have denied this have simply shown a lack of realism.

[...] [I]t is now appropriate to discuss some of the issues surrounding the concept of political legitimacy.

Theories About Political Legitimacy

The rise of the modern state was accompanied in the seventeenth and eighteenth centuries by a good deal of speculation and theorizing about the ways in which the authority exercised by the state could be justified. Expressed in one way, this is the problem of political obligation. Why should citizens feel obliged to obey the orders of the government? Expressed in another way, it is the problem of political legitimacy. Why should the actions of the government be regarded as the legitimate exercise of political power? Some of the most impressive works in the history of political thought have been addressed to these questions. Writings of this kind deal with the moral basis of political authority. Writings of a rather different kind deal with the sociological and practical bases of authority in the modern state. The most famous example of this second kind of theorizing is the work of Max Weber in the early years of the twentieth century.

Weber was a sociologist—indeed one of the founders of that discipline—whose contributions to political analysis were limited in number and significance. His best-known contribution is directly relevant to this chapter, however, as it was a classification of the sources of political legitimacy. Weber asked what it is that makes people accept that a political regime enjoys legitimate authority and he produced three answers. Each of these, he claimed, was an 'ideal type' to which actual situations approximated, with the possibility that any particular regime might be supported by more than one type of legitimacy. In this analysis, as in his other contributions to social science, Weber was careful to avoid the claim that sociological or political categories resembled watertight compartments. He maintained that patterns of social and political behaviour are too complex to be fitted into watertight categories, but that categorization is nevertheless an essential aid to understanding so long as it is recognized that each category represents only an ideal type of behaviour or relationship.

Weber's first type of political legitimacy is that based on tradition and inheritance. Traditional legitimacy is the legitimacy enjoyed by tribal chiefs, princes and kings. In this kind of regime the essential factor that ensures compliance with the orders and laws of government is personal loyalty to the chief or king or ruling family. In such regimes public administration tends to be in the hands of a ruling class defined by birth and upbringing, while key positions such as chief of police are often given to members of the ruling family such as the king's younger brother. Among modern states, Saudi Arabia and Kuwait conform most closely, though not completely, to this ideal type.

Weber's second type of political legitimacy, described by him as 'legal-rational', is that enjoyed by the governments of most modern states. In this kind of regime loyalty is given not to a person or a ruling family but to an impersonal set of institutions, the powers of which are defined (except in the United Kingdom) by a written constitution. In one example, namely the United States, recruits to the national army pledge themselves 'to defend the United States Constitution against its enemies, internal or external'. Public administration in regimes of this type is characteristically in the hands of trained specialists, recruited by an open competition based on merit, showing substantial neutrality as between the political parties competing for power. Public compliance with the orders and laws of government is based not on loyalty to persons but on general acceptance of the procedures by which these orders and laws are produced.

It is an obvious aspect of world history that the past three centuries have been marked by a widespread transition from regimes enjoying political authority of the traditional kind to regimes enjoying political authority of the legal-rational kind. However, there is a joker in the pack in the form of a third type of political authority, appearing irregularly and unpredictably. This is what Weber called 'charismatic authority', depending on the personal qualities of a political leader who appears as a kind of hero or saint and inspires his followers to accept his rule. Napoleon was an example, as were Mussolini, Hitler, Mao Zedong and Ayatollah Khomeini. Fidel Castro and Colonel Gaddafi are contemporary examples. Public administration in this type of regime is in the hands of people who are neither members of a traditional ruling class nor neutral bureaucrats recruited on the basis of merit, but followers of the leader who have faith in his wisdom, his vision and the religious creed or ideology that he promotes and manipulates.

The concept of charismatic leadership is frequently misused to apply to popular leaders like John F. Kennedy and Pierre Trudeau, whose actual authority was essentially legal-rational in character. However, these names draw attention to a feature of political life that Weber did not discuss, since he was suggesting ideal types of authority rather than writing descriptively about it. This feature is the role that 'humanly significant leadership', to use John Schaar's phrase (see Schaar 1981: 40–3), can sometimes play in enhancing political authority.

Margaret Thatcher is perhaps a more interesting example than Kennedy or Trudeau, as in the 1980s she persuaded millions of British voters to accept mass unemployment in their country without blaming the government for it. She changed people's attitudes. Winston Churchill would be a better example still, as during the Second World War he changed people's behaviour. His leadership and rhetoric inspired British citizens to do things that they would otherwise have been unlikely to do, such as continuing to work while bombs were falling around them or volunteering to spend their spare time drilling as members of the Home Guard.

The most remarkable example of humanly significant leadership in the democratic state is undoubtedly the leadership of Charles de Gaulle. His achievements were so great that he could be said to have exercised both charismatic and legal-rational authority. He exercised charismatic authority to acquire power both in 1944 and in 1958, to secure the adoption of a completely new constitution in the latter year, to change that constitution when he wanted the president (namely himself) to be directly elected, and to end the civil war in Algeria by granting independence to that country. At the same time, de Gaulle was careful to follow constitutional procedures whenever this was possible, deviating from them only to secure direct election for the presidency, which could not have been achieved by purely constitutional means.

One of the problems of the charismatic form of political authority, as noted by Weber, is that authority may die when the leader dies. It is not easy to pass this kind of authority on to heirs, as can be done in the case of traditional types of authority. It may, however, be possible to convert charismatic authority into a form of legal-rational authority, a process that Weber called 'the routinization of charisma'. The most outstanding example of this is again the career of Charles de Gaulle. During the early years of his rule commentators referred to the Fifth Republic as 'de Gaulle's Republic' and commonly predicted that it would give way to a Sixth Republic when he retired from the scene. In practice, the constitution of the Fifth Republic has proved to be durable, almost certainly the most successful France has had, and succeeding presidents have, without serious controversy, exercised powers that were previously thought to be dependent on de Gaulle's personal qualities.

The Limitations of Weber

Weber's contribution to the understanding of the sources of political authority is generally accepted as useful. It is, however, only a limited contribution to a complex topic, because Weber directed his attention only to the legitimacy of regimes. This is important, but a study of the conditions in which political authority is seriously challenged in the modern state would reveal that it is only in a minority of cases that the dissenters object to the regime itself. This happened in 1989–90 in Poland, Czechoslovakia, Hungary, East Germany and Romania, where Communist Party regimes were overthrown in quick succession by popular demonstrations and revolts. However, these were exceptional events in that, first, the Communist regimes had been imposed by Soviet power rather than emerging internally, and second, these regimes had been both brutal and conspicuously inefficient.

A more common cause of challenges to political authority in recent years has been the decision by leaders of particular ethnic and cultural groups in society to query or reject the legitimacy of governments dominated by other such groups. Challenges of this kind may be called challenges to the legitimacy of the political community. Another common cause of challenges to political authority has been the rejection of specific government policies by groups who are affected by them. Challenges of this kind may be called challenges to the legitimacy of policies.

Challenges to the legitimacy of the political community arise when there is a lack of congruence between community, territory and government. In an age of self-determination it is important that the citizens of a state should believe that they are rightly ruled, even if not well ruled, by leaders drawn from their own community. Colonial regimes do not qualify, and Northern Ireland is a classic example of a political unit that is perceived as colonial, and therefore as illegitimate, by a sizeable proportion of its citizens. Since the late 1970s we have seen violent challenges to political authority mounted by Basque nationalists in Spain, Palestinians in the West Bank and the Gaza Strip, Muslims in Lebanon, Tamils in Sri Lanka, Kurds in Turkey and Iraq and Sikhs in India. The ideology involved in such cases is that of nationalism, which can in one form be the cement that holds a political community together and in another form be the explosive that tears it apart.

Challenges to political authority based on objections to specific government policies have also been widespread in recent years. The Americans who burned their draft cards during the Vietnam war were not revolutionaries who wanted to replace the American constitution with a different form of government, but simply radicals who objected passionately to conscription to fight in a war they regarded as unnecessary and unjust. The Americans who bombed twenty-eight abortion clinics during 1986 were not even radicals, but religious zealots wanting to protest about the liberality of the laws regarding abortion. Pickets from the British mineworkers' union who fought the police during the long miners' strike of 1984–5 did not want to abolish Parliament, only to make the government's policy of closing uneconomic pits unworkable. Supporters of the Welsh Language Society who bombed television relay stations did so in protest against the British government's refusal to authorize a television channel using Welsh. German feminists who placed a bomb in the West German Constitutional Court were protesting about the toughness of German abortion laws at that time. French farmers who periodically block highways with farm tractors or dumps of manure do so to protest about agricultural policies. Canadian Indians who barricaded one of Montreal's main bridges for two months in 1990 took this action to protest against a plan to build a golf course over an old Indian burial ground. Anti-nuclear demonstrators who engage in civil disobedience do so to express their outrage at the possibility that nuclear weapons might be used. Examples could be multiplied to produce an extremely long list, for political authority in the modern state is not so secure as some textbooks would lead readers to assume.

In order of generality, the reasons why people reject political authority can be therefore categorized as:

1. objections to the composition and boundaries of the political community
2. objections to the constitutional arrangements within the community
3. objections to specific policies pursued by the government.

Challenges to authority in categories 1 and 3 are much more common than challenges in category 2 because most people are not political theorists. To get involved in activities that may involve personal sacrifice, most people need to be motivated by some kind of direct interest. They have such an interest if they are subject to government by a group whom they regard as alien, or if they are outraged by specific policies of the government. They can be mobilized for political action by leaders who play on these feelings and interests. It is more difficult to mobilize people for action in support of a better constitution. The cultural or material interests of citizens are prejudiced indirectly, rather than directly, by institutional inadequacy. Leaders of dissent on this ground cannot appeal simply to community or group interests, but must try to educate their fellow-citizens to a higher level of political awareness and sophistication.

It follows from these arguments that as Max Weber's contribution to the understanding of political authority deals only with the character of the regime, its value must be regarded as limited. It was useful in its way and in its time, but we now have more experience of popular involvement in politics on which to base our generalizations.

Legitimacy and the Economic System

Another approach to the problem of political legitimacy has been developed by several writers of neo-Marxist inclinations, of whom the most prominent are Jürgen Habermas and Claus Offe. One of the central features of Marxist analysis is the conviction that the political and economic systems of any society are so intimately linked that one of them cannot sensibly be studied in isolation from the other. Marx and Engels believed that the capitalist economic system is fundamentally unjust and exploitative, that workers in an advanced capitalist society would realize this, and that when capitalism moved into a state of crisis (as it inevitably would) the workers would seize control of the government and use their newly acquired political power to transform the economic system from capitalism to socialism. The problem for contemporary Marxists is that this prediction has not been validated by events. The workers have seized power only in the relatively backward societies of Russia, China and Cuba, while the more advanced capitalist societies have grown more and more prosperous and less and less class divided.

An early attempt to explain this predictive failure was made in the 1930s by Antonio Gramsci, the leader of the Italian Communist Party. Gramsci's argument was that within capitalist societies the social and political values of the capitalist class enjoy what he called an 'ideological hegemony'. These values are promulgated through the educational system, the mass media, popular novels and the cinema, so that the great majority of citizens come to accept them as natural. They emphasize the virtues of hard work and thrift and suggest that the poor themselves (rather than the system), are largely to blame for their poverty. They endorse competitive individualism as a way of life and they propagate the view that con-flicting interests could be accommodated through the free competition of parties and group spokesmen in the political system. In these ways workers are socialized into accepting the capitalist system, despite its manifest inequalities, and are led to believe that democratic political institutions could alleviate the problems of the working class. This bourgeois ide-ology, spread throughout society, prescribes the channels and limits within which political conflict is normally confined. As the French Marxist, Nicos Poulantzas, put it:

> The dominance of this ideology is shown by the fact that the dominated classes live their conditions of political existence through the forms of dominant political discourse: this means that often they live *even their revolt* against the domination of the system within the frame of reference of the dominant ideology.
>
> (Poulantzas 1973: 223)

Another explanation of the predictive failure of Marxism was developed in the 1970s by Habermas and Offe. Their argument had three main themes. First, it was declared that in western industrial societies the capitalist system had been largely legitimized in the eyes of the workers by the liberal-democratic state. In Offe's words, this process of legitimation can be defined as one by which 'the capitalist state manages, through a variety of institutional mechanisms, to convey the image of an organization of power that pursues common and general interests of society as a whole, allows equal access to power, and is responsive to justified demands' (Offe 1975: 127). This image disguises the dominant role of the capitalist class in society and in the formation of state policy, but it serves to keep the workers quiescent and willing to accept the authority of the state.

The second argument is that the liberal-democratic state has adopted various policies and tactics to protect both its own legitimacy and that of the social order. The most important of these policies is the development of welfare services designed to shelter disadvantaged groups from the inevitable hardships resulting from the operation of the capitalist system. In this way the groups with the most right to feel aggrieved are pacified. The hard edges of capitalism are softened by welfare spending.

Alongside this strategy, the state has protected itself by ensuring that those forms of social conflict that are most likely to upset sizeable groups take place outside the institutions of the state itself. Thus, group conflicts over taxation or import duties are resolved in Parliament or Congress but conflicts over wage levels, which upset the losers much more directly, take place in other arenas. It is true that these conflicts are resolved in a framework of rules that are to some extent determined by the state, but so long as no significant group challenges the rules themselves the state is protected from the wrath of losing groups in the bargaining process. The point is to safeguard the appearance (or illusion) of state neutrality in class conflicts. As Offe has put it, the 'capitalist welfare state bases its legitimacy on the postulate of a universal participation in consensus formation and on the unbiased opportunity for all classes to utilize the state's services and to benefit from its regulatory acts of intervention' (Offe 1972: 81).

Third, these writers claimed that in the late capitalist state this whole system of legitimation has begun to break down. Pressures within the system have led to the extension of social benefits in one form or another—student loans or grants, subsidized housing, health services, unemployment benefits, pensions, etc.—to virtually the whole population. The inevitable consequence of this, which European democracies were facing in the 1970s, would be to create a fiscal crisis by overloading the burden of public expenditure. Governments would then find themselves in a cleft stick. If they cut social expenditures they would alienate large numbers of citizens who had become dependent on them, thus reducing the ability of the state to legitimize the system. If they did not do this they would have to raise taxes or run a deficit, either of which would have deleterious effects on the economy.

The overall consequence of this kind of crisis, in Offe's view, would be the development of new kinds of group conflict in society, not so much between classes, in the old Marxist sense, as between sections. These might include conflicts between those dependent on social benefits and those who perceive themselves as paying for them, conflicts between depressed and prosperous regions, conflicts between generations, conflicts between ethnic minorities and the dominant community. Such conflicts would no longer be confined to the channels regarded as legitimate in a liberal-democratic state and the consequence of this would be that the outcomes of the conflicts would lack legitimacy in the eyes of the losers and the general public (see Offe 1980: 8–11). The general effect would be to undermine the whole process by which the democratic state legitimizes an unjust economic system, and thus to reduce the authority of the ruling classes in that society.

The belief that western societies were heading for a fiscal crisis in the 1970s was not confined to writers with Marxist sympathies. In 1978 two non-Marxist political scientists made a substantial impact on academic opinion with a book entitled *Can Government Go Bankrupt?* (Rose and Peters 1978). A central concept of this book was 'government overload', defined as a situation in which 'the national product grows more slowly than the costs of public policy and the claims of take-home pay, and there is not enough money in hand to meet both public and private claims' (Rose and Peters 1978: 29–30). This was said to be an immediate and serious problem in Italy, Sweden and the United Kingdom, while other western industrial states would be heading towards the same problem if the economic trends of the 1970s continued.

Governments facing this kind of dilemma have only three possible courses of action. One is to make policy changes to restrain the growth in public expenditure, a policy which is certain to be unpopular with bureaucrats, social workers and all those citizens who benefit from the social services that are affected. A second possibility is to maintain growing public expenditures by raising taxation, a course that would reduce the level of disposable personal incomes, be unpopular with most citizens and have a depressing effect on the economy. A third option is to dodge the issue by letting public expenditures rise without increasing taxation, which would increase the national debt and only postpone the task of getting to grips with the problem.

According to Rose and Peters, any of these options is likely to reduce public confidence in their government and to provoke a decline in political authority. Citizens could be expected to become cynical about government, unwilling to cooperate with it, and reluctant to comply with its edicts unless they are forced to do so. Governments would therefore become less effective and a cycle of declining authority would be initiated, to which the authors gave the label 'political bankruptcy'.

How much truth is there in these various theories about the relationship between the economic system and the level of political authority? To begin with Antonio Gramsci, the answer must be that his theory about the ideological hegemony of bourgeois values in capitalist society is undoubtedly correct. Since the end of the Second World War, the social values of the 'consumer society' have become dominant in all western industrial states. Capitalism has had such a beneficial effect on the living standards of the great majority of citizens in these states that alternative values have lost their attraction to all but a small minority. The revolutionary changes in eastern Europe in 1989 and 1990 have shown that forty years of brainwashing by socialist governments failed to convert their citizens to socialist values. Public ownership and central economic direction in these societies was a conspicuous failure, as it was in the Soviet Union, and people reacted accordingly. Radicals may regret that Gramsci was so penetrating, but the validity of his insight can hardly be denied.

The neo-Marxist argument that the capitalist system has been legitimized in the eyes of the workers by the liberal-democratic state is also both valid and helpful. There can be no doubt that political authority in the modern state is enhanced by democratic institutions. In past eras, when the functions of the state barely extended beyond foreign affairs, defence, customs duties and the maintenance of internal order, democracy might have been desirable but was not actually necessary. Governments could carry out their limited duties effectively so long as they had the support of the bureaucracy and the army, without needing much support from the general public. This could also be said of many developing countries today. But in modern industrial societies where the state regulates all aspects of public life, provides services for all its citizens and spends nearly half the national income, all sections of the community have to feel that they have some influences over government decisions if they are to acquiesce in government policies and cooperate willingly with government agencies. The modern state depends upon the cooperation of its citizens and this is a central fact of political life. It is beyond dispute that modern states with dictatorial systems of government have had to use stronger measures of coercion to secure public compliance with laws and policies than democratic states have needed.

The argument that welfare policies adopted by modern governments protect their legitimacy and that of the social order is also undoubtedly valid. If proof is needed, it is provided by examples of the partial breakdown of political authority among groups affected by prolonged unemployment, a tragic condition for which unemployment benefits can never be an adequate compensation. In Britain, unemployed workers engaged in riots and fights with the police during the period of mass unemployment immediately after the end of the First World War, and did so again in the depression years of the early 1930s. The large-scale unemployment of 1980–1 produced more riots, accompanied by widespread looting of shops, in twenty-seven urban areas in the summer of 1981. There was a racial element in the 1981 riots, for the first and worst of them (in Brixton and Liverpool) were fights between blacks and the police, and many of the subsequent disturbances were started by black teenagers. But most of the participants in the later riots were white and unemployment was clearly a major factor.

The final set of arguments examined in this section of the chapter, namely those relating to fiscal crisis and political overload, are particularly interesting in that they suggest that the modern state may be running into unavoidable problems as a consequence of its acceptance of responsibility for protecting its citizens against many of the hazards of life. People have higher expectations of what their government can do for them than were entertained by earlier generations. The efforts by governments to meet these expectations have put a heavy burden of costs on the national exchequer, which cannot easily be met unless the national economy is constantly growing, so that enhanced revenues are available to meet increasing costs.

The concern about fiscal overload arose during the 1970s because that was a bad decade for the industrial economies of the western world. A period of continuous economic growth since 1945 was checked by the four-fold increase in oil prices imposed by the Arab states in 1973, and western economies fell into a period of stagnation and growing unemployment accompanied by inflation. These conditions pushed several countries towards a position of fiscal overload, which might have had the serious political consequences predicted by some social scientists had the stagnation continued through the following decade. Fortunately, the last two decades of the century were years of almost continuous economic growth, so the predicted crisis did not develop. However, although the predictions made in the 1970s were unduly pessimistic, the analyses pointed to a significant potential problem. If western economies fall again into serious recession there will doubtless be renewed concern about the possibility that the problems created by fiscal overload might lead to a withdrawal of public confidence in government and a consequent decline in political authority.

Even without serious recession, there is, in Habermas's opinion, a danger that the legitimation of political authority by economic growth and welfare policies will be thought inadequate by some groups in society, either because (like the homeless or some ethnic minorities) the system has not worked for them, or because (like anti-nuclear protestors or radical environmentalists) the economic aims of the modern state are thought to be incompatible with moral principles that ought to govern the relationship between human beings and the natural world.

It may be concluded that the bearing of economic issues on political authority in the modern state is quite important. It is not as dominant as Marxists believe, but it certainly cannot be ignored as Max Weber and others seemed to assume. To understand the character and bases of political authority, we have to take both economic and non-economic factors into account, together with sociological factors like the composition of the political community. We have also, as suggested above, to consider not only the legitimacy of political, economic and social systems but also the legitimacy of particular policies, that may either elicit popular support or lead to public protests and cynicism. The maintenance of authority is central to the whole process of government, and an understanding of the factors supporting or diminishing that authority is therefore central to the understanding of how states are governed.

References

Arendt, H. (1968) *Between Past and Future*, New York: Viking Press.

Carter, A. (1979) *Authority and Democracy*, London: Routledge & Kegan Paul.

Cassinelli, C. W. (1961) 'Political authority: its exercise and possession', *Western Political Quarterly*, 14: 635–46.

Michels, R. (1930) 'Authority', in *Encyclopedia of the Social Sciences*, vol. 2, New York: Macmillan.

Offe, C. (1972) 'Political authority and class structures: an analysis of late capitalist societies', *International Journal of Sociology*, 2: 73–108.

Peters, R. S. (1958) 'Authority', *Proceedings of the Aristotelian Society*, 32: 207–24.

Poulantzas, N. (1973) *Political Power and Social Class*, London: New Left Books and Speed and Ward.

Rose, R. and Peters, G. (1978) *Can Government Go Bankrupt?*, New York: Basic Books.

Schaar, J. H. (1981) *Legitimacy in the Modern State*, New Brunswick, NJ: Transaction Books.

Sennett, R. (1980) *Authority*, New York: Knopf.

Reading 3.3

Democracy

Anthony H. Birch

The Word 'Democracy'

The word 'democracy' comes from the Greek and literally means rule by the people. It is sometimes said that democratic government originated in the city-states of ancient Greece and that democratic ideals have been handed down to us from that time. In truth, however, this is an unhelpful assertion. The Greeks gave us the word, but did not provide us with a model. The assumptions and practices of the Greeks were very different from those of modern democrats. The Greeks had little or no idea of the rights of the individual, an idea that is tied up with the modern concept of democracy. Greek practice granted the right of political participation to only a small minority of the adult inhabitants of the city. When those granted this right were able to take political decisions, they did so by a direct vote on issues, which is very different from the system of representative government that has developed in the west in the past two centuries. 'Modern men', asserts Sartori, 'want another democracy, in the sense that their ideal of democracy is not at all the same as that of the Greeks' (Sartori 1987: 279).

Greek democracy was poorly regarded by all the Greek philosophers and historians whose writings have survived, including Plato, Aristotle and Thucydides. They depicted it as government by the ignorant or government by the poor. It was subsequently held in general disrepute for over two thousand years. During the English civil war of the seventeenth century the Levellers briefly raised the banner of democracy, but they were a small group who had little or no influence on events. The founders of the American constitution shared in the generally poor view of democratic government. In *The Federalist*, James Madison, assuming that democracy involved direct rule by citizens, wrote that 'democracies have ever been found incompatible with personal security, or the rights of property; and have in general been as short in their lives as they have been violent in their deaths' (Hamilton et al. 1901: 48). The Founding Fathers talked of creating a republic, based on representative institutions, not a democracy; the leaders of the French Revolution talked of a republic also; and in Britain people described their system as one of representative and responsible government.

The term 'democracy', in its modern sense, came into use during the course of the nineteenth century to describe a system of representative government in which the representatives are chosen by free competitive elections and most male citizens are entitled to vote. In the United States this state of affairs was reached in the 1820s and 1830s, as the franchise was extended state by state. In France, there was a sudden leap to adult male suffrage in 1848, but parliamentary government was not established securely until 1871. In Britain, parliamentary government was secure from 1688 onwards, but the franchise was not extended to the majority of male citizens until 1867. Democracy is therefore a fairly new phenomenon in world history, though it is spreading.

Democratic institutions and practices have been firmly established for four decades or more in about 30 of the 192 states that now exist. In addition, there are younger but seemingly secure democratic regimes in Spain, Portugal and South Africa, an uncertain number of regimes that are best described as partially democratic, such as those of Cyprus, Mexico and Malaysia, and a very large number of regimes (mostly in eastern Europe and Latin America) that have freshly claimed the title of democratic since 1990. This last category will be discussed below under the heading of 'Democratization'.

In defining and discussing democracy in the twentieth century, there have been two sources of confusion. One source of confusion is that the term has been used not only to describe a system of government but also to describe other social relationships. Thus, Americans have said that their country not only has a democratic set of political institutions but also has or is a democratic society. Some socialists have advocated industrial democracy. Communists used to describe the Communist Party states of eastern Europe as people's democracies.

However, this kind of confusion does not pose serious problems so long as language is used with some precision. Thus, a democratic society, in the American sense, is one without hereditary class distinctions, in which there is something approaching equality of opportunity for all citizens. The term 'democratic' is used to indicate a degree of social equality, not a form of government. Industrial democracy, a term coined by Sidney and Beatrice Webb in the early years of the twentieth century, means a form of workers' control within industrial plants.

The term 'people's democracies' is an essentially misleading one that was coined in the aftermath of the Second World War. No sensible person has ever been deceived by this into thinking that these Soviet-controlled states were democratically governed in the accepted sense of the term. Clearly the citizens of the states themselves had no such illusion.

It follows that we need not be concerned about these extensions of the term 'democracy', but should focus our attention on the other source of confusion, namely the vagueness of the terms commonly used to define a democratic political system, the difficulty of clarifying these terms in a value-free way, and the array of partially incompatible justifications for democracy advanced by democratic theorists. It is because of these difficulties that the concept has to be regarded as currently contestable.

Definitions of Democracy

If we start from the dictionary definition, that democracy means the rule of the people, we immediately run into the problem of how, in practical terms, to define the people and how to define the meaning of rule. Does 'the people' mean the whole adult population, or only those who possess enough property to give them what nineteenth-century politicians called a stake in the country? Does it matter if women are excluded from the franchise, as they were until after the Second World War in several European countries that were universally recognized as democratic, including France and Switzerland? Can one say that a system is partially democratic if the right to participate in politics is confined to one section of the population? The South African regime under apartheid, for example, rested on democratic institutions for its white citizens, but not for the majority of its people, who are black or coloured. Would the answer to this question be different if the great majority of South African citizens were white? In practice, the answers that people give to these questions depend on their political values, so it is impossible to formulate a value-free definition of 'the people'.

This is even clearer in regard to the question of what is meant by 'rule'. If ruling is taken to mean the activity of reaching authoritative decisions that result in laws and regulations binding upon society, then it is obvious that (apart from occasional referendums) only a small minority of individuals can be rulers in modern, populous societies. So for the dictionary definition to be operational, ruling must be taken in the much weaker sense of choosing the rulers and influencing their decisions. But how weak can this sense be and still remain meaningful? Is it essential to a democracy that governmental decisions, though made by only a small minority of politicians, should nevertheless reflect or embody the popular will? If so, how can the popular will be defined and how can it be identified in practice? The answers that people give to these and various similar questions clearly depend on their values and ideals.

It follows that we cannot arrive at an objective and precise definition of democracy simply by elucidating the intrinsic meaning of the term, in so far as it might be said to have an intrinsic meaning. We are therefore left with two alternatives. On the one hand, we can start with the observation of political practice and common usage, which leads to a definition in terms of institutions and processes and leaves the question of justification to a distinguishable (though not entirely separate) intellectual exercise. On the other hand, we can spell out our democratic ideals and consider what the practical implications of these are. Some theorists of democracy have taken the first approach, which can best be called the empirical approach, while others have taken the second, best called the idealist approach. Others again have tried to blend the two approaches.

In discussing theories of democracy, there is another distinction that is very relevant, namely the distinction between theories about parliamentary democracy and theories about American democracy. Because American political scientists occupy a rather dominant position in the discipline, it is sometimes forgotten that, among democracies, the United States is a unique case. All other securely democratic states have political systems based on the principle that sovereignty inheres in the national parliament or assembly. The controversies about democracy in these countries are essentially controversies about the selection and functions of representatives in this parliament.

The United States, in contrast, has a political system based on the principle that sovereignty inheres in the people. The US constitution begins with the words 'We the People of the United States ... do ordain and establish this Constitution.' Members of Congress, Senators, the president and the judges are all regarded as deriving their authority from the people. In view of this difference, it will be convenient, in what follows, to deal with theories about American democracy separately from theories about parliamentary democracy.

American Democracy

Simplifying somewhat, it can be said that Americans have defined their democracy in three different ways: a populist way, in terms of the rule of the people; a pluralist way, in terms of competition between sections and pressure groups; and an institutional way, in terms of a set of institutions and processes. All three versions had their origins in the thought and writings of the Founding Fathers of the American republic.

A belief in the principle of popular sovereignty was common to all the Founding Fathers, whether they were relatively conservative or relatively radical. One of the latter, James Wilson of Pennsylvania, declared in 1787 that:

> in our governments, the supreme, absolute, and uncontrollable power remains in the people. As our constitutions are superior to our legislatures, so the people are superior to our constitutions ... In giving a definition of what I meant by a democracy ... I termed it, that government in which the people retain the supreme power.
>
> (quoted Padover 1963: 19)

Madison and Jefferson, while sceptical of democracy because of its Greek connotation of direct rule, were quite clear that the American republic must have frequent elections so that the people could keep the politicians in check. They and their colleagues were, indeed, much more sceptical than British and French liberals have been of what could be expected of politicians. Thus, Madison declared that 'it is in vain to say that enlightened statesmen will be able to adjust ... clashing interests. Enlightened statesmen will not always be at the helm' (Hamilton et al. 1901: 47). Jefferson believed that unless politicians and public officials were kept under the direct eye of their constituents, the result would be 'corruption, plunder and waste' (quoted Birch 1975: 227). Alexander Hamilton observed more than once that men love power. Thomas Mason said that 'From the nature of man, we may be sure that those who have power in their hands ... will always, when they can ... increase it' (quoted Dahl 1956: 8).

This scepticism about the motives and behaviour of politicians underlies the American belief in frequent elections. Hamilton said it was essential that representatives should 'have an immediate dependence on, and an intimate sympathy with, the people. Frequent elections are unquestionably the only policy by which this dependence and sympathy can be effectually secured' (Hamilton et al. 1901: 290). Jefferson was of the same opinion, declaring that legislators should have to submit themselves 'to approbation or rejection at short intervals' and saying that the executive (by which he meant a state governor or the president) must be 'chosen in the same way ... by those whose agent he is to be' (quoted Padover 1969: 27). The president, be it noted, was regarded by Jefferson as an agent of the people; a view that has never been taken of a prime minister in a parliamentary system of democracy. In fact, the several state constitutions that existed between 1776 and 1787 all provided for frequent elections of legislators: in Connecticut and Rhode Island elections were held every six months; in South Carolina, every two years; and in the other ten states, every year. The decision to have biennial elections to the US House of Representatives, which is more frequently than in any other national legislative chamber in the world, followed naturally from these assumptions and practices.

This belief in popular sovereignty and frequent elections did not at first lead American theorists and leaders to identify their system of government as democratic. They preferred to call it republican, both because of the eighteenth-century tradition of republicanism among advanced thinkers and because the term was thought more appropriate to the balanced constitution that had been adopted in 1787 than the term democratic, with its connotations of lower-class dominance. (For a discussion of republican rhetoric during the early years of the republic, see Hanson 1985: Chapters 2 and 3.) It was not until the Jacksonian period that the term democratic came into widespread usage, and at first it had partisan connotations.

By the 1860s it had gained general acceptance, however, and the belief in popular sovereignty was reflected in Lincoln's famous definition of democracy as 'government of the people, by the people, for the people'. As Sartori has pointed out, this phrase defies exact analysis. The three concepts in the phrase can be interpreted in a variety of ways; Stalin could have used it to characterize his regime without doing violence to the wording; and the phrase as a whole has rhetorical value rather than logical meaning (Sartori 1987: 34–5). It has rhetorical value because it reflects a strain in the American political tradition that all Americans can recognize; a strain that has been otherwise identified as faith in the common man. When Woodrow Wilson inspired popular enthusiasm for democracy during the First World War—which he described as a war to make the world safe for democracy—much was said about the twentieth century being the century of the common man. Padover reports that in the six years following the end of Wilson's presidency in 1921, 'there were, in the United States, no less than 120 books in print with "democracy" or its derivatives in their titles' (Padover 1963: 29).

There is another strain in American democratic thought that is also important, namely the pluralist strain. The origins of this, like the origins of the populist strain, can be found in the writings of the Founding Fathers. In *The Federalist* no. 10, Madison argued that the size and diversity of the proposed federation would safeguard the rights of minorities by making it difficult for any coherent majority to be formed.

> Extend the sphere, and you take in a greater variety of parties and interests; you make it less likely that a majority of the whole will have a common motive to invade the rights of other citizens; or if such a motive exists, it will be more difficult for all who feel it to discover their own strength, and to act in unison with each other.
>
> (Hamilton et al. 1901: 50)

In *The Federalist* no. 51, Hamilton repeated this argument.

> In the federal republic of the United States ... the society itself will be broken into so many parts, interests, and classes of citizens that the rights of individuals or of the minority will be in little danger from interested combinations of the majority.
>
> (Hamilton et al. 1901: 287)

This suspicion of majority rule runs through a great deal of political debate in the United States. It goes along with the attachment to the separation of powers between the legislature and the executive that operates at both federal and state levels of government. It adds up to a preference for weak government that has no clear equivalent in other democratic states. In parliamentary regimes there have been some groups at some periods who have favoured laissez-faire economic policies (as in Britain in the mid-nineteenth century) or have shown suspicion of state power (as in France in the Third Republic), but the dominant strain in theories of parliamentary democracy has been a preference for government that has the capacity for firm leadership, though being responsible to elected representatives for the way this leadership is exercised.

In the post-war period these early theories about sectional pluralism were given a new emphasis by writers who argued that disciplined national parties were undesirable and probably impossible to achieve in a society as large and heterogeneous as the United States. And, following that, writers like Earl Latham (1952) and David Truman (1951) developed a new form of pluralism which hinged on the activities of organized interest groups rather than on pressures from geographical sections. American government, it was urged, is democratic because policy making is an arena for conflict between organized groups, which represent all relevant interests and ensure that the outcome would be a series of compromises which took these interests into account. All citizens were free to organize and join such groups, and the politicians responsible for reaching decisions would be influenced not only by the activities of existing groups but also by the knowledge that new groups would undoubtedly be formed to defend any interest that was presently unrepresented, if decisions were reached that were harmful to that interest.

This line of argument was in part persuasive, because one of the characteristics that stands out in American politics is the openness of the system to group pressures and the vigour of the conflicts between interest groups. However, the argument was open to the criticism of being complacent in its assumption that all interests are adequately represented, because it is evident that some groups are much more influential than others, while some categories of people, such as the homeless, have no effective group to look after their interests.

In general, it seems clear that scholars of the pluralist school are broadly correct in their insistence that conflict between group pressures is a central characteristic of American politics, but controversial when they equate this with democracy. To populists, it is not good enough to show that power is divided between competing elites and pressure groups, when democracy, properly defined, would be a system in which power belonged to the common people.

Without necessarily accepting the superiority of the populist approach, it must be conceded that there are grounds for doubting the claim that a pluralistic dispersal of political influence in a political unit can be equated with democracy. Imagine an American city divided on ethnic lines, as New York, for example, was during the 1950s. Suppose that in the government of this city representatives of the Irish community tended to have a dominant influence on issues relating to the police and the appointment of magistrates; that representatives of the Jewish community tended to have a dominant influence on policy regarding education and the social services; and that representatives of the Italian community tended to have a large say in decisions about highways and the award of construction contracts. This would be a pluralistic system, but it would not be a fully democratic system if representatives of the black community lacked influence over any area of policy. Nor would it be fully democratic unless the representatives of the various communities were answerable to the electorate for their actions.

Some writers of the pluralist persuasion are more cautious than others in their claims. It is fair to say, however, that the pluralist view of democracy rests upon the three propositions that the United States is democratic, that the American political system is pluralistic, and that pluralism equals democracy, it being possible to start with any of these propositions and move to the other two, as if moving round a circle. And it is not unreasonable for critics to be sceptical about the third of these propositions, even while accepting the first two. One might well take the view that the American system is both pluralistic and democratic, but that its democratic character depends on more than its pluralistic dimension.

Parliamentary Democracy

The debates over the definition of democracy in countries enjoying parliamentary systems have been more limited in scope than the American debates. Very few writers in these countries have adopted populist definitions or pluralist definitions. The great majority have defined democracy in institutional and procedural terms, as parliamentary government with free competitive elections and a wide franchise. However, the normative theories by which they have justified democracy have varied considerably.

In discussing European ideas about democracy it is appropriate to begin with French ideas, because the French have influenced more countries that have remained democratic than the British have done. The British have certainly planted parliamentary institutions in nearly all their former colonies, but it is only in a few cases that these countries have remained democratic for more than a few years after the achievement of self-government. The French, in contrast, have influenced the growth of democratic institutions and practices throughout most of continental Europe.

A discussion of French democratic ideas has to begin with the theories of Jean-Jacques Rousseau. It is, of course, arguable whether Rousseau should be regarded as a democrat. He did not believe in representative government, because he did not think that people's wills could be represented by others. His ideal revolved around direct self-government in small communities, and even there he did not apparently think it important that all adults, or even a majority of adults, should be entitled to participate in political decisions. He wrote admiringly of the government of Geneva, where he had spent his youth, even though less than 10 per cent of the residents of that city had the right to participate. He is, nevertheless, important, because he developed a vision of popular self-government that has influenced the ideas of subsequent generations and affected the way they regard politics in large communities where representation is the norm.

One of the main keys to Rousseau's thinking is his commitment to the idea of civic virtue. Whereas most democratic theorists in both the United States and Britain have thought in terms of the protection and promotion of individual interests through political action, Rousseau considered that in an ideal polity individuals should put their personal interests on one side when they participated in politics, and commit themselves instead to the promotion of the communal welfare. He postulated the possibility that citizens could have two levels of consciousness, leading to two types of political will.

On the one hand, they would be conscious of their own individual or group interests, leading to a set of 'particular wills' to promote measures favourable to those interests. On the other hand, they could, in the right conditions, be led to think in terms of the interests of the community as a whole, leading to a 'real will' to promote measures that would protect these shared interests. The particular wills of citizens would be diverse and to some extent mutually incompatible; their real wills, on the other hand, would merge into a consensus that Rousseau called the 'general will'. It followed that if the laws of the state were based on the general will, they would not restrict the liberty (properly defined) of citizens, who would be forced to obey only laws that they had prescribed for themselves. It was in this way, Rousseau declared, that people could resolve the most fundamental problem of politics, that of how to achieve freedom while being bound by the laws of the community.

Rousseau was not naive enough to believe that this ideal state of affairs could easily be achieved. On the contrary, he set out some quite stringent conditions for its achievement. The community must be small enough for its active citizens to meet and cast their votes directly, rather than through representatives. Members of the community must be educated to accept what Rousseau called a civil religion—'a purely civil profession of faith of which the sovereign should fix the articles, not exactly as religious dogmas, but as social sentiments without which a man cannot be a good citizen' (Rousseau 1913: 121). The laws to be determined by the general will must be general in their scope, not regulations on specific matters which would be bound to divide citizens according to their particular interests. The formulation of the questions to be put to the sovereign body, namely the assembly of citizens, must be left to a statesman described as the legislator.

It is obvious that when Rousseau wrote of the laws he was thinking of a small body of laws on fundamental questions of state, not of a mass of detailed legislation such as regulate the affairs of industrial societies in the twenty-first century. It is also made clear that in his ideal state the day-to-day business of government would be conducted not by the sovereign assembly, but by a body of public officials answerable to the sovereign assembly (see Rousseau 1913: Book III, Chapters 16–18).

This very brief sketch is intended only to indicate the character of Rousseau's vision of an ideal self-governing community, not to serve as a guide to his rich and rewarding philosophy of politics. Rousseau's ideas have had a profound influence on subsequent thought in many countries, including most notably the philosophies of Kant, Hegel and numerous followers of Hegel in Germany and, much later, the social ideas of the English Idealists. It is Rousseau who was the originator of what is now called the positive concept of liberty [...].

Within France, Rousseau has always been a controversial figure, revered by some and reviled by others. What French attitudes to democracy have in common with Rousseau's ideas is the assumption that democracy is to be advocated in collective terms rather than in the individualistic terms common in the United States and Britain. French republicans tended to see the French revolution and the later extensions of the franchise as nation-building activities. Although French revolutionaries talked of the rights of man, they did not share the American belief in popular sovereignty. The doctrine of the revolutionaries was not that the French people were sovereign and that their views were represented in the National Assembly. The doctrine was that the French nation was sovereign and the National Assembly embodied the will of the nation. The 1789 *Declaration of the Rights of Man and of the Citizen* stated that members of the Assembly should not be 'bound by the instructions of their constituents', while the 1791 constitution said clearly that 'the representatives elected in the departments will not be representatives of a particular department but of the whole nation, and they may not be given any mandate'.

This doctrine marked a turning point in continental European ideas about political representation. Before this, the political representative had been viewed on the continent as a delegate, so that there were three parties in the representative process: the principal, the representative, and the authority to whom representations were to be made. According to the new theory promulgated by the French revolutionaries, political representatives were no longer to be thought of as intermediaries of this kind but were to contrive, in their collective capacity, to act as the voice of the nation. This theory clearly differs from both the populist view of democracy and the pluralist view of democracy; it is a European but not an American theory. It views the elected representative as an independent maker of national laws and policies, not as an agent for his constituents or for sectional interests.

This French view has been generally accepted in Europe. The French constitutional provisions that prohibited mandates and instructions were subsequently copied or followed in the constitutions of most of the countries of western Europe, including those of Belgium in 1831, Italy in 1848, Prussia in 1850, Sweden in 1866, Austria in 1867, Germany in 1871, Switzerland in 1874, the Netherlands in 1887, and Denmark in 1915. Similar provisions are included in the 1948 constitution of Italy and the 1949 Basic Law of the German Federal Republic.

In Britain, which has no written constitution, the same attitude is embodied in the constitutional doctrine that sovereignty belongs to Parliament, there being no mention of the people, and also in the conventions that protect the privileges of Members of Parliament (MPs). In the 1950s, for instance, the Committee of Privileges of the House of Commons found that a serious breach of privilege had been committed by the editor of a national newspaper (with a circulation numbered in millions) who had published the private telephone number of an MP and advised those of his readers who disagreed with the views of the MP to telephone him and say so. The committee insisted that MPs must be free to say what they pleased in the House without the fear that it might lead to their being pestered in this way. The editor had to apologize to the House and could conceivably have been sent to prison for his offence.

It is unnecessary to follow the vicissitudes of French democratic thought since the revolution, but two general points about it should be noted. The first is that the French, unlike the British, have not had protracted arguments about the extent of the franchise. This was based on a property qualification from 1791 to 1848; was then extended to all male citizens; and was extended to women in 1946 as the result of the changed status of women brought about by the Second World War rather than as the consequence of a debate about democracy.

The other point is that French debates have been influenced by the ideological factionalism that was for long a characteristic of political life. In the Third and Fourth Republics the existence of a multi-party system meant that every government was based on a coalition, while the weakness of party discipline increased the frequency with which these coalitions fell apart. In the life of these two regimes, totalling 81 years, France had 118 different governments, with an average duration of only eight months each. Some theorists were quite happy with this situation, feeling that it had the desirable result of keeping the executive in check. Others were critical, feeling that the representatives were spending much of their time on political intrigues and factional disputes rather than advancing the interests of the nation. The Chamber of Deputies in the Fourth Republic was sometimes described as a 'house without windows' for this reason.

The situation changed with the establishment of the Fifth Republic in 1958. De Gaulle was called to power because French governments had been unable to deal effectively with the political crisis and civil war in Algeria. He then adopted the tactic of appealing directly to French electors, over the head of the National Assembly, by holding referendums on critical issues. Two of these dealt with Algeria, the result being that de Gaulle's favoured policies were endorsed and he claimed that he had a mandate from the nation to grant independence to that territory. He also claimed a popular mandate for a constitutional revision to provide for the direct election of the president, and succeeded in carrying this through, although the use of a referendum in these circumstances was not authorized by the constitution.

The present system of government in France is a hybrid system, not only in the sense that it combines some of the features of normal parliamentary democracy with a strong executive presidency that is not answerable to parliament, but also in the sense that it has broken with the traditional republican doctrine that the National Assembly (and only the National Assembly) embodies the will of the nation. De Gaulle claimed on occasion to speak for the national will himself, while on other occasions he declared that the electorate had done so. He saw himself on these latter occasions in the role of Rousseau's legislator, putting a simple question to the people and eliciting a large majority in favour of a course of action that would probably not have emerged from factional debates in the Assembly. De Gaulle is not normally regarded as a democratic theorist, but the undoubted success of his approach to democratic government has added another strand to the French political tradition.

The history of the development of democratic government in Britain differs from the French case in three significant ways. First, Britain had a liberal culture and a constitution based on the doctrine of parliamentary sovereignty for nearly two centuries before the system became democratic. Second, British politicians and theorists engaged in a debate over the extent of the franchise for the greater part of the nineteenth century. Third, British liberal theories were more individualistic in their assumptions than French theories.

From 1688 onwards the British political system was liberal in two senses. First, it was established that ultimate power rested with Parliament rather than with the king. Whereas most European states, including France, were ruled in the eighteenth century by monarchs who claimed absolute powers, the British king depended on Parliament for the passage of laws and for finance. As taxation could not be authorized for more than 12 months, Parliament had to meet at least once a year—a sharp contrast to the position in France before the revolution, when the Estates-General (the three legislative bodies meeting simultaneously) had not been summoned for 175 years.

Second, Britain had a liberal regime from 1688 onwards in the sense that there was substantial freedom of speech, freedom of the press, and freedom of political association. Along with these freedoms, British residents had the right to trial by jury and they had a judiciary whose members were appointed for life and were independent of both the legislature and the executive government. In the eighteenth century, Britain had the most liberal regime in the world.

This regime was, however, far from being democratic. Fewer than 5 per cent of adult citizens were entitled to vote, constituencies were wildly unequal in size, the electoral process was highly corrupt, and wealthy land owners controlled almost half the seats in the House of Commons. Various radical reformers objected to this system and argued in favour of franchise reform, on the ground that all citizens should have equal political rights. The French Revolution stimulated demands for reform, particularly among the working classes. Tom Paine's book, *Rights of Man*, published in 1792 and sold about 200,000 copies within 2 years (see Brown 1918: 84). From this period until the major parliamentary Reform Act of 1832, there was constant agitation for radical changes in the electoral system, based on a belief in natural rights and popular sovereignty. (For a fuller outline of these radical movements, see Birch 1964: Chapter 3.)

British legislators were to some extent influenced by these agitations and demonstrations in industrial areas, but were quite unable to accept the validity of demands that invoked the concept of natural rights. They were more willing, however, to accept the proposals for reform put forward by the Utilitarians, based, as those were, on the concept of interests. In the view of Jeremy Bentham and his collaborator, James Mill, the key to good government could be found in two propositions. The first is the principle of 'self-preference', by which it was affirmed that all men, including legislators, know what will promote their own happiness and try to maximize this. The second is the principle of 'utility' by which it was claimed that 'the right and proper end' of government is to promote 'the greatest happiness of the greatest number' of citizens (Bentham 1838–43: vol. 9, p. 8).

These propositions, if accepted, established a case for parliamentary reform which was quite independent of cloudy ideas like natural rights. The unreformed Parliament of the early years of the nineteenth century could not be expected to maximize the happiness of the general body of citizens, it was said, for its members were drawn from a very narrow section of society and would reflect the interests of only that section. If Parliament were to promote the general welfare, the franchise must be extended so that elected members were drawn from all sections of society. The logic of the argument pointed to universal suffrage, though Mill, anxious to make his ideas acceptable to a middle-class male audience, declared that it would be enough to give the vote to men over the age of 40.

This theory had philosophical limitations and, as a prescription for action, was not without ambiguities and difficulties. For one thing, it is not easy to see why a process of free election in geographical constituencies should automatically produce a House of Commons that would be a microcosm of the interests of the whole citizen body. Some interests, being those of a minority in each constituency, might never be represented at all. The assumption that women had no interests of their own, not represented by male members of their family, is clearly faulty. Beyond this, there is the problem presented by the differences in the intensity with which pains and pleasures are felt or anticipated. If such differences were ignored by legislators, as Bentham suggested, the interests of the majority would always be put first, even if the majority were only mildly in favour of a proposed policy or law while the minority felt that it threatened their wellbeing in a quite drastic way.

Despite these shortcomings, the Utilitarian theory acquired a great deal of influence in Britain in the first half of the nineteenth century. It did so largely because it met the needs of influential groups. The manufacturers of the northern industrial towns and the traders and craftsmen of London were alike in wanting fairly radical reforms in the system of parliamentary representation. The theories of the Whigs, though somewhat supportive of reform, were too moderate and too aristocratic in tone for them; the views advanced by Tom Paine and his followers were unacceptable because they insisted on the dangerous doctrine of natural rights of man. The Utilitarian theory had the advantage of being radical without seeming revolutionary; it was apparently logical and apparently hard-headed; it was admirably suited to be a vehicle for the claims of the new middle classes.

These middle-class groups were given the vote by the Reform Act of 1832. At about the same time, the principle of ministerial responsibility to Parliament was established, while the procedure by which the Reform Act was passed seemed to establish the dominance of the House of Commons over the House of Lords. The system therefore became more liberal; but was still undemocratic because the property qualification for the franchise excluded the great majority of the population.

The system was democratized in the period 1867–85, when (in two bites) the franchise was extended to include nearly all adult male citizens, the distribution of seats was reformed to provide something much nearer to equality in the size of constituencies, and effective measures were taken to stop electoral corruption. The campaign leading up to these reforms, however, was conducted in the name of liberalism rather than that of democracy. It was marked by caution and by openly expressed doubts about the political reliability of the working classes. There was precious little rhetoric about the intrinsic wisdom of the people, as had long been commonplace on the other side of the Atlantic.

Reformers placed their faith not in this but in the view expressed by John Stuart Mill (son of James Mill) that political reform would lead to the gradual education of the masses; that granting men the right to vote would develop their sense of social responsibility and would stimulate them to understand political problems and prepare themselves to take part in political life. The younger Mill's views therefore stressed the possibility of civic education rather than just the simple representation of interests. In this way he was more of an idealist than his father or Bentham had been. However, he was a rather cautious idealist, recommending that the extension of the franchise to working-class citizens (provided they paid taxes and could pass a literacy test) should be accompanied by the granting of multiple votes to citizens who had a higher education or were working in skilled or managerial occupations (J. S. Mill 1946: Chapter 8).

In 1865 William Gladstone summarized the cautious liberalism of the period by offering a definition of the attitudes of the two main parties to the franchise question. The Liberal attitude, he said, was 'trust in the people, only qualified by prudence', while the Conservative attitude was 'mistrust in the people, only qualified by fear' (quoted Bullock and Shock 1956: 143). In the event it was a Conservative government that took the plunge by introducing the Reform Act of 1867.

Universal suffrage was not established until women were granted the vote, which was done in two instalments, in 1918 and 1926. However, it was generally accepted that the reforms of 1867–85 made the British system democratic. Moreover, these reforms, having been supported by both major parties, and not leading to any serious problems, were quickly accepted by all shades of opinion as having been desirable. Lord Bryce, writing in 1920, said: 'Seventy years ago the word "democracy" awakened dislike and fear. Now it is a word of praise' (Bryce 1920: vol. 1, p. 4).

Since 1920, with the franchise issue settled, there have been three other developments in British democratic theory that deserve mention. First, the political ideas of the English Idealists influenced the attitude to democracy taken by several theorists in the inter-war period. The Idealist social philosophers, writing in the last two decades of the nineteenth century, introduced some of Rousseau's notions to British intellectual circles. They advocated what has become known as the positive concept of liberty [...]. They and (more particularly) their followers also developed a less individualistic and more uplifting view of the purpose of representation than had been common in the nineteenth century.

One such theorist was A. D. Lindsay of Oxford. In a book called *The Essentials of Democracy*, published in 1929, he said this:

> The purpose of representative government is to maintain and preserve different points of view, in order to make effective discussion possible ... it is democratic in so far as it is recognized that anyone ... has something special and distinctive to contribute ... But this belief that everyone has something to contribute does not mean that what everyone has to say is of equal value. It assumes that if the discussion is good enough the proper value of each contribution will be brought out in the discussion.
>
> (Lindsay 1935: 40–1)

About the same time, Harold Laski wrote in similar terms: 'The underlying thesis of parliamentary government', he said, 'is that discussion forms the popular mind and that the executive utilizes the legislature to translate into statute the will arrived at by that mind' (Laski 1928: 13). Ernest Barker of Cambridge followed the same trend when he wrote that the real basis of democracy is the 'discussion of competing ideas, leading to a compromise in which all the ideas are reconciled and which can be accepted by all because it bears the imprint of all' (Barker 1942: 41).

Peter Bachrach has suggested that Lindsay and Barker, along with J. S. Mill, should be regarded as the authors of the 'classical theory of democracy' (Bachrach 1969: 4). This is quite implausible, both because there is no classical theory and because Lindsay and Barker were not particularly influential. They are quoted here only because their views indicate the width of the Atlantic Ocean in regard to democratic theory. The predominant tendency in Britain in this field has always been to favour pragmatic Utilitarian views, but those British theorists who did briefly (because their views did not survive the Second World War) develop more idealistic theories produced ideas that were far removed from the idealism of American populists.

A second line of argument in Britain has revolved around the theory of the electoral mandate, developed by Labour Party spokesmen. This theory states that each party has a duty to present the electorate at a general election with a detailed manifesto setting out the policies that the party proposes to follow, and the legislative changes it proposes to introduce, if it wins the election and forms the next government. The incoming government would then be entitled to claim that it had a mandate from the electors to carry out its promises and would therefore be acting democratically in using party discipline to press these policies through Parliament.

To some extent, this theory reflects the traditions and practices of the British trade-union movement, which has always believed that leaders should not only be elected but also be mandated to pursue specific policies endorsed by the rank-and-file members. Beyond this, however, it can be and has been claimed that the theory is the most appropriate one for a country whose politics are dominated by two highly disciplined national parties. It is said that individualistic theories of representative government like those of the Utilitarians are outdated in a situation in which the role of the voters is not to get their individual interests represented but simply to decide which of the two main parties should govern the country for the next four or five years. This may be a restricted choice, but if the parties are democratically organized (as the Labour Party is), so that all who are interested in party policy can play a part in framing it, then the ordinary citizen can have a continuing role in the democratic process and the policy of a party winning a general election can reasonably be regarded as reflecting the will of the majority.

This theory has some plausibility in the context of a parliamentary system dominated by two disciplined parties. It is, however, highly controversial and much academic opinion is against it. The theory runs contrary to the accepted constitutional doctrine that the government of the country has a responsibility to protect and advance the interests of the whole nation, not just to look after its own political supporters. The theory also seems to be incompatible with the fact that the victorious party at a general election in Britain rarely gets the support of a majority of voters and virtually never gets that of a majority of electors.

In reviewing the theory of the electoral mandate in the early 1960s I reached the conclusion that it had little descriptive validity, citing as evidence the results of sample surveys of public opinion and voting behaviour. These showed that in the 1950s there was a poor match between opinions on policy issues and voting behaviour. In the 1950 general election in a London constituency, 41 per cent of Labour voters agreed with Conservative policy positions, while in the 1955 election in Birmingham 39 per cent of Labour voters had pro-Conservative policy positions as against only 34 per cent who had pro-Labour policy positions (see Birch 1964: 120–1).

It was also shown that most voters decide how to vote on the basis of factors other than their view of the rival election manifestos; the authors of a study of voting in Birmingham in the 1951 election concluded that 'the maximum proportion of voters whose vote was primarily decided by an issue or issues cannot have been more than 10 per cent, and may have been much smaller' (Milne and Mackenzie 1954: 139). These data suggested that it would be unrealistic, as well as controversial on constitutional grounds, to interpret election results as conferring a mandate for the victorious party to pursue the particular policies listed in its election manifesto.

Is there any reason to revise this verdict? The answer to this question has to be a little ambiguous. The constitutional argument against the mandate theory remains, and the argument in terms of the opinions of voters can still be put. A 1970 survey showed that only four out of sixteen policies set out in the Labour Party's manifesto had the support of a majority of Labour voters (Rose 1976: 309). In 1982 a leading student of voting behaviour reported that 'for at least the last fifteen years people have voted Labour despite its policies' (Crewe 1982: 37). A 1987 survey found that only about a third of the voters favoured four of the central proposals put forward in the manifesto of the victorious Conservative Party (Oliver 1989: 128).

In view of these rather powerful arguments against the mandate theory, why is it suggested that the evidence of recent years is slightly ambiguous? The reason is that there has been a growing tendency for politicians to place more stress than previously on the claim that they have a mandate for certain specific policies. The behaviour of the House of Lords has been one reason for this. Their Lordships have adopted the convention, quite voluntarily, that they will not mutilate or reject government Bills to which the ruling party committed itself in its last election manifesto, though they might mutilate or reject other Bills. In consequence, Conservative ministers in the 1980s were heard arguing that their government had a mandate for such policies as the compulsory sale of municipal housing or the abolition of the Greater London Council, about which the Lords had reservations.

Another relevant development is that British electors have become more volatile since the 1960s, apparently more willing to switch votes between parties in reaction to specific policies carried out or promised. This does not mean that the theory of the electoral mandate is much more convincing, because voters are not any more likely to endorse the whole platform of the party they support at the polls. However, it does mean that parties are apt to place more emphasis on specific policies they have designed to attract votes, and to claim that they have a mandate to implement such policies if they win the election.

The consequence of these developments is that, although the theory of the mandate, in its strong form, may have been undermined by empirical evidence, British politicians still talk about mandates to do this or that, and are likely to continue to do so. The theory of the mandate may be dead, but it won't lie down.

If British government is viewed in comparative perspective, it can be said that the mandate theory at least has the merit of drawing attention to one of the most democratic features of the system. One of the strengths of British democracy is the existence of a closer connection between electoral behaviour and government policies than can exist in a system fragmented by the separation of legislative and executive powers, or competition between numerous parties. British electors have the opportunity to base their vote on the plans of the rival parties, with some expectation that these plans will be carried out by the winner, and that must be regarded as a distinct advantage in democratic terms even if only a minority of electors actually decide on this basis. British general elections give the public a more meaningful influence over future government policies than congressional elections in the United States, parliamentary elections in Italy (where every government is a coalition), or federal elections in Canada (where the parties do not publish detailed manifestos). Perhaps this aspect of the British system should be called 'manifesto democracy', to avoid the awkward connotations of the term 'mandate'.

Another controversy about democracy that has occurred in Britain is a controversy about intra-party democracy. This has been essentially a controversy within the Labour Party rather than between parties, but it raises a question of theoretical interest. Up until 1981, leadership selection and policy determination in the Labour Party were effectively in the hands of the parliamentarians. In 1981, the rules were changed so as to provide that the parliamentary leader would be chosen by an electoral college in which the Labour MPs would have only 30 per cent of the votes, the rest being divided between the local party branches (30 per cent) and the affiliated trade unions (40 per cent). It was also provided that sitting MPs would no longer have an automatic right of re-nomination, but could be deselected by their constituency party branches. The object of the changes was to give the unions and the party activists in the country more power to influence party policy and the behaviour of Labour MPs.

This objective would not be thought controversial in the United States, but it provoked a storm of controversy in Britain. Within months of the changes, twenty-five Labour MPs had left the party in protest and joined the new Social Democratic Party. They believed, as did many constitutional commentators, that giving extra-parliamentary organizations the power to influence party policy in Parliament contravened the principles of parliamentary democracy. R. T. McKenzie had declared in his magisterial book on the party system that if the extra-parliamentary organizations of the Labour Party 'attempted to arrogate to themselves a determining influence with respect to policy or leadership they would be cutting across the chain of responsibility from Cabinet, to Parliament, to electorate, which is a fundamental feature of the British parliamentary system' (McKenzie 1955: 588). In a much later article he said that 'intra-party democracy, strictly interpreted, is incompatible with democratic government' (McKenzie 1982: 195).

The vigour with which this view was expressed by McKenzie, an academic supporter of the moderate wing of the Labour Party, reflected his concern that radical party activists might gain the upper hand in struggles over party policy. However, the general principle involved has the support of most theorists of parliamentary democracy, in Britain as in continental Europe. It underlay Edmund Burke's famous 1774 speech to the electors of Bristol asserting that MPs should not surrender their judgement to the views of their constituents [...].

The modern justification for this principle is that party leaders, when in office, have to balance the doctrinal aims of their party with a myriad of conflicting pressures, financial problems, and international developments. It is the responsibility of these leaders to get the balance right and to answer for their decisions to Parliament, and subsequently to the electorate. It would be wrong, so the argument goes, for leaders to be subject in this difficult task to instructions or threats from party committees whose members do not have the same duty of governing the country, are not engaged full-time in this activity, do not have expert advice from the bureaucracy, and are not answerable either to Parliament or the electorate. The position of ministers in a parliamentary system is very different from that of US Members of Congress and Senators, who do not have executive responsibilities, and this is one of the reasons for the differences between European and American democratic theories. Europeans are rarely populists, in the American sense, and while in the nineteenth century this was partly because Europeans were more sceptical about the political wisdom of the people, in the late twentieth century it is mainly because of the constitutional differences between a parliamentary system and one based on the separation of powers. These transatlantic differences are so great that any attempt to generalize about democracy which ignores them must inevitably be inadequate.

Democratization

The 1990s saw a dramatic increase, indeed a doubling, in the number of countries claiming to have democratic regimes, and a direct consequence of this has been a renewed interest by scholars in the process of democratization. This interest is renewed rather than new because earlier decades saw two attempts by American theorists to generalize about the matter. One of these was the theory that there is a necessary relationship between the growth of free enterprise on the one hand and the development of democratic government on the other. The more ambitious of the writers who suggested this reflected the long-standing American tendency to believe that the destiny of the world is to see a convergence of all societies towards the American way of life.

This theory was always simplistic and historical experience gives little support for it. When Germany followed the British and American examples by rapidly industrializing its economy in the period between 1871 and 1914, it did so under an autocratic system of government, not a democratic one. Despite the growth of a large and well-educated middle class, said by theorists to be the main factor that links economic progress with democracy, Germany did not become democratic (apart from the brief and messy interlude of the Weimar Republic) until pushed into doing so by the American, British and French occupying powers after 1945. Equally, Japan's industrialization and economic progress did not lead to democratic politics until General MacArthur and his colleagues imposed democratic institutions on the country after its surrender. More recently the newly industrialized societies of eastern Asia, led by Singapore, South Korea and Taiwan, have achieved very high rates of economic growth with political systems that have been somewhat undemocratic. The Asian countries with the longest experience of democracy, namely India and Sri Lanka, have remained economically backward.

The other attempt to generalize was that by behaviouralist scholars who tried to find statistical correlations between the growth of democracy and a number of other variables. As Paul Cammack has pointed out, and as four or five behaviouralists admitted in the period from 1985 to 1991, this whole effort was unsuccessful (Cammack 1994: 174–5). Having learned from those mistakes, recent scholars have simply used historical methods, producing case studies of democratization in various areas with only modest attempts to generalize about them.

History shows that it is easier to establish democratic institutions than to develop the political conventions and practices that are needed to build a stable system of democratic government. The latter requires not only a system of free elections but also free mass media, freedom to organize political parties, a non-partisan judiciary, a readiness of voters to accept electoral defeat, a readiness of governing elites to hand over power to their rivals, and a willingness of the military to refrain from using their power to intervene in the democratic process. Some examples of failure follow.

After the defeat of Tsarist Russia and the Austro-Hungarian Empire in the First World War, nine successor states in eastern and south-eastern Europe were established with democratic institutions. Of these, only Czechoslovakia remained democratic until 1939. In the other eight, democracy gave way to authoritarian government of one kind or another in the following order: Bulgaria, June 1923; Poland, May 1926; Lithuania, December 1926; Yugoslavia, January 1929; Austria, March 1933; Estonia, March 1934; Latvia, May 1934; and Romania, February 1938 (see Bermeo 2003: 23). It should be noted that none of these moves to authoritarian systems was caused by ethnic cleavages in society, economic collapse, mass revolution or civil war, all of which have led to democratic breakdowns elsewhere. In these eight states the cause was either the unwillingness of the military to keep out of politics or manoeuvres among ruling elites to keep themselves or their friends in power (Bermeo 2003: Chapter 2).

Another wave of newly independent democratic institutions came into being in consequence of the decolonization of European empires in the period 1945–65. In Africa the results have been highly discouraging for democrats. The former Belgian Congo (now Democratic Republic of the Congo) has been a political shambles since the early 1950s, with dictatorship, ethnic violence and periods of civil war. In Portuguese East Africa (now Republic of Mozambique) independence was followed by a period of civil strife, while Angola has seen a protracted civil war lasting since 1976. The former British colonies have seen their parliamentary institutions disrupted by ethnic conflict, military takeovers and personal dictatorships, while Nigeria, the most tragic case, had a civil war that cost up to one million lives. They have also been affected by widespread corruption that has held back economic development and wasted vast amounts of international aid. The former French colonies have been the most stable, partly, perhaps mainly, because the French colonial administrators stripped power from tribal leaders and developed a French-educated elite to whom they could transfer power. Another reason was that after the colonies had nominal independence they retained close economic ties with France, which also provided their new governments with military support in what was often called a neo-colonial relationship. But these states have had long periods of single-party dominance and their claims to be democratic are questionable.

A quite different set of factors has created problems in South America. In that continent, which has seen numerous moves towards democratization, institutional arrangements have been more significant than ethnic cleavages in leading to reversions to authoritarian rule. Because of the natural influence of US ideas and examples, democratic reformers have generally favoured directly elected presidents. However, the US system has several disadvantages for a newly democratized state that, unlike the United States in its early decades, needs strong central government to cope with the myriad problems of the modern world. It provides for two centres of power, the executive and the legislative, each of which enjoys democratic legitimacy but which may be far from agreement. As Linz and Valenzuela (1994) have pointed out, it is often the case that the presidents owe their majority to the support of large urban centres while legislative houses are more representative of the very different interests of rural areas and small towns. There is no democratic principle to resolve conflicts arising from this kind of difference, so that there is a recurrent temptation for the president to seize power by organizing mass demonstrations or for the military to intervene on one side or the other (Linz and Valenzuela 1994: 7–8).

If no single party has a majority in the country, which is quite common in all systems, a parliamentary system can produce a coalition cabinet, but there cannot be a coalition president. A presidential election produces a winner-take-all situation, and frequently a loser who loses all, having no other office to fall back on. Another disadvantage is that presidential systems normally provide for fixed terms of office, unlike parliamentary systems which are much more flexible. If a new development provokes a crisis, a parliamentary system can respond by a cabinet reshuffle, the replacement of the prime minister by one of his or her colleagues, or a general election focused on the issue in question (Linz and Valenzuela 1994: 8–10).

Yet another disadvantage of the US system is the principle that if a president dies in office the vice-president automatically takes over for the duration of the president's term. This worked well enough in the United States in 1945 and 1963, when exceptionally talented vice-presidents acceded to office, but it is an inherently risky system. It contributed to the downfall of democratic regimes in Brazil in 1964, Uruguay in 1973, and Argentina in 1976, after death had elevated vice-presidents who had different policies from or were thought to be less efficient than their predecessors (see Bermeo 2003: Chapters 3, 4 and 6). This is no place for a catalogue, but it seems clear that a preference for directly elected presidents has played a part in the chequered political history of South American countries, with periods of democracy, one-party government and military dictatorship following one another, not necessarily in that order.

Since 2003, a new focus of interest in democratization has followed President Bush's repeated assertion that he would like to promote democracy throughout the Middle East and sees no reason to believe that Muslim societies cannot support democratic political systems. In fact there are two reasons to be doubtful about this, one theological and the other sternly practical.

The theological reason is that a basic doctrine of the Islamic religion is that all the laws humankind needs are to be found in the Koran and a very early volume of judicial elaborations of Koranic law. The democratic view that a parliament or congress can be a sovereign law-making body therefore conflicts with a fundamental Islamic belief; all that such assemblies can properly do is to interpret the laws that already exist. The current constitution of Iran is strictly correct by Islamic standards. Iran has an elected Parliament that passes laws, but it also has a Council of Guardians, composed of unelected religious leaders, that has the power to nullify these laws if they are deemed to conflict with Koranic law. It was not really surprising that during the 2005 parliamentary election campaign the Council of Guardians was able to disqualify numerous candidates, including thirty-five sitting Members of Parliament, on the grounds that they were unfit to interpret Koranic law.

The practical reason is simply that moderate leaders of Muslim states are afraid that democratic elections and all the liberalizing moves that go with them would increase the influence of fundamentalist groups whose aim is to destabilize the system and push their countries into open opposition to the United States and the western alliance. Egypt, under American pressure, held a general election in 2005 that was more free than it has held for a generation. The main fundamentalist organization, the Muslim Brotherhood, was illegal with many of its leaders in prison. It nevertheless fielded numerous candidates as independents and they shocked the government by getting almost 20 per cent of the popular vote. The government subsequently jailed a candidate who had challenged President Mubarak for the presidency, tightened its emergency laws, and summarily postponed local elections that were due to be held in April 2006.

Of course, successful democratization in a Muslim country is only improbable, not impossible. Turkey has had a nominally secular regime since 1928 and has recently developed a largely democratic parliamentary system. It has had to cope with nationalist agitation and occasional terrorist attacks from its sizeable Kurdish minority, its record on human rights is controversial, and its secular regime is unpopular with other Muslim states. But its leaders have displayed great determination in maintaining their commitments.

In this, Turkey may be compared with India, where commitment of the governing elite to democratic principles has survived every kind of problem since the country achieved independence in 1947. India has Muslim, Sikh and Tamil minorities totalling over 210 million people. It has experienced three major wars with Pakistan, a border conflict with China, civil conflict in Kashmir, a nationalist revolt in Punjab, terrorist attacks on Delhi and Mumbai, and the assassination of two prime ministers. That its democratic parliamentary system has remained intact is a great tribute to its leaders and an encouragement to all who believe, as I do, that democracy is the best form of government yet devised. The problem for social scientists, however, is that Turkey and India have very little in common apart from human commitment. In 1994 Alistair Edwards concluded that 'general questions about democratization are unanswerable. The infinite variety of conditions, actually present or counterfactually posed, which might facilitate or impede such a process can produce only bewilderment' (Edwards 1994: 101).

The period since 1945 has certainly seen progress in a democratic direction, for nearly all European states outside the Balkans now have democratic systems that seem stable, while in the developing world democratic ideals and ambitions have become more widespread. A Freedom House report has indicated that between 1980 and 2004 22 states in the developing world embarked on a process of democratization (Karatnycky and Ackerman 2005). However, prediction is difficult and the passage of time since Edwards' (1994) conclusion was reached has revealed little to challenge it.

References

Bachrach, P. [1967] (1969) *The Theory of Democratic Elitism*, London: University of London Press.

Barker, E. (1942) *Reflections on Government*, London: Oxford University Press.

Bentham, J. (1838–43) *Works*, ed. J. Bowring, Edinburgh: William Tait.

Bermeo, N. (2003) *Ordinary People in Extraordinary Times*, Princeton, NJ: Princeton University Press.

Birch, A. H. (1964) *Representative and Responsible Government*, London: Allen & Unwin.

———(1975) 'Some reflections on American democratic theory', *Political Studies*, 23: 225–31.

Brown, P. A. (1918) *The French Revolution in English History*, London: Allen & Unwin.

Bryce, J. (1920) *Modern Democracies*, New York: Macmillan.

Bullock, A. and Shock, M. (eds) (1956) *The Liberal Tradition*, London: Black.

Cammack, P. (1994) 'Democratization and citizenship in Latin America', in G. Parry and M. Moran (eds) *Democracy and Democratization*, London: Routledge.

Crewe, I. (1982) 'The Labour Party and the electorate', in D. Kavanagh (ed.) *The Politics of the Labour Party*, London: Allen & Unwin.

Dahl, R. A. (1956) *A Preface to Democratic Theory*, Chicago, IL: University of Chicago Press.

Edwards, A. (1994) 'Democratization and qualified explanation', in G. Parry and M. Moran (eds) *Democracy and Democratization*, London: Routledge.

Hamilton, A., Jay, J., and Madison, J. [1787] (1901) *The Federalist*, New York: The Colonial Press.

Hanson, R. L. (1985) *The Democratic Imagination in America*, Princeton, NJ: Princeton University Press.

Karatnycky, A. and Ackerman, P. (2005) *How Freedom Is Won: From Civic Resistance to Durable Democracy*, New York: Freedom House.

Laski, H. J. (1928) *The Development of the Representative System in our Times*, Geneva: Inter-Parliamentary Union.

Latham, E. [1952] (1965) *The Group Basis of Politics*, New York: Octagon.

Lindsay, A. D. [1929] (1935) *The Essentials of Democracy*, London: Oxford University Press.

Linz, J. and Valemzuela, A. (eds) (1994) *The Failure of Presidential Democracy*, Baltimore, MD: Johns Hopkins University Press.

McKenzie, R. T. (1955) *British Political Parties*, London: Heinemann.

———(1982) 'Power in the Labour Party: the issue of intra-party democracy', in D. Kavanagh (ed.) *The Politics of the Labour Party*, London: Allen & Unwin.

Mill, J. S. [1859] (1946) *On Liberty*, Oxford: Blackwell.

———[1861] (1946) *Considerations on Representative Government*, Oxford: Blackwell.

Milne, R. S. and Mackenzie, H. A. (1954) *Straight Fight*, London: Hansard Society for Parliamentary Government.

Oliver, D. (1989) 'The parties and Parliament: representative or intra-party democracy', in J. Jowell and D. Oliver (eds) *The Changing Constitution*, Oxford: Clarendon Press.

Padover, S. K. (1963) *The Meaning of Democracy*, New York: Praeger.

Rose, R. (1976) *The Problem of Party Government*, Harmondsworth: Penguin.

Rousseau, J. J. [1762] (1913) *The Social Contract*, London: Dent.

Sartori, G. (1987) *The Theory of Democracy Revisited*, Chatham, NJ: Chatham House.

Truman, D. (1951) *The Governmental Process*, New York: Knopf.

Reading 3.4

Introduction to *Authoritarianism Goes Global: The Challenge to Democracy*

Larry Diamond, Marc F. Plattner, and Christopher Walker

T HE QUARTER-CENTURY SINCE THE COLLAPSE of communism has been marked by three trends, the most recent of which has caught many observers by surprise. The first was the "democratic surge" that began with the "third wave" of democracy in the mid-1970s and kept pace into the first half-decade of the new century. Although democracy's momentum slowed in the mid-2000s, the overall pattern from 1990 to 2005 was clear. Continuing a trend that had begun well before the Cold War ended, the list of countries categorized by Freedom House as "electoral democracies" grew from 76 in 1990 to 119 in 2005. During this same period, the countries rated Free by Freedom House grew from 65 to 89, indicating a significant expansion in the number of countries that had established democratically accountable systems.

In the mid-2000s, a second trend came into view. Authoritarian regimes that had regained their footing reacted to democratic forces pushing for governance systems that were more accountable and responsive—and less corrupt. As part of this "backlash" against democracy, repressive regimes began to apply measures meant to limit independent voices and institutions, including civil society groups and the media. While the outlines of systematic resistance to democracy had begun to emerge in the early 2000s, the backlash really took off in reaction to the popular uprisings known as "color revolutions." These mostly peaceful citizen uprisings against rampantly corrupt authoritarian regimes swept out incumbents in Georgia, Ukraine, and Kyrgyzstan in 2003, 2004, and 2005, respectively. Remaining repressive regimes, seeing what might be coming their way, responded by beginning to apply fuller restraints on freedoms of expression and association, with special emphasis on progressively narrowing the space available to nongovernmental organizations.

The signs of this squeeze (in some places it was sharp enough to be called a crackdown) were visible from the outset, yet for a while at least the whole thing seemed relatively circumscribed and episodic. Writing in the *Journal of Democracy* in 2006, Carl Gershman and Michael Allen characterized the backlash as a "problem that involves a relatively limited number of countries—approximately 20 out of the more than 80" where democracy assistance was being provided at the time.[1] Most of what the authoritarians were doing was domestic in focus: They forced local activists and democracy-oriented organizations in countries as diverse as Egypt, Russia, Venezuela, and Zimbabwe to contend with rafts of obstructive new laws and regulations, but authoritarian maneuvers within regional or even global settings had not yet begun.

Writing at about the same time as Gershman and Allen, Thomas Carothers foreshadowed some of the more acute challenges that were gaining steam. He noted that, in addition to the restrictive measures being pursued by undemocratic regimes, the broader international context for promoting democracy was changing.[2] Greater resistance and less receptiveness to external support for democracy were taking root. Since then, the global context has changed even more dramatically, and so too has the environment for supporting democracy.

The third and most recent trend in the post–Cold War context is one that has emerged from the backlash but is distinct from it. We might most aptly call it the "authoritarian surge." Led by the "Big Five" authoritarian states of China, Russia, Iran, Saudi Arabia, and Venezuela, the authoritarian powers have taken more coordinated and decisive action to contain democracy on a *global* level.[3]

Over the course of this period, authoritarian governments have become bolder and more adept at stopping dissent before it starts. Restrictions on democratic voices at home have become increasingly sophisticated. Repressive governments have learned how to use the forms of law to repress independent civil society, while also developing sophisticated techniques to manipulate the media, both traditional and new. Even more striking than the refinement of domestic repression is the extent to which these regimes have learned to project influence beyond their own borders.

Authoritarianism has gone global. The characteristic features of the present authoritarian surge include amply funded media initiatives such as Russia's RT, China's CCTV, and Iran's Press TV. Each enjoys a global reach and projects messages that seek to undermine Western and U.S. prestige while shaping attitudes toward democracy. The new challenge to democracy is also evident in the authoritarians' efforts to alter the democracy and human-rights mechanisms of key rules-based institutions, including the Organization of American States, the Council of Europe, the Organization for Security and Cooperation in Europe, and international bodies concerned with the governance of the Internet. These regimes and their surrogates are increasingly seeking to insinuate themselves into the democratic political space with the goal of influencing—whether openly or furtively—the political dynamics of countries in one world region after another.

The extent of the authoritarian challenge forces us to confront the disconcerting prospect that the most influential antidemocratic regimes are no longer content simply to contain democracy. Instead, they want to roll it back by reversing advances dating from the time of the democratic surge. Just a decade ago, few political observers could even have imagined such a development.

In order to aid the cause of coming to grips with this challenge to democracy, the International Forum for Democratic Studies at the National Endowment for Democracy organized an effort to study the new authoritarian activism and grasp its inner workings. This volume is a product of that intensive project, which was carried out during the years 2014 and 2015.

The present book is meant to stand on its own, though it is also worth mentioning that it builds on earlier essay collections published in the *Journal of Democracy* since the close of the Cold War. Taken together, these volumes illuminate key trends and offer a guide to the shifting landscape that democracy and efforts to promote it have had to cope with over the last several decades. In their editors' introduction to *The Global Resurgence of Democracy* (1996), Larry Diamond and Marc F. Plattner recognized democracy's significant achievements up to that time and concluded on a note of "qualified optimism" about democracy's prospects. Diamond and Plattner observed that "for the near term, and perhaps for some time to come, democracy will benefit from the absence of any alternative regime form that could appeal across regions and cultures."[4] Twenty years later, it remains true that no such alternative has emerged. Some might wish to nominate China's developmental-authoritarian model, with its stress on economic growth without political rights, as a candidate. Yet China's own troubles with political repression, social restiveness, and general uncertainty (economic and otherwise) make its system an unlikely one for direct export.

In 2001, when the world political landscape had begun to shift in unpromising ways, *The Global Divergence of Democracies* examined the challenges that were then taking shape and asked how the behavior of China and Russia might affect democratic prospects.[5] In the years since, each of these leading authoritarian states has not only become more authoritarian, but has taken the lead in countering democratic developments.

[...]

Authoritarianism's "Big Five"

[...] Under Xi Jinping, who became head of the party-state in 2012, China has become increasingly assertive in pursuing its economic and strategic interests. While the Chinese Communist Party (CCP) is willing to work abroad with any type of regime, it denounces "universal values" and calls instead for state sovereignty and noninterference. Nathan observes that "for now, at least, China displays no missionary impulse to promote authoritarianism." Yet this does not mean that the world's largest authoritarian state exerts no adverse effect on democracy.

[...] [There are] six ways in which Beijing objectively works against liberal democracy. First, there is the sheer power of its example: China is the model *par excellence* for illiberal regimes that wish to achieve economic growth while preserving authoritarian rule. Second, the Chinese regime can be said to promote this model through the propaganda—meant to burnish China's international image—that it steadily pumps out via foreign media outlets. Third, China is a world leader in developing and teaching the technologies and techniques of censorship and political repression. Fourth, [...] Beijing aims to "roll back existing democratic institutions or to stifle sprouts of democratic change in territories where it enjoys special influence." Fifth, China provides diplomatic support, favorable economic access, and investment opportunities to authoritarian regimes that function as key economic and strategic partners. Sixth, Beijing works with other illiberal powers to change the norms governing international organizations, the goal being to block outside scrutiny of authoritarian practices. But [...] "China's influence on the fate of democracy in the world, and its ability— if it wants to—to promote authoritarian transitions beyond its borders will depend on how the democracies perform."

[...] [T]he Putin regime's system of personalized power [...] is already in decay; the Kremlin's top priority is to shore it up. With this objective in mind, the regime uses the "Putin Doctrine" to legitimize harsh authoritarian measures at home and abroad. Domestically, there are crackdowns on political opponents, civil society activists, and independent media outlets. Foreign policy, too—be it the invasion of Ukraine, the annexation of Crimea, or the recent intervention in Syria—is bent to the task of sustaining personalized power and the *sistema* (as Russians call it). Belligerence and adventures in the countries on Russia's periphery and overseas are intended to distract the Russian public from the country's acute social and economic problems and to allow Putin to pose as a restorer of national greatness.

The specific aims of Russian international policy include containing Western influence both inside and outside Russia, undermining cooperation among Western democracies, and building a pro-Kremlin lobbying network in the West. Moscow also seeks to bolster fellow illiberal states by exerting influence within regional organizations such as the Eurasian Economic Union, the Collective Security Treaty Organization, and the Shanghai Cooperation Organization. Within these bodies, the Kremlin actively shares techniques for information warfare and propaganda with like-minded regimes. While the future remains uncertain, [...] "the Kremlin will not mellow with time"—any signs of backing down from its current strategy could be interpreted as weakness. This situation will push the Russian regime closer to its tipping point and, as it becomes more desperate, will turn it toward even harsher authoritarian measures, including more intensive repression at home and provocation beyond its borders.

[...] Despite [Iran's] authoritarianism and brutal repression, a young and vibrant movement of democratic advocates has persisted since the 1979 Islamic revolution. Although Iran's authoritarian rulers have been forced to accommodate these liberal voices to a degree, power remains highly concentrated in the hands of a narrow elite. [...] Supreme Leader Ayatollah Ali Khamenei appoints the head of the judiciary; chooses members of influential political bodies; has representatives in every institution; controls the country's key mass-media outlets; and selects all Friday-prayer leaders and dictates the agenda of their weekly sermons. Despite these efforts to dominate every aspect of life in Iran through propaganda and even raw force, [...] the populace remains restive while "cracks in the regime have become more apparent." [...] [W]hile some observers see the regime's "cracks" as belonging to a shrewd strategy of "repressive tolerance"—one in which the regime lets dissidents waste their energy on relative trivia while saving its own energy for truly crucial fights—others believe that even small acts of resistance can chip away at the edifice of clerical authoritarianism.

The Islamic Republic of Iran's key domestic priority is regime survival, and its international policy aims at forging alliances with partners around the world who share its agenda of containing democracy. [...] [I]nternational recognition and legitimacy have always been the goal of Iran's leaders. "As Iran's international isolation over its nuclear program has tightened," Alex Vatanka writes, "Tehran has upped the ante in the race to influence global public opinion." The landmark July 2015 nuclear deal between Iran, the United States, and five other world powers will significantly affect how Iran engages the rest of the world. Whether the Iranian regime comes to behave—as Western advocates of the deal hope it will—in a more open and liberal manner as a result of this rapprochement remains a large question with serious implications for democracy both within Iran and beyond its borders.

As part of the broader trend of authoritarian cooperation, Iran has sought to build ties with like-minded nondemocratic countries, especially China and Russia. Iran's desire to collaborate with other illiberal powers reflects both its economic and its diplomatic needs, according to Vatanka. As it expands its surveillance techniques and cyberspace-policing strategies, Tehran looks to Beijing for new ideas. Meanwhile, following China and Russia, Iran has built an extensive international media presence, as the clerical regime projects its own form of "soft power" into countries in the Middle East, the Balkans, and elsewhere. Through these actions, Iran and its authoritarian partners have formed a "common bond." The thread that unites them is their shared quest to hang on to power. In forming alternative blocs in the global arena, [...] these countries seek to undermine democratic norms, share technology to limit free speech online, and utilize international broadcasting to promote their illiberal values.

[...] Venezuela's slide into authoritarianism under the late President Hugo Chávez and his handpicked successor, Nicolás Maduro [...] [can be described] in terms of the spread of "autocratic legalism" at home and the creation of an international strategy meant to armor the *chavista* regime against criticism from abroad. [...] Chávez, a former army officer who was elected president in 1998 after having led a failed coup attempt in 1992, leveraged Venezuela's vast oil resources to build an "alliance of tolerance." The countries that benefit from Venezuela's largesse—in Latin America and beyond—are generally unwilling to criticize the Venezuelan government for its human-rights violations or undemocratic governance.

[...] Venezuela's rulers have concentrated their power through the "use, abuse, and non-use of the law." Both Chávez and Maduro have used procedures that are constitutional in form in order to pass laws that are autocratic in nature—a ploy that has served to shield them from criticism even as they have drawn ever more power into the executive branch. This trend of autocratic legalism has exerted especially harmful effects on Venezuela's civil society, independent media, and political opposition. The sharp falloff in world oil prices has put the regime under excruciating economic pressure, but Maduro continues to pursue Chávez-inspired soft-power initiatives. Perhaps most prominent among these is Telesur, a state-funded regional outlet that uses both traditional and new media to spread throughout Latin America messages hostile to the West in general and the United States in particular.

Much like Venezuela, the Kingdom of Saudi Arabia is heavily reliant on oil revenues. It also is currently beset by high unemployment and a good deal of domestic uncertainty. These domestic pressures, coupled with the monarchy's ongoing fear of Arab Spring–style political mobilization, have led to a shift in Saudi Arabia's regional foreign policy. [...] The Kingdom's authorities are worried by the threat of "ideological mobilization incited from abroad" and remain anxious that Saudis might imitate the popular-protest tactics that rocked the Arab world in 2010 and 2011, when long-entrenched and seemingly secure autocrats found themselves run out of their own capitals almost overnight.

The Saudi regime's counterdemocratic activities [...] are basically defensive in intent. The monarchy is most concerned to guard itself and the smaller countries that line its edges against destabilizing external influences. Thus Riyadh seeks to suppress democratic forces that it fears could open the way to rivals such as the Shia radicals of Iran (about a tenth of all Saudis are Shia, and they reside near the oil fields) or the Sunni radicals of the Muslim Brotherhood. The Saudis' main tool is money: The Kingdom uses its petrodollars to help its regional allies buy arms and stabilize their economies. Riyadh also has in hand a new antiterror code—like all Saudi laws, it is the decree of an absolute monarch who rules a polity with no elections and only an appointed, largely advisory parliament—that can support the task of suppressing dissent at home. Such policies [...] may not come accompanied by heaping helpings of explicitly antidemocratic rhetoric, but it is clear that their "ultimate effect has been damaging to the spread of democratization and political pluralism." Looking ahead, it remains likely that the Saudi authorities will stick to their status quo policy despite swelling domestic pressures for change and the deep political shifts that are underway in the region.

Arenas of "Soft-Power" Competition

The size, location, and political and economic clout of the "Big Five" countries mean that any attempt to analyze the authoritarian resurgence must reckon with them. But such an analysis must also consider the critical "soft-power" arenas in which authoritarian regimes today are projecting influence regionally and globally. The second part of this volume therefore focuses on the strategies and methods that authoritarian states utilize to advance their agendas at home and abroad. It includes chapters covering the authoritarian influence on international norms, election observation, civil society, international media, and the Internet, respectively.

[...] Long-held assumptions about the historical trajectory of norms [...] are being tested. Thanks to their determination and assiduous cooperation with one another, the authoritarians have achieved a dismaying degree of success in reshaping international bodies founded to promote human rights and democracy into forums more favorable to regimes that have scant regard for either.

In pursuing this goal, the authoritarians have challenged the universality of democracy and sought to erode liberal-democratic norms, replacing them with new counternorms that emphasize "state security, civilizational diversity, and traditional values." Sensing an opportunity in the rise of counterterrorist and security concerns since 9/11, authoritarians have grown increasingly assertive. They have expanded their own blacklists of domestic terror suspects and enlisted the help of their fellow authoritarians in repressing any groups or individuals whom they deem a threat. [...] "[R]espect for civilizational diversity" is the counternorm pushed by regional groups such as the Shanghai Cooperation Organization (whose members include China, Russia, and four Central Asian states). A third counternorm, pioneered by Russia, is the emphasis on defending "traditional values." [...] [C]ivil society has borne the brunt of these three antidemocratic counternorms.

The color revolutions that shook Georgia, Ukraine, and Kyrgyzstan from 2003 to 2005 made authoritarians elsewhere fear the possible rise of prodemocracy mobilizations in their own countries. Out of this fear came the crafting of a "counterrevolutionary playbook" that targets NGOs and democracy monitors." Authoritarian tactics include new legal restrictions on foreign funding for civil society groups, plus the promotion of "pseudo-NGOs" and "zombie election monitors" that serve to sow confusion and lend illiberal governments a façade of legitimacy. In order to further bolster their influence abroad, authoritarian regimes have created new regional bodies that challenge democratic norms while promoting illiberal counter-norms. Hard cash helps too: China and the wealthy Gulf states have not been afraid to reinforce counternorms with flows of aid and investment money.

Such efforts [...] "have turned a world that was once relatively favorable to the spread of democratic norms into one where authoritarians can push back—and have learned to do so in innovative ways." The focus of such authoritarian efforts is no longer merely preserving authoritarianism at home, but reshaping the international norms that stigmatize such governance. [...] [D]emocratic states must remain committed to liberal values and a rules-based international order. Only then can the West and its allies hope to succeed in stemming the tide of the authoritarian resurgence.

[...] Following the onset of the post-1974 third wave of democratic transitions, [...] nonpartisan citizen election monitoring became key to promoting accountability and citizen participation during elections. More recently, however, with the decline in confidence in democracy, authoritarian regimes have become more assertive in the electoral realm, just as they have in the areas of communications and international organizations. These regimes have learned to employ a variety of tactics—including denial of access to information, cyberattacks, abuse of legal powers, electoral fraud, and manipulation of results—to undermine citizen election-monitoring efforts. In a typical ploy, state-run media can pump out disinformation, dwelling on the findings of authoritarian-friendly monitors while ignoring or marginalizing the reports of independent monitors. Public understanding is distorted while incumbents manufacture positive coverage for themselves and loudly lay claim to electoral legitimacy.

To illuminate the extent of the new challenge in this sphere, [...] case studies of recent elections in three countries—Azerbaijan, Zimbabwe, and Venezuela—[...] show how authoritarians utilize these tactics to manipulate electoral processes. [...] Without credible elections, both democracy and stability are at risk.

[...] Edmund Burke and Alexis de Tocqueville [praised] what would come to be known as "civil society." [...] [When] the Bolsheviks [...], seized power in Russia during the First World War, [...] [t]hey insisted that the public sphere must be "unitary and univocal," then set about taking over or crushing all independent organizations. [...] [T]he Bolsheviks loathed independent organizations "because they gave people the power to control their own lives, because they encouraged independent thought, and because they made people more critical of state power." Driven by this antipathy, Soviet rulers systematically destroyed all independent organizations—even apolitical ones. After 1945, the Soviet Union's communist satellite regimes in Central and Eastern Europe did the same thing in their own countries. Even today, communist powerholders in China and North Korea act out repressive policies first conceived and enforced by Lenin and his Bolsheviks.

Ironically, however, [...] "Lenin did not see that by attempting to control every aspect of society, totalitarian regimes would eventually turn every aspect of society into a potential source of dissent." After communism ended, people regained a degree of control that made possible a return to what Václav Havel called the "independent life of society." Yet the work required was often arduous, and the obstacles daunting: Independent initiatives and the legal infrastructure that enabled them had been wiped out, and many in these societies opposed efforts to rebuild them.

Countries such as Poland managed to break out of this pattern and become places where civil society could flourish again. Others, such as Russia, were weighed down by long histories of stubborn state efforts to suppress freedom of association, and remained places where independent civic organizations aroused much mistrust and suspicion. [...] "[T]he return of the KGB to power has been marked by the slow but systematic elimination of all kinds of independent groups and organizations from Russian society." This includes a series of repressive laws restricting foreign funding and handing the Kremlin authority to shut down any foreign organizations deemed "undesirable." Fear tactics such as these threaten to erode Russia's already fragile civil society. Moreover, [...] they could spread beyond Russia and make other postcommunist societies centers of hostility to a free and robust associational life.

[...] [T]he fall of the Berlin Wall ushered in an era of unprecedented civic engagement. Following the 9/11 terrorist attacks, however, the climate for civil society grew increasingly frigid. Concerns grew that civil society organizations might be linked to terror groups. Moreover, as we have seen, the color revolutions fed authoritarian governments' already robust readiness to fear anything that could promote prodemocracy mobilization. Thus came the limits and bans.

Governments invoke national security and state sovereignty while protesting that they desire only to improve the effectiveness of development assistance, promote transparency, and keep civil society reasonably accountable to national laws and standards. Although international law contains a variety of mechanisms designed to protect civil society, these are undermined by "exceptions that permit national governments to enact restrictions under certain circumstances." [...] [T]hese circumstances include restrictions that are "prescribed by law," seek to fulfill a "legitimate aim," or are deemed "necessary in a democratic society"—a set of large loopholes indeed. But we should make no mistake: With regime security foremost in mind, authoritarian governments have been imposing restrictions on civil society groups' ability to receive funds from abroad in order to weaken the opposition and suppress independent associations.

[...] Under Putin, the Kremlin, through control and deft use of television, has expanded its efforts to promote an alternative political reality for Russian—and increasingly international—audiences. As a result, the political process in Russia today has come to resemble a reality television show starring Putin as the "superhero-czar." Russian coverage of the war in Ukraine highlights this system's main aims—to insulate Putin and his allies from negative coverage while making his opponents look bad. This strategy has granted the Kremlin control over all forms of discourse, paving the way for it to blur the lines between fact and fiction in order to suit its needs. Kremlin-controlled channels deliberately spread cynicism among Russians and make them vulnerable to conspiracy theories.

Beyond Russia's borders, the Putin regime advances its interests by making allies of parties across the political spectrum, doling out moneymaking opportunities, and waging an information war against its critics. Perhaps the regime's most potent weapon in this war is RT, the Kremlin's international television broadcaster, which is a force not only via the airwaves but also on social media. Lavishly funded and active in a number of languages, RT has entered into editorial partnerships with a variety of countries, including Argentina and Syria (where Putin has become the mainstay of the Assad regime). Brimming with anti-Western content, RT "muddle[s] the information space and sow[s] doubt and confusion." Through censorship and the use of modern media, [...] the Kremlin "has created a cynical citizenry, shaped by propaganda and conspiracy theories, that is bereft of hope." Perhaps most distressing is the example that Russia has set for other authoritarian regimes seeking to maintain control through media manipulation.

Like Russia under Putin, China under Xi Jinping has built up a formidable media apparatus with broad reach and refined its foreign-propaganda strategy. [...] Since Beijing's brutal response to the 1989 Tiananmen Square protests, China's image has suffered. To undo the lingering reputational damage of the Tiananmen crackdown, the Chinese Communist Party works tirelessly—especially among the large diaspora of "Overseas Chinese"—via the Internet and other media to portray itself favorably while isolating critical voices. To sway elite non-Chinese audiences abroad, the Beijing regime has (as of 2015) created more than a thousand Confucius Institutes and classrooms worldwide to teach Chinese language and culture on college campuses in dozens of countries. The goal, writes Brady, is to "raise awareness of China's social, economic, and political stability, and the nation's incredible economic growth."

Although Beijing has already invested billions of dollars in these soft-power initiatives, Xi Jinping has pledged to spend still more on them. Given China's size and growing political ambition, its international mass-media gambits must be taken very seriously. Brady writes that since Xi announced the launch of a new global media strategy in 2014, "China's foreign-propaganda efforts have taken on a new level of assertiveness, confidence, and ambition." The same ambition can be seen in Beijing's efforts to get more of China's almost 1.4 billion people online even as authorities keep censoring the Internet and doing their best to strangle the possibility of any meaningful political speech or organization.

[...] Once trumpeted as "tools of liberation," cyberspace technologies are now being harnessed by authoritarian regimes to repress opposition and shrink civic space. Deibert sheds light on the arsenal of cyberspace-control techniques that authoritarians have developed and suggests responses. [...] [T]hree "generations" of information controls [exist]. The first generation includes "defensive" strategies that seek to restrict access to information; the second consists of legal regulations intended to constrain the private sector; and the third relies on "offensive" techniques, such as surveillance and targeted cyberattacks. [...] [A] fourth generation of information controls could be added to this list: the expanding role of authoritarian regimes in Internet-governance forums. Even more worrisome is the growing use of regional groups such as the Shanghai Cooperation Organization and the Gulf Cooperation Council to reshape online norms.

[...] [T]he driving forces behind the authoritarian cybersurge [are many]. One driver is the emphasis on protection against extremism and terrorism—especially in response to new threats from groups such as the Islamic State and Boko Haram. While cybercrime and terrorism are genuine threats, authoritarian regimes often overstate them to justify their use of repressive practices in policing cyberspace. Another driver is the growing spread of digital technology across the global South. The spread itself is not the problem, but it does carry with it the risk that authoritarian regimes will turn the newly accessible technologies into new tools of political repression. By sharing "best practices" and expanding their cooperation with one another, authoritarians have become more assertive in seeking to tighten their grip on cyberspace. To counter this threat, [...] democratic states must develop export controls, "smart sanctions," and a monitoring system to identify rights violations. Ensuring a "free, open, and secure cyberspace [...] should loom as an urgent priority."

[...] [T]oday's authoritarian regimes have turned the tables on the democracies by exploiting the opportunities presented by globalization and integration since the end of the Cold

War. [...] "Although authoritarian regimes are today integrated in many ways into the global system, they have not become more like the democracies; rather, they have developed policies and practices aimed at blocking democracy's advance." Over time, the authoritarians have "jiu jitsu–like" systematically turned integration against the democracies, seeking to hollow out the democracy and human-rights components of the most important regional and global rules-based institutions.

A critical part of this effort has been the creation of an "authoritarian toolkit" that includes government-organized nongovernmental organizations (GONGOs), "zombie election monitors," and well-funded international media enterprises, such as China's CCTV and Russia's RT. Through dedicated authoritarian learning, as well as the development and application of simulated instruments of democracy, authoritarian regimes have effectively hijacked the concept of "soft power." [...] "[A] renewed struggle between democracy and authoritarianism has emerged." So far, however, the democracies have not taken seriously the authoritarian challenge to the democratic order. If, in the end, the democracies continue to rely on a reactive approach that allows the autocrats to maintain the initiative, "we can expect the grim prospect of an even greater erosion of democratic space in the years to come."

Looking Forward

Authoritarian influence has been growing at a time when the United States and the European Union have scaled back their own ambitions with respect to supporting democracy and the values underlying it. Hence, more than a quarter-century after throngs of jubilant Germans tore down the Berlin Wall, the trajectories of influence of the world's leading democratic and antidemocratic powers are moving in opposite directions. The challenge presented by regimes in Moscow, Beijing, Tehran, Caracas, and Riyadh is being taken to an entirely new level by virtue of their projection of illiberal values and standards beyond their own national borders.

Lately, the leading authoritarian regimes have been riding high. Perhaps it is no surprise that the authoritarian surge has taken off at a time when malaise seems to grip the world's leading democracies. Some of their weakness in the face of the growing authoritarian challenge likely stems from the global economic crisis and the lingering loss of confidence that it has bred in the West. More generally, the established democracies have been distracted and at times even consumed by their own internal political debates and challenges. But the democracies underestimate the authoritarian challenge at their peril. Ironically, in the era of globalization—a phenomenon that many had assumed would give democracies an advantage in world affairs—it is the undemocratic states that have been the nimblest at exerting influence, especially in critical "soft-power" arenas. The democracies, quite simply, need to take the authoritarian challenge far more seriously than they have so far, and improve their game.

Over the past half-decade, as the authoritarian surge has taken clearer shape, four of the "Big Five" countries have been supported by high oil revenues. With the price of oil having moved much lower in 2015, it remains to be seen how Venezuela, Russia, Saudi Arabia, and Iran will manage over the longer haul. All suffer too from the scourge of corruption, which for each is a way of life but also a running sore and even an Achilles' heel.

Given low oil prices, Venezuela and Russia already are facing stiff challenges, which are increasingly raising questions about their regimes' legitimacy. China, unlike the others, does not depend on oil exports, yet it has its own serious problems. This was made glaringly clear during the latter half of 2015, when turmoil beset the Chinese economy amid a grave stock-market tumble. Much of the Chinese system's allure and prestige since the late Deng Xiaoping's stint as paramount leader (1978–92) has been based on the country's prodigious export-led economic growth. But should this growth ever slow, as inevitably it must and as it has recently shown signs of doing, many of those who have been drawn to the Chinese model of authoritarian governance will cast a colder eye upon it and its coercive ways. Presiding over growth and prosperity is easy. The test comes when times get tough and a system's capacities for resilience and self-correction are sorely tried. It remains to be seen how China's rulers, and indeed all the Big Five's authoritarian elites, will respond if they have to cope with long periods of poor economic growth. The Chinese Communist Party has relied heavily on a vast and repressive coercive apparatus even during times of prosperity; during times of hardship the system as it is presently configured may be pushed past its breaking point.

[...] The established democracies have been slow to recognize the determined challenge that today's authoritarians present, perhaps out of hope that these regimes will be undone by their flaws. But given the resilience that the authoritarians have displayed so far, it would be rash for the democracies to underestimate the seriousness of the dangers that they pose.

Notes

1. Carl Gershman and Michael Allen, "The Assault on Democracy Assistance," *Journal of Democracy* 17 (April 2006): 36–51.
2. Thomas Carothers, "The Backlash Against Democracy Promotion," *Foreign Affairs* 85 (March–April 2006): 55–68.

3. Christopher Walker, "The New Containment: Undermining Democracy," *World Affairs* 178 (May–June 2015): 42–51.

4. Larry Diamond and Marc F. Plattner, "Introduction," *The Global Resurgence of Democracy* (Baltimore: Johns Hopkins University Press, 1996).

5. Larry Diamond and Marc F. Plattner, "Introduction," *The Global Divergence of Democracies* (Baltimore: Johns Hopkins University Press, 2001).

Chapter 3

1. Define the concept of power.
2. How does legitimacy affect authority?
3. Define and illustrate democracy.
4. What pattern of state power defines authoritarianism?
5. Can a democratic form of government function as an authoritarian state?

Chapter 4

Embedded States
Social, Economic, and Global Substructures

H ow do the social and economic environments of political systems shape the dynamics of state power? Having presented the state, its types of power, and the democratic and authoritarian patterns of control, the next readings examine some of the effects of the social, economic, and global environments. The first three readings examine the character and function of civil societies and economic systems constituting infrastructures of political systems. This perspective explains why democratic states tend to be nationalistic, wealthy, law abiding, and stable, whereas authoritarian states tend to be more divided over national identity, ethnicity, and economic inequality. In general, the strength of a state depends on how culturally cohesive, modernized, and productive its society is. The four readings survey the interdependence among four factors and the stability of states. Just how these can strengthen or weaken states underscores their importance.

Nationalism is one of the basic elements giving identity to a modern state. Nationalism refers to a cultural identity and its association with the community supporting the institutions of a state. These include 1) language and cultural norms; 2) social traits, such as kinship or ethnic heritage; and 3) institutional heritages, such as local, regional, or national political affiliations. Nationalist sentiments can be a source of conflict between states as they assert their identity or as a source of internal division, as in the case of Belgium, which is divided between the Dutch-speaking north and the French-speaking south.

Ethnic identities, once thought to be diminishing as modernization progressed, are now intensifying. Accommodating ethnicity issues challenges the cohesion of states, such as the demand of Scotland to abandon its union with the United Kingdom, which currently incorporates English, Irish, Welsh, and Scottish identities. Some states consist of even larger numbers of ethnic groups, such as Nigeria with over 100. Multiculturalism occurs when diverse cultures exist within a single state. The survey of the experiences with ethnic differences in Canada, the Netherlands, the United Kingdom, and France brings out how multiculturalism can impact political culture in previously predominantly homogeneous states. Philosophers of multi-culturalism divide between giving preference either to individuals or to ethnic groupings.

Economic systems are another bedrock of any political system. Growth generates rising incomes, enriches personal development, and fosters legitimation of relations between state and political economy. When progress toward equality and prosperity fades, internal conflict is likely to break out, causing a loss of support for political leaders and institutions. Conflict and instability signal that it is imperative to reformulate the social and economic bases of growth. Our reading provides an illustration of this with a case study recording the conflictual and dysfunctional UK politics of the 1970s. After over 20 years of postwar social democratic growth, 1970s Britain experienced a collapse of that political-economic settlement. The result was political and economic crises. The lack of industrial growth; rising prices, especially for fuel; wage demands that resulted in serious industrial unrest; and demands from industry for help culminated in a crisis of governability. This case study outlines political responses to the economic crisis and the shift toward a new governing formula of Thatcherite neoliberalism. This case underscores the critical role of capitalist growth as the basis of political stability and, in turn, the central role of the state in adjusting the relationship among capital, labor, and the state to ensure that growth.

The final reading reviews the challenges that globalization presents to nation-states. These range from environmental issues, economic policies, human rights protection and transnational military involvements, to patterns of global communications. The impact of increasing importance of multinational firms, major changes in international finance, and the central roles of multinational and international political and economic organizations such as the World Bank, World Trade Organization (WTO), and the European Union (EU) are most significant. In addition, the increasing role of global communications and media and the often-overlooked role of NGOs add to a daunting list of recent but fundamental forces bringing profound challenges to the goals of state autonomy and their democratic traditions.

Reading 4.1

Nationalism and the National State

Anthony H. Birch

THE ENTIRE LAND SURFACE OF THIS planet, with the single exception of Antarctica, is now divided for purposes of government into territories known as national states. This is a relatively recent development in human history. Only two hundred years ago, there were fewer than 20 states with the shape and character that we should now recognize as deserving description as national states, with the rest of the world being divided between a host of very small principalities and city-states, a few untidy empires, and large areas that were the home of tribal communities who lived without fixed territorial boundaries. By 1945 there were 51 national states and by 2000, following the virtual end of colonial empires, there were 192. Today the only relics of empire are a few miniscule territories such as Gibraltar, the Falkland Isles, Martinique and Guadeloupe. The transformation has come about largely because the doctrine of nationalism has both triumphed in Europe and been exported to the rest of the world.

Because of this transformation, in the contemporary world we all live under the political authority of the national state within whose borders we reside. Political authority is a concept which raises a host of interesting questions and problems. Of course, in the practical experience of day-today life, everyone knows what the authority of the state means to the citizen. In the simplest terms, it means the ability of the state to make and enforce laws binding upon its inhabitants, including the ability to take their money in taxation, to confine them in prison, and (providing they are citizens) to conscript them into the armed forces. There are, however, important questions about the character, bases and limits of this authority [...]. There are also problems about its justification that have been discussed by political philosophers over the centuries, most notably by Hobbes, Locke and Rousseau. It is beyond the scope of this book to discuss this kind of problem, and it must be emphasized now that the fairly brisk and concise account of the nature of political authority [...] can be brisk and concise only because these large normative questions have been left to the several hundred other authors who have addressed them.

The term national state is itself a conjunction of two terms that are best dealt with separately, with the definition of the first raising more difficulties than that of the second. It is true that the question of how to define the state has led political theorists and constitutional lawyers to produce a variety of alternative definitions and generalizations. The difficulty of producing a simple and agreed definition arises from the fact that in the modern world the state is an abstraction, that is deemed to exist independently of the individuals and institutions that exercise state power. This assumed independence is a fairly recent development in human history, for in pre-modern times the state was frequently identified with its ruler, but it is not now a matter of controversy. But although one cannot see a state, in any concrete sense, one can see the manifestations of the state's existence, which have to be divided into external and internal manifestations. Seen from the outside, a state is a legal entity possessing sovereign independence, having unfettered control over its own territory, defining its own citizenship rules, and equal in international law to all other states. Seen from the inside, a state manifests itself in a collection of public institutions, legislative, executive, administrative and judicial, having the power to govern the territory and all its inhabitants. There is no conflict between these exterior and interior manifestations, however; rather, they are like two sides of the same coin. As the nature of the modern state, viewed in this double way, is fairly clear, it is not intended to pursue the problem of providing a precise short definition of it.

The one controversy regarding the state that will be addressed in this book is that raised by the Marxist generalization that the actions of the state are severely circumscribed by the need to protect the interests of the dominant economic class in society, which in the modern democratic state means the capitalist class. [...]

The term nation raises more problems than the term state. It refers to a community of people rather than to a set of institutions, but the definition of who constitutes a nation involves conceptual difficulties that, in turn, lead to practical problems. Thus, the Irish are everywhere recognized as a nation, but what about the Northern Irish? Given that the English and Scots are both nations, can there also be a British nation? If the Palestinians are a nation, in spite of never having governed themselves, is this also true of the Kurds, the Sikhs, the Tamils, the Karens and the Chins? The French-Canadians living in Quebec seem to constitute a nation, but how should we describe the English-Canadians who also live in Quebec?

Because the term nation is different in character from the term state, there was some discussion in 1919 about whether the new international organization that was being created should be called the League of Nations or the League of States. The second of these alternatives would have been more logical and more precise, but the doctrine of nationalism had achieved such a hold on people's minds by 1919 that the first alternative was chosen. In 1945 the United Nations Organization was created without any debate on this point.

In this chapter we shall discuss in turn the concept of nationalism, the concept of nationhood, and the concept of national integration.

The Concept of Nationalism

[...] [P]olitical concepts can be divided into three broad categories. There are age-old concepts that have both political and other usages, such as power and representation. These terms are widely used by the public at large and tend to be applied to political life in more than one way, so that differing usages have to be distinguished. There are a number of precise technical concepts that have been developed by political scientists and are used only in scholarly communications within the discipline. Somewhere between these, in terms of precision, there are concepts that have no usages outside of politics but have entered into the general currency of political debate. The concept of nationalism falls into the third category. It has been developed only in the past two centuries; it has a basic meaning that is not contestable; but it is often used loosely in public discourse and confused with related but different concepts such as national identity or patriotism.

The confusion of nationalism and national identity, for instance, is quite common in general speech. Scottish people in England or North America who celebrate St Andrew's Day, wear the kilt and eat haggis might well be described by their neighbours as 'real Scots nationalists'. However, Scottish people in Scotland would be described in that way only if they supported the eventual secession of Scotland from the United Kingdom, and this way of using the term is more correct. The Scottish people abroad are displaying symbols of national identity, which is a sentiment, whereas supporters of the Scottish National Party are invoking the principles of nationalism, which is a doctrine or ideology.

Like several other terms ending with 'ism', such as liberalism, conservatism and socialism, nationalism is a normative doctrine that embodies a particular set of assumptions and beliefs about politics. The essence of nationalism is a belief about the social basis of political authority. The prevailing assumptions of eighteenth-century Europe were that government could properly be based on force, in the conquest of empires, or on heredity or marriage, in the government of principalities and monarchies. In contrast to these assumptions, nationalists asserted the view that the only proper form of government is one in which the boundaries of the state correspond to the boundaries of a society and the rulers of the state are members of that society. It was wrong, in terms of nationalist doctrine, for the Poles to be ruled by Russians, the Greeks to be governed as part of the Ottoman Empire, the southern Italians to be ruled by Spanish or French aristocrats, the Hungarians to be ruled by Austrians, and the Germans to be divided between scores of principalities.

The development and spread of this doctrine in Europe during the nineteenth century led to the emergence of two types of nationalist movement. On the one hand, there were movements for the national independence of peoples under imperial rule; for the independence of Greeks from Turkish rule, of Poles from Russian rule, of (later) the Irish from British rule. The generic form of the aims of this type of nationalist movement can be expressed in the proposition that 'the Ruritanian people ought to be liberated from foreign domination so that they can govern themselves'. On the other hand, there were movements to unite under a single government people who were said to belong to a single society but were actually divided for political purposes between a number of rulers. This type of movement had its intellectual origins in what is now Germany, where nationalist theories were developed in reaction to a situation in which German-speaking people were divided between over a hundred jurisdictions. (For the intellectual origins of nationalist theory, see Kedourie 1961; Birch 1989: Chapter 2.) Another obvious example is that of the Italian nationalist movement, whose aim was to unify Italy under Italian rulers. The generic form of the aims of this type of movement can be expressed in the proposition that 'the Ruritanian people ought to be united under a single Ruritanian government'.

Underlying these two types of nationalist movement is a general theory about good government that has been neatly summarized by Elie Kedourie in the three propositions 'that humanity is naturally divided into nations, that nations are known by certain characteristics which can be ascertained, and that the only legitimate type of government is national self-government' (Kedourie 1961: 9). This is the doctrine, in a nutshell, and in historical terms it has been an extremely successful doctrine. If asked to name the political doctrines that have reshaped the world, most people in the west would probably name liberalism, democracy and socialism. In practice, however, only a minority of political regimes are liberal, democratic or socialist, whereas the whole world is now politically organized on nationalist principles.

To say that the doctrine has been successful is not to say that it is free from ambiguities. On the contrary, nationalism is a doctrine marred by a central ambiguity, namely the extreme difficulty of defining the social unit that has the right to govern itself. Johann Herder and J. G. Fichte believed that a nation should be defined in terms of its language and culture, a view which led in time to the German nationalist objective of uniting all people who spoke German under the same government. Such a view, if relied on as a guide to practice, would extend German boundaries to include Austria, part of former Czechoslovakia, part of Switzerland and a small part of eastern France. Leaving aside Switzerland, this was precisely Hitler's aim, but it is not a view that commands widespread assent. Other nationalists have specified ethnicity as the proper basis of nationhood, or religion (as in the cases of Pakistan and Israel), or shared historical experiences (as in the case of Switzerland), or shared commitment to a set of political ideals (as in the United States). It is evident that there is no agreed definition of the basis of nationhood to validate the second of Kedourie's three propositions, and that without that the first of the propositions seems suspect. To elucidate the matter further, it is necessary to enquire into the concept of nationhood.

The Concept of Nationhood

The difficulty of defining this concept can best be illustrated by tabulating three groups of concepts, one sociological, one cultural and the third institutional:

Sociological Concepts	Cultural Concepts	Institutional Concepts
Kinship group	Language	Municipality
Tribe	Literature	County
Ethnic group	Religion	Province
Community	Culture	State
Society	Civilization	Empire

The concepts in these three columns all refer to entities that can be identified by charting personal relationships or consulting documentary sources. There is sometimes room for controversy about how to categorize people of mixed ethnic origins or how to specify the boundaries of a community, but in general these concepts are clear and unlikely to lead to misunderstanding. The great difficulty about the concept of nationhood is that it seems to spread across all three columns. In ideal terms, a nation can be described as a society that has a distinctive culture and also possesses its own state. However, as a definition for social scientists, this has the crippling disadvantage that it renders the proposition that every nation ought to have its own state purely circular. One cannot say that 'every A ought to have B' if the definition of A includes B.

It would be logically acceptable to say that every society with a distinctive culture is a potential nation, but this would not in practice be true unless a further variable is added to the equation. This further variable is the existence of a territory with agreed borders that could reasonably form the geographical basis of a self-governing state. There are American political writers commonly described as black nationalists who assert that American blacks constitute a distinct community with a distinctive culture that should be protected and passed on to new generations, and a reasonable argument can be made for this point of view. However, American blacks cannot be described as a potential nation in the absence of an agreed territory that they can call their own.

If we continue to approach the concept of nationhood from the sociological end of the equation, we might define a nation as a community or society of people who share a distinctive culture, live together in an identifiable territory in which they constitute a clear majority, and either govern themselves today or have done so in the not-too-distant past or have a credible claim to do so in the not-too-distant future. The limitation on historical distance is necessary because circumstances change so much over the centuries. The people of Athens governed themselves twenty-five hundred years ago, but it would not be reasonable to use this historical fact as a reason for describing modern Athenians as a nation, because for several centuries their identity has been merged into the larger identity of the Greeks. Equally, it is fruitless to try to predict what social and political developments may take place in the next two thousand years. We can only take account of the foreseeable future, which in terms of politics is the near future.

It is also possible to approach the concept of nationhood from the other end of the equation, from the existence of statehood. The idea of a British nation followed, and was created by, the union of England, Wales and Scotland in the newly constituted British state. The idea of a French nation preceded the French Revolution, but the reality of a national identity embracing all citizens of the French state was a product of the revolution, the political changes made by the revolutionaries, and the deliberate process of socialization into nationhood that was adopted (on the wishes and orders of the government) in the French educational system. As that early nation-builder, Napoleon Bonaparte, said in 1805:

> So long as children are not taught whether they must be republicans or monarchists, Catholics or free thinkers, etc., the state will not constitute a nation but will rest on vague and shifting foundations, ever exposed to disorder and change.

> (quoted Herold 1955: 118)

Throughout tropical Africa, the question of nationhood is best approached from the state rather than the sociological end of the equation. The new states that emerged as a consequence of the end of colonial rule in the 1950s and 1960s had borders that had been imposed by the colonial powers with little regard to existing social geography. The loyalties of the citizens of these new states were tribal loyalties for all but a tiny minority of educated and westernized leaders, and the creation of national identities and national loyalties has been one of the tasks of the new post-colonial governments.

Political scientists call this process nation building or national integration, and there are so many modern states in which the development of a sense of nationhood has depended upon this process that Kedourie's three propositions have to be called into question. It is not that Kedourie was wrong in summarizing the essence of nationalist theory in this fashion. It is, rather, that the assumptions underlying nationalist theory are sociologically inaccurate. Humanity is naturally divided into sexes and perhaps into races, but these are the only divisions produced by nature. The divisions into societies, cultures, religions and nations have been brought about by human activities, with the divisions sometimes being accidental by-products of economic enterprise and geographical mobility, sometimes the product of deliberate action by preachers, teachers, poets, philosophers, politicians and soldiers.

Social groupings have changed remarkably over the centuries, with a general tendency for smaller groups and communities to merge together into larger societies. Thus, we now say that the British are made up of the English, the Welsh, the Scots and some of the Northern Irish, but fourteen hundred years ago the groups who combined to become the English were known as Angles, Saxons, Jutes and Frisians. It follows from all this that nationalism is an artificial and contrived theory, involving a degree of sociological mythology rather than being based squarely on sociological and historical facts. Many nationalist movements have reflected this in their propaganda. Thus, when Mazzini bolstered his arguments for Italian unity in the 1860s by writing eloquently about Italy's glorious past in the days of the Roman Empire, he conveniently overlooked the fact that the regional divisions within Italy, both then and when Mazzini was active, were so great that northern and southern Italians could barely understand each other's dialects. The process by which national societies and identities are established out of diverse social groups is known as national integration, and this needs a little elaboration.

National Integration

With a handful of exceptions, modern nations are an amalgam of historical communities that have been brought together by various economic, social and political developments that can be bracketed under the general name of national integration. Some of these developments are unplanned whereas others are devised by political leaders and implemented as government policies.

The unplanned component of the integrative process has been given the name of social mobilization by Karl Deutsch (1953) and his colleagues. In brief outline, this is the process by which the development of a commercial and industrial economy induces agricultural workers to leave their villages to seek work in the growing centres of trade and industry, thus eroding the social communities of rural areas and mobilizing the workers for absorption into the larger national society. Kinship links become weaker, local languages and dialects give way to the dominant national language, local customs and cultures lose their hold. As smaller economic concerns are swallowed by larger ones, as means of transport improve, and as mass media of communications are established, the integrative process continues, until everyone in the country watches the same television programmes, admires the same popular heroes and supports the same political leaders.

It would be a mistake to think that the process is entirely automatic, however. It is given a large helping hand by governmental decisions about language and education. National governments ruling over a society that is accepting a commercial and industrial economy can hardly avoid the need to designate an official language for legislation, administration and commerce. As has been said, the state can be blind but it cannot be deaf; it may ignore differences of race among its citizens but it cannot ignore differences of language. The normal pattern has been to establish the language of the governing classes as the official language of the whole country.

This move is invariably followed, however, by the decline of other languages, for it is not natural for people to be bilingual and the experience of history shows that the stronger language in an area always tends to drive out the weaker one. (On this, see Laponce 1987.) If local languages decline to the point of extinction or near extinction, like Breton in France, Gaelic on the mainland of Scotland, or Cornish in England, this is a cultural loss to be set against the political, economic and social advantages of linguistic unity. Some states are forced by circumstances to recognize more than one language as official, but the recent histories of Canada and Belgium show that this can be politically expensive.

Compulsory education is also a planned move that is integrative in its effects, often intentionally. This is both because instruction is normally given in the official national language and because the teaching of history and (where it is in the curriculum) civics tend to strengthen feelings of national identity and loyalty. The importance of education in this respect is illustrated by the examples of Canada and Northern Ireland. In Canada the fact that the French schools in Quebec teach a rather different version of Canadian history from that taught in the rest of Canada is one of several factors that have weakened the process of national integration and contributed to the possibility that Quebec may secede from the federation. In Northern Ireland, with a few recent exceptions, Protestant children attend Protestant schools and Catholic children attend Catholic schools, which until the 1990s have taught different versions of Irish history and Anglo-Irish relations, so that to some extent children have been socialized into conflict.

In addition to their language and educational policies, national governments also pursue a variety of tactics designed to minimize the political effects of ethnic and religious cleavages within society and thus to strengthen the authority of the government. One obvious initiative is the creation of symbols of national identity. Flags, anthems and uniforms all serve this purpose. In recent years new states of the developing world have thought it important to establish national airlines, sometimes at great expense, to emphasize their independence. As Kenneth Minogue has pointed out, new names for towns, new palaces for rulers and even new capital cities have been thought necessary parts of what he calls 'the equipment of a proper nation' (Minogue 1967).

Another form of nation building (as the planned parts of the process of national integration are sometimes called) is the establishment of political institutions seen to represent all sections of society. In relation to class divisions, this is achieved by the adoption of universal adult suffrage. In relation to regional divisions, it is sometimes achieved by the device of giving peripheral regions more-than-proportional representation in national institutions. Scotland and Wales have more Members of Parliament than England, in proportion to their relative populations. The Senates of Australia and the United States give the smaller states more members than their populations deserve, and in Canada there are elaborate conventions to ensure that the peripheral areas are represented in the federal Cabinet and Quebec is fully represented in the Supreme Court. In relation to ethnic cleavages, minorities are often given the support of legal bans on ethnic discrimination, insistence on unsegregated schools and (in the United States and India) measures of positive discrimination in certain areas of employment.

Of course, the process of national integration does not always proceed smoothly. Occasionally, the measures adopted rebound, as when American white parents rioted in Boston to prevent their children being sent by bus to unsegregated schools, or when Mrs Gandhi was assassinated by the Sikh bodyguards she had appointed to demonstrate her confidence in the loyalty of the Sikh minority. More frequently, the cleavages in society are just too deeply rooted for integrative measures to have their desired effect. Canadian efforts at national integration have failed to prevent Quebec from demanding either full or substantial independence. French and Spanish attempts at nation building have failed to stop Breton and Basque nationalists from attacking public buildings and (in Spain) public officials with bombs. Elaborate Belgian attempts to maintain a linguistic balance between Flemish-speakers and French-speakers have failed to prevent a deterioration in relationships between the two communities since the 1960s. A widespread revival of ethnically based minority nationalist movements in the 1970s has put paid to the hopes of many that political cleavages other than those based on economic cleavages were losing their force. Much more could be said about the process of national integration, about the various theoretical justifications of it that have been put forward, and about the recent tendency for some theorists to move away from that position in order to justify policies of multiculturalism. Enough has been said, however, to define and illustrate the concept itself.

References

Birch, A. H. (1989) *Nationalism and National Integration*, London: Unwin Hyman.

Deutsch, K. W. (1953) *Nationalism and Social Communication*, New York: Wiley.

Herold, J. C. (ed.) (1955) *The Mind of Napoleon*, New York: Columbia University Press.

Kedourie, E. (1961) *Nationalism*, London: Hutchinson.

Laponce, J. A. (1987) *Languages and Their Territories*, Toronto: University of Toronto Press.

Minogue, K. R. (1967) *Nationalism*, London: Methuen.

Reading 4.2

Ethnic Cleavages, Multiculturalism, and the National State

Anthony H. Birch

T HE LAST THREE DECADES OF THE twentieth century saw the growth of two very different trends in world politics that were anticipated by only a few politicians and writers before the 1970s. Although this book is concerned with political concepts and theories rather than with historical developments as such, these trends must be outlined because they have brought with them a new emphasis in political studies involving the concepts of ethnicity, multiculturalism and globalization.

Ethnicity and Ethnic Conflict

From the 1860s to the 1960s nearly all liberal and socialist political theorists both antici- pated and welcomed the growing diminution in the political significance of religious, cultural and ethnic cleavages within national societies, leaving economic and class differences as the most important issues in political debate. This was an entirely rational point of view, because conflicts deriving from religious, cultural and ethnic cleavages are usually more difficult to resolve than conflicts deriving from economic cleavages, whether the latter be between regions of the country or classes within society. One reason for this is that people are locked into their religious, cultural and ethnic groups, having no wish to change even if they could, whereas people can hope to escape from a depressed region or class by indi- vidual mobility. If they cannot themselves escape, they can hope that their children will do so. A second reason is that it is easier for governments to mitigate economic cleavages, by a process of incremental adjustment, than it is for them to mitigate religious, cultural or ethnic conflicts.

In the twentieth century the growth of industry, urbanization and prosperity in western societies has been accompanied, everywhere except in the United States, by a decline in the intensity of religious feelings. Whatever the moral consequences of this, its political benefits have been demonstrated by the marked decline of political conflicts exacerbated by religious cleavages in Europe (with the exception of the Balkans and Northern Ireland) and, in contrast, their continuance in the United States, where twenty-eight abortion clinics were bombed by religious zealots in 1986 and individual surgeons performing legal abortions were subjected to murderous attacks in the 1990s.

Similarly, the growth of political integration in most developed western societies has led to the decline of minority languages, with some of them becoming virtually extinct. [...] [T]his trend is best regarded as a cultural loss but a political benefit.

In contrast, political conflicts based on ethnic cleavages have become considerably more widespread since the early 1970s. The concepts of ethnicity and ethnic identity are somewhat elastic and have led to occasional disagreement among journalists and scholars. Such disagreements are not really significant, however, as they all derive from the simple fact that ethnicity, like other forms of group identity, is a social construction that can be self-defined or defined by others in more than one possible way. Any individual's ethnic identity can be defined in terms of heredity or upbringing or culture, chosen according to which seems most salient in the circumstances of the time. The present author, for example, is English, Scottish, French and Irish in terms of heredity, wholly English by upbringing and culture, British, Canadian and European by citizenship, and has other group identities that in some circumstances are more relevant than any of these, such as being male in a dance hall or white on a visit to South Africa.

The recent growth or revival of ethnic conflicts within several national societies, leading to the emergence of minority nationalist movements, is the consequence of social, economic or political changes that have made ethnic identities seem more salient than other identities or loyalties that are national in scope. A good example is the decision of 840,000 Scottish electors to vote for the Scottish National Party in October 1974, as against only 64,000 who had done so ten years earlier. This did not mean that they had ceased to be British or socialists or liberals or conservatives, only that the discovery of a vast oil field in the Scottish part of the North Sea made their identity as Scottish seem more salient to them. The 1970s saw new or renewed claims by ethnic minorities in several other states for forms of cultural autonomy or political independence. France experienced demands for autonomy from Bretons and Corsicans, Spain more violent demands from Basques and milder claims from Catalans. Quebecois nationalists demanded independence from Canada. The people of East Bengal rebelled against the Pakistani government and secured independence as Bangladesh. In the 1980s, India had to cope with Sikh nationalists and Sri Lanka with Tamil nationalists.

In the 1990s ethnic conflicts became increasingly violent. In the Balkans, age-old conflicts between Serbs, Croats and Albanians flared into civil war. In east central Africa, conflicts between Tutsis and Hutus led to genocide in Rwanda and massacres in Burundi. Civil war in Zaire (now the Democratic Republic of Congo) brought ethnic groups into conflict and led, by 1999, to a confused situation of near-anarchy in the eastern part of the country. In March 2000 it was reported that five ethnic groups there had relapsed into a pre-colonial state of tribal warfare, raiding each other's villages with spears and bows and arrows. The same month saw brief but murderous riots in Nigeria between Muslim Hausas and Christian Ibos.

In the context of this book, the most relevant question is how far this revival of ethnic conflict has affected the state system. The answer is that its impact was modest until 1990 but has since become appreciable. Until 1990, the Irish, the Algerians and the Bengalis of Bangladesh were the only ethnic minorities within an established national state to achieve political independence from it in the twentieth century, but since 1990 the Soviet Union has split into fifteen constituent parts, Yugoslavia has disintegrated, Czechoslovakia has split in half, and altogether twenty-three successor states have been given international recognition as independent, with Kosovo on its way to becoming the next. These developments have led some writers to speculate that the world system of national states is beginning to disintegrate along ethnic lines. As early as 1979, Dov Ronen predicted that the nation-state is likely to disappear as the main unit of political organization and to be replaced by a world order composed of 'hundreds, maybe thousands, of social and political frameworks' (Ronen 1979: 179). Following the break-up of the Soviet Union and Yugoslavia, John Naisbitt put this view into the present tense, declaring that 'we are moving towards a world of a thousand countries. ... The nation-state is dead' (Naisbitt 1995: 40).

For two quite different reasons such a view, although understandable, is very questionable. One reason is that this untidy planet contains something between 6,000 and 15,000 ethnic groups (depending on the defining criteria adopted), the great majority of which are so intertwined by migration and intermarriage and so interdependent in economic terms that it would not be feasible for them to be separated into self-governing territories. A handful of existing states may well be partitioned along lines that are more or less ethnic in character, but ethnicity in itself cannot reasonably be proposed as either a better or a more probable basis for political jurisdiction than the existing state system, imperfect though this is.

A second reason which makes the concept of the end of the nation-state unlikely is that existing states, in addition to possessing organized armies, have a variety of political tactics available to them that can be grouped under the heading of system maintenance devices. Minority areas can be given regional councils and/or representation in national institutions, as Scotland and Wales have long had fuller representation in the British Parliament than the size of their populations justifies. Belgium has invented a complex system whereby certain powers over cultural matters are given to linguistic councils that are largely, but not entirely, territorial in jurisdiction. Tito held Yugoslavia together not only by force and his control of the Communist Party but also by giving politicians from each of the main ethnic groups some fairly conspicuous positions in national authorities. By one means or another, national states have many ways of maintaining their integrity and authority.

It cannot, therefore, be concluded that the revival of ethnic politics is breaking down the state system around the world, though it may do so in particular localities. As Anthony Smith noted in 1995,

> As of now, the national state remains the only internationally recognized structure of political association. Today, only duly constituted 'national states' are admitted to the United Nations and other international bodies, though aspirant ethnic nations may be admitted as observers.

> (Smith 1995: 104)

It can also be observed, however, that the revival of ethnic politics is making the political process more complex in many states. The distribution of political authority has in some countries been complicated by the devolution of powers to regional authorities, such as for Scotland and Wales within the United Kingdom and for Catalonia and the Basque country within Spain. Government spokespersons in both countries have claimed that these measures have taken the wind out of the sails of minority nationalist movements wanting independence, but the fact remains that the creation of regional assemblies provides fora in which nationalist movements may thrive in the future, so that the constitutional equilibrium is potentially less stable than it was. A more widespread development has been the growth in influence of ethnic pressure groups claiming privileges of one kind or another for their groups. There has also been a tendency for a new generation of liberal writers to advocate policies of multiculturalism in place of the policies of national integration advocated by previous generations of liberals.

Multiculturalism

The concept of multiculturalism was first publicly articulated by Pierre Trudeau, Prime Minister of Canada, in 1971. He did this in response to complaints about the title and report of the Royal Commission on Bilingualism and Biculturalism, which had laboured from 1963 to 1969 to propose ways of remedying certain French-Canadian grievances. Spokespersons for ethnic groups that were neither French nor British in origin, such as the large Ukrainian community in the western provinces, argued that this report ignored their own distinctive cultures. In answer, Trudeau proclaimed that Canadian society, though officially bilingual, was multicultural rather than bicultural in character, and his government quickly established an administrative agency with funds to promote multiculturalism. In its early years this agency devoted much of its resources to the provision of grants for community centres organized on ethnic lines, for ethnic festivals, and for similar activities designed to encourage the maintenance of diverse immigrant cultures. Some politicians and public servants turned these policies into a kind of ideology, arguing that cultural diversity is a positive advantage for society and should therefore be encouraged by the government. This naturally provoked controversy among social scientists.

The main argument in favour of the principle was that it differed from the American belief in promoting social unity by way of the melting pot and would therefore help to maintain Canadian distinctiveness from its large southern neighbour. One sociologist noted that 'in the absence of any consensus on the substance of Canadian identity or culture, multiculturalism fills a void' (Weinfeld 1981: 94), while another said that multiculturalism 'helps to define a distinct collective identity and thus to differentiate Canadians from Americans' (Breton 1986: 50).

As against this, Porter argued that multicultural policies encourage ethnic separation, maintain and perhaps strengthen barriers to upward social mobility, and thus perpetuate what he called the vertical mosaic and others have called the cultural division of labour (Porter 1975, 1979). Brotz alleged that the principle of multiculturalism corrupted liberal-democratic and egalitarian ideals 'by projecting the ideal of Canada as some kind of ethnic zoo where the function of the zoo keeper is to collect as many varieties as possible and exhibit them once a year in some carnival where one can go from booth to booth sampling pizzas, wonton soup and kosher pastramis' (Brotz 1980: 44). Kallen complained that 'by stressing the particularistic, expressive functions of immigrant ethnocultures, the multicultural policy shortchanges the goal of national unity and ... the goal of ethnic equality' (Kallen 1982: 169).

While sociologists differed in their assessments of multiculturalism as an ideal and a policy, Canadian voters hardly differed at all. Overwhelmingly, they disliked it. In 1990–1 an extraordinary national survey of public opinion on this and other issues was commissioned by the federal government under the name of *The Citizens' Forum on Canada's Future*. By having open telephone lines, inviting written comments and briefs and sponsoring discussion groups the energetic committee in charge managed to secure the opinions of about 400,000 citizens. Nearly 80 per cent of the telephone calls and nearly 60 per cent of the letters and written briefs expressed hostility to the government's policy of multiculturalism, while most of the other comments were ambiguous or uncertain and only a handful expressed support for it. The final report on the survey stated that most citizens wanted better integration of immigrants through language training and 'assistance in transferring foreign degrees and qualifications to meet Canadian standards', while most members of cultural minorities wanted 'to play their full role in the country as equal members of society –no more and no less'. The conclusion of the committee was that 'federal government funding for multiculturalism activities other than those serving immigrant orientation, reduction of racial discrimination and promotion of equality should be eliminated' (Citizens' Forum 1991: 128–9).

The government had actually moved in this direction during the late 1980s and it moved further following this report. It seems fair to conclude that the belief that the promotion of cultural diversity should be a policy objective of governments in liberal societies has been pretty well discredited by the Canadian experiment. This conclusion was strongly supported by a best-selling book written by a Canadian novelist who argued that it was a mistake for the government to promote policies likely to have the effect of artificially preserving the traditional cultures of immigrants or their ancestors, often in stereotypical versions, although the values and manners of immigrants or their children normally change as they adapt to their new society (see Bissoondath 1994: Chapters 5 and 6).

By this time, Trudeau's vision of multiculturalism, which he had declared 'might become a brilliant prototype for the moulding of tomorrow's civilization' (Trudeau 1977: 179), had been written into the constitution. The Charter of Rights and Freedoms of 1982 included an article stating that: 'This Charter shall be interpreted in a manner consistent with the preservation and enhancement of the multicultural heritage of Canadians'. As the word 'heritage' can hardly apply to a controversial policy introduced only eleven years earlier, it must be taken to refer to the long-standing arrangements whereby Canadian governments have passed special laws designed to protect the interests of French-Canadians, one of the nation's two founding European peoples, and the Indians and Inuit, who had arrived from Asia thousands of years earlier. It is therefore relevant to consider how successful these arrangements have been.

Francophone Canadians were given constitutional protection for their language by the British North America Act of 1867 and have acquired additional privileges since the growth of a Quebec independence movement. Since the 1980s Quebec provincial governments have been able to insist that all migrants to the province from outside Canada must have their children educated in French, that French must be the language of business in all sizeable firms, that French must be the dominant language on public hoardings and must be at least equally prominent in shop windows and on labels on merchandise for sale. In such ways the group rights of francophone Quebecois have been given legal priority over the individual rights of other residents, though equivalent measures in any of the other nine provinces would be struck down by the courts as contrary to the Canadian Charter of Rights. In the same period Quebec has been given substantial financial advantages under the tax equalization arrangements, and some Quebec industries and firms have been given special help by federal government.

Supporters of these policies point out that Quebec has a vibrant francophone culture, and that in two provincial referendums a majority of voters have opted to stay in Canada rather than secede. Sceptics note that in spite of all these incentives the majority in the 1995 referendum amounted to less than 1 per cent of the voters and that there would have been no majority at all had it not been for what the leader of the secessionist party called 'the ethnic vote', the 'ethnics' in question being the million or so English-Canadians who had their homes in Quebec.

Regarding the Indians and Inuit, now known by the legal title of aboriginal peoples, the record is less ambiguous. The hope that they would become fully integrated into Canadian society has not been realized, and in the 1970s government policies reflecting this hope were widely criticized as having involved distinct cultural losses for inadequate social and economic benefits. Opinion moved in favour of giving these peoples more independence to protect their cultural traditions and the 1982 Charter of Rights contained an article giving constitutional protection to 'the existing aboriginal and treaty rights of the aboriginal peoples of Canada'. As nobody knew (or even claimed to know) what these rights were, this was equivalent to entrenching a blank cheque, and a further article specified that a Constitutional Conference should be held in 1984 to identify and define the rights in question. This conference failed, as did further conferences in 1985 and 1987, and the attempt to reach agreement was then abandoned. However, at the 1984 meeting the federal government produced a document stating that the aboriginal peoples have 'the right to self-governing institutions', subject to agreements to be negotiated with the federal and provincial governments, and many Indian politicians have taken this to imply that they have a right to full independence. While this ambition is understandable, the Indians are divided between so many reserves that it can never be fully achieved. At the end of the 1970s Canada had 573 Indian Bands occupying 2,287 reserves, only 13 per cent of which had populations of over 1,000 (Gibbins and Ponting 1986: 242–3), while very many of them consisted of a few blocks in urban or suburban areas. A few large reserves in sparsely populated areas of northern Canada have been given substantial political autonomy in 'land claims agreements', after years of difficult and expensive negotiation, while many bands elsewhere have acquired some degree of municipal administrative devolution. However, no general policy is geographically possible and as a general policy is what many Indian leaders think they have been promised, political debate on the matter tends to be fruitless.

One consequence is that there have been prolonged stand-offs in which militant Indians have blockaded public highways outside their reserves on the ground that proposed commercial developments there would violate territory inhibited by the spirits of their ancestors, and the police have been unable to uphold the law because of political fears that this might provoke widespread violence. Another consequence has been financial. Although total government expenditures on Indian policy have been sufficient to provide every Indian family on the reserves with an annual income equal to the average non-Indian family in Canada, so much of it has gone to public officials, Indian politicians, expert advisers, and fiscally unaccountable band councils that tens of thousands of Indians on reserves live in dire poverty with high rates of disease, substance abuse and suicide. It is a story of almost complete political failure.

In view of this record, it is impossible to take seriously the claim that Canadian policies towards ethnic minorities can be an example to the world. Some Canadian scholars have defended multiculturalism as an ideal, notably Will Kymlicka and Charles Taylor, but Canadian practice has had some success only in regard to the large francophone minority. The problem of dealing with a society of settlers with two founding peoples instead of one is unique to Canada and the Canadian technique is better put under the heading of 'asymmetrical federalism' than that of 'multiculturalism'.

Australia is the only other country to have pronounced multiculturalism to be its national policy, which it did in 1973, but in practice Australian policies with that label have been very different from Canadian policies. Instead of encouraging the maintenance of cultural diversity, they were designed to facilitate the integration of newcomers into Australian society and have been rather successful in pursuing this objective. Australia has managed to achieve more economic equality between ethnic groups than exists in Canada and also to gain greater public understanding and acceptance of its ethnic policies.

European Debates

In Europe, debates about multiculturalism have developed more recently than in Canada and Australia and the term has been used to describe a bundle of practices more than a doctrine or national policy. British and Dutch practices in regard to recent immigrants from non-European countries have been more multicultural than French policies, and the comparisons are interesting. Dutch immigrants since 1945 have been overwhelmingly Muslim and come mainly from Turkey, Morocco and Suriname (formerly Dutch Guiana), with smaller numbers from Somalia and Iraq. The Netherlands has for long had a political and social policy known as 'pillarization', whereby the Protestant, Catholic and socialist groups in society have each had their own pressure groups and political parties, with an elaborate electoral system of proportional representation which ensured that every government was a coalition of several parties. Religious schools have been given state financial support and when substantial numbers of immigrants were recognized as settlers, rather than temporary guest workers, state schools offered classes in their languages of origin.

The growth of a substantial Muslim minority, numbering between 5 and 6 per cent of the population, has given Muslims the opportunity to become a fourth 'pillar', and to a limited extent this has happened. There are many Islamic primary schools and some secondary schools given government financial support. The Netherlands has a privately financed Islamic university and other post-secondary institutions with government finance that offer courses for Muslim students, including imams.

There is no problem about girls in state schools wearing headscarves in the Muslim style, and the courts have decided that Muslim women workers can be banned by their employers from doing this only if they come into direct contact with customers, as in the case of waiters and shop assistants. There has been no problem about the construction of traditional mosques, except that in the smaller towns they have not been allowed to have minarets because of town planning rules that religious buildings (of whatever denomination) cannot be higher than secular buildings. Muslims have been active in politics and have achieved proportionate membership in city councils and the lower house of the Dutch parliament, where in 2006 they had 10 out of 150 members.

Dutch policies may therefore be described as largely multicultural, but since 2000 there has been a public reaction to this based on the realization that many Muslim imams and politicians were in open opposition to the very liberal Dutch social attitudes and policies regarding sexual matters, gay rights and soft drugs. A populist party developed that favoured a revision of national policy, including changes in immigration policy that would hinder a growth in the size of the Muslim minority. However, in the 2002 national election campaign this party's leader, Pim Fortuyn, was assassinated in a parking lot. The party was quite unlike the large National Front in France and the miniscule British National Party, which are both right-wing anti-immigrant organizations. The Dutch party was centrist in orientation and its leader was an openly gay sociologist. His concern was to protect Dutch liberal policies from being undermined by socially conservative Muslim influence.

The assassin did not deny his guilt and, though not himself Muslim, stated that his motive had been to protect Dutch multiculturalism from a new party that seemed intolerant of Islamic beliefs.

In 2004 the Dutch got another shock when a well-known film director, Theo Van Gogh, was shot, stabbed and had his throat cut, in a public street with many witnesses, because he had made a documentary criticizing practices towards women in Muslim societies. The assassin was an Islamic fundamentalist of Moroccan origin who made no attempt to evade arrest and clearly wanted the murder to be well publicized as a warning to others who might be inclined to criticize Islamic practices. The immediate consequence of this event was a brief breakdown of public order, with non-Muslim gangs or mobs attacking Muslim schools and centres while Muslim gangs or mobs retaliated by attacks on Christian schools and centres. Altogether twenty public buildings on both sides were set on fire or otherwise badly damaged.

Death threats were then made against Ayaan Hirsi Ali, who had largely written the script for the documentary, herself a Somalian refugee who had been elected to the Dutch parliament and was well known as a politician. She had to go into hiding with police protection, and eventually decided to emigrate to the United States to escape the threats and stress. It emerged that the assassin had been associated with a terrorist group known as the Hofstad Group, nine of whose members were later convicted and imprisoned.

A consequence of this change in the political climate is that the Dutch government has revised some of its policies. After Van Gogh's murder, a parliamentary report declared that 'multiethnic society had been a dismal failure; huge ethnic ghettos and subcultures were tearing the country apart and the risk of polarization could only be countered by Muslims effectively becoming Dutch' (Fekete 2004: 20). In 2005 the Amsterdam Free University was given a special government grant to train imams in Dutch culture and Christianity.

In 2005 also the Dutch revised their immigration rules to insist that foreigners wanting to settle in the Netherlands have to pass a 'civic integration test' in Dutch language and culture, taken in their country of origin, as a condition of securing an entry permit. This new rule is rather clearly aimed at Muslims, both in its list of those exempt from its provisions and in some of the questions asked. The exemptions include citizens of EU member states, Switzerland, Norway, Canada, Australia, New Zealand, Japan and the United States. The exempt also include asylum seekers and people covered by the provisions for family reunion. However, all those exempt will have to take an integration test after their arrival in the Netherlands. The questions asked in the tests include some about Dutch values, including a readiness to accept gay marriage and affectionate public behaviour between gay couples, which are contrary to Islamic doctrine. The new rule specifically includes religious leaders coming to work in the Netherlands and young resident foreigners who have to go abroad to take the test when they reach the age of 17. It seems that the Netherlands is moving away from its previous commitment to multicultural policies.

British Policies and Practices

British experience regarding non-European immigrants since 1945 has been greatly affected by the fact that they have nearly all come from former colonies whose residents had British nationality and unrestricted rights of immigration until these were somewhat, but not greatly, curtailed by the Commonwealth Immigrants Act of 1962. By 2003 Britain had just over a million citizens of Afro-Caribbean origin, about 900,000 Hindus and Sikhs, and 1.6 million Muslims, mainly from Pakistan and Bangladesh.

As members of these ethnic minorities had British citizenship on arrival or soon afterwards, the government saw no need to develop special policies for them. It was, however, concerned to prevent racial discrimination and to that end introduced the Race Relations Act of 1965 supported by all parties and extended in 1968. This legislation is as comprehensive in scope as similar legislation in any other democracy. The 1965 Act established a national Race Relations Board and the 1968 Act added a Community Relations Commission. In 1976 these two bodies were replaced by a Commission for Racial Equality, with wider powers. There are numerous local branches of the Commission and other bodies with similar aims, so that altogether Britain has a small army of people working to improve relations between the host society and immigrant communities.

British society has long been exceptionally liberal and tolerant. There are, for instance, no identity cards, no laws to ban people calling themselves by any name they choose, no laws against trespassing on private land unless damage is caused, and no requirement for private schools and clubs to be registered or subject to government inspection.

The Commonwealth immigrants had presumably migrated to improve their living standards and official concern about them was related to this ambition rather than to cultural matters. The major concern to prevent racial discrimination in employment and housing was followed by concern about educational achievement. When cultural issues did arise, they were dealt with on a piecemeal and often local basis rather than as important issues of national policy. For instance, general laws about the slaughtering of animals had for long (since the 1920s) been subject to local exemptions to enable Jewish abattoirs to slaughter in the kosher manner, and similar exemptions were made for Islamic abattoirs in the 1960s. There have been no objections to Muslim girls wearing their traditional headscarves at school. The insistence of Sikhs on wearing turbans instead of caps or helmets caused some argument, but it was settled in favour of the Sikhs more quickly and with far fewer public protests than the same question had been settled in Canada, the other main destination for Sikh migrants. Town planning regulations, a municipal matter, have very rarely been used to hinder the construction of mosques and temples in traditional styles, as has happened to some extent in the Netherlands and to a large extent in France.

However, in 1981, there was a long week of rioting and looting, partly racial in origin, that affected twenty-seven urban areas in England. The main reason for the widespread incidence of the violence was a short-term growth of mass unemployment, which had reached its highest level since the 1930s and had particularly affected young people. However, the first riot occurred in Brixton, a south London neighbourhood largely populated by Jamaican immigrants, and this was precipitated by a cultural factor as well as by unemployment. During the late 1970s many West Indian immigrants had been converted to Rastafarianism, a millenarian creed that had emerged in Jamaica in the 1920s and is essentially a creed of underprivileged black people in a world dominated by whites. The creed holds that the blacks of Jamaica were descendants of slaves whose homeland was Ethiopia, and it takes its name from the family name of the former Emperor Haile Selassie of Ethiopia, Ras Tafari. White society is regarded as corrupt as well as oppressive and is known to Rastafarians as 'Babylon'. The creed promises that, come the millennium, Babylon will collapse and the blacks will go back to Ethiopia, idealized as a 'promised land'. In the mean time, blacks should not work in the white economy, should have contempt for white institutions and should smoke marijuana to induce relaxation and passivity while awaiting the great day.

Knowing of this, the police in parts of south London made extensive use of their 'stop and search' powers to search West Indians for drugs. This practice led the latter to accuse the police of racial profiling to which the police response was, in effect, 'of course'. In April 1981 the police decided to descend on Brixton in force to search for drugs in what was known as Operation Swamp. This caused great resentment and led to three days of rioting, in which young black residents attacked the police with stones and fire-bombs and set fire to shops owned by whites. An official report showed that 401 police officers were injured while 204 vehicles and 145 shops and offices were destroyed or damaged. No figure was given for the number of rioters injured.

The disturbances spread to the Toxteth area of Liverpool, where they were more prolonged and worse. The riots in other areas were less serious, with looting as their main cause, but many thousands of young people, white as well as black, were involved in them. (For a report on the police and political violence, see Birch 1990: Chapter 17.)

Following a judicial report criticizing police insensitivity, tactics were changed. Street patrols in black neighbourhoods were largely replaced by closed-circuit television cameras. The worries about the possibility of crime during the three-day Notting Hill Festival, held every August with reggae bands, dancing in the street and so forth, were replaced by police cooperation with the Afro-Caribbean organizers. By the late 1990s this had become the largest ethnic festival in Europe, with over 200,000 people enjoying themselves. In 1985 there had been short local riots in districts of Birmingham and north London, but since then there have been no public disturbances involving Afro-Caribbean groups and unemployment has ceased to be a problem except briefly around 1991. By 2000 about one-third of Afro-Caribbean men were living with white partners. The general conclusion must be that the integration of Afro-Caribbean immigrants into British society should be regarded as successful.

Asian immigrants have not made headlines in the same way. In 1979 there was a large street fight in a Sikh area of west London, provoked by a gang of white skinheads and eventually won by the Sikhs, with the police trying vainly to separate the two groups and incurring injuries to eighty-one officers for their pains. However, until 2001 this was the only riotous assembly involving Asians, and widespread complacency about their situation was reinforced by the publication of statistics showing that, in areas of comparable economic status, Asians were doing rather better than whites in school examinations.

However, in 1996 a leading student of ethnic relations, John Rex, suggested that this complacency was misplaced in respect of working-class Muslim immigrants. He observed that there was 'mostly in London, a professional and business Muslim bourgeoisie' who interacted well with British elites but did not fully understand the alienation of Muslim workers in the industrial north (Rex 1996: 232). He noted that in the woollen textile city of Bradford (Yorkshire), where about one-quarter of the population are Muslim, protests about some obscure passages in a novel that were apparently blasphemous about the Islamic religion led to public bonfires of the book. The author (Salman Rushdie) was a British writer of Indian origin, and there were some protests in India and Pakistan, but the demonstrations in Bradford lasted longer although 'it is extremely unlikely that many of these young people in Bradford had read Rushdie's book' (Rex 1996: 235). The demonstrations had been organized by imams and teachers but the sizeable participation in them clearly indicated feelings of social alienation. Rex also noted that in the early 1980s twelve Pakistani youths in Bradford had been prosecuted for possessing offensive weapons in the shape of gasoline bombs, 'but were actually acquitted when they argued in court that the bombs were for self-defence' (Rex 1996: 234).

In 1991, meetings had been held in the Bradford area to protest against British participation in the first Gulf War because Iraqis were Muslims. This was logically absurd because the war was fought in defence of two other Muslim states, Kuwait and Saudi Arabia. Rex's warnings were underlined in the summer of 2001 (before 9/11) when rioting of two or three days broke out in textile industry towns. It started in Oldham (Lancashire), where a man of 62 taking a short cut through a few blocks regarded as Muslim was beaten up by youths, groups of whom then wrecked a pub said to be favoured by anti-immigrant groups, set fire to newspaper offices and fought the Greater Manchester police. It spread to Bradford, where white-owned shops were vandalized and the police felt it necessary to defend a chapel. In December 2001 a fair number of British Muslims went to Afghanistan to fight against the allied invasion and nine of them were captured by US troops and sent to Guantanamo Bay. And in 2006 it was reported that others had gone, or tried to go, to Iraq to join the insurgents. No figures could be given, but police statements indicated that scores of suspects had been stopped, many at Manchester Airport, on some such pretext as passport irregularities.

One of the 2005 London Underground suicide bombers (himself from Leeds, near Bradford) made a video before his death justifying his behaviour by saying that it was a response to British fighting in Afghanistan and Iraq that had killed numerous Muslims. This attitude reflects the traditional Islamic belief that being Muslim involves not only a religious identity but also a political one. Historically, the division of humanity into religious faiths predated its division into national states by many centuries, and Muslims tend to regard it as also logically prior, with Islam shaping a whole way of life and Muslims belonging to the worldwide community of 'Ummah'.

What of British policies towards religion and education? There is a privileged state church in England whose spiritual leader is responsible for the coronation of monarchs, but it has suffered more than most churches from religious decline in recent decades and surveys in the early 1990s showed that no more than 4 per cent of nominal members attended church on an average Sabbath.

Before 1944 many schools were owned by churches although their running expenses were largely paid by county or city councils. However, when the Education Act of 1944 was negotiated a deal was offered whereby ownership would be taken over by the local councils but the schools would have to provide two periods of religious instruction (RI) for each class every week. The Protestant churches all accepted this deal but the Roman Catholic Church refused, so that Catholic schools became wholly private. The instruction is by law non-denominational and in practice a great many schools share the responsibility around the staff, with the result that largely irreligious students get RI twice a week from largely irreligious teachers. In areas of mixed ethnicity part of the time has often been spent on creeds other than Christianity, and in 2004 this uneven move in a multicultural direction was made official by a new National Framework for Religious Education issued by the Department for Education and Skills. This called for children, as appropriate, not only to study the six main religions within British society, namely Christianity, Buddhism, Hinduism, Judaism, Islam and Sikhism, but also not to ignore less common creeds like the Baha'i faith, to give equal respect to the views of religious and non-religious pupils, and to deal with secular philosophies such as humanism (London *Independent*, 29 October 2004; see also Preece 2005: 38).

Another move in a multicultural direction had been made in 2001 when the government introduced an Education White Paper on 5 September making clear that government grants would henceforth be available for independent faith-based schools if local circumstances made this appropriate. The Secretary of State defended this change of policy on the ground that accepting grants would ensure that such schools taught the national curriculum and would be subject to government inspection. She mentioned schools from minority faiths and it was generally understood that she was thinking of the 80 or so Islamic schools that were financed by Saudi-Arabian institutions. This new policy has led to the development of a limited number of state-funded religious schools of the Christian, Muslim, Hindu and Jewish faiths, but the policy remains controversial.

In January 2005 the Chief Inspector of Schools expressed his concern that 'many young people are being educated in faith-based schools, with little appreciation of their wider responsibilities and obligations to British society'. He mentioned Islamic schools in particular, saying that a traditional Islamic education 'does not entirely fit' children for life in modern Britain, and that the government must monitor such schools to make sure that pupils are taught about 'other faiths and the wider tenets of British society' (*Manchester Evening News*, 17 January 2005). On 26 July 2005 Tony Blair gave a press conference on the issue at which he was met with a barrage of hostile questions reminding him of the experience of state-financed Protestant and Catholic schools in Northern Ireland, which had socialized generations of young people into sectarian conflict and intermittent violence. Faced with this undeniable truth, Blair completely lost his normal eloquence and could say only that 'I hadn't realized that you all felt so strongly'.

The only significant grievances of a religious kind have been those coming from Muslim spokesmen, and in respect of Muslims the British position is a little paradoxical. A comparative study by two American academics has shown that the British state has done markedly more than the state in France or Germany to look after and advance Muslim requirements for the exercise and preservation of their religion. The study concludes that on the issues of 'religious instruction in state schools, state aid to religious schools, and mosque building Britain has been remarkably accommodating to Muslims' (Fetzer and Soper 2005: 60). At the same time, another American academic has discovered in the course of interviews with moderate Muslims in leading positions in six European countries that the British are much more likely than the others to regard Islamic values as 'inherently incompatible' with the values of their host country (Klausen 2005: 87). This has more to do with the varieties of Islam prevalent in their homelands than with policies in Britain, but it is not irrelevant.

Grievances sometimes voiced by Muslim spokesmen in Britain are not very serious. It is complained that the Race Relations Acts do not cover Muslims because the courts have decided firmly that they do not constitute a race. This is an entirely logical decision and it makes little practical difference as only a handful of converts are white, all other resident Muslims being covered as Indians, Pakistanis, Arabs, or whatever. The complaint simply reflects the wish, already mentioned, for Islam to be regarded as a form of political identity as well as religious identity. Another complaint, following the Rushdie affair, is that the British law against blasphemy covers only the Christian religion. This is true but makes little practical difference as the law is virtually obsolete. It would perhaps make sense to abolish it, but there are scores of obsolete laws on the Statute Book and the British tradition is to let them lie dormant rather than spend parliamentary time tidying them all up. In any case, it is highly unlikely that a British jury would have convicted the author of this difficult work (in which the offending passages occur in a dream or fantasy) so if the law were changed in the direction wanted by zealous Muslims, the probable consequence would be to replace a rather theoretical grievance by a series of controversies and complaints about court procedure and juries.

Exactly the same may be said about the proposal to add a law banning 'religious hatred' to the large arsenal of laws already available to bring prosecutions for expressing racial hatred, for 'offensive behaviour' for 'behaviour whereby a breach of the peace might be caused', and so on. Very few such prosecutions are ever brought, because of the deep attachment of the British people, including police, lawyers and judges, to the value of free speech. The Blair government, anxious to please Muslim organizations after the London bombings, introduced a Bill of this nature to Parliament, but a backbench revolt led to its defeat in 2006.

French Policies and Practices

France is a fascinating country, in this as in many other ways. As Walzer (1997) and Jennings (2000) have pointed out, it has had many waves of immigration and has a high level of ethnic diversity but still regards itself as a monocultural society (Walzer 1997: 8; Jennings 2000: 375).

This belief derives from the republican tradition, starting from the original Revolution of 1789, rooted in the thought of the Enlightenment, and having survived repeated clashes with monarchs and the Roman Catholic Church. One aspect of this tradition is that all citizens should be regarded as equal, with no mention of ethnicity or class or religion in censuses and other government documents. Another aspect is that the system of state schools should consciously prepare children for citizenship and should inculcate republican virtues. Another is that the separation of church and state should be vigorously observed. There is no place in this ideal for individual citizens to have loyalties to intermediate groups or organizations between themselves and the state, nor is there any place for the idea of minority rights. In view of this, it is natural for French intellectuals to have open contempt for the novel concept of multiculturalism, which they tend to regard as a new form of tribalism, likely to cause social disintegration on Lebanese lines, and totally un-French (Jennings 2000: 587–9).

This republican (sometimes called Jacobin) tradition has lasted as an ideal for over two centuries, although during that period France has experienced regime changes, violent or peaceful, in 1815, 1830, 1848, 1852, 1870, 1940, 1944, 1946 and 1958; has been invaded three times and occupied for four years; and has been through an appalling civil war in Algeria. That the ideal has survived through all these crises indicates the tenacity with which it has been held.

Of course, the practice of government in France, though organized on more of a national plan than public administration in Britain has ever been, is not quite as uniform as the republican model suggests. A French scholar has outlined some of the complexities in an article entitled 'Multiculturalism in France' (de Wenden 2003), using the term to cover an assortment of administrative variations rather than a doctrine. She notes that in the three Rhineland *départments* that were under German rule from 1870 to 1918 religious affairs are still governed by 'an agreement between the state and the three faiths of Roman Catholic, Protestant and Jewish' as the area was not governed by France when the legal separation of church and state was enacted in 1905 (de Wenden 2003: 83). She points out that in Alsace the German language is used in local administration, that in the Perpignan region street and town names are displayed in Catalan as well as in French, and that since 1968 the teaching of regional languages has been authorized in schools and universities of Brittany and Corsica (de Wenden 2003: 83). The arrival of millions of non-European immigrants has led to the recognition of cultural mediators in industrial suburbs and municipal housing blocks built for the immigrants, and Algerian groups, being familiar with French administrative styles, have been particularly successful in getting state subsidies for cultural activities (de Wenden 2003: 85).

It is doubtful whether these marginal inconsistencies justify the author's conclusion that 'the rise of claims to be different means that the republican model of integration has no other choice but to negotiate with multiculturalism' (de Wenden 2003: 86). This whole question was thrown into relief by the 'affair of the headscarves' that began in 1989. To explain this affair some historical introduction is necessary.

From the founding of the Third Republic in 1870 until the 1960s, the most important cultural division in society was that between the church and its sympathizers on the one hand and the secular or anti-clerical groups on the other. As the influence of the church waned, this source of anxiety for republicans has gradually been replaced by anxieties about the impact of non-European immigrants, most of whom are Muslim. Although France has received many non-Muslim immigrants since 1945, mostly from the Caribbean territories and former colonies in West Africa and Indo-China, it is clear that they have been outnumbered by Muslims, mainly from North Africa. Although precise statistics are not available, it is believed that between 5 million and 6 million Muslims now live in France, between 9 and 10 per cent of the population and thus a higher proportion than in any other western country. Since the 1980s, two political crises have developed involving them, of which the affair of the headscarves was the first.

When a universal system of state education was introduced in the early years of the Third Republic, the Catholic Church encouraged faithful girls to attend school wearing conspicuous symbols of their religion. As the church had always been opposed to the republican form of government and had indeed campaigned for the choice of a monarch rather than a president as head of state when the new regime began life, the wearing of religious symbols was taken to be a form of political demonstration. As such, it was naturally resented by teachers and school administrators with republican sympathies, and in 1904 the Ministry of Education published a regulation, affecting the entire national system, that banned the wearing of religious symbols in school. The official justification for this ban was the principle of *laïcité*, meaning secularity, that was part of the theoretical basis of the French state. As all state agencies were secular institutions, there was no place in them for religious symbols.

Suddenly, in 1989, three Muslim girls from North Africa produced a great shock by arriving at school wearing the *hijab*, the Muslim headscarf. The headmaster banned them from attendance and the response of the French public to news of the challenge 'was almost unanimously hostile, not to say at times hysterical' (Jennings 2000: 584). Other girls challenged the ban and the Minister of Education, seeking calm, asked the highest administrative court, the Conseil d'Etat, for an advisory ruling. The ruling was that girls should be permitted to wear the headscarf provided that it was not ostentatious or worn in local circumstances that made it an act of provocation or propaganda, the decision to be made by the local education authority. This compromise lasted uneasily until 1994, when a teenager reacted to a local ban by announcing that she was taking the local authority to court on the ground that it was violating her human rights. This caused a crisis that was both legal and political.

Unlike Anglo-Saxon countries, France does not have a common law system that can cope with novel challenges. French law is based on the Napoleonic Code, and any observant tourist will know that even a notice banning spitting or smoking bears details of the statute and clause authorizing the ban. Because the headscarf ban was based only on an administrative regulation, not a statute, French courts could not handle a case regarding it unless a law was passed. As teachers, public opinion and all political parties favoured the ban, parliament duly enacted one.

The consequence of the challenge was therefore an empathic reassertion of the French belief in *laïcité* and their rejection of the view that the growth of religious minorities in society should lead to the adoption of multicultural policies. This may not last for ever in regard to headscarves, as the new law is worded in a way that may make possible a future move to the flexible position favoured by the Conseil d'Etat in 1989, but the general principle of monoculturalism remains intact.

The other political crisis involving ethnic minorities erupted in late 2005, when tens of thousands of residents of industrial suburbs, mainly of African origin, rioted in protest over high unemployment rates (reaching 40 per cent among young men) as well as poor housing and inadequate social services. The riots lasted for three weeks, spread widely across France from their origin in the industrial suburbs around Paris, and were TV spectaculars, with about 10,000 cars and 500 public buildings set on fire. The reaction of the government was to introduce measures to moderate the exceptional rigidity of French labour laws, in ways that would make it easier for employees to hire unemployed young people without being committed to keeping them for life, but this proposal met with so many hostile demonstrations by trade unionists and students that the government abandoned the plan. The reaction of the police was to put the events into perspective by publishing figures showing that disorderly behaviour by young people after dark was not uncommon: from 1 January 2005 to mid-November, about 28,000 cars and 17,500 trash cans had been set on fire in France, with about 9,000 police cars stoned.

An academic reaction was to take comfort from the two facts that the rioters were multiethnic and, although the majority were Muslim, the degree of religiosity among the immigrant Muslim community was not high. A sociologist had reported that observance of Muslim rules of behaviour was now 'minimal among young people'. Few of them observed the ban on alcohol, the requirement of daily prayer, or the insistence on halal food. They tended to fast during the first three days of Ramadan (though not for the month), but 'this is frequently the only individual rite observed by young people' and their 'degree of theological knowledge is generally negligible' (Roy 1994a: 57). The realistic general French reaction to the riots was to regard them as a consequence of poverty and unemployment, similar in character to the British riots of 1981, and not therefore requiring any modification of policies relevant to cultural divisions.

Philosophical Approaches to Multiculturalism

The two most sophisticated analyses of this kind are by the British political theorists Brian Barry (2001) and Bhikhu Parekh (2000). Barry's basic position in *Culture and Equality* is the classical liberal one, a product of Enlightenment thought and therefore of the views underlying both the French and American revolutions, that a liberal state should treat all citizens as equal before the law. He accepts that a state may properly give special assistance to groups lacking certain opportunities or resources, provided that the assistance should be available to all citizens needing it for the reasons specified and that it should be temporary, ceasing to be given when the need is alleviated (Barry 2001: 12–13). He asserts that the wish of multiculturalists to give special privileges to groups defined by their ethnicity and culture, so that the help would not be generally available to citizens and not temporary in duration, amounts essentially to a rejection of Enlightenment ideals about politics (Barry 2001: 13 and 15).

Barry very carefully criticizes a whole set of arguments used by writers favouring multicultural policies, designed to give special rights and permanent help to groups defined by a culture which is not that of the majority, and his analysis is entirely consistent with his basic assumptions about the character of the liberal state.

A quite different approach is made by Parekh in *Rethinking Multiculturalism: Cultural Diversity and Political Theory*. He begins by asserting that most classical political theorists have made individualistic assumptions about the proper relationship between the citizen and the state, without paying adequate attention to the role of culture in shaping individual desires and beliefs. Although human character is not completely determined by culture, the culture in which people are raised 'shapes them in countless ways', influences their 'modes of reasoning' and leads them to assess their 'options in certain ways' (Parekh 2000: 170). Different cultures have different views about sex and gender relationships, about death, about the nature of religion, and so forth, and there is no universal criterion for evaluating the differences (Parekh 2000: Chapter 4). All cultures should therefore be treated with equal respect.

In regard to politics, Parekh accuses liberals of attaching too much importance to liberalism and of being unfair to groups within society with non-liberal beliefs. At one point, he defines the latter as including 'conservatives, socialists, communists, Marxists, religious communities, indigenous peoples, long-established ethnic communities and newly-arrived immigrants' (Parekh 2000: 112). This is much too sweeping and includes several groups defined simply by their political opinions rather than by their cultures. This distinction is vitally important to any discussion of liberal democracy, which depends upon the ability and readiness of voters to change their opinions from time to time. If voters are so bound by their cultures that they cannot or do not do this democratic institutions will fail, as they failed, sometimes tragically and bloodily, in former colonies of tropical Africa where the electorate was divided by tribal loyalties.

Parekh goes on to discuss the virtue of cultural diversity, which he says is wrongly defended by other liberal theorists on instrumental grounds, that in this way or that it produces beneficial consequences, and must be defended as simply a good in itself, essential to human freedom (Parekh 2000: 165–71). And in the second half of his book he presents a long and thoughtful discussion of ways to make cultural minorities feel fully part of their nation as a political entity. Noel O'Sullivan (2004) has offered a philosophical critique of Parekh's position, noting that it is weakened by its failure to define a cultural community, by its assumption of certain Enlightenment values that he criticizes in other liberal thinkers, and by optimistic assumptions about the existence of universal moral truths that will prevent political disagreements between cultural groups leading to conflict and even violence (O'Sullivan 2004: 48–54).

While Parekh's book is written at a high level of generality, its year of publication also saw the publication of a report entitled *The Future of Multi-Ethnic Britain* prepared by a commission of which he was chair, and frequently (though incorrectly) known as the Parekh Report. The commission was established by the Runnymede Trust, 'a think-tank devoted to the cause of promoting racial justice in Britain' (Runnymede Trust 2000: viii). This report, 399 pages long, includes a vast list of desirable changes in government policy. In the present context, its most relevant feature is the insistence that 'colour-blind and culture-blind approaches don't work' (Runnymede Trust 2000: 80–7). The problem about this, put starkly, is the belief that membership of a certain racial or cultural group in itself entitles a citizen to special rights and assistance. This may be reasonable in respect of a country that imported slaves or has indigenous peoples who were conquered by settlers, but it is hardly reasonable in respect of a country whose cultural minorities consist mainly of people who (or whose ancestors) freely migrated in search of better living conditions. Taxpayers of the host society cannot be expected to accept such a view. It conflicts with liberal principles and could be put into practice only if the British system of democratic government were replaced by a dictatorship of social workers.

Conclusions Regarding Multiculturalism

This is a confusing concept. In the hands of Canadian liberals, it started as a guide to the distribution of government subsidies and quite quickly changed to being a label to distinguish Canadian society from the apparently similar society south of the border. It has been thought to have the magical quality of protecting Canada against terrorism, so that when 17 Muslim Canadians were arrested on plausible charges of planning mass murder in Toronto, a leading journalist wrote a syndicated column under the heading 'Terror plot allegations hurt our multicultural dream' (Can West News Service, 6 July 2006).

In the hands of Parekh (2000) it is a novel philosophical understanding of human nature. Its most common use is as an omnibus title for a package of government policies, but our outline of Dutch and British policies shows that they are characterized by inconsistency and are liable to change at short notice. They do not add up to a doctrine, as communism or socialism or conservatism are doctrines.

It seems fair to conclude that while 'multicultural' is quite a convenient adjective for students of politics to use, 'multiculturalism' the noun is so vague and uncertain in meaning that it is entirely unhelpful.

References

Barry, B. (2001) *Culture and Equality: An Egalitarian Critique of Multiculturalism*, Cambridge, MA: Harvard University Press.

Birch, A. H. (1990) *The British System of Government*, 8th edn, London: Unwin Hyman.

Bissoondath, N. (1994) *Selling Illusions: The Cult of Multiculturalism in Canada*, Toronto: Penguin.

Breton, R. (1986) 'Multiculturalism and Canadian nation-building', in A. Cairns and C. Williams, *The Politics of Gender, Ethnicity and Language in Canada*, Toronto: University of Toronto Press.

Brotz, H. (1980) 'Multiculturalism in Canada: a muddle', *Canadian Public Policy*, 6: 41–6.

Citizens' Forum (1991) *Citizens' Forum on Canada's Future*, Ottawa: Canadian Government Publishing Center.

Fekete, L. (2004) 'Anti-Muslim racism and the European security state', *Race and Class*, 46(1): 3–29.

Fetzer, J. S. and Soper, J. R. (2005) *Muslims and the State in Britain, France and Germany*, Cambridge: Cambridge University Press.

Gibbins, R. and Ponting, J. R. (1986) 'An assessment of the probable impact of Aboriginal self-government in Canada', in A. Cairns and C. Williams (eds) *The Politics of Gender, Ethnicity and Language in Canada*, Toronto: University of Toronto Press.

Jennings, J. (2000) 'Citizenship, republicanism and multiculturalism in contemporary France', *British Journal of Political Science*, 30: 575–98.

Kallen, E. (1982) *Ethnicity and Human Rights in Canada*, Toronto: Gage.

Klausen, L. (2005) *The Islamic Challenge: Politics and Religion in Western Europe*, Oxford: Oxford University Press.

Naisbitt, J. (1995) *Global Paradox*, London: Nicholas Brealey.

O'Sullivan, N. (2004) *European Political Thought since 1945*, Basingstoke: Palgrave.

Parekh, B. (2000) *Rethinking Multiculturalism: Cultural Diversity and Political Theory*, Cambridge, MA: Harvard University Press.

Porter, J. (1975) 'Ethnic pluralism in Canadian perspective', in N. Glazer and D. Moynihan (eds) *Ethnicity: Theory and Experience*, Cambridge, MA: Harvard University Press.

_____(1979) 'Melting pot or mosaic: revolution or reversion', in J. Porter (ed.) *The Measure of Canadian Society*, Toronto: Gage.

Rex, J. (1996) *Ethnic Minorities in the Modern Nation State*, London: Macmillan.

Ronen, D. (1979) *The Quest for Self-Determination*, New Haven, CT: Yale University Press.

Roy, O. (1994a) 'Islam in France: religion, ethnic community or social ghetto?', in B. Lewis and D. Schapper (eds) *Muslims in Europe*, London: Pinter.

Runnymede Trust (2000) *The Future of Multi-Ethnic Britain*, London: Profile Books.

Smith, A. (1995) *Nations and Nationalism in a Global Era*, Cambridge: Polity Press.

Trudeau, P. (1977) *Federalism and the French Canadians*, Toronto: Macmillan.

Walzer, M. (1997) *On Toleration*, New Haven, CT: Yale University Press.

Weinfeld, M. (1981) 'Myth and reality in the Canadian mosaic: "affective ethnicity"', *Canadian Ethnic Studies*, 13: 80–100.

de Wenden, C. W. (2003) 'Multiculturalism in France', *International Journal on Multicultural Societies*, 5(1): 77–87.

Reading 4.3

Economic Policy

Jim Tomlinson

T HE MID-1970S ARE COMMONLY SEEN AS a watershed in post-war economic policy. The 'golden age' of the 1950s and 1960s came to an end in a period of 'stagflation' and crises over public spending, borrowing and the exchange rate. The 'Keynesian' consensus about how to conduct economic policy was fundamentally challenged by the sharp rise in both inflation and unemployment coupled to a major loss of financial confidence. Subsequently, both Conservative and New Labour politicians and their academic allies have seen ideological advantage in painting the period in the worst possible light. If historical distance is unlikely to lend enchantment to our view of the period, it does at least allow some perspective, and such perspective is what this chapter seeks to offer. In assessing Labour's economic policy in this period, the discussion is divided into four sections. The first deals with Labour's inheritance from the Heath period (1970–4), the second with the Government's policy responses to the problems it faced, the third with the outcomes of those policies, and the final part attempts to set these years in a broader perspective of post-war economic policy evolution. The focus throughout is on macro-economic policy, other issues only being discussed if they bear on this macro aspect.

The Inheritance

On coming to power all governments say that they have inherited an economic mess from their predecessors. But few governments have received such a poisoned chalice as awaited the Labour Government in March 1974. Following its 'U-turn' in 1972 the Heath Government had embarked on an unprecedentedly expansionary fiscal and monetary policy and allowed the exchange rate to float—which meant, in practice, to sink. This put the economy on a path of sharply rising public spending, fiscal deficits and money supply. Some minor attempts were made to slow down the rate of growth in November and December 1973, but the impact of these expansionary policies was to be felt for several years into Labour's term of office.

Second, the new Government took office at a time of the worst industrial relations crisis since the 1920s. The dispute with the miners had led to the imposition of a three-day week over most of industry. In addition, as an accompaniment to fiscal expansion and increasing inflation, there was a surge in pay under way, especially in the public sector. The Conservative Government's attempt to counter wage inflation had led to an agreement on threshold payments, which tied permitted wage increases to the inflation rate and consequently institutionalised inflation. This locked the new Government into a wage–price spiral.

Externally, the world-wide economic expansion of 1970–3 had meant a sharp deterioration in both the terms of trade (the price of imports relative to exports) and the balance of payments. These trends were capped by the quadrupling of oil prices agreed by OPEC in December 1973. This imparted both a powerful inflationary impact via its effects on costs and simultaneously a deflationary one by requiring the oil-importing economies (which included Britain in 1973) to redistribute resources towards exports in order to pay for the higher priced oil.

Last but not least was the very rapid increase in import penetration in manufactures. Imports' share of the home market rose from 15 per cent in 1970 to 22 per cent in 1974 (and was to rise to 30 per cent by 1980).[1] The early 1970s' growth was fuelled by the rapid expansion of demand in Britain, the competitive weakness of many domestic suppliers, and the reduction in barriers to trade, especially because of entry into the EEC in January 1973. The rapid rise in imports, not offset by a parallel rise in exports, led not only to a marked deterioration in the current balance of payments, but perhaps even more importantly to the profit squeeze on the private sector which formed a key backdrop to Labour's problems in managing the economy.[2]

In sum, when Labour took office almost every economic indicator was moving adversely: inflation was around 10 per cent, the balance of payments had moved sharply into the red after recording a current surplus in 1971, the exchange rate was falling after floating from June 1972, and the public sector deficit was at a peacetime high. The last of these was perhaps the most intractable of the legacies of the 'Barber boom'. Not only was the deficit itself a key factor in financial confidence in British economic management, but the rise in interest on the debt meant that many of the great battles to cut public spending under Labour did no more than offset higher payments to holders of government paper.[3]

Towards the end of 1973 the Conservatives recognised that the pace of expansion since the spring of 1972 was unsustainable and began to tighten both fiscal and monetary policy. In retrospect it is clear that a cyclical peak had been reached in May 1973, but the downturn was mild before Labour came into office. Thus Labour inherited a condition of 'stagflation' that largely justifies the new Chancellor's assertion that 'my predecessor left me an economy on the brink of catastrophe'.[4]

The Government Response

The Labour Government was poorly prepared for the scale of the economic problems it faced—as indeed were governments in all countries in the 1970s. In opposition Labour had been crucially concerned with the relationship with the unions, partly because of the unhappy development of that relationship under the previous Labour Government of 1964–70, partly because in the early 1970s it was apparent that industrial relations and wage inflation were the key issues of the time. Labour had agreed a 'social contract' with the unions designed to deal with the problems of the early 1970s rather than the much worse conditions after 1974. In return for policy concessions from the government, the TUC had promised to exercise restraint on the wage front, but without any intention of conceding the case for a formal incomes policy. The social contract was then 'insipid and toothless', a papering over of the cracks between the leadership of the Party and trade union opinion.[5]

Initially this contract had little effect, as unions sought to stay ahead of accelerating price inflation. But in 1975 union leaders 'looked into the abyss' of hyperinflation, and after reaching a peak of almost 30 per cent in the summer of that year, wage inflation slowed down. The Government was able to negotiate an agreement with the TUC on the basis of a flat-rate increase of £6 per week. Although this limit was widely exceeded, it did have a significant impact, especially notable in the public sector where the Government tightened the purse strings, but the process of deceleration was generally aided by the sharp rise in unemployment, which more than doubled between 1974 and 1976, and the squeeze on profits in the private sector. In 1976 a further agreement was reached with the TUC, aided by the novelty of making tax cuts dependent on restraint in wage claims. But the Government's attempt to extend further the life of this beefed-up social contract was met with decreasing enthusiasm and then outright opposition from the trade unions, now that the immediate crisis was seen to be past. Down to 1978 and despite these tensions the policy can be seen as facilitating the reduction of inflation without a rise in unemployment, which stabilised from 1976. But in 1978–9 the Government sought to achieve an unrealistic 5 per cent wage target, which could be made effective only in the public sector, where low-paid workers had already borne much of the brunt of the social contract. The result was the 'Winter of Discontent', as union members sought at least to maintain their real wage at a time when inflation was running at 8–10 per cent per annum. In retrospect, this limit of 5 per cent must be seen as a grievous error, the Government failing to recognise the strength of feeling among rank and file union members, and the inability of union leaders to contain such powerful discontent.

Alongside the social contract Labour had committed itself to a radical departure in industrial policy. In particular it was envisaged that Labour would create a National Enterprise Board to take a controlling share in a large number of large manufacturing firms. Such proposals for 'competitive public enterprise' originated on the right of the Party as an alternative to 'old-fashioned' sectoral nationalisations as far back as the 1940s. They gained support from wide sections of the Party in the early 1970s, but even before Labour came to office it was apparent that many in the leadership of the Party were worried about the hostile reaction to such proposals from the private sector. The radical version of the NEB proposals was spelt out in *Labour's Programme* of 1973, but even as early as August 1974 with the publication of *The Regeneration of British Industry* the tone had shifted markedly. The stance was no longer one of government attempting to change industry's behaviour by heavy controls, but of co-operation in a joint enterprise of recovery.[6] In a macro-economic context these proposals, even as watered down, were significant for the way they added to the loss of private sector confidence and thus put downward pressure on investment, an issue that was very important in the crisis of the mid-1970s.

Earlier episodes of incomes policy had been based on the economists' argument that if this instrument was used to contain inflation, demand management, especially fiscal policy, could be used to maintain full employment. But such a happy division of labour proved unfeasible in the mid-1970s. The social contract proved insufficient to contain inflation, and so fiscal policy could not be used to pursue full employment. Almost from the beginning, therefore, fiscal policy was downgraded to a supporting role, essentially seeking to aid the effectiveness of the social contract. Despite increasing unemployment the March 1974 budget was mildly deflationary. In contrast, that of November 1974 was slightly expansionary, but with the main aim of easing company finances, which had been hard hit by the fact that they were being taxed on paper profits on stock whose price had only risen because of inflation.

By 1974 Britain was undoubtedly suffering from a serious profits crisis, significantly worse than other OECD countries, and particularly noticeable in manufacturing. This profit squeeze had existed in milder form since the 1960s, but the recession of 1974–5 brought levels to an all-time low, and government action was inescapable. Profits reached their lowest point in 1975, and then recovered, partly because of government action and partly as a normal consequence of the upturn of the cycle. The link between profits and investment is not a straightforward one, but the reversal of the profit squeeze does seem to have facilitated a degree of investment recovery after 1976. However, it has been plausibly argued that the still depressed levels of investment were insufficient to support full employment of the labour force. However difficult the circumstances, Labour's response to the profit problem may reasonably be labelled 'too little, too late'.[7]

Crucial in the evolution of fiscal policy for the whole period of the Labour Government was the budget of April 1975. In it the Chancellor, Denis Healey, argued:

> I fully understand why I have been urged by so many friends both inside and outside the House to treat unemployment as the central problem and to stimulate a further growth in home consumption, public or private, so as to start getting the rate of unemployment down as fast as possible. ... I do not believe it would be wise to follow that advice today. ... I cannot afford to increase demand further when 5p in every pound we spend at home has been provided by our creditors abroad and inflation is running at its current rate.[8]

For a Labour Government to give priority to reducing inflation by cutting public spending when unemployment was so high marked a turning point in post-war economic policy. As Britton notes, 'in the circumstances it was a very un-Keynesian budget'.[9] Also very important to the development of fiscal policy was the cash limits policy announced in July 1975 and embodied in the February 1976 White Paper. Cash limits gave priority to containing the financial consequences of rising public spending, and had the unexpected consequence of underpinning the sharpest ever peacetime fall in public spending, amounting to 6.9 per cent between fiscal 1976–7 and 1977–8.[10] The April 1976 budget was framed explicitly to try and gain support for the social contract, with a stabilisation of public spending allied to conditional tax cuts. Further public expenditure cuts were announced in July and December, the last as part of the deal with the IMF that figures so largely in accounts of this Government (see below for further discussion).

The cuts in public spending planned from 1975 onwards had a differentiated pattern. In the light of the squeeze on private sector profits not only was tax relief to companies greatly extended, but also industrial subsidies shot up. To some extent history was repeating itself; in the 1960s Labour had sought to encourage private investment by large subsidies, and indeed it was the perceived failure of this policy which fuelled the call for more direct government control over that sector as embodied in the idea of the NEB.[11] Now, in much less favourable macro-economic circumstances, the policy was tried again. Coupled with the rising payments on debt, the switch of public spending was away from social programmes, especially where this involved capital as opposed to current spending; most conspicuously 'the party is over' was an accurate summary of the position for local authority housing spending which was never again to reach the heights it reached in the early 1970s. Many of the problems of underinvestment in public infrastructure, which were to plague Britain into the twenty-first century, began in the mid-1970s.[12]

Another very important feature of spending policy in the 1970s was linked to the broader debate about de-industrialisation which gathered pace in this period. Historically Labour had been a party which gave high priority to industrial modernisation.[13] This continued in the 1970s—for many the radical industrial policy was about finding new ways to pursue this agenda, given what was seen as the incorrigible complacency and ineffectiveness of privately owned companies, especially with regard to their willingness to invest. Historically, too, Labour had seen such modernisation as the necessary underpinning for its aim of 'social justice', especially secured by expanding government social programmes. But in the climate of slowing growth in the 1970s there appeared to some to be a direct clash between resources going to higher investment and resources for public spending. Such a view animated the Treasury desire to curb public spending growth and boost company finances. But perhaps most strikingly it affected the outlook of key figures in the TUC, whose views in the context of the social contract were especially important for the Government.

Most interesting in this regard is Hugh Scanlon, leader of the engineering union and a key figure in union discussions with the Government. While he tended to put his weight behind many of the policies of the left in the Labour Party in this period, as the leader of a largely private manufacturing union he was very much concerned with industrial investment, and attracted to the position which argued that public, social spending had to be held back to finance such investment.[14] In public discussions Scanlon and other TUC leaders were willing to face up to the logic of this argument. For example, the 1975 *TUC Economic Review* noted that in the context of the need to 'increase productive investment ... there could be little scope for real increases in consumption at the present time'. The following year, in discussing the social contract Scanlon argued that economic recovery would only come 'on the basis of a viable, efficient manufacturing industry with emphasis on those who make and sell and, if necessary, somewhat less emphasis on those who serve'.[15]

As well as sympathising with the Government's fiscal priorities, Scanlon was lukewarm on the radical industrial policy partly because he did not see how it could guarantee the shift in resources he wanted to secure. Yet the kind of strategy he desired was difficult to deliver in this period. In 1974–5 the threshold agreements inherited from the Conservatives protected households against the slump, while the Government was trying to stabilise the public sector deficit: the result was a big financial squeeze on the private sector. As we have seen the Government then came to the rescue with measures of tax relief, but already considerable damage had been done to both investment and employment. From a union point of view, advocacy of squeezing consumption in order to pay for investment was never likely to be a popular policy; to do so when the recession was depressing incomes was perhaps wholly politically implausible. From this perspective, analysis of the social contract which emphasises the strains put on the trade unions by their leaderships' attempts to subordinate the unions' policy to national economic priorities appears all the more crucial to understanding the 1970s.[16] The first serious recession since the war was not an environment in which giving priority to industrial investment was likely to find much ready support.

On 28 September 1976 Callaghan made his famous speech asserting that the option of spending Britain's way out of recession 'no longer exists, and that insofar as it ever did exist it only worked on each occasion since the war by injecting a bigger dose of inflation into the economy'.[17] As a description of postwar policy this seems to be entirely inaccurate, but at the time and subsequently it has been regarded as a hugely important symbol of Labour's renunciation of 'Keynesian' policies. In fact it is difficult to see it in that light. Not only was the speech made during the 'crisis of confidence' period which led up to the IMF visit, and to be seen very much as aimed at trying to restore confidence, but it did not portend a move away from Keynesian policies. On the contrary, not only was policy moving away from 'Keynesianism' well before the speech, but in 1977 and 1978 the direction of fiscal policy was to become *more* expansionary as the economic environment improved.

Down to the autumn of 1976 the fall in the exchange rate, which gathered pace in 1975, was not regarded as a problem, as it aided the balance of payments. In the spring of 1976 the authorities seemed to encourage a further fall, but the decline in the pound's value got out of hand in the summer of 1976. This led to the IMF deal in December 1976, by which Britain was granted further support for the pound in return for a 'Letter of Intent' on future policy which included public spending cuts, only agreed after a major crisis in the Cabinet and the Government. Politically the IMF episode was undoubtedly of major importance, in arousing opposition to what can be regarded, according to taste, as either an illegitimate interference in a national government's policy decisions or a stark demonstration of the incompetence of Labour in managing the economy.[18]

But in economic terms the episode is a puzzle. As we have seen, it is a myth to suggest that Labour reversed its policies sharply only in response to the IMF's demands. The major arguments within the Government about the priority to be accorded to full employment in framing fiscal (and monetary) policy took place in 1974 and 1975, and by 1976 policy was clearly set on according priority to inflation, coupled to trying to encourage support for the social contract. The evidence suggests this stance had already led to the economy starting to recover well before the IMF arrived. Output bottomed out in August 1975, inflation started to fall from the same month and the balance of payments to improve (for the whole of 1976 the current account deficit was less than a third of that of 1974). The public sector finances were improving from early 1976 as cash limits started to have their impact. Yet until the end of the year the pound would not stop falling. Undoubtedly there was a major loss of financial confidence in the mid-1970s, and the issue was not so much Labour's policies as the need for that confidence to be boosted by the granting of the IMF's seal of approval to Labour's 1975 reversal of priorities.[19]

The size of the PSBR and the inflationary splurge of 1975 underpinned financial market views that Labour Governments are prone to extravagance. In the summer of 1976 there was what *The Economist* referred to as a 'gilt strike', which exposed the weakness of any govern-ment with a large borrowing requirement.[20] The floating exchange rate meant there was no 'anchor' against inflationary policies as had existed in the 1950s and 1960s. In these circum-stances policy credibility could only be restored by an outside agency trusted by financiers; this was the role of the IMF.

If it is inaccurate to see the IMF as the major instigator of Labour's policies, it remains to be asked where these policies did come from. Partly this is a matter of the internal politics of the Labour Party. While never a whole-heartedly Keynesian party, Labour in the 1950s and 1960s was united around a belief that full employment could and should be achieved by active demand management. While there were long-term doubts about the capacity of such demand management to achieve faster growth, the basic idea that fiscal policy could be effectively used to achieve full employment was only just beginning to come under serious critical scrutiny in the 1970s.[21] The stagflation of 1974–6 was a body-blow to such assumptions, and sharply divided Labour economic opinion. On the left an 'Alternative Economic Strategy' emerged which, in macro-economic terms, wanted to expand demand but protect the external account by import controls. But also on the left (though overlapping with elements on the right) were people like Scanlon who, it has been suggested above, wanted to give a higher priority to industrial investment and was willing to sacrifice Labour's traditional social agenda in doing so, unlike advocates of the AES.

On some sections of the right there was a nascent 'monetarism' that believed the central concern should be to reduce inflation and government borrowing to hold back government spending to expand the scope for increases in both take-home pay and investment. But others on the right argued that while financial confidence could not be ignored, the basic social democratic commitment to full employment and high spending was sustainable with a little trimming.[22] These divergent views emerge fairly clearly in the agonised discussions of 1976, both at the time of the July cuts and the IMF visit. Ultimately, however, what mattered in that period was what seemed likely to resolve the crisis quickly. As Thompson suggests:

> one is left, though, with the overwhelming impression that in this period economic ideas and economic philosophies proved influential to the extent that they contributed to political survival. When they did so they were embraced or modified, when they did not they were jettisoned. Economic policy did not so much bear the imprint of ideas as the scars of expediency.[23]

But if this is a period of disarray in Labour's economic doctrine, what of the institutions of policy making? Here, of course, the key role was played by the Treasury. The Treasury in the 1970s sustained its position as the most important department in Whitehall, and possessed an ability to shape the agenda that its opponents found very hard to shake. As the Cabinet diarists of the 1970s make clear, opposition to the Treasury line always lacked intellectual weight because no minister other than the Chancellor had access to sufficient resources to make a well-grounded alternative case.[24] In Cabinet the Chancellor, always in the end receiving support from the Prime Minister, was able to dominate economic discussion and face down opposition. But recognition of this power should not lead us to think of the Chancellor as a mouthpiece of the carefully crafted, consistent and monolithic 'Treasury View' as opponents such as Benn suggest.[25]

First, it is clear that Labour's Chancellor in the 1970s, Denis Healey, was not a simple mouthpiece for an institutional position. He (like the PM, and former Chancellor, Jim Callaghan) was critical of quite a lot of what the Treasury did, especially its forecasting errors and the policy mistakes that such errors could lead to.[26] In this environment he was willing and able to make up his own mind on many important issues.

Second, it seems clear that, like everyone else in this period, the Treasury found it hard to navigate its way through the crisis of the mid-1970s. Not only did much of its forecasting appear error strewn, but it suffered a huge blow when it appeared to have lost control of public expenditure, perhaps its most central function. While the degree of loss of control may have been exaggerated, the fact that such an allegation could plausibly be made by a previous government economic adviser (Wynne Godley) suggests how far the Treasury found itself under pressure in the mid-1970s.[27]

This pressure partly found its expression in a sense of panic, notably over the negotiations over the IMF agreement in late 1976. And, far from being a monolith, there is evidence of serious divisions of opinion within the Treasury in this period, some linked to doctrinal disputes, especially concerning the continuing relevance of Keynesian policies, others more pragmatic, such as how to respond to the loss of financial confidence in 1976.[28]

Last but not least, the Treasury seems to have made serious errors of judgement in this period. First there was the confusion about the level of public expenditure, which allowed critics to allege erroneously that the share of such spending was reaching the 'dangerously' high level of 60 per cent. Even more important, there was what Healey calls a 'muddle' on exchange rate policy, especially on the extent to which a depreciation was to be welcomed as a means of restoring competitiveness, or feared as a harbinger of future inflation.[29] Such confusion was especially important in the crisis of 1976, because it was initial Treasury (and Bank of England) support for depreciation of the pound which began the process which eventually led to the accelerated decline of the currency, and the battle to restore financial confidence eventually achieved only through the political humiliation of the IMF visit.

If the Treasury was divided and rattled by the problems of economic management in the 1970s, that is hardly surprising. If the Labour leadership was similarly affected, we may feel that this was only to be expected; the Party had always contained an often uneasy combination of economic opinions, and even before coming into office had been sharply divided over the key area of industrial policy and able to produce only a highly fragile agreement on wages. To be then faced with a macro-economic crisis, which nothing in earlier experience could be used as a helpful precedent in solving, was bound to lead to deep arguments. In the event, and after much division and dispute, the Government managed to agree economic policies which kept it surprisingly intact; for all Benn's invocation of the horrible example of 1931, no such political disaster came close to occurring in the 1970s. Healey's 'eclectic pragmatism' proved to be sufficiently agile to keep the economy, and the Government, on a path which, in retrospect, appears defensible as dealing with some success with a disastrous legacy combined with unprecedented external adverse conditions, and in circumstances where the norms of post-war economic understanding appeared to have disintegrated.

Outcomes

In assessing the outcomes of Labour's period in office, it is important to look in a comparative context because the economic problems facing the British Government were far from unique, and similarly the dilemmas and difficulties in responding to the deterioration in the international economic environment were strongly paralleled in other West European countries. In this section comparisons are made with the West European 'Big Three': West Germany, France and Italy.

Inflation rates are shown in Table 4.3.1. Plainly there was a marked upward trend everywhere in the first part of the 1970s, except in West Germany, with Britain on average not as bad as Italy (or, the OECD figures suggest, Spain). Inflation was an international phenomenon, and though in Britain it threatened to get out of control in 1975, in fact the upward trend was sharply reversed after that year.

Table 4.3.2 on public expenditure shows the rapid expansion of the 'Barber boom' of the early 1970s reversed after 1975, and the share of public spending in GDP lower in Britain than elsewhere by 1979. Perhaps it is particularly striking that the share of GDP taken by public spending was considerably lower in Britain than in 'virtuous' Germany by the end of the decade.

Table 4.3.3 shows the fiscal balance; these are the unadjusted 'headline' figures. They show that France had a much better performance, Italy much worse, Germany surprisingly not much different. These are 'headline' figures, upon which much contemporary attention was focused. But much of the increase was not due to policy decisions, but to the automatic effects of the economic cycle. If the cycle is taken into account, and we adjust the numbers for the impact of the recession, the main increase in the deficit was under the Conservatives in 1970–3, the trend being flat thereafter. There is also the huge issue of inflation adjustment to these raw numbers, with the 'burden' of the debt much reduced by the rise in prices.[30]

TABLE 4.3.1 Inflation in the West European 'Big Four' 1972–9 (Percentage Change from Previous Year in Private Consumption Deflator)

	France	Italy	West Germany	Britain
1972	6.3	6.4	5.7	6.5
1973	7.4	13.8	6.3	8.5
1974	14.8	21.3	7.0	16.9
1975	11.8	16.6	6.2	23.7
1976	9.9	17.7	4.2	15.8
1977	9.4	17.5	3.6	14.8
1978	9.1	13.2	2.7	9.0
1979	10.7	14.5	3.9	13.6

Source: OECD, *Economic Outlook,* 47, 1990, Table R11

TABLE 4.3.2 Public expenditure in the West European 'Big Four', 1972–9 (Total Outlays of Government as a Percentage of GDP)

	France	Italy	West Germany	Britain
1972	38.3	38.6	40.8	39.3
1973	38.3	37.8	41.5	40.4
1974	39.3	37.9	44.6	44.9
1975	43.4	43.2	48.9	46.6
1976	43.9	42.2	47.9	46.3
1977	43.7	42.5	48.0	43.8
1978	44.6	46.1	47.8	43.3
1979	45.0	45.5	47.7	42.7

Source: OECD, *Economic Outlook,* 47, 1990, Table R15

TABLE 4.3.3 Government Surpluses and Deficits in the West European 'Big Four', 1972–9 (General Government Financial Balances as a Percentage of GDP)

	France	Italy	West Germany	Britain
1972	+0.8	8.6	0.5	1.3
1973	+0.8	7.9	+1.2	2.7
1974	+0.1	7.8	1.3	3.9
1975	2.2	12.9	5.6	4.6
1976	0.6	9.8	3.4	5.0
1977	0.8	8.6	2.4	3.4
1978	2.1	10.4	2.4	4.4
1979	0.8	10.2	2.6	3.3

Source: OECD, *Economic Outlook,* 47, 1990, Table R14

In comparative terms one of the curious features of the 1970s is that Britain's relative growth performance improved. This reflected the fact that the golden age of the 1950s and 1960s had seen a process of 'catch-up' by the major continental West European countries, but by the 1970s that process was more or less complete. West European growth rates slowed down sharply, while the British rate decelerated much less from a lower starting point. Britain's performance in the 1970s was helped by the exploitation of North Sea oil, which Crafts suggests added about 0.5 per cent to annual expansion. Labour productivity in manufacturing stands out for its poor performance in the 1970s, though by this date manufacturing was only 30 per cent of total output. The causes of this poor performance are contentious. Some have argued that it reflected the exhaustion of increasing returns from the early 1970s spurt in investment. Others see it as a consequence of labour hoarding as employers anticipated a cyclical revival which never came.[31] In any event, this nadir of manufacturing productivity performance should not obscure that fact that for the economy as a whole this was a period of sharp recession followed by substantial recovery, but with the trend performance understated by the unsustainable peak of 1973.

Conclusions and Implications

In the 1980s accounts of this Labour Government suggested that the events surrounding the IMF crisis of 1976 formed a key turning point in post-war British politics. Holmes typified this argument in suggesting that 'the change in attitudes and ideologies after 1976 was possibly the most profound ... since that engendered by the 1945–51 Labour government ... the post-1976 change of approach saw reducing inflation regarded as the prime policy objective ahead of full employment'.[32] This now seems mistaken in two respects. First, the shift towards giving primacy to inflation began well before the IMF visit, 1976, going back to at least Healey's budget of 1975, as noted above. Second, this shift in objectives was much less profound than this quotation posits; as Burk and Cairncross persuasively counter, 'economic policy in the last years of the Labour government differed little from what it had been before the arrival of the IMF'.[33] Once the IMF seal of approval had been given, and the exchange rate strengthened, Labour started to reflate the economy and to limit inflation by continuing with the social contract. Keynesianism was not dead.

This is not to suggest nothing changed in the 1970s. In the broadest terms an important part of the social democratic 'project' did suffer mortal blows in the 1970s, the part which saw expanding public spending—'tax and spend'—as the centrepiece of social democratic egalitarianism.[34] The year of 1976 saw the end of the upward trend in spending and taxing which had (with interruptions) characterised the previous three-quarters of a century—an upward trend that was not to be restarted until the beginning of the next century.

If at the macro-economic level 1976 was not the historic turning point early commentators suggested, it did mark the beginnings of a notable improvement in economic performance. As Gardener argues: 'the story of the years 1977 and 1978 is one of paradox. The statistics now available suggest success, but attitudes at the time spoke of failure.'[35]

It is not only attitudes of the time that spoke of failure; for many superficial analysts as well as political opponents the whole period of the Labour Government remains one spoken of in absurdly exaggerated terms of breakdown and disaster. How did such views gain so much credence? Part of the answer is to be found in the contemporary panic which surrounded the economic instability of these years. Evidence of this panic can be found in the pages of such respectable journals as *The Economist*, which as early as March 1973 was suggesting inflation was threatening 'Latin American modes of both price inflation and societal decay'. A year later the *Banker* was suggesting that Britain faced the last chance 'for the parliamentary system to cope with Britain's economic problems'. By summer 1975 *The Economist* was suggesting that 'Britannia's dream of apocalypse is horribly close to coming true'.[36]

Such arguments were not the result of sober economic analysis so much as part of a wider 'great fear' on the part of many in Britain. As Johnson suggests, 'in 1974–76 important sections of the middle classes did lose confidence. For the first time parts of the Establishment began seriously to consider the alternatives to our present forms of parliamentary democracy.' Johnson goes on to suggest that 'a future social historian may well experience some difficulty in comprehending the cacophony of the Great Fear'.[37] But the historian also needs to explain why this immediate overreaction to events of the 1970s has been replicated in so many later accounts.

Part of the explanation lies in the exaggerated accounts of long-run economic 'decline', in which the 1970s are represented as a culmination of the disastrous post-war economic trends brought about by Keynesian social democracy. This, of course, was the key historical narrative of Mrs Thatcher, and one she used to great effect in securing her leadership role.[38]

But the highly political use of stories about the 1970s is not of course confined to the Conservatives. For New Labour exaggerated stories about the 1970s provide a useful counterpoint to contemporary 'prudence'; for New Labour the suggestion that the 1970s were a disastrous period serves to emphasise the distance travelled between the 'Old' and the 'New'. But to compare a more realistic account of the 1970s with Labour under Blair/Brown suggests considerable similarity as much as stark difference. The label 'monetarily-constrained Keynesianism'[39] has been applied to the Wilson–Callaghan years, and this is a not inaccurate characterisation of economic policy around the end of the century under New Labour. In the 1970s Labour was faced with a world recession at the beginning of its period in office, and this forced a focus on monetary and fiscal tightening to beat inflation, which was then relaxed after 1976 as inflation seemed to be under control. Under New Labour the sequence has been reversed. Having established its anti-inflationary credentials in the first term, the second brought a recession in which Keynesian policy (the overriding of the automatic stabilisers) was vigorously pursued. Also, in a direct reversal of the mid-1970s, the automatic stabilisers were augmented by a substantial expansion of public capital spending. In the earlier period, because inflation was high financial markets lost confidence in the Government's policies, and this was not to be restored until the IMF gave its seal of approval. Under Gordon Brown there seems to have been no such loss of credibility despite fiscal deficits which are projected to rise to over 3 per cent of GDP, and with debt rising to

43 per cent of GDP (in excess of the limits for each of these figures under the Growth and Stability Pact of the European Union).[40]

It is interesting to compare the fiscal experience of the 1970s with Brown's golden rules for fiscal prudence. First, because of inflation, the debt/GDP ratio fell fast, from 48.8 to 40.6 per cent between 1974 and 1979. Second, the overall fiscal deficit was larger than investment spending only because capital spending fell from 4.8 to 2.6 per cent of GDP. But even this lower figure is significantly *above* public investment under New Labour, even in 2007–8, when it is projected to rise to 2.2 per cent of GDP, from the very low level of 0.9 per cent in 2001–2.[41]

In sum, while the public finances did deteriorate sharply in the early to mid-1970s, this was quickly corrected, in part because Labour accepted the Treasury analysis of the likely consequences in terms of resources for investment and exports, and later because of the loss of financial confidence. Recent work in international political economy has emphasised that financial markets usually employ rather simple judgements on financial credibility.[42] If a government combines high inflation and big fiscal deficits confidence will soon be lost; hence the crisis of 1975–6. But if inflation is under control, which it clearly is in New Labour's second term, the scale of fiscal deficit which will induce a loss of confidence is much less clear, and the scope for 'Keynesian' policies seemingly becomes substantial. To put this point slightly differently; high inflation in the 1970s forced a (temporary) reversal of Labour's priorities towards bringing inflation down. As long as the rate of price increase stays down (and the current threat in 2003–4 seems to lie more with deflation), Keynesianism, in the sense of counteracting recession with budget deficits, appears a realistic option for a government to choose. In this long-term perspective, the crisis of the 1970s appears much more conjunctural, and much less systemic than most discussions of the period allow.

Notes

1. Williams, K., Williams, J. and Thomas, D., *Why are the British Bad at Manufacturing?* (Routledge and Kegan Paul, London, 1983), pp. 18–19.
2. Ormerod, P., 'Incomes Policy', in Artis, M. and Cobham, D. (eds), *Labour's Economic Policies, 1974–79* (Manchester University Press, Manchester, 1991), p. 65. This book provides by far the best account of Labour's economic policies, albeit focused on the macro-economy.
3. Browning, P., *The Treasury and Economic Policy, 1964–1985* (Longman, London, 1986), pp. 71–2.
4. Healey, D., *The Time of My Life* (Penguin, London, 1990).
5. Thompson, N., *Political Economy and the Labour Party* (UCL Press, London, 1996), p. 234.

6. Forester, T., 'How Labour's Industrial Strategy got the Chop', *New Society*, 6 July 1978; Wickham-Jones, M., *Economic Strategy and the Labour Party: Politics and Policy-Making, 1970–1983* (Macmillan, London, 1996), ch. 6.

7. Brown, C. and Sheriff, T., *De-industrialisation in the UK: a Background Paper*, National Institute Discussion Paper 23 (National Institute for Economic and Social Research, London, 1978), pp. 27–31; Sawyer, M., 'Prices Policies', in Artis and Cobham (eds), *Labour's Economic Policies, 1974–79*, pp. 77–9; Ormerod, P., 'Incomes Policy', in ibid., pp. 168–9.

8. Commons, Hansard, 15 April 1975, col. 282; Harmon, M., *The British Labour Government and the 1976 IMF Crisis* (Macmillan, Basingstoke, 1997), p. 95.

9. Britton, A., *Macroeconomic Policy in Britain 1974–1987* (Cambridge University Press/NIESR, Cambridge, 1991), p. 25.

10. Pliatzky, L., *Getting and Spending: Public Expenditure, Employment and Inflation* (Basil Blackwell, Oxford, 1982), Table A.1.

11. Tomlinson, J., *Modernising Britain? The Economic Policies of the Labour Governments 1964–70* (Manchester University Press, Manchester, 2003).

12. Clark, T., Elsby, M. and Love, S., 'Trends in British Public Investment', *Fiscal Studies*, 23, 2003, pp. 305–42.

13. Tomlinson, *Modernising Britain? The Economic Policies of the Labour Governments 1964–70* and Tomlinson, J., *Democratic Socialism and Economic Policy: The Attlee Years 1945–51* (Cambridge University Press, Cambridge, 1997).

14. Minkin, L., *The Contentious Alliance* (Edinburgh University Press, Edinburgh, 1991), pp. 170–3.

15. *TUC Economic Review* (TUC, London, 1975), p. 58; TUC, *The Social Contract 1976/77* (TUC, London, 1976), p. 28.

16. Brown, W., 'Industrial Relations', in Artis and Cobham (eds), *Labour's Economic Policies, 1974–79*, pp. 213–28.

17. Callahan, J., Speech at Labour Party Conference, in *Labour Party: Annual Conference Report* (Labour Party, London, 1976), p. 182; Benn refers to this as a 'most patronising lecture'. *Against the Tide: Diaries 1973–76* (Arrow, London, 1989), p. 615.

18. Ludlam, S., 'The Gnomes of Washington: Four Myths of the 1976 IMF Crisis', *Political Studies*, 40, 1992, pp. 713–27.

19. Allsopp, C., 'Macroeconomic Policy: Design and Performance', in Artis and Cobham (eds), *Labour's Economic Policies 1974–79*, pp. 31–4; Burk, K. and Cairncross, A., '*Goodbye, Great Britain*': The 1976 IMF Crisis (Yale University Press, New Haven, CT, 1992).

20. Keegan, W. and Pennant-Rea, R., *Who Runs the Economy?* (Temple Smith, London, 1979), chs 4, 5.

21. Thompson, *Political Economy and the Labour Party*, chs 14–16.

22. Barnett, J., *Inside the Treasury, 1974–79* (Andre Deutsch, London, 1982), p. 103; Dell, E., *The Chancellors* (HarperCollins, London, 1996), ch.14; Healey, *Time of My Life*, p. 431.

23. Thompson, *Political Economy and the Labour Party*, p. 239.

24. Benn, T., *Against the Tide: Diaries 1973–76* (Arrow, London, 1989); Castle, B. *The Castle Diaries 1974–76* (Weidenfeld and Nicolson, London, 1980).

25. For example, *Against the Tide*, p. 593.

26. Healey, *Time of My Life*, pp. 380–1, 401–2, 433–5, 449–50.

27. Pliatzky, *Getting and Spending*, pp. 130–42.

28. Barnett, *Inside the Treasury, 1974–79*, p. 103; Browning, *The Treasury and Economic Policy, 1964–1985*, ch. 14; Young, H. and Sloman, A., *Yes Minister* (BBC Publications, London, 1982), p. 25.

29. Healey, *Time of My Life*, pp. 433–5; Pliatzky, *Getting and Spending*, pp. 156–63.

30. Allsopp, 'Macroeconomic Policy', pp. 24–8.

31. Middleton, R., *Government versus the Market* (Edward Elgar, Cheltenham, 1996), p. 465; Crafts, N., 'Economic Growth in the 1970s', in Coopey, R. and Woodward, N. (eds), *Britain in the 1970s: the Troubled Economy* (UCL Press, London, 1996), pp. 81–5.

32. Holmes, M., *The Labour Government, 1974–79* (Macmillan, London, 1985), p. 182.

33. Burk and Cairncross, 'Goodbye, Great Britain', p. 228.

34. Clark, T., *The Limits of Social Democracy? Tax and Spend under Labour, 1974–1979*, Working Papers in Economic History No. 64/01 (LSE, 2001).

35. Gardener, N., *Decade of Discontent* (Basil Blackwell, Oxford, 1987), p. 214.

36. *The Economist*, 31 March 1973; *Banker*, March 1974; *The Economist*, 17 May 1975.

37. Johnson, R., *The Politics of Recession* (Macmillan, London, 1985), pp. 131, 130.

38. Cannadine, D., 'Apocalypse When? British Politicians and British "Decline" in the Twentieth Century', in Clarke, P. and Trebilcock, C. (eds), *Understanding Decline* (Cambridge University Press, Cambridge, 1997), pp. 261–84.

39. Fforde, J., 'Setting Monetary Objectives', *Bank of England Quarterly Bulletin*, 23, 1983, pp. 200–8.

40. Barrell, R., Kirby, S., Riley, R. and Weale, M., 'The UK Economy', *National Institute Economic Review*, 184, April 2003, pp. 40–1.

41. Allsopp, 'Macroeconomic Policy', p. 26; Jackson, P., 'Public Expenditure', in Artis and Cobham (eds), *Labour's Economic Policies, 1974–79*, p. 79; Barrell *et.al.*, 'The UK Economy', p. 40.

42. Mosley, L., 'Room to Move: International Financial Markets and National Welfare States', *International Organization*, 54, 2000, pp. 737–73.

Reading 4.4

Globalization and the National State

Anthony H. Birch

G LOBALIZATION IS A RATHER NEW CONCEPT in political discourse and in the social sciences. Malcolm Waters reports that the first sociological article to include the word in its title was published in 1985 and that by February 1994 'the catalogue of the Library of Congress contained only 34 items with that term or one of its derivatives in the title', none of them published before 1987 (Waters 1995: 2). In the late 1990s the term became fashionable, however, and by the turn of the millennium it had appeared in scores of books and hundreds of articles. There is no point in trying to itemize or categorize these very numerous references, because the concept is not in itself contentious. It is simply an omnibus term used loosely as a shorthand label for any or all or, most commonly, some combination of five rather different trends in world affairs that can easily be enumerated.

One such trend is a growing concern and international action about environmental problems of global significance, including threats to rare species, global warming and the dangers of nuclear fallout. Another is the growth of a world market as the consequence of lower transport costs and the widespread reduction of customs duties, coupled with the creation of the World Trade Organization to protect trade agreements and to reduce non-tariff barriers to trade. A third is the establishment of international courts to protect human rights, either in specific regions or more widely. A fourth is a new view that liberal governments, or coalitions thereof, should have the right, and perhaps the duty, to intervene in the internal affairs of other states if the latter are guilty of gross suppression of human rights within their territories. A fifth is the very rapid growth of worldwide means of communication, leading to the possibility of the globalization of culture.

In considering the impact of these developments on the theory and practice of modern democracy, [...] it is vital to distinguish speculation from fact. As the chief arena for the exercise of democratic politics is the government of the national state, the following brief review will focus on the extent to which these globalizing developments have actually diminished the authority and powers of national states and the effect of the changes on the character and extent of democracy.

Environmental Issues

Growing concern about environmental issues in the last decades of the twentieth century led to a number of international conferences and agreements, but the impact of these on the status and powers of national states has been varied. Conference agreements depend very largely on the decisions of national governments for their implementation. A concerted effort to limit the impact of national rivalries on the extraction of minerals from the seabed led to elaborate recommendations being hammered out at the Law of the Sea Conference in the 1980s, but several powerful states, including the United States and Britain, simply refused to be bound by all of the recommendations made. The bio-diversity treaty signed in Rio in 1992 was an ambitious attempt to protect rare plants and species, but when the United States refused to sign there was nothing that other governments could do. The signatories to the Montreal Protocol of 1988 promised that between 1989 and 2000 they would halve the emission of chemicals dangerous to the ozone layer, but progress in this field depended entirely on the actions of individual state governments, most of which failed to meet the targets. The Kyoto Convention of 1997 contains enforceable provisions but it was not until 2005 that it was ratified by a sufficient number of states to activate it and it is not yet clear how effective these provisions will be. The international agreement on the non-proliferation of nuclear weapons, hailed as a very significant achievement by western politicians and mass media in 1997, did not stop India and Pakistan from conducting test explosions of nuclear bombs in 1998. However, this is not to deny that there is a move towards international action on environmental matters, because clearly there is, and clearly it is important. The point is simply that this move has not yet undermined the authority of national states.

A Global Economy

On this topic, again, there are facts, speculations and controversies. It is true that since 1950 international trade has expanded much more quickly than world production (*Economist*, 27 November 1999: 21); that more than half of this trade is accounted for by the actions of multinational corporations (see Gray 1998: 62); that electronic means of communication enable billions of private dollars to be transferred between countries every day in foreign exchange speculations; and that, with one or two exceptions like Cuba and North Korea, the whole world has moved or is moving towards a market economy. It is also a fact that supranational institutions like the European Union (EU) and worldwide institutions like the World Trade Organization (WTO) now protect trading agreements and make it difficult for individual countries regulated by them to erect trade barriers unilaterally.

On this basis of fact it has been said that economic globalization has eroded the independence of national states. As John Gray has pointed out, some writers have been very emphatic about this. Keniehe Ohmae, for instance, has asserted that 'in a borderless economy, the nation-focussed maps we typically use to make sense of economic activity are woefully misleading' (Ohmae 1995: 19–21). Susan Strange has said that 'the authority of the governments of all states ... has been weakened ... by the single global market economy' (Strange 1996: 13–14). Manuel Castells has declared that 'bypassed by global networks of wealth, power and information, the modern nation-state has lost much of its authority' (Castells 1997: 354). This kind of assertion (and there are numerous other examples) can only be analysed by breaking down the generalizations on which it is based.

One claim that has questionable foundations is that the growth of large transnational corporations has undermined the authority of national governments. This is questionable because it has always been true that governments have had to consider the possible impact of their taxation policies and labour laws on the behaviour of international investors. There is nothing new about this. Another questionable claim is that the vast daily movements of capital by electronic means have destroyed the ability of governments to control their exchange rates. British experience between 1945 and 1979 showed rather clearly that political attempts to protect the international value of their currency, for some time by 'fixed' exchange rates under the Bretton Woods Agreement and always by tight exchange controls, could only postpone the devaluation of sterling by a year or two, not prevent it, if international trading balances made devaluation appropriate.

Bilateral treaties on customs duties necessarily limit the freedom of national governments to change the duties unilaterally so long as the treaties are respected, but this has always been true and in any case history is replete with examples of treaties being revoked or broken. The only significant new developments are, first, the role of the International Monetary Fund (IMF) and World Bank, second, the growth of the European Union, and third, the role of the WTO.

The IMF and World Bank make very large loans to developing countries, together with occasional short-term loans to industrialized countries experiencing temporary financial difficulties, such as Britain in 1976–7 and South Korea in 1998–9. The money comes mainly from the United States and other western countries and the loans are accompanied by conditions about economic policy that reflect the beliefs and policies of these countries. The loans that have been made to Russia since 1990, for instance, have been conditional upon that country moving towards a market economy. In that kind of way, the IMF and the World Bank have reduced the independence of the recipient governments, but this is simply the price of getting the loans.

The European Community (EC, the economic arm of the EU) is an unprecedented move towards the economic integration of the member states. By joining it, these states have surrendered their powers to negotiate and control their own tariffs and have increasingly lost control over agricultural policies, fisheries, open or concealed subsidies to industry, and various aspects of labour law, in the interests of creating a 'level playing field' for internal competition. The EC has been immensely successful in its two main original aims of increasing prosperity through the creation of a large tariff-free market and increasing agricultural production through modernization. On the political level, it has made a major war between member states unthinkable and, since its enlargement into the European Union under the Maastricht Treaty of 1992, has taken steps towards the development of common policies on immigration, refugees and policing.

These developments add up to a significant surrender of national independence by the member states. However, moves towards greater integration are hampered by the fact that the EC and EU are elitist rather than democratic organizations and have failed to gain majority support among their citizens. Numerous surveys have shown that national loyalties remain much stronger than any sense of European identity (see Birch 1998: 223) and the *Economist*, a generally pro-European journal, concluded in 1997 that 'the EU's deepest problem of all is the disenchantment of its citizens' (*Economist*, 31 May 1997).

The WTO is different again. It is a young institution, having come into existence in January 1995 with the objective of enforcing the decisions made by trading nations subscribing to the General Agreement on Tariffs and Trade (GATT), that had grown in coverage and membership in successive instalments since its inception in 1948. Its enforcement procedure provides for any of its 135 member states to launch a complaint against another member state for alleged violation of an agreed rule, and for a panel of three officials to hear arguments from both sides and reach a decision that, subject to appeal to another panel of three officials, is then legally binding on the states concerned. If the state that loses the argument declines to comply with the ruling, the other state may impose tariffs on imports from the loser equivalent in total value of lost trade to the estimated loss to the winning state resulting from the continuance of the banned practices. This amounts to a loss of national independence, though the fact that the losing state cannot be forced to comply, but only forced to expose its exporting firms to financial loss, somewhat reduces the direct impact of the punishment.

WTO procedures cannot by their nature be subject to direct democratic controls, but they have offended democrats who believe in open decisions, openly arrived at, by the secrecy in which the decision-making panels work. In this respect the WTO compares very poorly with the United Nations. The UN Security Council and General Assembly are not exactly democratic bodies either, but debates in both bodies are conducted in the full light of publicity so that citizens the world over can observe what their national representatives are saying and make informed judgements on their behaviour. In contrast, the WTO panels operate behind closed doors and produce only brief justifications of their decisions.

In the first five years of its existence, the WTO produced a number of decisions that have been very controversial and have increased the scope of its authority in ways that were not generally anticipated. Because its responsibilities extend only to trade, it has not felt able to take account of widely held values other than free trade, such as the protection of the environment, the protection of threatened species, or the protection of public health by food safety regulation. Many measures adopted by governments to protect these other values can be shown to have an adverse effect on some trading interest or another, and each time a trading nation has appealed to the WTO on this basis the decision has favoured the appellant. For example, when four Asian states challenged provisions of the US Endangered Species Act that forbade the sale in the United States of shrimp caught in ways that kill sea turtles, the WTO required the United States to amend its statute. Conversely, when the United States attempted to reduce air pollution by requiring oil refineries to produce clean gasoline if it was to be sold in the American market, Venezuela successfully appealed to the WTO on the ground that this rule discriminated against Venezuelan refineries.

When the US administration appealed against an EC ban on the import of beef from hormone-injected cattle, the WTO upheld the appeal on the ground that the Europeans had no scientific proof that the beef would endanger human health. This infuriated the Europeans, well aware that no scientists had predicted that the improved feeding stuff fed to British cattle in the 1980s might produce the epidemic of 'mad cow disease' (bovine spongiform encephalitis: BSE) that has led to many human deaths so the European Community refused to comply with the ruling. As a result, the United States imposed crippling (100 per cent) tariffs on a range of European products.

These and several other decisions mean that the WTO has acquired, or (as some would say) arrogated to itself, the power to deny national governments the right to make their own laws and regulations to protect their citizens. It is the first, and so far the only, worldwide organization to have this kind of power, which necessarily involves a reduction in the extent of democracy. Controversy over this has been heightened by allegations that the power has been used to protect the profits of large corporations at the expense of what most liberals would regard as the public interest. In addition to the rejection of arrangements and laws designed to protect the environment or public health, the WTO decided in 1999 that the agreement whereby the EU gave a protected market for bananas to farmers in former European colonies in the Caribbean was contrary to its rules, following an appeal by the United States that this discriminated against a slightly different type of banana produced in parts of central America by a US company using industrialized farming methods. As this would probably throw tens of thousands of small farmers in the Caribbean into bankruptcy and devastate the economies of several small island nations, the decision further upset Europeans, who did not fail to note that the US administration acted not to help US farmers (who do not grow bananas) but simply to enhance the profits of a large American transnational corporation operating in foreign countries. In consequence of these developments, there was widespread concern that the world conference held in Seattle in December 1999 to launch a new round of trade negotiations might result in a process that enlarged still further the scope of WTO authority.

Happily for nationalists and democrats, this conference turned out to be a complete fiasco. The various heads of government invited to dignify the conference by their presence all declined the invitation. The steering committee that met in Geneva failed to agree on an agenda. The leader of the US delegation upset some of the other delegations by insisting on chairing the conference herself. And when the delegates arrived in Seattle they found the streets blocked by about 100,000 demonstrators carrying placards denouncing the WTO.

On the first day the delegates were unable to get to the conference hall. On the second the Mayor of Seattle declared a state of emergency that authorized the police to get tough. On the third day, with several hundred demonstrators behind bars (and denied legal representation) the conference finally got down to business. On the fourth it came to an end without reaching agreement on anything at all, even a final communiqué.

So ended the attempt to launch a millennium round of trade negotiations. The hope of critics that the fiasco might lead to a reform of the WTO in one way or another has not been realized, but more and more states have been admitted to membership. The organization now has 149 members, of which well over half are developing societies. In November 2001 a meeting at Doha (Qatar) launched a new round of conferences with the specific aim of helping poor countries by reducing barriers to their export of agricultural products and textiles. However, in September 2003 a much heralded world conference in Cancun (Mexico) resulted in complete failure. The European Union refused to make major changes to its agricultural policies; the United States refused to reduce its subsidies to the cotton industry; Japan refused to reduce its help to rice farmers. On the other side, many poor countries saw the pro-poor slogans of the Doha round 'as an excuse for making demands of the rich world while doing nothing to lower their own trade barriers' (*Economist*, 20 September 2003). They refused even to reduce barriers to trade with each other, which according to the World Bank would have brought them great economic benefits. The conference ended acrimoniously.

A slightly more positive world conference was held in Hong Kong in December 2005. It was agreed to eliminate export subsidies on agricultural exports by the end of 2013; the United States agreed to reduce help to its cotton industry; and there was general agreement that the rich countries should give a large package of aid and trading concessions to the thirty-two countries deemed to be 'least developed'. However, all this added up to only a small step towards world free trade.

In July 2006 another meeting of the world's trade ministers was held in Geneva, for 'what was billed as a final attempt to salvage the Doha round of global trade talks'. The failure of this meeting led *The Economist* to predict that bilateral and regional trade deals (of which there are more than 250) may 'replace multilateralism as the organizing principle of world trade' and that the WTO 'may eventually lose its legitimacy as an arbiter of trade disputes' (*Economist*, 8 July 2006).

Human Rights and International Justice

Another relevant development is the move to establish international tribunals and courts with the power to prosecute individuals for offences against human rights, even if these offences were committed within their own countries and did not violate national laws. The first example of this was the 1945 decision of the victorious powers in the Second World War to establish International Military Tribunals in Nuremburg and Tokyo to hear allegations of 'crimes against humanity' committed by German and Japanese leaders and soldiers during the war. This was an unprecedented and controversial action, because the crimes for which people were prosecuted were not known to either national laws or international law at the time that the events took place. In effect, the victorious powers were acting as legislators, prosecutors and judges in a process that contravened most liberal assumptions about the nature of justice, but was nevertheless widely accepted by liberals because the behaviour in question had been so horrific. These tribunals did not affect the authority of national governments because at the time Germany and Japan, having surrendered unconditionally, were occupied territories with no governments of their own.

In 1948 the proclamation of the Universal Declaration of Human Rights by the General Assembly of the United Nations set out some general principles that could be used as standards of reference in future cases, though it was over-ambitious in scope and for this reason was not suitable for adoption as a legal code. The provisions of the Declaration will be examined in Chapter 10; at this point it is sufficient to note that its adoption (by 48 votes to nil, with 8 abstentions) did not make it binding on national governments and that it was not accompanied by any provisions for its enforcement.

The Declaration was followed in 1950 by the publication of a shorter and more modest document entitled the European Convention for the Protection of Human Rights and Fundamental Freedoms. This was produced by the Council of Europe, a rather odd body established in 1949 by agreement of ten western European governments, of which seven had been Allies; Ireland and Sweden had been neutral; and Italy had been on both sides in the war. The Council had vague aims and was denied any real powers because some of its founding members, notably Britain, were reluctant to hand over any of their sovereign authority to it. This reluctance was justified by Ernest Bevin, the British Foreign Secretary, in the memorable phrase: 'Once you open that Pandora's Box, you'll find it full of Trojan Horses' (quoted in Nugent 1991: 16). However, in 1959 the Council, now swollen to fifteen members, created the European Court of Human Rights to adjudicate complaints brought before it by citizens, including complaints about the behaviour of their own national governments. This was a highly significant step, being the first occasion on which national governments voluntarily surrendered part of their sovereignty to an international court of justice. European states have signed on to this court's jurisdiction one by one over the years, with seven having done so by 1984 and twenty-eight by 1994. As the Court has no direct powers to implement its decisions, it can be (and has been) argued that the reduction in sovereignty is limited. The strength of this argument can be judged in the light of three examples from the 1980s involving the United Kingdom.

A 1985 decision of the Court that British immigration laws discriminated against women in one respect resulted in an immediate change in British law to comply with the judgement. Another decision held that the human rights of parents had been violated when their son was caned in school without their permission. This led to protracted debate, but in the end the British Parliament banned all forms of corporal punishment in state schools. In 1989 the Court decided that the British Prevention of Terrorism Act violated human rights because it permitted the police to detain suspected terrorists for up to four days before bringing them before a court, as against twenty-four hours for people suspected of other crimes. However, this judgement was declared to be unreasonable by the British government on the ground that it took insufficient account of the threat to British lives posed by the murderous activities of the Irish Republican Army, and no change was made to British law.

Overall, the European Convention and European Court must clearly be counted as successful and important. Most states that subscribe to it have added some or all of the articles of the Convention to their own constitutions, so that they can be implemented by national courts with the European Court needed only to hear appeals, and in 1999 Britain (which has no written constitution) followed this example by adding several of the Convention's provisions to its own laws. An immediate result of this was a decision by a Scottish court that the practice whereby some Scottish magistrates (known confusingly as sheriffs) were appointed for only annual terms of office did not give them sufficient independence of the executive to be acceptable under these new rules. As British judicial procedures are out of step with those of most other western European countries, they may face further legal challenges.

In 1993 and 1995, the UN Security Council established two new military tribunals on the lines of the Nuremburg and Tokyo tribunals, one to try persons accused of war crimes in the conflicts following the break-up of Yugoslavia, the other to try persons accused of genocide in Rwanda. By the spring of 2000 a little over twenty suspects had been arrested by NATO troops in Bosnia and tried by the new tribunal in The Hague. This seems like a form of globalization, but as Bosnia had never had an effective national government it is not clear whether these actions represent an infringement of national sovereignty. In 1999, during the conflict in Kosovo (to be discussed below), the tribunal named several suspects to be arrested for crimes against humanity, including President Milosevic of Yugoslavia. As Kosovo, unlike Bosnia, was still a province within Yugoslavia, such action was clearly a violation of Yugoslav sovereignty. In the event, NATO military action led to the de facto separation of Kosovo from what remained of Yugoslavia; there followed a domestic revolution in Belgrade; and the new regime eventually yielded to EU and American pressure by handing Slobodan Milosevic over for trial. The trial itself was hardly a success, as Milosevic proved to be at least as good at defending himself as the prosecutors were at establishing his guilt, many of the charges had to be dismissed, and after nearly two years he died of natural causes in March 2006 while the trial was nowhere near conclusion.

The situation in Rwanda is very different, as in 1994 between 500,000 and 800,000 members of the Tutsi minority were slaughtered by the Hutu majority, in the world's first case of genocide since the Holocaust. The Tutsis were victorious in the subsequent civil war and a vast number of Hutus were arrested. However, it has proved impossible for either the international tribunal or the Rwandan courts to try more than a small proportion of them. The international tribunal, set up in 1995, had to be restructured in 1997 after a UN inspection revealed gross mismanagement and financial irregularities, and by August 1999 it had still secured only seven convictions. The Rwandan courts have done better, but by 2005 about 120,000 suspects were still in makeshift prison camps awaiting trial.

A development of very much greater potential importance took place in 1998, namely the decision by a large international conference in Rome to recommend the establishment of a world court of justice to be entitled the International Criminal Court, with power to exercise jurisdiction over infringements of human rights anywhere in the world if these were not being prosecuted by national courts. The recommendation was approved by a majority of 120 votes to 7, but did not come into force until 2005 because it required ratification by at least sixty national parliaments.

Soon after this conference, in October 1998, an astonishing attempt was made to jump the gun on this process when a Spanish high court judge applied to British authorities to extradite General Pinochet, the former president of Chile, to stand trial in Spain for crimes against humanity that he had ordered his police and troops to commit in Chile. This application threw the British judicial authorities into confusion. A London magistrate found the extradition papers to be in order, but when this was appealed against the Lord Chief Justice allowed the appeal on the dual grounds that the Spanish courts had no jurisdiction over crimes committed in Chile by a Chilean citizen and that, in any case, a retired head of state travelling on a diplomatic passport was exempt from extradition.

When an appeal against this decision went to Britain's highest court, the House of Lords, the case had to be heard twice because the deciding vote at the first hearing was cast by a Law Lord who should have disqualified himself from the case on grounds of a conflict of interest. The second hearing eventually produced seven somewhat varied judgments, with a majority of six to one deciding that extradition was possible. On the general question of whether a retired head of state could be prosecuted internationally, the majority reached a slightly ambivalent conclusion. They upheld the traditional principle of international law that a state itself, its government and its serving head of state are absolutely immune from international prosecutions, but they yielded to the moral demand for legal action against breaches of human rights by removing this immunity from retired heads of state in respect of actions they had authorized while in office. On the particular question of whether British courts could authorize the extradition of Pinochet, they concluded that only two of the thirty-five charges were relevant, these being allegations of torture in two incidents in the final months of his presidency, after Britain had ratified the 1984 UN Convention against Torture on 8 December 1988.

In all the circumstances, the seven Law Lords 'made a strong plea to the Home Secretary to reconsider the exercise of his discretion in allowing extradition proceedings to continue' (Fox 1999: 690). However, the Home Secretary rejected this plea, the case went back to three further court hearings, and Pinochet was kept under arrest until March 2000, when he was freed because a panel of medical experts reported that the 84-year-old man was mentally unfit to stand trial.

This case can be considered both in itself and in terms of its wider implications about international justice. In itself, it is a prime example of what games theorists call a negative-sum game. Relations between Chile and Britain were damaged; the Spanish government was embarrassed; the reputation of the English judicial system was tarnished; British taxpayers had to pay the substantial costs involved; and nobody benefited directly apart from the British lawyers who made a small fortune by arguing on both sides of the case.

In terms of wider issues, the case has established a precedent for international action to enforce the Convention against Torture. After the Law Lords had made their final decision, spokespersons for the Swiss, French and Belgian governments all indicated that Pinochet could be tried in their own courts for authorizing torture. However, in terms of procedure the Pinochet precedent is entirely unhelpful. If it were followed, then any of several thousand high court judges in 192 states would be entitled to apply for the extradition of some suspected citizen of the other 191 states from any of the remaining 190 that the suspect happened to be visiting. This would be so chaotic and absurd that national courts may be expected to use the establishment of the ICC as a reason for rejecting any such application.

The ICC now has an official prosecutor, a Canadian lawyer appointed by the UN, and early in 2006 it issued its first indictments. These are of five leaders of a particularly brutal gang called the Lord's Resistance Army, operating in the extreme north of Uganda. There is little doubt of their guilt, but considerable doubt about whether the Ugandan authorities will be able to arrest them and some doubt about whether they would hand them over to the ICC if they do. The UN Security Council has given the prosecutor the names of 51 Sudanese whom it suspects of rape and murder in the Darfur region, but this has not been followed up. The creation of the ICC is clearly a move towards the globalization of justice, but it remains to be seen how effective it will be.

Transnational Military Incursions and the Case of Kosovo

It is generally accepted that the principles of the modern state system of international relations date from the 1648 Treaty of Westphalia. This ended the Thirty Years War, the worst and last of the religious and dynastic conflicts that had ravaged much of Europe. The main principle established was that each national state should be regarded as legally independent and equal in status, with no right to interfere in the internal affairs of another state. It has been reasonably claimed that this principle gave order to the international system and has prevented the occurrence of numerous wars that might otherwise have been fought.

It is possible to argue that the increased number of transnational incursions made in violation of this principle since 1970 is an example of the move towards globalization. In 1971, for instance, the Indian army crossed the border to help East Bengal (now Bangladesh) to secure independence from Pakistan. In 1978 Vietnam sent troops into Cambodia to get rid of the murderous Khmer Rouge regime. In 1979 Tanzania sent troops into Uganda to depose the tyrannical Idi Amin and force him into exile. In 1983 the Americans invaded Grenada, claiming that its left-wing regime threatened naval security, and in 1989 they invaded Panama, said to be acting as a pipeline for drugs destined for American cities. However, these five incursions had certain similarities that prevented them from having a lasting impact on international opinion or the world order. They were all sudden incursions by one state into the territory of an immediate neighbour; they were all justified (more or less plausibly) as being in the national interest of the invading state; they were all quickly successful; and they achieved their objectives without great loss of life or material damage.

The 1999 war over Kosovo was very different. The territory involved is a landlocked province of no strategic or economic importance, very distant from the United States, which was the chief organizer of the campaign. The conflict was justified by the aggressors not in terms of national interests but in terms of humanitarian objectives; it was embarked upon not suddenly but only after a period of negotiations and threats; it was expensive in terms of lives and material damage; and it was said by some to usher in a new period of world history, in which national sovereignty would be no protection for governments that grossly violated the human rights of their citizens. It is therefore appropriate to outline the history and character of the conflict.

Kosovo is a territory with a tortured history. It was conquered by the Turks in the fourteenth century and remained part of the Ottoman Empire until the second half of the nineteenth century. Its rulers converted the majority of its citizens to the Muslim faith, but the territory nevertheless remained of great historical and symbolic importance to its Christian neighbours in Serbia, partly because Kosovo had been the 'cradle of the medieval Serbian monarchy' (Hagen 1999: 58), partly because it had been the scene of a great historic battle between the Serbs and the Turks, partly because it contains the religious centre and main cathedral of the Serbian branch of the Christian Orthodox Church. In 1912 the Serbs conquered Kosovo, massacred many of its Muslim citizens, and incorporated the territory into Serbia. It remained as a province of Serbia (and therefore part of Yugoslavia when that state was created) until 1941, when the Germans invaded Yugoslavia and Kosovo was transferred to Albania, then an Italian colony. When Mussolini fell in 1943 the German army marched into Albania and Kosovo and 'raised an SS division among the Kosovar Muslims' which carried out murderous attacks on anti-Nazi Serbian groups (Hagen 1999: 60). It follows from this all-too-brief outline that Kosovo has for much of its history been the scene of bitter ethnic and religious conflict and that there has never been a Kosovar nation.

Ethnic conflict was largely suppressed from 1948 to 1968 under Tito's government, but in 1968 violent demonstrations by Albanian-speaking and largely Muslim groups persuaded Tito to grant the province a measure of political and cultural autonomy. This continued until 1989, when Tito's successor, Slobodan Milosevic, centralized power in Belgrade and filled most administrative positions in Kosovo with members of its ethnic Serb minority. This led in turn to demands from the Albanian-speaking majority for Kosovar independence, at first peaceful but later, by 1997, led by an armed resistance movement called the Kosovo Liberation Army (KLA). The KLA, easily acquiring arms from neighbouring Albania, waged a violent campaign to end Serbian control of Kosovo much as the IRA was fighting to end British control of Northern Ireland and the ETA (the militant wing of the Basque independence movement) was fighting to end Spanish control of the Basque region in northern Spain. The KLA was therefore classified by the CIA as a terrorist movement.

By the summer of 1998 the Yugoslav army was deployed in Kosovo to suppress the KLA and the US administration was warning the Yugoslav government to use less brutal ways of doing this. The warnings had no effect and in the coming months the Americans were joined by British and French governments in expressing growing concern about attacks on Kosovar civilians and the destruction of their homes. NATO was involved as an organization and in early February 1999 a conference convened in Rambouillet (France) gave Milosevic an ultimatum (with an early deadline) to the effect that he must withdraw his army from Kosovo or face NATO military intervention. The deadline was ignored, as were subsequent deadlines, so that the NATO leaders painted themselves into a corner, leaving themselves no choice but to carry out their threats or make NATO a laughingstock. In late March the bombardment started, the product of western miscalculations and a clear breach of international law.

Now, many governments have employed 'gunboat diplomacy', being a small threat of violence (by naval or other forces) made to secure a modest concession. James Cable's careful analysis of 211 examples of this tactic between 1919 and 1979 showed that it can be successful if, but only if, the small threat is backed up by a larger threat (Cable 1981). A gunboat in an estuary is likely to secure the wanted concession only if the threatened government knows that a larger fleet of warships offshore will enforce much more painful concessions if the first threat is defied. In the case of Kosovo the larger threat could only be that of a land invasion, but Madeline Albright (US Secretary of State) promptly removed that by declaring that US troops would in no circumstances be used in a land war. This blunder ensured that the bombardment would have to be prolonged if it were to succeed. It also emboldened the Yugoslav army to do exactly what NATO leaders had hoped to prevent, namely to engage in a campaign of 'ethnic cleansing' that forced most ethnic Albanians to take refuge in the mountains or over the border into Macedonia or Albania. It is estimated that about 500,000 took to the mountains and 800,000 went over the border.

The concept of ethnic cleansing requires a word of explanation. It is a campaign by the ethnic majority in a given territory to drive the members of an ethnic minority from their homes and land in order to secure something approaching ethnic homogeneity in the territory. It is quite different from genocide, which is a campaign of mass murder undertaken to eliminate a minority, whether to 'purify the race', as the Nazis tried to justify the massacre of 6 million Jews and Gypsies, or to ensure tribal domination, which was the Hutu motive in murdering over half a million Tutsis in Rwanda. At one stage President Clinton attempted to justify the bombardment of Yugoslavia under international law by declaring that the Yugoslavs were guilty of genocide in Kosovo, with 100,000 ethnic Albanians already buried in mass graves, but this statement revealed conceptual misunderstanding as well as being statistically inaccurate. When UN inspectors examined the graves it was found that they contained only a handful of bodies, and by the end of 1999 it was clear that the total number of deaths in Kosovo was under 10,000, some of them caused by the KLA or NATO. This is horrific enough, but it is nothing like genocide.

A feature of the bombardment was that, to avoid the possibility of NATO casualties, the bombers flew above the level of anti-aircraft missiles, namely above 15,000 feet, from which height it was impossible for them to hit small moving targets such as Yugoslav armoured vehicles. Inevitably, many civilians were killed. As attacks on Kosovo were not helping the people they were intended to help, the bombardment increasingly concentrated on Belgrade and other Serbian cities, causing great damage. After eleven weeks concern over industrial damage, combined with diplomatic pressure from Moscow, persuaded Milosevic to accept a compromise peace whereby he agreed to withdraw the Yugoslav army from Kosovo and to offer no opposition to its replacement by NATO troops, but there was no agreement about the political future of the province. *The Economist* greeted this with the headline 'Messy war, messy peace' and concluded that the whole Kosovo campaign had 'turned into a disaster' (*Economist*, 12 June 1999: 15–16).

When NATO troops took control of Kosovo, they soon faced several problems. One was their inability to prevent some of the returning Kosovar Albanians from wreaking revenge on the Serbian minority in the province (about 10 per cent of the population) by murder and their own form of ethnic cleansing. By January 2000 three-quarters of the Kosovar Serbs had fled out of the province to escape these reprisals. Another problem was the absence of an effective civilian administrative apparatus, as most of the senior police, judges and civil servants had been Serbs. A third was a shortage of financial help to rebuild the province, and in December 1999 the new NATO Secretary-General, Lord Robertson, said that without substantial aid the allies look like 'losing the peace'.

Beyond all these problems there was a basic contradiction in NATO policy that has been well articulated by Michael Mandelbaum. As he points out, the refusal of the western allies to support independence for Kosovo means, in effect, that the alliance had 'intervened in a civil war and defeated one side, but embraced the position of the party it had defeated on the issue over which the war had been fought. This made the war, as a deliberate act of policy, a perfect failure' (Mandelbaum 1999: 5).

If the Kosovo affair was in itself misconceived and bungled, is it likely, nevertheless, to be the first of a series of forceful transnational actions by some states to protect the human rights of minorities in other states? The questions that this possibility raises have been addressed in a short but considered article by Kofi Annan. He declared that the conflict in Kosovo

> has cast in stark relief the dilemma of so-called 'humanitarian intervention'. On the one hand, is it legitimate for a regional organization to use force without a UN mandate? On the other, is it permissible to let gross and systematic violations of human rights ... continue unchecked? The inability of the international community to reconcile these two compelling interests in the case of Kosovo can be viewed only as a tragedy.
>
> (*Economist*, 18 September 1999: 49)

Considering prospects for the twenty-first century, Annan gave a cautious welcome to the use of international force to prevent humanitarian disasters, but only on condition that such measures should be universal in their application, should receive the approval of the

UN Security Council and should be accompanied by a commitment to preserve peace in the affected region after the end of fighting. He noted that national attitudes towards the definition of national interests would have to change if these conditions were to be met, but did not venture any prediction about when or whether such a remarkable change might come about (*Economist*, 18 September 1999: 50).

Since then, in September 2005, the UN has agreed in principle that state governments have 'a duty to protect' their citizens, and that a clear failure to carry out that duty may justify international intervention. There is one case that qualifies under this new provision, namely the gross violation of human rights in the western Sudanese region of Darfur. This has led to the displacement of over 3 million people from their homes to live in desperate conditions in tented refugee camps, to deaths estimated to be over 300,000, and to the flight of tens of thousands of refugees over the border into Chad. The African Union has sent about 7,000 peacekeeping troops to the region, but they are insufficient in number and lack the money, transport facilities and supplies to make much difference to the situation. Kofi Annan has called for a UN peacekeeping force of 14,000 or more to go to Darfur, but the Sudanese government has refused entry to a UN military assessment mission and there is little that the UN can do in face of opposition from the legal government of the area.

Global Communications and Culture

It is obvious that since the 1950s there has been a vast increase in the volume of international communications, by radio, satellite television, cheap air travel, telephone calls made inexpensive by fibre-optic cables, mobile phones, email and the Internet. There are questions about how far this development has produced a global culture and how far it has changed the conduct of politics.

One important unifying development has been a reduction in the number of languages commonly used and, beyond that, the increased spread of knowledge of English. Linguistic concentration has been a long-term process resulting from industrialization and mass migrations, and it has been greatly hastened by modern communications. Jean Laponce estimated in 1987 that only 69 of the 2,000 or so languages thought to exist were spoken by more than 4 million people (Laponce 1987: 67–8) and that many of the others were spoken by only a handful. For instance, only 3 of the 53 Indian languages listed for Canada were actually spoken by more than 5,000 people (Laponce 1987: 58), and a similar situation exists in Australia. Moreover, in many ex-colonial territories English or French is still the dominant language among political and social elites: in India and Pakistan, for instance, which have local languages spoken by many millions, English remains the dominant language at cabinet meetings and in the civil service (see Laponce 1987: 204–7). In addition to these long-term developments, the exploding use of satellite television and the Internet has further spread an understanding of English. The market for international news services carried by satellite television is dominated by CNN, Sky News and the BBC, all of them broadcasting entirely or mainly in English, while the multilingual Euronews has a much smaller audience (see Waters 1995: 149–50).

The answer to the question of whether these developments in communication and language have contributed to the emergence of a global culture depends on the perspective and timescale of the observer. Given a western perspective and a short timescale, say of the past century, these positive factors may be supplemented by a marked reduction in differences of lifestyle caused by recent economic developments. In the poorer agricultural areas of the world, the move from subsistence farming to cash crops has drawn millions into the market economy, their welfare depending somewhat upon commodity trading in London, New York and Tokyo. In newly industrializing areas the growth of branch plants of large American, Japanese and European firms has led to the development of mass production techniques in textiles and electronic goods. In developed industrial societies, rising standards of living have led to some homogenization of consumer demands and fashions. All of these developments have been said to be indications of a globalization of culture on western, and particularly American, lines.

If we turn from economics to values and beliefs, however, the picture is rather different. In the first place, the capacity of the United States to lead the world in social values has been somewhat undermined by an increasing clash of attitudes in American intellectual circles. In the 1940s, 1950s and 1960s a great many American universities offered survey courses to undergraduates on Western Civilization, which were unifying in their message. However, in the 1970s and since, these courses were challenged as Eurocentric, male-dominated and even racist in character, so that they have increasingly been replaced by courses in Black Studies and Women's Studies.

Post-modern theorists have challenged the whole idea that literary critics can identify the great works of western literature and provide criteria by which new writing can be assessed. This kind of intellectual scepticism has even spread to discussions of science and technology. J. W. Grove has said that 'postmodern scholars now feel secure enough to patronize scientists for their absurd belief in objectivity, truth and other holdovers from the Enlightenment' (Grove 1999: 384). Radical feminists have argued that science is the product of a male-dominated society. The American philosopher Sandra Harding, for example, has described modern science as 'Eurocentric, androcentric, racist and imperialist and inadequately linked to projects for advancing democracy' (quoted in Grove 1999: 387).

Another development that undermines the case for the existence of a global culture is the growth of religious sects and extremist groups since the early 1990s. Strange sects in North

America and East Africa have gone in for mass suicides and mass murder. A sect in Japan has released poison gas in the Tokyo subway system. Australian and other Christian missionaries in India have been harassed and threatened by Hindu extremists. The growth of Ultra-Orthodox Jewish groups in Israel has led to rising political tension between them and the liberal majority. Riots between Muslim extremists and Christians in parts of Indonesia killed thousands of people in the winter of 1999/2000 and caused the destruction of many churches and mosques. [...]

A third, and politically most important factor, is the growth of Islamic fundamentalism and the emergence of a new kind of terrorism that derives part of its motivation from this. Terrorism of all kinds has become so much the focus of world news and attention since 2001 that an entirely new chapter on the subject has been added to this edition. One of the intellectual consequences of this development is that it forces us to consider the whole question of cultural beliefs and assumptions from a global rather than a western perspective and with a timescale that encompasses a millennium rather than merely a century.

If we do this it immediately becomes obvious that the people of this planet have long been divided between four major cultures or civilizations plus others that are either less clearly defined or of less worldwide importance. The four major cultures or civilizations are the Chinese, the Indian, the Islamic and the European. The others include the Buddhist and the Japanese.

The Buddhist faith is quite distinctive and was once widespread in eastern Asia, but has declined in relative influence except in Thailand, Cambodia and Sri Lanka. Japanese culture was subject to both Chinese and Buddhist influences but has long been distinctive, though its history has been rather a mystery to the outside world until quite recently and the culture has not spread beyond the islands of Japan. The cultures of tropical Africa, though permeated by Islam in the north and by European influences in former colonies, are in themselves difficult about which to generalize or to classify. There are of course questions about the identity of the four major civilizations. Should the first be called Chinese or Confucian, to include the societies of Vietnam, Singapore and Korea and people of Chinese ethnic origin in other states? A fair case can be made for either alternative, but I prefer the former because the differing political and economic systems of the various countries have made a difference to the values and behaviour of their ethnic Chinese communities. Some aspects remain fairly constant, such as the importance of the extended family and the acceptance of a familial duty to support elderly relatives. But any migrant or visiting western business executive will find customs among the Chinese of Singapore much less of a cultural shock than customs in mainland China. Western executives doing business in China may find it particularly difficult to adjust to the customs of exchanging gifts before reaching a deal and using a paid intermediary when approaching public officials. Such customs raise questions of business ethics and possibly even legal allegations of corrupt practices in the homeland of the executive's head office.

A similar question may be asked about whether Indian culture should be called Hindu, to include the large expatriate communities in Trinidad, Britain, Fiji and elsewhere. I would again prefer the geographical term to the religious. One of the problems of westerners doing business in India is of coping with the caste system that plays such a large part in Indian society, but is not of much relevance among overseas communities of Indian ethnicity. Social values among international migrants tend to be modified over the generations, as Neil Bissoondath has insisted.

Three questions may be raised about the name I have given to the fourth major culture listed above. One is whether the title should be Christian rather than European, which I would reject as outdated in view of the striking decline in the Christian faith in much of contemporary Europe. Another is whether American society is properly included under the title of European, which may seem strange to Americans because so much of their education stresses their history as a society that contrasts to the class-bound societies of Europe. But, as Lewis (1995) has suggested, to the rest of the world American civilization is seen as essentially European in character and this is undoubtedly correct. A third question is whether Latin America should be bracketed with North America in this classification. It is certainly possible to argue that Latin America is culturally distinct from the United States, but so much of Latin American culture has been influenced by Spanish and Portuguese colonists that in a broad classification such as the current one I regard the title of European as reasonably appropriate.

That Islamic culture is distinct is quite clear. The renewed western interest in it in the past few years owes a lot to the growth of global terrorism, but this is unfortunate and potentially misleading, not only because [...] terrorist activities have been carried out over the centuries by many groups from other cultures but also because it may detract from the great contributions that Muslim architects and scholars have made to the world. It was, after all, Islamic mathematicians of the tenth century (when Europe was in the Dark Ages) who developed trigonometry and algebra (an Arabic word).

For any discussion of global culture, a global perspective is needed, and this suggests that much recent speculation is too narrowly focused.

Global Communications and Political Action

In the arena of global communication there have been important developments, of which the most interesting are the impact of television news programmes on public attitudes to foreign policy and the impact of email and Internet usage on transnational pressure groups.

The problem about television news is that it depends on visual images, and bad news is more visually interesting than good news. An ever-increasing proportion of television news is devoted to disasters like earthquakes, floods, terrorist bombings, famine in Somalia, civil wars in Africa, or destroyed villages in the Balkans. This leads to public demands for transnational intervention, based on moral feelings rather than on assessments of national interest. This may be desirable in humanistic terms but, as Joseph Nye has pointed out, quick responses urging intervention may change to dismay if casualties among troops of the viewers' own country are subsequently depicted (see Nye 1999: 32). This was dramatically emphasized in the case of the UN mission to relieve the famine in Somalia. American public support for this evaporated overnight when US television showed the bodies of American soldiers being dragged through the streets by trucks driven by members of local gangs, and the whole mission was quickly terminated. The relatively new American practice of sending the bodies of US troops killed in action back to their homeland, where their arrival is also shown on television, has made this kind of reaction more likely. It was a reason for the decision to use only high-level bombing or guided missiles in the Kosovo campaign, and it raises the whole question of how far it is realistic for political leaders to press for a new world order in which liberal democracies will use military force to protect human rights in other countries.

The impact of email and Internet usage on the organization and tactics of pressure groups has been truly remarkable. Within national societies it has proved possible to rally more citizens for demonstrations using these cheap and rapid means of communication than was previously feasible, a notable example being the growth of demonstrations devoted to animal welfare and environmental issues in Britain. However, the impact on transnational groups has been much more dramatic, in terms of both their number and their variety. Some of them, like Médecins Sans Frontières, are concerned mainly with the delivery of aid and services and are only tangentially involved in politics, while others, like Amnesty International and the Council of Canadians, are entirely devoted to political campaigns. They are so varied in character that in the 1990s a new collective name was coined for them; they are now usually known as non-governmental organizations (NGOs). In itself, this is an absurdly imprecise term that could logically cover any private concern in the world, from a retail store to a football club. In the current literature about world affairs, whether academic or journalistic, it is just accepted as meaning citizens' organizations that are involved, directly or marginally, with campaigns about issues of public concern. Some more sensible nomenclature will doubtless emerge in due course, but for the time being we have only this ambiguous omnibus label.

The number of NGOs active across national borders has grown at a remarkable pace in the past few years. According to the *Yearbook of International Organizations*, it grew from about 6,000 in 1990 to about 21,000 in 2005. Most of them are concerned with environmental issues, consumer issues and issues that can be broadly described as humanitarian or liberal in character. They tend to be organized by well educated and fairly young people who are adept at using the Internet and talented at handling the mass media. Greenpeace, one of the earliest and most successful of them, is a good example. Its ultimate aim is de-industrialization; in the words of its Executive Director, it regards the modern economy as 'a fire-breathing vampire of petroleum which is slowly cooking our planet' (letter in *The Economist*, 11 December 1999). As this would drastically reduce living standards, it could get little public support in itself, but Greenpeace organizers have shown great skill in taking up other issues, like nuclear testing or ocean pollution, that have attracted large numbers of idealistic supporters. In 1998 Greenpeace shocked business leaders by threatening a worldwide boycott of Shell petroleum that induced that firm to abandon its plan to dispose of a North Sea oil platform by sinking it, which was both legally and scientifically permissible. Other NGOs, or coalitions thereof, have mobilized European opinion against genetically modified foodstuffs and against the export of powdered baby food (deemed less nutritious than mother's milk) to African countries. Hundreds of NGOs in many countries pushed their governments to outlaw landmines, in a successful campaign led by the Canadian government. This was an interesting case in that the Canadian Department of External Affairs used the Internet to encourage NGOs in other countries to press their governments to act in this way.

To the question of whether the increased international activities of NGOs have undermined the power of national states, the answer must be 'not greatly, so far'. They have certainly embarrassed police forces and magistrates by staging demonstrations involving civil disobedience, but they have had little direct impact on state policies. For example, the much-publicized protests by Greenpeace against the French government for carrying out nuclear tests in the Pacific, against the British government for dumping nuclear waste into the Atlantic, and against the US Navy for carrying nuclear arms into Canadian waters, did not change official policies.

On one very important issue NGOs have successfully defended the sovereignty of national governments. This was the defeat of the proposed Multilateral Agreement on Investment (MAI). The campaign against this was led by the Council of Canadians, alarmed when they found that the proposed agreement contained a clause modelled on a little-publicized but highly significant provision of the 1987 North Atlantic Free Trade Agreement (NAFTA). Under this provision a commercial firm which finds its activities in a foreign country frustrated by government legislation or regulations passed after the signing of the Agreement can sue the government involved for compensation that is not limited to the investments made but can also include compensation for the loss of anticipated profits in future years. Under this provision a firm in California has proposed to sue the government of British Columbia for $15 billion, this sum representing the profits that the firm thinks it might have made if its tentative plan to pipe water from British Columbian reservoirs to the parched areas of southern California had not been frustrated by an Act of the British Columbian legislature forbidding the export of fresh water from the province. When the Council of Canadians publicized the equivalent clause in the MAI by sending it to the other NGOs around the world, the latter successfully put pressure on many of their own governments to turn down the whole proposal.

The future role of NGOs in world politics is hard to predict. They may have more impact on international organizations than directly on national governments. The World Bank regularly consults NGOs regarding its projects. The UN has a fair number of 'accredited' NGOs which advise UN officials on policy. There is a proposal to create a second chamber of the UN General Assembly, possibly to be called the People's Assembly, in which the views of NGOs can be articulated. This may be a pipe-dream, since it is unclear who would decide which of the thousands of NGOs would be represented in it, but some move towards regular international conferences of NGOs is quite likely. How far this should be regarded as an extension of democracy is another question.

Conclusions

It is clear that the new developments outlined in this chapter have complicated the political world and to some degree challenged the authority of national states. However, as David Held has suggested (Held 1991: 210–12), this change has to be put into historical perspective. In 1950 the world contained 54 recognized states, of which 5 in eastern Europe were so dominated by the Soviet Union that their independence was little more than nominal. By 2000 there were 192 recognized states. It follows that for three-quarters of the existing states the second half of the twentieth century was a period in which national independence dramatically increased. Cracks appeared in the state system in the last years of the century, but it would be an exaggeration to say that the state or the system is in decline.

At the UN each state has one vote. The International Court of Justice can arbitrate between states if requested to do so, but state governments frequently refuse to refer their disputes to it. The member states of the EU have surrendered some of their authority to the collectivity, but only over some fields of action. There is a European passport, but residents qualify for it only by being citizens of one of the member states, and the ways that new residents can acquire citizenship are not uniform. There has long been a commitment for EU states to work towards common policies towards the outside world, but this has not prevented Britain from differing from the majority on the question of sanctions against South Africa under apartheid, Britain and France from taking opposite sides regarding sanctions against Iraq, Germany from having a more friendly relationship with Croatia than have most other members, Italy a more friendly relationship with Libya, Greece a less friendly relationship with Turkey. Each member state has a veto over the admission of new members, and in 1994

Spain used the threat of vetoing the admission of Sweden, Finland and Austria to get fishing regulations changed to allow Spanish fishing boats access to British and Irish waters. Even within the EU, national states and governments retain considerable power.

In the economic field, if we leave aside the EC as unique and lacking global implications, the main development that has actually reduced the authority of states, as distinct from merely having an influence on government policies, is the North American Free Trade Agreement of 1987. For the first time in the modern age, this gives commercial corporations the same legal status as governments. Moreover, although at the time of writing this has yet to be established beyond doubt, the terms of the Agreement appear to give corporations an enforceable advantage over governments in cases of dispute. If provisions modelled on NAFTA were to be extended to the other countries of Central and South America, as was at one time proposed by the Clinton administration, this would involve a partial loss of sovereignty by 19 additional states.

The WTO is in principle different from this, as only national governments and the EC can be parties to disputes dealt with by the organization. The readiness of many governments to act on behalf of sizeable corporations reduces the practical significance of this distinction but does not eliminate it, as is shown by the readiness of the EC to allow some of its firms to pay the cost of defiance of WTO rulings. For this, it helps that EC policy-makers are more insulated from domestic pressures than is the average democratic government.

If the principles enshrined in NAFTA were to be included in a new version of the MAI, and this were to gather much more international support than the original version, the result would be a partial loss of national independence on a global scale. If the world were to move in this direction, it must be asked how this would affect the theory and practice of democracy. The answer can only be discouraging for democrats. As the fiasco in Seattle illustrated, the main political actors in such a world would be not elected politicians but corporation directors, international bureaucrats and the leaders of countless NGOs. In some sense the NGOs may represent the opinions of consumers and informed citizens, but NGO leaders are appointed by a variety of procedures and many of them are, in effect, self-appointed. They may or may not be accountable to their members for their actions and they are certainly not accountable to parliaments or electors. As public accountability is the essence of democracy, the transfer of authority over economic issues from national governments to international institutions appears to involve a democratic loss and no democratic theories have yet been developed to justify it.

The war over Kosovo is a precedent for international action to protect human rights. In pure logic, the arguments used by NATO leaders to justify the bombardment of Belgrade might also be used to justify the bombing of Beijing over the question of Tibet, of Moscow over Chechnya, of Rangoon over the treatment of political dissidents and ethnic minorities, and of an uncertain number of African cities. The arguments could be a prescription for wars that could destroy civilized life on this planet.

In reality political leaders are unlikely to be so negligent about their own national interests. In the summer and early autumn of 1999 no government was willing to take action against Indonesia regarding the gross abuses of human rights that its troops were committing in East Timor. This would have been legally much easier to justify than the Kosovo campaign, because Indonesian sovereignty over East Timor had never been recognized while Yugoslav sovereignty over Kosovo had never been disputed. The reasons for inaction were entirely practical. Indonesia is a large state with a large army and its stability is important to the western powers because they (especially the United States) have enormous investments there. The 'international community' therefore took no action until the Indonesian government gave permission for peacekeeping units to arrive.

It is also relevant that American opinion is divided, at all levels, about the wisdom of embarking on forcible interventions overseas for humanitarian reasons. Peter Rodman, a former State Department and White House official, has pointed out that 'ethnic conflicts are a swamp', far from easy to resolve (Rodman 1999: 51). Joseph Nye, Dean of Harvard's Kennedy School of Government, has said that the United States 'should generally avoid the use of force except in cases where our humanitarian interests are reinforced by the existence of other strong national interests' (Nye 1999: 32). E. N. Luttwak, of the Center for Strategic and International Studies, has said that international intervention to impose cease-fires in local wars is often misguided, as it is apt to give the combatants a respite to recuperate and re-arm, so that the conflict can be resumed with renewed vigour when the peacekeeping forces are withdrawn (Luttwak 1999: 36–44). American voters are apt to withdraw support for a venture that leads to numerous American casualties.

To conclude, exploring the concept of globalization in this chapter has led us into a discussion of diverse developments and a rather confusing debate. At the level of practice, it seems that the world, or at any rate the industrialized part of it, is staggering, partly as a result of economic forces and partly by the intention of politicians, towards more complex political arrangements. The process is hesitant, uncertain and controversial, and it will take decades, if not centuries, to bring about a state of affairs that could be reasonably described as a new world order. In the meantime, we have a more complex political world with an increased and increasing number of actors having meaningful roles in political dramas.

Commenting on this, Michael Keating concluded that 'the state has not faded away, or even retreated', but has lost its uniqueness as the 'arena in which policy differences are negotiated and resolved'. This has poor implications for democracy, for 'it brings into question the whole purpose of politics as a means of reconciling economic needs with social and cultural ones and the nation-state as the institutional forum which not only provides the mechanisms for this but legitimizes the outcomes' (Keating 1996: 39–40). Held posed the question: 'If the efficacy of the system of representative democracy is being strained and eroded in the face of global interconnectedness, what mechanisms could ensure accountability in the new international order?' (Held 1991: 225). He could offer no answer to the question. Ever since the 1950s, political science students have been made acquainted with the 'systems theory' approach to the study of democratic politics [...], whereby pressure groups are said to articulate public interests and values and political parties to aggregate them, so that voters can be presented with more-or-less coherent clusters of policies between which to choose. It is a simplistic model, but not at all worthless, and it illustrates a basic problem, for democrats, of the globalizing developments here discussed. The world has an ever-increasing number of transnational pressure groups that articulate particular interests and ideals, but there is no prospect of transnational political parties to aggregate them, let alone of global elections to legitimize the decisions that emerge.

At a more theoretical level, the years around the turn of the millennium present an extraordinary paradox in the character of world politics. The growth of supranational and international institutions and the moves towards a world system of justice represent a development of the humanistic and rationalistic ideals that characterized the Enlightenment of the eighteenth century and inspired both American and French revolutionary leaders. Simultaneously, the revived incidence of ethnic and religious conflicts represents a rejection of Enlightenment ideals in favour of a much older kind of tribal and religious rivalry. The attempts to reconcile these divergent trends by liberal thinkers and politicians who favour supranational government by bureaucrats and judges for large issues combined with popular government in small ethnic or cultural communities for minor issues involve a further paradox. This is that such a development would involve the gradual destruction of liberalism's greatest achievement in the past two centuries, namely the establishment of democratic systems of government in national states that are virtually all to some extent multi-ethnic.

How, if at all, these paradoxes will be resolved in the future can only be a matter of conjecture. It is not within the capacity of political scientists to make predictions about the long-term future and in the remainder of this book we shall therefore concentrate on problems that are within our capacity, namely the conceptual and theoretical problems involved in the study of democratic politics within the modern national state.

References

Birch, A. H. (1959) *Small-Town Politics*, London: Oxford University Press.
———(1998) *The British System of Government*, 10th edn, London: Routledge.
Bissoondath, N. (1994) *Selling Illusions: The Cult of Multiculturalism in Canada*, Toronto: Penguin.

Cable, J. (1981) *Gunboat Diplomacy*, London: Macmillan.

Castells, M. (1997) *The Power of Identity*, Oxford: Basil Blackwell.

Fox, H. (1999) 'The Pinochet case no. 3', *International and Comparative Law Quarterly*, 48: 687–702.

Gray, J. (1998) *False Dawn: The Delusions of Global Capitalism*, London: Granta.

Grove, J. W. (1999) 'The face of science at the end of the twentieth century', *Queen's Quarterly*, 106: 383–92.

Hagen, W. W. (1999) 'The Balkans' lethal nationalisms', *Foreign Affairs*, 78(4): 52–64.

Held, D. (1991) 'Democracy and the global system', in D. Held (ed.) *Political Theory Today*, Stanford, CA: Stanford University Press.

Keating, M. (1996) *Nations Against the State*, London: Macmillan.

Laponce, J. A. (1987) *Languages and their Territories*, Toronto: University of Toronto Press.

Lewis, B. (1990) 'The roots of Muslim rage', *Atlantic Monthly*, 266(3): 47–60.

——(1995) *Cultures in Conflict*, New York: Oxford University Press.

Luttwak, E. N. (1999) 'Give war a chance', *Foreign Affairs*, 78(4): 36–44.

Mandelbaum, M. (1999) 'A perfect failure: NATO's war against Yugoslavia', *Foreign Affairs*, 78(5): 2–8.

Nugent, N. (1991) *The Government and Politics of the European Community*, 2nd edn, London: Macmillan.

Nye, J. S. (1999) 'Redefining the national interest', *Foreign Affairs*, 78(4): 22–35.

Ohmae, K. (1995) *The End of the Nation-State: The Rise of Regional Economics*, London: HarperCollins.

Rodman, P. W. (1999) 'The fallout from Kosovo', *Foreign Affairs*, 78(4): 45–51.

Strange, S. (1996) *The Retreat of the State*, Cambridge: Cambridge University Press.

Waters, M. (1995) *Globalization*, London: Routledge.

Chapter 4

1. Identify four sources of social supports contributing to state unity and/or division.
2. What are ethnic cleavages?
3. Why do high inflation and huge fiscal deficits undermine citizens' support for a governing political party?
4. Define and illustrate the concept of globalization.
5. How does globalization affect state authority and the global economy?

Chapter 5

Theorizing Patterns of Domination and Conflict

THEORIES OF STATE DRAW ON VARIOUS philosophical traditions to interpret and expose patterns of political power. The following readings are applications illustrating the most important theories of state, namely, pluralism, elite theory, Marxism, and constructivism (culture). Attention to the philosophical starting points of each exemplary reading will make clear the importance of the meta-theoretical foundations of research in political science.

Our first reading illustrates the positivist philosophical foundations that facilitate identification of pluralism and democracy. It does this by looking for the ways interest groups mobilize around policy goals linked to their special group and then lobby legislators and executive office holders. As Robert Dahl notes, democratic policymaking is the rule of minorities, as special interests rise, succeed, and then dissipate. Such groups, for example, may represent workers in a trade union wanting a wage increase or the emergence of citizen groups upset with proposed housing projects in their neighborhood. Pluralism as a theory of power is optimistic about democracy, since it holds that citizen participation and contestation usually achieve policy goals and maintain elite accountability to citizen's needs.

The second and third readings exemplify two different types of philosophical realism, philosophical approaches holding that structural processes shape power. In the second reading, Hanlon focuses on how organizational processes allocate influence. He examines David Graber's recent book on the rationalization or bureaucratic organization of modern ways of living, complementing the commodification of relations through market processes. This combination creates and reproduces individualism, competitiveness, and private property. The focus on the intensification of rationalized organizations and their effects is a concern of neo-institutional approaches, a school of theories popular in comparative politics today.

The third reading asks how capitalists' rule without an identifiable class-conscious capitalist ruling class being in command. Fred Block develops a structural analysis to explain how capitalism functions as a legitimate mode of "rationality," expanding on a perspective appearing as commonsense yet operating in the service of the ruling class. His analysis starts by shifting our attention away from businesses or the state as such. Instead, he proposes that capitalism dominates because this mode of production and consumption benefits society. The state, moreover, depends for its own legitimacy and authority on the success of this system. This structural positioning of the capitalist economy gives it overwhelming importance to the success of the capitalist system, thereby removing any need for capitalists to have their own class consciousness. The system's successes also undercut class consciousness among the working class and hinders anti-capitalist sentiment among citizen beneficiaries.

Our final reading uses an interpretive approach to investigate whether the expansion of China as a global power will be interpreted as an intolerable threat to America's global dominance, leading to war. Graham Allison focuses on whether the cultural heritages are the drivers of interest and policy. He cites the famous "Thucydides's Trap" to deduce a possible outcome. This refers to the Greek historian's hypothesis explaining the reasons for the war between Sparta and Athens, proposing that the cause was the Spartans interpretation that Athens's rising prominence was an unacceptable threat. Allison then asks if the United States of America will see the rise of China in a similar way, as a threat that leads to war. His survey of the civilizational, historical, and recent cultural developments in both China and America predicts growing conflict, raising serious concerns about the future relations between the two states. While this conclusion is unsettling, it is important to critically examine how the analytical foundations of any analysis, in this case the role of culture shape issues, arguments, and projected outcomes.

Reading 5.1

Pluralism

Anthony H. Birch

P LURALISM IS AN AMERICAN THEORY ABOUT the impact of sectional and group conflict on
policy making. It occupied a central place in political debate in the 1950s and 1960s, but
it is an enduring concept in American political thought, having been formulated in one form
by the founders of the republic and still current in a modified form. As a theory, pluralism
has been defined and redefined, supported by empirical studies, criticized and attacked as
misleading. It no longer has such a central place in debate as it had a few years ago, but it has
featured in so much of the writing about American politics that it clearly deserves a chapter
in this book. Moreover, its use has spread from the United States to other countries, some
writers having said that all democratic systems are pluralist in character. To some extent, the
concept of pluralism is an American intellectual export.

Sectional Pluralism in American Thought

[...] [T]he first pluralist thinkers in the United States were Madison and Hamilton. They were
writing to advocate the proposed transition from a loose confederation of states to a federal
union. Their arguments were a combination of empirical hypotheses and normative assertions. They have been subjected to an elaborate logical analysis by Robert Dahl (see Dahl
1956: Chapters 1 and 2) and I am indebted to Dahl for this analysis. In so far as Madison and
Hamilton's writings were relevant to pluralism, however, I think their points can be summarized without injustice in the form of four empirical hypotheses, one normative assertion and
a conclusion. The empirical hypotheses were as follows:

1. That politicians are not normally motivated by altruism or a concern for the public
   interest. On the contrary, they enjoy the exercise of power and can be expected to maximize it if given the opportunity to do so.

2. That a conflict of interests in society is inevitable and will necessarily lead to the development of factional disputes. As Madison put it:

   > A landed interest, a manufacturing interest, a mercantile interest, a moneyed
   > interest, with many lesser interests, grow up of necessity in civilised nations. ...
   > The regulation of these various and interfering interests forms the principal

task of modern legislation, and involves the spirit of party and faction in the necessary and ordinary operations of the government.

(Hamilton et al. 1901: 46)

3. That factions within society will, if not checked by others, seek to maximize their own interests at the expense of others.
4. That factions will be led or represented by politicians who can be expected to use their power to promote factional interests.

The normative assertion was that Americans ought to organize their system of government so as to minimize the possibility that leaders of any one faction could dominate the others, which Madison said would lead to a deprivation of rights.

The conclusion was that joining the thirteen states into a federal union would be desirable on the ground that, by multiplying and diversifying the factions, the danger of any one faction gaining a position of dominance would be greatly reduced. Hamilton's assertion to this effect in paper 51 of *The Federalist* bears repetition because it was so clear; it was that 'society itself will be broken into so many parts, interests, and classes of citizens that the rights of individuals or of the minority will be in little danger from interested combinations of the majority' (Hamilton et al. 1901: 287).

This line of argument was given a new emphasis in the 1850s by John C. Calhoun, the influential southern politician who was concerned that northern politicians, if they gained control of Congress, might use their majority to abolish slavery. Calhoun took the view that representative government could only safeguard the interests of geographical minorities if it were based on the principle of the 'concurrent majority' (see Calhoun 1943: 28). He asserted that this view was to some extent recognized in the US Constitution, by the equal representation of each state in the Senate and by the clause requiring the agreement of three-quarters of the states before any constitutional amendment could be passed. The essence of his message was that this principle should be extended by convention so that a numerical majority in Congress would never use its power to pass measures which deprived some of the states of rights that they considered essential to their wellbeing. If northern politicians refused to accept such a convention in regard to slavery, Calhoun warned, the result would be to upset the delicate equilibrium of American politics and probably to lead the southern states to secede from the union.

It is possible to argue either that the American civil war justified Calhoun's view, for the war was an undeniably tragic event, or that it rendered his extreme version of geographical pluralism obsolete by demonstrating the power that a national majority could exert. After the civil war somewhat less was heard about this type of pluralism, and the improvement of communications and the trend towards the nationwide organization of industry made

American society more homogeneous. Nevertheless, the ideas of sectional pluralism did not die out, and were reaffirmed in 1950 by Herbert Agar, who wrote as follows:

> Successful federal policies will tend to follow Calhoun's rule of concurrent majorities. Every interest which is strong enough to make trouble must usually be satisfied before anything can be done. This means great caution in attempting new policies, so that a whole ungainly continent may keep in step.
>
> (Agar 1950: 690)

A. N. Holcombe held a similar viewpoint, arguing that disciplined national parties (as then being advocated by many political scientists) were undesirable and probably unworkable in a large and heterogeneous society like the United States. The price of union, it was said, was the acceptance of the right of minorities to veto policies that they found intolerable (Holcombe 1950). This was a fairly straightforward application of the doctrine first advanced by Madison and Hamilton. Dahl came close to this position when he suggested that the distinction between dictatorship and democracy could be described as one 'between government by a minority and government by minorities' (Dahl 1956: 133).

Not everyone in the post-war period shares the values implied by this quotation, for some critics have wanted firmer national leadership than has normally been given. However, it is true as a matter of fact that political power in the United States is more decentralized than in any other modern democratic state, with the exceptions of Canada and Switzerland. Sectional interests with a geographic base have more influence on national policy than is normal elsewhere, and the extent of congressional log rolling for regional and local interests in regard to the budget, appropriations and defence contracts would be thought shocking in most other democracies.

Pressure-Group Pluralism

After 1950, an emphasis on the sectional and geographical basis of American pluralism was replaced by an emphasis on the role of organized pressure groups, however based, on governmental decision making. In 1952, Latham's book on *The Group Basis of Politics* asserted that the pressure group is 'the basic political form' (Latham 1965: 10) and that the political process is essentially a struggle between such groups:

> The legislature referees the group struggle, ratifies the victories of the successful coalitions, and records the terms of the surrenders, compromises, and conquests in the form of statutes ... The legislative vote on any issue tends to represent

the composition of strength, i.e. the balance of power, among the contending groups at the moment of voting. What may be called public policy is the equilibrium reached in this struggle at any given moment.

(Latham 1965: 35–6)

The 1950s saw the publication of many books and articles with a similar emphasis[...] The most influential of them was Truman's book, *The Governmental Process*, which sought to synthesize the results of numerous specialized studies so as to provide a 'systematic conception of the role of interest groups in the political process' (Truman 1951: VIII–IX). It will be noted that Truman preferred the term 'interest group' to the term 'pressure group'. He did this because he thought that the latter term had become part of 'the language of political abuse' (Truman 1951: 38) whereas the former term was more neutral. However this may have been in 1951, it would be a great pity to follow him in this usage today. The terms are equally capable of being used in a neutral way, as they usually are by political scientists, and it is much more helpful to use 'pressure group' as a generic term, to describe all organized groups that try to exert pressure on the process by which policies are made and implemented, while distinguishing between the two sub-categories of interest groups and promotional groups.

An interest group, in this usage, is a group that has the function of defending or advancing the material interests of its members, while a promotional group is one that exists to promote a particular value or cause. Thus, in regard to defence policy there is a useful distinction to be drawn between groups defending the interests of firms (and their employees) working on defence contracts and other groups, like those opposed to nuclear arms, whose members share an attitude or moral conviction about the proper nature of the policy. In regard to the law on abortion, there is a similar distinction between groups representing the interests of doctors, nurses and the owners of abortion clinics and other groups whose members simply have convictions about the rights and wrongs of abortion. The distinction is reflected in the financial and other resources available to the groups and, frequently, in the tactics of pressure they employ. Interest groups are more likely to be consulted by government agencies and thus to have an inside track in the decision-making process, while promotional groups are more likely to rely on public campaigns and demonstrations. 'Pressure group' is clearly the most appropriate generic term and it will be used in what follows.

The main thrust behind the pressure-group pluralists of the 1950s was methodological. They believed that there was an unhelpful tendency among political scientists to depict the role of pressure groups as being in some sense outside the basic process of government, or at any rate on the periphery of it. In contrast, the pluralists' view was that such groups were at the heart of the policy-making process. 'The institutions of government', Truman declared, 'are centres of interest-based power' (Truman 1951: 506). Is this true of the presidency, the

Supreme Court, the State Department? Truman's answer is in the affirmative: 'The political structure of the United States ... has adopted characteristic legislative, executive, and judicial forms through the efforts of organized interest groups' (Truman 1951: 513).

This statement seems like an exaggeration, an attempt to redress the methodological balance that goes too far the other way. Pressure groups are important, but they are not all-important. There was, moreover, an element of complacency in the suggestion that the American democratic system automatically registers a state of approximate equilibrium between conflicting pressure groups. In Truman's version the concept of a 'potential interest group' was introduced to serve a function analogous to that of 'the invisible hand' in Adam Smith's writings, namely to guarantee that the clash of private interests would not produce consequences that would upset the system. Another balancing factor was said to be the existence or likelihood of overlapping memberships between interest groups, widely defined so as to include potentially overlapping memberships in both actual and potential groups. One of Truman's conclusions was as follows: 'It is thus multiple memberships in potential groups based on widely held and accepted interests that serve as a balance wheel in a political system like that of the United States' (Truman 1951: 514).

This position went beyond the empirical evidence to produce what could be (and was) construed as a theory of American democracy in terms of an automatic balance of group pressures. The theory could be (and was) attacked by critics on the ground that it was smug, perhaps to the point of being Panglossian, and this line of criticism is understandable. In the 1950s the American system was rather obviously one in which some groups, such as those representing farmers or doctors or business interests, had more influence than others, such as those representing slum-dwellers or racial minorities or the consumers of medical or legal services. It is not clear that pluralist writers would actually have disagreed with this generalization, but their comments about equilibrium, balance, countervailing powers, potential interest groups and the like tended, by implication at least, to minimize its significance.

The fact is that the 1950s were years characterized by a good deal of political and other self-satisfaction in the United States. There was a fair amount of Panglossian writing in that decade, and a prize for pluralist complacency in this period might perhaps be awarded to Max Lerner for the following sentences in a book entitled *America as a Civilization*:

> [Power in the United States] is plural and fluid. It is many-faceted rather than uniform, it is dispersed among a number of groups. ... The pluralist, pragmatist and federalist character of American politics has compelled it to develop the arts of compromise and to achieve an equilibrium of conflicting powers in motion. ... The American system of power has become like a system of nebulae held together by reciprocal tensions in the intergalactic space.
>
> (Lerner 1957: 398, 405, 406)

Despite this kind of rhetorical exaggeration, writers in the pluralist tradition have pointed to an important dimension of American democracy. Thus, Truman said that 'the outstanding characteristic of American politics ... is that it involves a multiplicity of co-ordinate or nearly-co-ordinate points of access to governmental decisions' (Truman 1951: 519). Robert Dahl said much the same thing in his textbook on American government:

> When one looks at American political institutions in their entirety and compares them with institutions in other democracies, what stands out as a salient feature is the extraordinary variety of opportunities these institutions provide for an organized minority to block, modify, or delay a policy which the minority opposes.
>
> (Dahl 1967: 326)

These two generalizations are undoubtedly valid, though it is open to question whether this feature of the American system is entirely desirable. Should democrats be pleased, for instance, that the National Rifle Association has been able to hold up effective gun control for many years, against the apparent wish of the majority of citizens to see such control? Dahl's defence of pluralism is that it provides opportunities for groups of citizens to mobilize slack political resources for whatever interests and values they wish to press, and that it also limits the power of governing bodies. As he puts it, when 'one centre of power is set against another, power itself will be tamed, civilized, controlled and limited to decent human purposes' (Dahl 1967: 24). Charles Lindblom has gone rather further than this, arguing that pluralism is not only democratic, but also likely to produce more desirable policy outcomes than any more centralized system of policy making. It involves 'muddling through' rather than political planning, but the complexity of problems in modern industrial societies is so great that it is unlikely that planners can master them all and it is better to leave the outcome to what he calls 'partisan mutual adjustment' (Lindblom 1959, 1965).

In the 1960s the emphasis changed again, as the publication of Dahl's *Who Governs?* turned attention from the role of pressure groups in Congress to the distribution of influence in municipal politics. The background to this study was the publication of seven or eight surveys of community power structure by sociologists, all of which had reached the conclusion that power within American cities was dominated by an established elite of upper-class citizens. The upper class (variously defined) was said to have a ruling position in local society, the elected politicians and officials were said to follow the orders of the upper class, and each community, it was concluded, was therefore controlled by a power elite. Dahl and his junior colleague, Nelson Polsby, took the view that the methodology used in these studies was faulty and the conclusions were mistaken. Polsby produced a detailed and searching analysis of the studies which cast great doubt on their validity (Polsby 1963), while Dahl organized the study of power in New Haven [...] (see Dahl 1961).

[...] I believe that the methodology employed by Dahl and his colleagues was superior, by normal scientific criteria, to the methodology of their sociological predecessors. However, it is important to be precise about what was and what was not demonstrated by the New Haven study. It was demonstrated that the government of New Haven was an arena of conflict between small groups and factions, with different factions coming out on top in different areas of policy. It was also shown that the members of the city's social elite were not very active or powerful in the decision areas studied, so that it would be implausible to characterize the social elite as being also a political elite.

It was not shown, and not claimed, that all classes and groups in the city had equal power or equal access to the levers of power. It was not shown that the decision makers were not dominated by what may loosely be called middle-class values. It was not shown that there were no other potentially important areas of conflict in the city that had not reached the political agenda, either because (as Dahl would say) the would-be reformers in these areas had failed to mobilize enough resources to get the issues on to the agenda or because (as Bachrach and Baratz would say) the opponents of change had been able to keep the issues off the agenda. It was not shown, and not claimed, that New Haven was typical of all American cities or that its political structure should be regarded as a microcosm of the whole structure of American politics.

The New Haven study and the accompanying methodological analysis by Polsby (1963) exposed the weaknesses of the earlier studies of community power by stratification theorists and opened up an instructive debate [...] about the nature of political power and the problems of assessing it. However, Dahl and Polsby did not exhibit the complacency of some earlier pluralist writers, as Dahl was at pains to point out in a much later book. In this he said, among other things, that organizational pluralism is apt to contribute to the maintenance of political inequalities (Dahl 1982: 40–1).

Pluralism and Democracy

Under this heading it is pertinent to ask whether pluralist systems of government are necessarily democratic and, conversely, whether democratic systems of government are necessarily pluralist. The answer to the first question has to be negative. Pluralism is clearly compatible with democracy but incompatible with totalitarianism, for governments cannot exercise total control over society if autonomous organizations are permitted to exercise any substantial degree of social and political influence. However, most systems of government are neither democratic nor totalitarian. It is not difficult to imagine a system of government that is characterized by competition between organized groups for influence and power, but is nevertheless undemocratic, either because only a minority of citizens are permitted to participate in political life or because the dominant groups use the power of the state to exclude other relevant groups from the competition.

History provides numerous examples of just such a system, including Britain between 1688 and 1867, Germany under Bismarck, and France during the Second Empire. Looking further back, it can be argued that many pre-modern systems of government were pluralist without being democratic, characterized by political struggles between churches, land owners, farmers and merchants while excluding most citizens from political influence.

The answer to the question of whether democratic systems are necessarily pluralist depends upon how pluralism is defined. It is clearly not the case that all democracies are characterized by sectional pluralism with a geographical base, as envisaged by Madison and Hamilton and as exemplified by the American situation. Most European democracies are not only much smaller but also more homogeneous. They also (apart from Switzerland) have more centralized systems of government with, in consequence, fewer points of access for sectional pressure groups than exist in the United States. However, it would not be sensible to say that for these reasons countries like Britain, France, Denmark and Sweden are less democratic than the United States.

If pluralism is defined as Truman (1951) and Latham (1965) defined it, in terms of a political system in which pressure groups (however based) compete for influence on the decisions of the national government, then all modern democracies have a pluralist dimension. Pressure groups are more conspicuous in some democratic systems than in others and they exhibit a great deal of variety in terms of their organization, their resources and their political tactics, but in systems characterized by freedom of organization and political communication some pressure groups are bound to exist. There are important practical questions about how far the activities of pressure groups advance or detract from the public interest, but these are best regarded as local and particular questions to which general answers cannot be given. It has, for example, been plausibly said that the power exerted by trade unions was harmful to the British economy in the 1960s and 1970s, that the influence of industrial organizations has prevented Italy from establishing adequate environmental controls, and that the influence of agricultural groups kept food prices in the European Community unnecessarily high in the 1980s. Many similar generalizations could be cited, some apparently reasonable, others evidently biased, all of them involving some kind of value judgement. However, questions of this kind are essentially questions for specific applications of political judgement, not questions that can be resolved by conceptual or theoretical analysis.

This said, it can be added that some democratic systems are more obviously pluralist than others. The United States is the extreme case, not only because of its geographic sectionalism and its decentralized system of government, but also because, within Washington, the executive branch of the national government is weaker than its equivalent in other democracies. The separation of powers, combined with the weakness of party discipline in Congress, make it very difficult for the executive to get draft legislation translated into law if influential groups are opposed to it. The executive cannot even be sure of getting approval for the annual budget, which could be taken for granted in most parliamentary democracies. One of Dahl's many accurate comments on the federal government was that, to a large extent, 'the numerical majority is incapable of undertaking any co-ordinated action. It is the various components of the numerical majority that have the means for action' (Dahl 1956: 146).

This is a comment that would not be made about the national governments of Britain, France, Germany, Sweden, or Australia. Pressure groups are very influential in these countries, and often have direct access to the administration. In this area of policy or that, some groups might have more influence than their American equivalents can muster. But the results of their pressure can rarely be counted in parliamentary votes, and they can rarely prevent a government with a parliamentary majority from pursuing and implementing a policy once the government has made up its collective mind. It is partly these institutional differences, as well as the differences in their theoretical concerns, that have led American political scientists to place much more stress on the concept of pluralism than their colleagues elsewhere have done. However, the concept can be used in the analysis of almost any system of government.

References

Agar, H. (1950) *The Price of Union*, Boston, MA: Houghton Mifflin.

Calhoun, J. C. [1853] (1943) *Disquisition on Government*, New York: Peter Smith.

Dahl, R. A. (1956) *A Preface to Democratic Theory*, Chicago, IL: University of Chicago Press.

———(1961) *Who Governs?*, New Haven, CT: Yale University Press.

———(1967) *Pluralist Democracy in the United States*, Chicago, IL: Rand McNally.

———(1982) *Dilemmas of Pluralist Democracy*, New Haven, CT: Yale University Press.

Hamilton, A., Jay, J., and Madison, J. [1787] (1901) *The Federalist*, New York: The Colonial Press.

Holcombe, A. N. (1950) *Our More Perfect Union*, Cambridge, MA: Harvard University Press.

Latham, E. [1952] (1965) *The Group Basis of Politics*, New York: Octagon.

Lerner, M. (1957) *America as a Civilization*, New York: Simon & Schuster.

Lindblom, C. E. (1959) 'The science of muddling through', *Public Administration Review*, 19(4): 79–88.

———(1965) *The Intelligence of Democracy*, New York: Free Press.

Polsby, N. (1963) *Community Power and Political Theory*, New Haven, CT: Yale University Press.

Truman, D. (1951) *The Governmental Process*, New York: Knopf.

Reading 5.2

Total Bureaucratisation, Neo-liberalism, and Weberian Oligarchy

Gerard Hanlon

Review of

Graeber, D. (2015) *The utopia of rules: On technology, stupidity, and the secret joys of bureaucracy.* London: Melville House Publishing (HB, pp. 272, $21.55, ISBN 978-1-612193-74-8).

D AVID GRAEBER'S BOOK ON RULES AND bureaucracy examines the topic from a refreshing standpoint. Much management literature, since at least Bennis (1965), has made the claim that bureaucracy and competitive markets and/or change are somehow incompatible. The world needs to be post-bureaucratic—'bureaucracy must die' (Hamel, 2014), organizations must be more entrepreneurial (Drucker, 1984). These are the refrains we hear—if we are to survive and grow, creativity must be unleashed from the shackles of bureaucracy. A dominant neo-liberal motif has been to burn red tape—most recently one thinks of David Cameron's demands of the EU wherein if British membership is to continue, red tape (and perhaps reds) is to be burned—those dynamic commercial Brits taking on the sclerosis of bureaucratic Europe on our behalf. In reply, management scholars opposing such a position argue that bureaucracy and its rules protect us from unethical behaviour, arbitrary power, anti-democratic forces, and so on. Bureaucracy here equates with rational-legal authority and the rule of law. It may not be perfect but it at least defends the weak and the infirm, e.g. Du Gay's (2013) defence of bureaucracy as more ethical than post-bureaucracy. Building on Hennis (1988), Du Gay argues that the father of bureaucracy, Max Weber, sought to find a way through which personality would allow an individual to live ethically. The entrepreneurial or post-bureaucratic firm undermines such an ethic by encouraging an arbitrariness more closely associated with charismatic or traditional rule. Indeed, neo-liberalism itself is in the dock because it undermines ethics and subsumes life to something like Weber's instrumental rationality (see Gane, 2014—although importantly Weber [1975: 33] argued that the heuristic device of the ideal type known as rational economic man was an 'approximation' that was becoming more and more a reality as institutions altered to act as though it were true). Here, in my crude summary, bureaucracy, ethics, and Weber line up against post-bureaucracy, ethically neutral instrumental rationality, and neo-liberalism.

Graeber takes a different and more interesting tack. For him, bureaucracy increases under neo-liberal market conditions. It is 'an iron law of liberalism' that increasing *laissez-faire* increases bureaucracy [9] and that our so called era of post-bureaucratic organization is actually a period of 'total bureaucratisation' [18]. He usefully highlights the links between bureaucracy and the rise of the state, the contemporary market, and the modern corporation—pointing out along the way, that the two most bureaucratic countries are also perhaps historically the sites of the corporation—Germany and the USA. Bureaucracy is about putting shape on 'reality'; it is the enforcing of particular forms of order. In chapter three, he uses many examples from anthropology, fantasy, and history to argue bureaucracy is engaged in a struggle against play, heroic storytelling, narrative, and charisma. In the name of democratic rules, transparency, indifference and neutrality [183-86], bureaucratic societies seek to 'civilise' non-bureaucratic ones because seemingly impartial rules provide a neutral order. Something like this argument was made recently in the BBC documentary series *The Celts* which compared and contrasted Rome's rule bound order and the charismatic and traditional Celtic world. Bureaucracies are a structured game [190] and not much fun, unlike their less structured nemesis, unruly play. But the game of bureaucracy has been winning as ever more areas of life become rule bound. Ours is a world which increasingly sees play as threatening—as needing evermore structure. As the distinction between work and play collapses (Graw, 2010), unruly play is structured to resemble a game—is this not what the neoliberal Schultz's (1962) call for human capital as a never-ending investment in man implies—structure your activities to make them profitable? For Graeber [204], games and play also take us to one of the major schisms within the left—between those who see rules as freedom, because it reduces power to a transparent set of regulations, and those anti-authoritarians who see freedom largely in terms of improvisation and play. The problem for the former—as the proto-fascist Robert Michels (1915) understood—is that bureaucracy enables the holders of power to make up the rules. The problem of the latter is that like language play needs flexibility and some rules if it is to be progressive—but this too returns us to how many and who constructs them.

Graeber, from a management studies viewpoint, is a welcome challenge. Bureaucracy versus post-bureaucracy, or markets, or competition, or innovation, or entrepreneurship, etc. has recently been the field's dominant way of viewing organizational life. Here, to paraphrase, Graeber is saying these are largely the same thing. Furthermore, he is arguing that bureaucracy is an anti-democratic rule maintenance machine for a neo-liberal elite. At this juncture, his work takes on an interesting hue. It links to the growing scholarship on neo-liberalism and democracy put forward by Brown (2003, 2006), Streeck (2014), Biebricher (2015) and others. But it is also interesting for reasons concerned with the latent neo-liberalism of management's (indirect) founding father, Max Weber.

That neo-liberalism is rule bound seems beyond dispute. Biebricher (2015) has strongly argued different variants of neo-liberalism make use of rules and expertise to stifle democracy. For example, he suggests ordo-liberals use expert rules as a mechanism to restrict democracy because they believe the masses do not know what is in their own interests. As Megay (1970: 404-424) highlights, rules were to be used as a tool in a 'revolt of the elite' who were a 'natural aristocracy'. Indeed, one can see elements of this in the contemporary 'Greek' crisis wherein Jens Weidmann, the head of the Bundesbank (quoted in Streeck, 2014: 109), commented:

> In the event that a country does not keep to the budgetary rules national sovereignty would automatically pass to the EU level to the extent for the targets to be reached ... one example might be the right to implement—and not simply demand—tax increases or proportionate spending cuts ... Within such a framework, the EU level could secure the path to consolidation, even if no majority could be found in the national parliament concerned.

Or one can also think of the UK government's push to ensure legislation stopping future governments from running deficits. In these renditions democracy has to be curtailed by rules created via an elite 'expertocracy' (Müller, 2015: 6).

Hayek also develops such rule inflected structures. Following Carl Schmitt's repost to the attempts by the German left to commandeer the private property of the former Kaiser (Scheuerman, 1997), Hayek (1960: 54–71) argues general and self-binding rules need to be developed to stop a state acting on the whim of an electorate (or of experts—both of whom he distrusted). General rules would keep democracy at bay. Rules should be used to enable the free flow of capital, goods, labour etc. and thereby limit the capacity of democratically elected governments to initiate changes which damaged returns on property. If the electorate 'freely' undermined these returns, then property (and skilled labour) could move to where it could get a better return—hopefully the burden of such responsibility would chasten democrats. This 'interstate federalism' (Hayek, 1948: 255–272; Streeck, 2014: 97–102) shares many features with the current neo-liberal turn of the EU. Thus neo-liberals are not necessarily hostile to rules or to bureaucratic forms, even if Mises (1944:10 fn1) claimed they were un-American. Indeed, rules are used to instil authority and circumvent democracy with softer or harder forms of authoritarianism. Echoing Graeber, less play and more expert games lies at the heart of the supposedly dynamic, creative, free-flowing, bottom-up neoliberal economy.

But how does this link to the rules outlined in Weber's analysis of bureaucracy? Weber (1948: 197) clearly outlines how bureaucratic rules can be used by those lower in the hierarchy to appeal to a higher authority against decisions made by their immediate superiors. He (1948: 216–217) clearly links bureaucracy to rational justice rather than the 'Kadi-justice' of charismatic or traditional systems. And finally, he (1948: 224–225) clearly links it to a 'levelling of social differences' because it undermines ascribed power. Here, bureaucracy appears as an enabling force. But as is well known Weber does not stop there. Bureaucracy is not simply 'good' because it is '"Without regard for persons" (which) is also the watchword for the market' (Weber, 1948: 215). Like the law or the market, as a rational impersonal system bureaucracy is ethically neutral (Hennis, 1988: 90–103). Thus it can be beneficial to larger or smaller groups, to all or to the few. Graeber [14-21], for example, suggests during the post-war boom the bureaucratic corporate structure was built on an inter-class alliance between workers and managers which broke down when 'management' abandoned workers to side with an investor class. In this transition, to what we call neo-liberalism, the many were disempowered and the few were dramatically enriched as the organizational (and other) rules changed. Thus bureaucracy and rules are always the result of social re-composition—of the relations rather than the forces of production.

One can see this clearly in the twentieth century emergence of the American corporation. The shift from the 'Inside Contract' wherein hierarchical and unequal craft workers self-organized production according to forms of authority built on expertise, collegiality, community, age, gender, etc. to what became the bureaucratic corporate form (Buttrick, 1951; Williamson, 1952; Clawson, 1980; Englander, 1987). Here, one can surmise that these craft 'honorific arrangements' meant that the 'administration, therefore, runs less precisely and is more independent of superiors; hence, it is less unified and slower' (Weber, 1948: 214). The creation of bureaucracy was used to counter this 'independence' and to make administration quicker, more certain, dependent on superiors, and more anti-democratic. This is precisely the point made by Clawson (1980) and Stone (1973). Stone's examination of the steel industry is important in this regard. In fine detail, she lays out Graeber's claim that bureaucracy is not neutral and demonstrates how the emergence of the modern bureaucratic corporation, dominated by rules and procedures, was the outcome of social struggle into which were built class, ethnicity, gender, and age related forms of power.

For management research, Graeber's essential point is that the bureaucracy versus the post-bureaucracy-entrepreneurial firm is a misplaced argument. Today both are essential elements of neo-liberal social re-composition. Central here he argues is the blurring of the public and the private. Government bureaucratic reregulation has enabled corporate bureaucracies access public funding on a monumental scale; so, too, have the trade bureaucracies, the WTO, IMF, World Bank, G8, EU, NAFTA. They have opened up large elements of the Global South to bureaucracies such as Goldman Sachs, American Insurance Group, etc. Furthermore, he argues, we are complicit in this because through these bureaucracies we act as though we believe trade is free, the market is free, and corporations fair and transparent. He goes on to add that the expansion of the market is really an expansion of more 'people in offices to administer things' [32]. Thus in reality it is the opposite of everything the free market is supposed to be. He also claims the same is true for the demise of the labour theory of value (a view of value adhered to by those working under the Inside Contract). Bureaucracies managed by leaders such as Andrew Carnegie forcefully espoused the notion that efficient bureaucracies headed by men of leadership created wealth, not labour. As such, these leaders should justly take the rewards. Adding this to Michels' (1915: 13) famous suggestion that the organization implies 'a tendency to oligarchy' and the way to deliver elitism was through control of the bureaucracy—we thus have oligarchy. Neo-liberalism necessarily creates a world of ruled and rulers because of 'the technical indispensability of leadership' (Michels, 1915: 400). Thus Mount misses the point when he claims the new oligarchs have emerged because the neo-liberal reforms 'have not been neoliberal enough' (2013: 11). Quite simply, at the heart of neo-liberalism is a bureaucratic oligarchy. Herein lies the rub for Graeber. More markets mean more bureaucracy and more oligarchy. Not an outrageous position—indeed it is increasingly espoused by theorists such as Wolfgang Streeck and Wendy Brown. The anti-democratic bureaucracy and the anti-democratic modern market reinforce one another to create our contemporary elite societies.

Of course this returns us to that other elite theorist, Max Weber (Titunik, 1997). The indirect father of much of management—leadership, bureaucracy, innovation, and entrepreneurship all bear his imprint—shared many similarities with neo-liberal thinkers. This is why he influenced them so much (Mommsen, 1974: 64; Gane, 2013; 2014). For example, Mises takes Weber's concept of instrumental rationality to apply it to all human action and to imbue it with values (Gane, 2013: 8–9). Schumpeter—not a neo-liberal—and the neo-liberals use Weber's concept of the static, planned, bureaucracy to posit the need for an innovator/entrepreneur. Leadership studies is, to a significant extent, based on Weber's concept of the leader as a charismatic figure (Beyer, 1999). And finally, organization studies examines or critiques Weber's bureaucracy more than perhaps any other single form. Weber is at the heart of the study of management, yet we misinterpret him.

Weber thinks in neo-liberal ways in two senses. Firstly, his concept of economic behaviour is heavily neo-liberal (Parson, 2003). Neo-liberalism critiques orthodox economics because it is static, it does not allow for error, and it does not have a temporal dimension. [...] [T]ime and uncertainty are central to neo-liberalism. The market is never static, the future always unknown, people make mistakes, and the market acts as an institution which teaches us over time. Those who learn best do well, those who cannot (or will not) suffer, and the market never achieves equilibrium (Hayek, 1948: 100). Thus, central to neo-liberal economics is a view of the market as an institution that teaches us that the future is important because we base future actions on learned experiences, and that uncertainty is a fundamental part of economic life (Hanlon, 2014). This view makes the entrepreneur/innovator the key subject because more than any other figure, she delivers the market's most urgent needs. This subject learns from the market what is in demand and provides it—it is not the scientist, the inventor, or the worker who shapes the economy but the entrepreneur. In his analysis of utility theory, wherein he favourably comments on the Austrian economist Carl Menger, Weber too stressed the future, uncertainty, and the role of the market as a learning mechanism (1975: 33). Indeed, he highlights the importance of uncertainty with a footnote mentioning Frank Knights' famous work *Risk uncertainty and profit* in this quote:

The calculations underlying trading activity will be called "speculative" to the extent to which they are oriented to possibilities, the realization of which is regarded as fortuitous and is in this sense uncalculable. In this sense the merchant assumes the burden of "uncertainty" (51). The transition from rational calculation to what is in this sense speculative calculation is entirely continuous, since no calculation which attempts to forecast future situations can be completely secured against "accidental" factors. The distinction thus has reference only to a difference in the *degree* of rationality. (1978: 159 fn 51, emphasis in original)

In light of this people learn in the marketplace (Weber, 1975: 29). The market and our behaviour within it are shaped by three forces. One, our needs and their satisfaction in light of limited supply; two, in contrast to orthodox economics, subjectively felt urgent needs are (or are not) satisfied and replaced or supplanted with other more urgent needs; and three, prior experience of subjective needs and efforts to attain them shape our future calculation of effort, spend, investment, and so on. Here need, temporal matters, learning, error, matter in a way that Menger would approve of. Thus Weber's sociological analysis of economic action shares very substantial overlaps with Menger's Austrian economics (Parson, 2003: 19). Furthermore, unlike orthodox economics, both Weber (1975: 28) and Menger (Parsons, 2003: 10) stress the importance of interaction and anticipation as central to the formation of price. Price is generated in uncertainty and time rather than as a given outcome of supply and demand. As is well known, the entrepreneur is a key figure in neo-liberalism, but Weber (1978: 92) too stresses their importance because future and uncertain needs need to be 'awakened' and 'directed' by entrepreneurs. In light of this, it is the entrepreneur, not the 'marginal consumer' of orthodox utility theory, who drives production. Here, one sees the outline of a tension between the bureaucracy and the entrepreneur/innovator. The bureaucracy sees planning as the solution to the fixed preferences of marginal utility and the entrepreneur/ innovator (or leader) sees the shaping and anticipating of fluid preferences as central to the pursuit of profit—crudely the bureaucracy versus the post-bureaucracy.

These tensions return us to Graeber's merging of bureaucracy and neo-liberalism because Weber is important to both concepts. The bureaucracy and its rules are necessary to deliver neo-liberalism through institutions such as the state, the corporation, the market, etc. But it is also the case that the bureaucracy allows an elite to dominate and, in many respects, force competition onto the rest of us whilst legitimating such actions through the discourses of leadership, entrepreneurship, or innovation—all important neo-liberal and Weberian concepts.

As is well known, Weber was interested in institutions and how they shape behaviour. Often the routines of life created discipline and, as suggested, whilst he (1975) accepted that the ideal type of economic man was an approximation to reality, it was one which was getting closer and closer to reality as institutions altered to accommodate this ideal type. Thus central to institutions like the state, the market, or the bureaucracy are rules which create routines. In his examination of the bureaucracy this worried Weber—he was concerned with oppressive stagnation and the emergence of the bureaucratic personality (Merton, 1940). This bureaucrat is characterised by obedience developed through 'habitual activity learned in public as well as in private organizations' (Weber, 1948: 229, emphasis in original). Obedient habits make bureaucrats susceptible to corporatism and the formation of unethical bureaucratic economies—a 'robber capitalism' (Weber, 1994: 89)—because they learn the wrong routines. Charismatic leadership is pivotal to undermining this form of bureaucracy and un-freedom in a democratic state (Burawoy, 2013: 752–753; Mommsen, 1974: 72–94). Yet this leadership also demonstrates Weber's neo-liberal democratic scepticism. On the issue of democracy and leadership, he supposedly expressed the following to General Ludendorff:

> In a democracy people choose a leader in whom they trust. Then the chosen leader says "Now shut up and obey me". People and party are now no longer free to interfere in his business. (Gerth and Mills in Weber, 1948: 42)

Weber affirms leadership in the face of bureaucratic capitalist societies but his affirmation allows a few to maintain their freedom and creativity. For the majority, they face a life of being subject to the rules and regulations of the bureaucratic organization (Mommsen, 1974: 93–94). In this manner, competitive-based leaders set the rules and regulations for organizations and societies. But this occurs alongside a world where the masses are dominated by bureaucratic un-freedom.

Furthermore, Weber sees that these twin features of bureaucracy and charismatic leadership—the 'double nature of what may be called the capitalist spirit' (Weber, 1978: 1118)—alter people in two neo-liberal ways. Bureaucracy externally regulates them through rules, rewards and punishments and charismatic leadership internally alters them by giving people new ambitions, desires and beliefs (Weber, 1978: 1115–1117). Thus the charismatic leader acts in ways Weber (and neo-liberals) also associated with the entrepreneur. His work suggests that, if managed by the right elite, bureaucracy and charismatic leadership can shape society, buttress markets, create competitive organizations, mould subjectivity, and protect individual freedom (for some). However, whilst bureaucracy is often presented as the opposite of competitive freedom (Mises, 1944), in actual fact what has occurred is a Weberian combination of neo-liberal management joined to bureaucracy to regulate and de-democratise and create increasing un-freedom for the many and freedom for the elite (Briebricher, 2015; Müller, 2015; Streeck, 2014).

This is clearly obvious in contemporary organizations with their unforgiving bureaucratic use of data to make labour compete and their infatuation with a culture that rewards the successful charismatic leaders and entrepreneurs—just think of the current obsession with Steve Jobs. Here Weber's competitive charismatic leadership and bureaucracy dominate the individual, the organization and the society. This takes place in a market society controlled by large organizations with competiveness, individualism, and private property at its base. In this vision, charismatic leaders alter the bureaucratic rules to change society, anchor competition, and reserve freedom.

Such a world is extremely close to neo-liberalism's entrepreneur. Mises (1996: 252) argues that uncertainty makes us all entrepreneurs. He enshrines (entrepreneurial) knowledge at the heart of social relations so that it creates development in the marketplace and the organization. Because of these attributes the entrepreneurial function is different to simple management. Management deals with 'subordinated entrepreneurial duties' (Mises, 1996: 304). However, in the actual functioning economy you cannot disentangle the two roles (Mises, 1996: 306; Metcalfe, 2006: 83–86). This inability to separate the roles increases in corporate bureaucratic capitalism. This has led some neo-liberals to argue that senior management takes on the entrepreneurial role of driving the economy. Elite management's subjective view and tacit knowledge grow in importance in an 'experimentally organized economy' (Eliasson and Eliasson, 2003). Senior management should act and be rewarded as entrepreneurs. It is they who have the subjective, intuitive, and tacit knowledge central to a bureaucratically filled economy (Eliasson, 1990; 2005; Eliasson and Eliasson, 2003). Here, following Hayek (1945), senior management need to act entrepreneurially because they can also only ever know a small part of the market—their knowledge, like that of everyone else, is incomplete hence they have to imagine the future and not rely on routine—they have to act as 'proxy entrepreneurs' (Foss et al., 2007; 1894). Furthermore, the entrepreneurial function entails the search for profit thereby allocating resources through anticipating the future needs of consumers. From this anticipation, profits or losses ensue which 'thereby shifts the ownership of the means of production from the hands of the less efficient into those of the more efficient' (Mises, 1996: 299).

As such, senior management becomes entrepreneurial through anticipation and the ability to match existing or new routines to this anticipation (Metcalfe, 2006; Foss et al., 2007). Thus the economy can continuously transform or develop itself through what we might call the 'entrepreneurial function of senior management'. Schumpeter's belief in equilibrium meant that knowledge could be concentrated which led him to forecast the demise of the entrepreneur and the rise of the behemoth corporation. However, in the neo-liberal vision, Schumpeter's 'invincible corporation' (Eliasson and Eliasson, 2003: 432) can no longer survive on routine innovation or 'subordinated entrepreneurial duties' and hence the necessary shift of major corporations to an entrepreneurial senior management found in areas of value capture, open innovation, or strategic acquisition. Thus the subjective imagination of the entrepreneur, who stands or falls by the actually realised value from their anticipated future, is transferred to the behemoth corporation (Eliasson, 1990; 2005). This is Graeber's 'total bureaucratisation'.

Central to this is the fact that here entrepreneurship is not creative. Rather it is about value capture (Burczak, 2002; Alvarez and Barney, 2006). Indeed, Kirzner explicitly comments:

> I view the entrepreneur not as a source of innovative ideas ex nihilo but as being *alert* to the opportunities that exist *already* and are waiting to be noticed. In economic development, too, the entrepreneur is to be seen as *responding* to opportunities rather than *creating* them; as *capturing* profit opportunities *rather than* generating them. (1973: 74, emphasis added)

Following Mises (1996), he sees entrepreneurial activity as the ethical inheritor of all wealth (Burczak, 2002). This wealth is then used to pay (or increasingly not pay) others their market price via transaction co-ordination e.g. capitalists, landowners, or workers. Building on Locke and Mises, Kirzner (1973) argues entrepreneurs display initiative and it is this human will—this imagining of profit to be captured and realised—that creates the product and not what flows through labour or capitalist risk—entrepreneurial activity is the key to wealth generation (Burczak, 2002).

Today, corporate bureaucracies supposedly house such entrepreneurial leadership and have used this vision and their economic power to legitimate a world wherein neo-liberal bureaucracy has created levels of inequality that even the Chief Economist of the Bank of England is concerned about and has referred to as corporations 'almost eating themselves'[1] as they snaffle labour's 'share'. This is what David Graeber entreats us to consider.

Graeber's book—whilst by no means perfect—usefully switches our attention to a different bureaucratic battle. Rather than analysing the bureaucratic firm versus the post-bureaucratic firm or the entrepreneurial economy versus corporatism, management scholarship would do well to heed his call and examine the bureaucratic firm as the Trojan horse of neoliberal (post-bureaucratic) oligarchy. As the most productive and efficient organizational form to date (Mills, 1951), it would be a surprise if elites relinquished bureaucratic power without a fight. Far more likely, they would harness such power to further entrench the elite societies neo-liberals have long since sought—Weber's bureaucracy and his elitism combine in neo-liberalism's oligarchic 'total bureaucratisation' (Hanlon, 2016).

---

1 See this interview with Andy Haldane, chief economist at The Bank of England: https://www.youtube.com/watch?v=-ZmUlTuyRPd8 [accessed 18 November 2015].

References

Alvarez, S. and Barney, J.B. (2006) 'Discovery and creation: Alternative theories of entrepreneurial action', *Fisher College Business Working Papers*, WP 2006-01-005 [http://www.ssrn.com/abstract=900200].

Bennis, W. (1967) 'The coming death of bureaucracy'. *Management Review*, 56(3): 19.

Biebricher, T. (2015) 'Neoliberalism and democracy', *Constellations*, 22(2): 255–266.

Brown, W. (2003) 'Neo-liberalism and the end of liberal democracy', *Theory and Event*, 7(1).

Brown, W. (2006) 'American nightmare: Neoliberalism, neoconservatism, and de-democratization', *Political Theory*, 34(6): 690–714.

Burawoy, M. (2013) 'From Max Weber to public sociology' [http://burawoy.berkeley.edu/PS/From%20Weber%20to%20PS.pdf].

Burczak, T. (2002) 'A critique of Kirzner's finders-keepers defense of profit', *The Review of Austrian Economics*, 15(1): 75–90.

Buttrick, J. (1951) 'The inside contract', *Journal of Economic History*, 12(3): 205–21.

Clawson, D. (1980) *Bureaucracy and the labor process: The transformation of US industry, 1860–1920*. New York: Monthly Review Press.

Drucker, P. (1984) *Innovation and entrepreneurship*. London: Routledge.

Du Gay, P. (2013) 'New spirits of public management ... 'Post-bureaucracy'', in P. Du Gay, P. and G. Morgan (eds.) *New spirits of capitalism? Crises, justifications, and dynamics*. Oxford: Oxford University Press.

Eliasson, G. (1990) 'The firm as a competent team', *Journal of Economic Behaviour and Organization*, 13: 275–98.

Eliasson, G. (2005) 'The nature of economic change and management in a new knowledge based information economy', *Information, Economics and Policy*, 17: 428–56.

Eliasson, G. and A. Eliasson (2003) 'The theory of the firm and the markets for strategic acquisition'. [http://www.snee.org/filer/chapters/177.pdf].

Englander, E. (1987) 'The inside contract system of production and organization: A neglected aspect of the history of the firm', *Labor History*, 28(4): 429–46.

Foss, K, N. J. Foss and P. G. Klein (2007) 'Original and derived judgement: An entrepreneurial theory of economic organization', *Organization Studies*, 28(12): 1893–1912.

Gane, N. (2013) 'The emergence of neo-liberalism: Thinking through and beyond Michel Foucault's lectures on biopolitics', *Theory, Culture and Society*, 31(4): 3–27.

Gane, N. (2014) 'Sociology and neoliberalism: A missing history', *Sociology*, 47(1): 1–15.

Graw, I. (2010) 'When life goes to work: Andy Warhol', *OCTOBER*, 132(Spring): 99–113.

Hamel, G. (2014) 'Bureaucracy must die', *Harvard Business Review*, November 4.

Hanlon, G. (2014) 'The entrepreneurial function and the capture of value: Using Kirzner to understand contemporary capitalism', *ephemera*, 14(2): 177–95.

Hanlon, G. (2016) *The dark side of management: A secret history of management theory*. London: Routledge.

Hayek, F.A. (1945) 'The use of knowledge in society', *American Economic Review*, 35(4): 519–30.

Hayek, F.A. (1948) *Individualism and economic order*. London: Chicago University Press.

Hayek, F.A. (1960) *The constitution of liberty*. London: Routledge.

Hennis, W. (1988) *Max Weber: Essays in reconstruction*. London: Allen and Unwin.

Kirzner, I.M. (1973) *Competition and entrepreneurship*. Chicago, University of Chicago Press.

Megay, E.N. (1970) 'Anti-pluralist liberalism: The German neo-liberals', *Political Science Quarterly*, 85(3): 422–42.

Merton, R. (1940) 'Bureaucratic structure and personality', *Social Forces*, 18(4): 560–568.

Metcalfe, J.S. (2006) 'Entrepreneurship: An evolutionary perspective', in M. Casson et al. (eds.) *The Oxford handbook of entrepreneurship*. Oxford: Oxford University Press.

Michels, R. (1915) *Political parties*. New York: Hearst's International Library Co.

Mills, C.W. (1951) *White collar: The American middle classes*. New York: Oxford University Press.

Mises, L. von (1944) *Bureaucracy*. New Haven: Yale University Press.

Mises, L. von (1996) *Human action—A treatise on economics, vol. 2*. Indianapolis: Liberty Fund.

Mommsen, W.J. (1974) *The age of bureaucracy: Perspectives on the political sociology of Max Weber*. Oxford: Basil Blackwell.

Mount, F. (2013) *Power and inequality in Britain now: The new few or a very British oligarchy*. London: Simon and Schuster.

Müller, J. (2015) 'Rule-breaking', *London Review of Books*, 37(16): 3–7.

Parsons, S.D. (2003) *Money, time and rationality in Max Weber—Austrian connections*. London: Routledge.

Scheuerman, W.E. (1997) 'The unholy alliance of Carl Schmitt and Friedrich A. Hayek', *Constellations*, 4(2): 172–88.

Schultz, T. W. (1962) 'Reflections on investment in man', *The Journal of Political Economy*, 70(5): 1–8.

Stone, K. (1973) 'The origin of job structures in the steel industry', *Radical America*, 7(6): 19–66.

Streeck, W. (2014) *Buying time: The delayed crisis of democratic capitalism*. London: Verso.

Titunik, R. (1997) 'The continuation of history: Max Weber on the advent of a new aristocracy', *Journal of Politics*, 59(3): 680–700.

Weber, M. (1948) *From Max Weber*, in H.H. Gerth and C. Wright Mills (eds.) London: Routledge and Kegan Paul.

Weber, M. (1975) 'Marginal utility theory and the so-called psychophsyics', *Social Science Quarterly*, 56(1): 21–36.

Weber, M. (1978) *Economy and Society, 2 vols*. Berkeley: University of California Press.

Weber, M. (1994) *Political writings*. Cambridge: Cambridge University Press.

Williamson, H.F. (1952) *Winchester: The gun that won the west*. New York: A. S. Barnes and Company.

Reading 5.3

The Ruling Class Does Not Rule: Notes on the Marxist Theory of the State

Fred Block

T HE MARXIST THEORY OF THE STATE remains a muddle despite the recent revival of interest in the subject.[1] Substantial progress has been made in formulating a critique of ortho- dox Marxist formulations that reduce the state to a mere reflection of economic interests. However, the outlines of an adequate alternative Marxist theory are not yet clear. This is most dramatically indicated by the continued popularity in Marxist circles of explanations of state policies or of conflicts within the state that are remarkably similar to orthodox formulations in their tendency to see the state as a reflection of the interests of certain groups in the capi- talist class. Many Marxists, for example, were drawn to interpretations of Watergate that saw it as a conflict between two different wings of the capitalist class.[2] This gap between theory and the explanation of actual historical events demonstrates that the critique of orthodox Marxist formulations has not been carried far enough. These earlier formulations—even when they have been carefully criticized and dismissed—sneak back into many current analyses because they remain embedded in the basic concepts of Marxist analysis.

This essay proposes two elements of an alternative Marxist theory of the state. The first element is a different way of conceptualizing the ruling class and its relationship to the state. This reconceptualization makes possible the second element—the elaboration of a structural framework that specifies the concrete mechanisms that make the state a capitalist state, whereas other structural theories have tended to analyze structures in an abstract and mystifying way.[3]

Although these two elements do not provide a complete Marxist theory of the state, they do provide a new way of thinking about the sources of rationality within capitalism. Contemporary Marxists have been forced to acknowledge that despite its fundamental irrationality, capital- ism in the developed world has shown a remarkable capacity to rationalize itself in response to the twin dangers of economic crisis and radical working-class movements.[4] Since the pres- ent historical period again poses for the left the threat of successful capitalist rationalization, the understanding of the sources of capitalism's capacity for self-reform is of the utmost polit- ical importance. The traditional Marxist explanation of capitalist rationality is to root it in the consciousness of some sector of the ruling class. In this light, capitalist reform reflects the conscious will and understanding of some sector of the capitalist class that has grasped the magnitude of the problem and proposes a set of solutions. The alternative framework being proposed here suggests that the capacity of capitalism to rationalize itself is the outcome of a conflict among three sets of agents—the capitalist class, the managers of the state apparatus, and the working class.[5] Rationalization occurs "behind the backs" of each set of actors so that rationality cannot be seen as a function of the consciousness of one particular group.

This argument and its implications will be traced out through a number of steps. First, I intend to show that critiques of orthodox Marxist theory of the state are flawed by their acceptance of the idea of a class-conscious ruling class. Second, I argue that there is a basis in Marx's writing for rejecting the idea of a class-conscious ruling class. Third, I develop a structural argument that shows that even in the absence of ruling-class class consciousness, the state managers are strongly discouraged from pursuing anticapitalist policies. Fourth, I return to the issue of capitalist rationality and describe how it grows out of the structured relationship among capitalist, workers, and state managers. Finally, I briefly analyze the implications of this argument for capitalism's current difficulties in the United States.

The Critique of Instrumentalism

The major development in the Marxist theory of the state in recent years has been the formulation of a critique of instrumentalism. A number of writers have characterized the orthodox Marxist view of the state as instrumentalism because it views the state as a simple tool or instrument of ruling-class purposes. First, it neglects the ideological role of the state. The state plays a critical role in maintaining the legitimacy of the social order, and this requires that the state appear to be neutral in the class struggle. In short, even if the state is an instrument of ruling-class purpose, the fact that it must appear otherwise indicates the need for a more complex framework for analyzing state policies. Second, instrumentalism fails to recognize that to act in the general interest of capital, the state must be able to take actions against the particular interests of capitalists. Price controls or restrictions on the export of capital, for example, might be in the general interest of capital in a particular period, even if they temporarily reduced the profits of most capitalists. To carry through such policies, the state must have more autonomy from direct capitalist control than the instrumentalist view would allow.

The critics of instrumentalism propose the idea of the relative autonomy of the state as an alternative framework. In order to serve the general interests of capital, the state must have some autonomy from direct ruling-class control. Since the concept of the absolute autonomy of the state would be un-Marxist and false, the autonomy is clearly relative. However, the difficult is in specifying the nature, limits, and determinants of that relative autonomy. Some writers have attempted to argue that the degree of autonomy varies historically, and that "late capitalism" is characterized by the "autonomization of the state apparatus." But these arguments have an ad hoc quality, and they share an analytic problem derived from the phase "relative autonomy from ruling-class control."

The basic problem in formulations of "relative autonomy" is the conceptualization of the ruling class. Relative autonomy theories assume that the ruling class will respond effectively to the state's abuse of that autonomy. But for the ruling class to be capable of taking such corrective actions, it must have some degree of political cohesion, an understanding of its general interests, and a high degree of political sophistication. In sum, the theory requires that the ruling class, or a portion of it, be class-conscious, that is, aware of what is necessary to reproduce capitalist social relations in changing historical circumstances. Yet if the ruling class or a segment of it is class-conscious, then the degree of autonomy of the state is clearly quite limited. At this point the theory of relative autonomy collapses back into a slightly more sophisticated version of instrumentalism. State policies continue to be seen as the reflection of inputs by a class-conscious ruling class.

The way out of this theoretical bind, the way to formulate a critique of instrumentalism that does not collapse, is to reject the idea of a class-conscious ruling class. Instead of the relative autonomy framework the key idea becomes a division of labor between those who accumulate capital and those who manage the state apparatus. Those who accumulate capital are conscious of their interests as capitalists, but, in general, they are not conscious of what is necessary to reproduce the social order in changing circumstances. Those who manage the state apparatus, however, are forced to concern themselves to a greater degree with the reproduction of the social order because their continued power rests on the maintenance of political and economic order. In this framework, the central theoretical task is to explain how it is that despite this division of labor, the state tends to serve the interests of the capitalist class. It is to this task—the elaboration of a structural theory of the state—that I will turn after a brief discussion of the division of labor between capitalists and state managers.

Division of Labor

The idea of a division of labor between nonclass-conscious capitalist and those who manage the state apparatus can be found in Marx's writings.[6] Two factors, however, have obscured this aspect of Marx's thought. First, Marx did not spell out the nature of the structural framework in which that division of labor operated, although he hinted at the existence of such a framework. Second, Marx's discussion of these issues is clouded by his polemical intent to fix responsibility for all aspects of bourgeois society on the ruling class. Even when Marx recognizes that the ruling class lacks class consciousness, he still formulates his argument in such a way as to imply that the ruling class as a whole is in conscious control of the situation. Marx used the idea of a conscious, directive ruling class as a polemical shorthand for an elaboration of the structural mechanisms through which control over the means of production leads to control over other aspects of society.

The tension in Marx's formulations is clearest in *The Eighteenth Brumaire* when he is explaining why the bourgeoisie supported Louis Bonaparte's coup d'état against the bourgeoisie's own parliamentary representatives. He writes:

> The *extra-parliamentary* mass of the bourgeoisie, on the other hand, by its servility towards the President, by its vilification of parliament, by the brutal maltreatment of its own press, invited Bonaparte to suppress and annihilate its speaking and writing section, its politicians and its *literati*, its platform and its press, in order that it might then be able to pursue its private affairs with full confidence in the protection of a strong and unrestricted government. It declared unequivocally that it longed to get rid of its own political rule in order to get rid of the troubles and dangers of ruling.[7]

The passage suggests a division of labor and a division of interest between the extra-parliamentary mass of the bourgeoisie, primarily interested in accumulating profits, and the parliamentary and literary representatives of that class, whose central concerns are different. Marx uses the notion of representation as a substitute for specifying the structural relationship that holds together the division of labor.

In an earlier passage, in a discussion of the petit-bourgeoisie, he states what is involved in the idea of representation:

> Just as little must one imagine that the democratic representatives are all shopkeepers or enthusiastic champions of shopkeepers. According to their education and their individual position they may he separated from them as widely as heaven from earth. What makes them representatives of the petty burgeoisie is the fact that in their minds they do not go beyond the limits which the latter do not go beyond in life, that they are consequently driven theoretically to the same tasks and solutions to which material interest and social position practically drive the latter. This is in general the relationship of the *political and literary representatives* of a class to the class that they represent.[8]

Marx here rejects the simple reductionism so common among his followers. For Marx, representation was an objective relationship—one did not need to be of a class to be its representative. And, in fact, representatives and their classes did not always see eye to eye, since their different positions could lead to different perspectives. In sum, representatives are *not* typical members of their classes, and it is a mistake to attribute to the class as a whole the consciousness that parliamentary or literary representatives display.

Marx's idea of representation suggests the geneal structural links between the capitalists and those who manage the state apparatus. Marx recognized that those in the state apparatus tended to have a broader view of society than the capitalists, although their view is still far short of a general understanding of what is necessary to reproduce the social order. After all, the state managers' preoccupation with the struggle for political power distorts their understanding. This is the source of the "parliamentary cretinism" that made Louis Bonaparte a better defender of the bourgeoisie's interests than that class's own representatives. But if neither the ruling class nor its representatives know what is necessary to preserve and reproduce capitalist social relations, why then does the state tend to do just that? The answer is that such policies emerge out of the structural relationships among state managers, capitalists, and workers.

Subsidiary Structural Mechanisms

When Marxists put forward a radical critique of instrumentalist views of the state, they usually do so to justify reformist Socialist politics. When one argues that the ruling class is diffused, lacks class consciousness and political sophistication, it seems to follow that if Socialists could gain control of the levers of the existing state, they would be able to use the state to effect the transition to socialism. The logic is impeccable—if the state is not inherently a tool of the ruling class, then it can be turned into a tool of the working class. This reformist view shares with instrumentalism a personalistic reductionism—either the ruling class controls the state personally and directly or it does not control it at all, in which case the state can be used for other purposes. Neither view recognizes the structural mechanisms that make the state serve capitalist ends regardless of whether capitalists intervene directly and consciously. However, once these mechanisms are understood, it is possible to construct a critique of Socialist reformism that is far more powerful than the critiques derived from the instrumentalist tradition.

Before considering the major structural mechanisms, it is necessary to consider a number of subsidiary mechanisms. The first of these includes all the techniques by which members of the ruling class are able to influence the state apparatus directly. Even though the members of the ruling class lack class consciousness, they are acutely aware of their immediate interests as capitalists and of the impact of the state on those interests. Capitalists, individually and in groups, apply pressure on the state for certain kinds of lucrative contracts, for state spending in certain areas, for legislative action in their favor, for tax relief, for more effective action to control the labor force, and so on. Needless to say, the pursuit of these various interests does not add up to policies in the general interest of capital. Even in the area of control of the labor force, where the common interest among capitalists is strongest, the policies that the capitalists demand might not even be in their own long-term best interest. Nevertheless, capitalists attempt to assure responsiveness by the state through various means, including campaign contributions, lobbying activities, and favors to politicians and civil servants. While these techniques are primarily used for increasing the state's receptivity to the special interests of particular capitalists or groups of capitalists, the overall effect of this proliferation of influence channels is to make those who run the state more likely to reject modes of thought and behavior that conflict with the logic of capitalism.

Included in the category of influence channels is the recruitment of ruling-class members into government service, and in recent years, into participation in various private policymaking groups that have a powerful impact on the formulation of government policies. Instrumentalists tend to see such individuals as typical members of their class, and their impact on the state is viewed as the heart of capitalist class rule. In the perspective being advanced here, this direct ruling-class participation in policy formation is viewed differently. For one thing, ruling-class members who devote substantial energy to policy formation become atypical of their class, since they are forced to look at the world from the perspective of state managers. They are quite likely to diverge ideologically from politically unengaged ruling-class opinion. More important, even if there were no politically engaged ruling-class members, there is still every reason to believe that the state and policymaking groups would advance policies that are in the interests of the ruling class. Marx's formulation cited earlier makes clear that one does not need to be of the ruling class to "represent" it politically; when there are no ruling-class individuals around, individuals from other social classes will eagerly fill the role of ruling-class "representatives."

All of the techniques of ruling-class influence, including direct participation, constitute a structural mechanism of subsidiary importance. The influence channels make it less likely that state managers will formulate policies that conflict directly with the interests of capitalists. But it is a subsidiary mechanism because, even in the absence of these influence channels, other structural mechanisms make it extremely difficult for the state managers to carry through anticapitalist policies. While instrumentalists argue that influence is the core of ruling-class control of the state, it is really more like the icing on the cake of class rule.

The same cannot be said of a second subsidiary mechanism—bourgeois cultural hegemony. The relevant aspect of cultural hegemony is the widespread acceptance of certain unwritten rules about what is and what is not legitimate state activity. While these rules change over time, a government that violates the unwritten rules of a particular period would stand to lose a good deal of its popular support. This acts as a powerful constraint in discouraging certain types of state action that might conflict with the interests of capital. However, simply invoking the existence of bourgeois cultural hegemony begs the problem of explaining how that hegemony is generated. Here, too, there must be specific structural mechanisms that operate to make "the ruling ideas" consistent with class rule. However, the task of explaining these structural mechanisms is beyond the scope of this essay.

Major Structural Mechanisms

A viable structural theory of the state must do two separate things. It must elaborate the structural constraints that operate to reduce the likelihood that state managers will act against the general interests of capitalists. An understanding of these constraints is particularly important for analyzing the obstacles to reformist Socialist strategies. But a structural theory must also explain the tendency of state managers to pursue policies that are in the general interests of capital. It is not sufficient to explain why the state avoids anticapitalist policies; it is necessary to explain why the state has served to rationalize capitalism. Once one rejects the idea of ruling-class class consciousness, one needs to provide an alternative explanation of efforts at rationalization.

Both tendencies can be derived from the fact that those who manage the state apparatus—regardless of their own political ideology—are dependent on the maintenance of some reasonable level of economic activity. This is true for two reasons. First, the capacity of the state to finance itself through taxation or borrowing depends on the state of the economy. If economic activity is in decline, the state will have difficulty maintaining its revenues at an adequate level. Second, public support for a regime will decline sharply if the regime presides over a serious drop in the level of economic activity, with a parallel rise in unemployment and shortages of key goods. Such a drop in support increases the likelihood that the state managers will be removed from power one way or another. And even if the drop is not that dramatic, it will increase the challenges to the regime and decrease the regime's political ability to take effective actions.

In a capitalist economy the level of economic activity is largely determined by the private investment decisions of capitalists. This means that capitalists, in their collective role as investors, have a veto over state policies in that their failure to invest at adequate levels can create major political problems for the state managers. This discourages state managers from taking actions that might seriously decrease the rate of investment. It also means that state managers have a direct interest in using their power to facilitate investment, since their own continued power rests on a healthy economy. There will be a tendency for state agencies to orient their various programs toward the goal of facilitating and encouraging private investment. In doing so, the state managers address the problem of investment from a broader perspective than that of the individual capitalist. This increases the likelihood that such policies will be in the general interest of capital.

Constraints on State Policies

This is, of course, too simple. Both sides of the picture—constraints and rationalization—must be filled out in greater detail to make this approach convincing. One problem, in particular, stands out—if capitalists have a veto over state policies, isn't this simply another version of instrumentalism? The answer to this question lies in a more careful analysis of the determinants of investment decisions. The most useful concept is the idea of business confidence. Individual capitalists decide on their rate of investment in a particular country on the basis of a variety of specific variables such as the price of labor and the size of the market for a specific product. But there is also an intangible variable—the capitalist's evaluation of the general political/economic climate. Is the society stable; is the working class under control; are taxes likely to rise; do government agencies interfere with business freedom; will the economy grow? These kinds of considerations are critical to the investment decisions of each firm. The sum of all of these evaluations across a national economy can be termed the level of business confidence. As the level of business confidence declines, so will the rate of investment. Business confidence also has an international dimension when nations are integrated into a capitalist world economy. Multinational corporations, international bankers, and currency speculators also make judgments about a particular nation's political/economic climate that determine their willingness to invest in assets in that nation. This, in turn, will affect the internal level of business confidence and the rate of productive investment.

Business confidence is, however, very different from "ruling-class consciousness." Business confidence is based on an evaluation of the market that considers political events only as they might impinge on the market. This means that it is rooted in the narrow self-interest of the individual capitalist who is worried about profit. Business confidence, especially because of its critical international component, does not make subtle evaluations as to whether a regime is serving the long-term interests of capital. When there is political turmoil and popular mobilization, business confidence will fall, and it will rise when there is a restoration of order, no matter how brutal. It was business confidence that responded so favorably to Louis Bonaparte's coup d'état, because he promised to restore the conditions for business as usual, despite negative implications for the political rights of the bourgeoisie. The crudeness of business confidence makes capitalism peculiarly vulnerable to authoritarian regimes that are capable of acting against the general interests of capital.[9]

The dynamic of business confidence as a constraint on the managers of the state apparatus can be grasped by tracing out a scenario of what happens when left-of-center governments come to power through parliamentary means and attempt to push through major reforms. The scenario distills a number of twentieth-century experiences including that of Chile under Allende. From the moment that the left wins the election, business confidence declines. The most important manifestation of this decline is an increase in speculation against the nation's currency. Reformist governments are always under suspicion that they will pursue inflationary policies; a high rate of inflation means that the international value of the nation's currency will fall. Speculators begin to discount the currency for the expected inflation as soon as possible.

This association between reformist governments and inflation is not arbitrary. Reformist policies—higher levels of employment, redistribution of income toward the poor, improved social services—directly or indirectly lead to a shift of income from profits toward the working class. Businesses attempt to resist such a shift by raising prices so that profit levels will not be reduced. In short, price inflation in this context is a market response to policies that tend to benefit the working class. The reformist government, faced with the initial speculative assault on its currency, has two choices. It can reassure the international and domestic business community, making clear its intention to pursue orthodox economic policies. Or it can forge ahead with its reform program. If it pursues the latter course, an increased rate of inflation and an eventual international monetary crisis is likely.

The international crisis results from the combination of continued speculative pressure against the currency and several new factors. Domestic inflation is likely to affect the nation's balance of trade adversely, leading to a real deterioration in the nation's balance-of-payments account. In addition, inflation and loss of confidence in the currency leads to the flight of foreign and domestic capital and increased foreign reluctance to lend money to the afflicted nation. The initial speculative pressure against the currency could be tolerated; the eruption of an acute international monetary crisis requires some kind of dramatic response. The government may renounce its reformism or cede power to a more "responsible" administration.

But if the government is committed to defending its programs, it will have to act to insulate its economy from the pressures of the international market by imposing some combination of price controls, import controls, and exchange controls.

Escalation in the government's attempt to control the market sets off a new chain of events. These new controls involve threats to individual capitalists. Price controls mean that firms lose the ability to manipulate one of the major determinants of profit levels. Import controls mean that a firm may no longer be able to import goods critical to its business. Exchange controls mean that firms and individuals no longer are able to move their assets freely to secure international havens. The fact that assets are locked into a rapidly inflating currency poses the possibility that large fortunes will be lost.

These are the ingredients for a sharp decline in domestic business confidence. Why should business owners continue to invest if they must operate in an environment in which the government violates the fundamental rules of a market economy?

A sharp decline in business confidence leads to a parallel economic downturn. High rates of unemployment coexist with annoying shortages of critical commodities. The popularity of the regime falls precipitously. The only alternative to capitulation—eliminating controls and initial reforms—is sharp forward movement to socialize the economy. The government could put people back to work and relieve the shortages by taking over private firms. However, the political basis for this kind of action does not exist, even where the leaders of the government are rhetorically committed to the goal of socialism. Generally, the reformist government has not prepared its electoral supporters for extreme action; its entire program has been based on the promise of a gradual transition. Further, the government leaders themselves become immersed in the political culture of the state apparatus, militating against a sharp break with the status quo.

The outcome of this impasse is tragically familiar. The government either falls from power through standard parliamentary means—loss of an election, defection of some of its parliamentary support—or it is removed militarily. Military actions that violate constitutionality meet formidable obstacles in liberal capitalist nations, but when economic chaos severely diminishes the legitimacy of a regime, the chances of a military coup are enhanced. When the militay intervenes, it does not do so as a tool of the ruling class. It acts according to its own ideas of the need to restore political order and in its own interests. Naturally the removal of the reformist government leads to a rapid revival of business confidence simply because order has been restored. However, it should be stressed that this revival of business confidence might not be sustained, since there can be substantial conflicts between the interests of the military and the capitalists.

The key point in elaborating this scenario is that the chain of events can unfold without any members of the ruling class consciously deciding to act "politically" against the regime in power. Of course, such a scenario is usually filled out with a great deal of editorializing against the regime in the bourgeois press, much grumbling among the upper classes, and even some conspiratorial activity. But the point is that conspiracies to destabilize the regime are basically supefluous, since decisions made by individual capitalists according to their own narrow economic rationality are sufficient to paralyze the regime, creating a situation where the regime's fall is the only possibility.

Rationalization

The dynamic of business confidence helps explain why governments are constrained from pursuing anticapitalist policies. It remains to be explained why governments tend to act in the general interests of capital. Part of the answer has already been suggested. Since state managers are so dependent upon the workings of the investment accumulation process, it is natural that they will use whatever resources are available to aid that process. In administering a welfare program, for example, they will organize it to aid the accumulation process, perhaps by ensuring certain industries a supply of cheap labor. Unlike the individual capitalist, the state managers do not have to operate on the basis of a narrow profit-maximizing rationality. They are capable of intervening in the economy on the basis of a more general rationality. In short, their structural position gives the state managers both the interest and the capacity to aid the investment accumulation process.

There is one major difficulty in this formulation—the problem of explaining the dynamic through which reforms that increase the rationality of capitalism come about. Almost all of these reforms involve an extension of the state's role in the economy and society, either in a regulatory capacity or in the provision of services. The difficulty is that business confidence has been depicted as so shortsighted that it is likely to decline in the face of most efforts to extend the state's role domestically, since such efforts threaten to restrict the freedom of individual capitalists and/or increase the tax burden on capitalists. If the state is unwilling to risk a decline in business confidence, how is it then that the state's role has expanded inexorably throughout the twentieth century?

Most theorists escape this problem by rejecting the idea that the capitalists are as short-sighted as the idea of business confidence suggests. Even if many members of the class share the retrograde notions implicit in the idea of business confidence, there is supposed to be a substantial segment of the class that is forward-looking and recognizes the value of extending the state's power. Theorists of corporate liberalism have attempted to trace many of the major extensions of state power in twentieth-century America to the influence of such forward-looking members of the ruling class. However, the position of these theorists ultimately requires an attribution of a high level of consciousness and understanding to the ruling class or a segment of it, and assumes an instrumental view of the state where state policies can be reduced to the input of certain ruling-class factions.[10]

There is, however, an alternative line of argument, consistent with the view of the ruling class and the state that has been advanced in this paper. It depends on the existence of another structural mechanism—class struggle. Whatever the role of class struggle in advancing the development of revolutionary consciousness, class struggle between proletariat and ruling class in Marx's view has another important function. It pushes forward the development of capitalism—speeding the process by which capitalism advances the development of the productive forces. This is conservative in the short term, but progressive in the long term; it brings closer the time when capitalism will exhaust its capacity to develop the productive forces and will be ripe for overthrow. Class struggle produces this result most clearly in conflict over wages. When workers are able to win wage gains, they increase the pressure on the capitalists to find ways to substitute machines for people. As Marx described the cycle, wage gains are followed by an intense period of mechanization as employers attempt to increase the rate of exploitation; the consequence is an increase in the size of the industrial reserve army, as machines replace workers. This, in turn, diminishes the capacity of workers to win wage gains, until the economic boom again creates a labor shortage. While this description applies particularly to competitive capitalism, the point is that workers' struggles—in Marx's theory—play an important role in speeding the pace of technological innovations. *Class struggle is responsible for much of the economic dynamism of capitalism.*

This pattern goes beyond the struggle over wages. From the beginning of capitalism, workers have struggled to improve their living conditions, which also means upgrading their potential as a labor force. For example, unbridled early capitalism, through child labor and horrendously long working days, threatened to destroy the capacity of the working class to reproduce itself—an outcome not in the long-term interests of capitalists. So working people's struggles against child labor, against incredibly low standards of public health and housing, and for the shorter day, made it possible for the class to reproduce itself, providing capitalism a new generation of laborers. In each historical period, the working class struggles to reproduce itself at a higher level of existence. Workers have played an important role, for example, in demanding increased public education. Public education, in turn, helped create the educated labor pool that developing capitalism required. Obviously, not every working-class demand contributes to the advance of capitalism, but it is foolish to ignore this dimension of class struggle.

In its struggles to protect itself from the ravages of a market economy, the working class has played a key role in the steady expansion of the state's role in capitalist societies. Pressures from the working class have contributed to the expansion of the state's role in the regulation of the economy and in the provision of services. The working class has not been the only force behind the expansion of the state's role in these areas. Examples can be cited of capitalists who have supported an expansion of the state's role into a certain area either because of narrow self-interest—access to government contracts, or because government regulation would hamper competitors—or because of some farsighted recognition of the need to coopt the working class. However, the major impetus for the extension of the state's role has come from the working class and from the managers of the state apparatus, whose own powers expand with a growing state.

Once working-class pressures succeed in extending the state's role, another dynamic begins to work. Those who manage the state apparatus have an interest in using the state's resources to facilitate a smooth flow of investment. There will be a tendency to use the state's extended role for the same ends. The capacity of the state to impose greater rationality on capitalism is extended into new areas as a result of working-class pressures. Working-class pressures, for example, might lead to an expansion of educational resources available for the working class, but there is every likelihood that the content of the education will be geared to the needs of accumulation—the production of a docile work force at an appropriate level of skill. Or similarly, working-class pressures might force the government to intervene in the free market to produce higher levels of employment, but the government will use its expanded powers of intervention to aid the accumulation process more generally.

This pattern is not a smoothly working functional process, always producing the same result. First, working-class movements have often been aware of the danger of making demands that will ultimately strengthen a state they perceive as hostile. For precisely this reason, Socialist movements have often demanded that expanded social services be placed under working-class control. However, working-class demands are rarely granted in their original form. Often, the more radical elements of the movement are repressed at the same time that concessions are made. Second, there can be a serious time lag between granting concessions to the working class and discovering ways that the extension of the state's power can be used to aid the accumulation process. There might, in fact, be continuing tensions in a government program between its integrative intent and its role in the accumulation process. Finally, some concessions to working-class pressure might have no potential benefits for accumulation and might simply place strains on the private economy. If these strains are immediate, one could expect serious efforts to revoke or neutralize the reforms. If the strains occur over the long term, then capitalism faces severe problems because it becomes increasingly difficult to roll back concessions that have stood for some time.[11]

These points suggest that the tendency for class struggle to rationalize capitalism occurs with a great deal of friction and with the continuous possibility of other outcomes. Nevertheless, the tendency does exist because of the particular interests of the state managers. Where there is strong popular pressure for an expansion of social services or increased regulation of markets, the state managers must weigh three factors. First, they do not want to damage business confidence, which generally responds unfavorably to an expansion of the government's role in providing social services or in regulating the market. Second, they do not want class antagonisms to escalate to a level that would endanger their own rule. Third, they recognize that their own power and resources will grow if the state's role is expanded. If the state managers decide to respond to pressure with concessions,[12] they are likely to shape their concessions in a manner that will least offend business confidence and will most expand their own power. These two constraints increase the likelihood that the concessions will ultimately serve to rationalize capitalism.

Major Reforms

This argument suggests that while some concessions will be made to the working class, the threat of a decline in business confidence will block major efforts to rationalize capitalism. Since business confidence is shortsighted, it will oppose even procapitalist reform programs if such programs promise a major increase in taxes or a major increase in the government's capacity to regulate markets. This leaves the problem of explaining the dramatic increases in the state's role that have occurred in all developed capitalist nations during the course of this century. The explanation is that there are certain periods—during wartime, major depressions, and periods of postwar reconstruction—in which the decline of business confidence as a veto on government policies doesn't work. These are the periods in which dramatic increases in the state's role have occurred.

In wars that require major mobilizations, business confidence loses its sting for several reasons. First, international business confidence becomes less important, since international capital flows tend to be placed under government control. Second, private investment becomes secondary to military production in maintaining high levels of economic activity. Third, in the general patriotic climate, it would be dangerous for the business community to disrupt the economy through negative actions.[13] The result is that state managers have the opportunity to expand their own power with the unassailable justification that such actions are necessary for the war effort. Some of these wartime measures will be rolled back once peace returns, but some will become part of the landscape.

In serious depressions and postwar reconstruction periods, the dynamics are somewhat different. Low levels of economic activity mean that the threat of declining business confidence loses its power, at the same time that popular demands for economic revival are strong. In such periods, the state managers can pay less attention to business opinion and can concentrate on responding to the popular pressure, while acting to expand their own power. However, there are still constraints on the state managers. Their continued rule depends on their capacity to revive the economy. As government actions prove effective in reducing unemployment, redistributing income, or expanding output, the political balance shifts. Pressure from below is likely to diminish; business confidence reemerges as a force once economic recovery begins. In short, successful reforms will tilt the balance of power back to a point where capitalists regain their veto over extensions of the state's role.

The increased capacity of state managers to intervene in the economy during these periods does not automatically rationalize capitalism. State managers can make all kinds of mistakes, including excessive concessions to the working class. State managers have no special knowledge of what is necessary to make capitalism more rational; they grope toward effective action as best they can within existing political constraints and with available economic theories.[14] The point is simply that rationalization can emerge as a by-product of state managers' dual interest in expanding their own power and in assuring a reasonable level of economic activity. The more power the state possesses to intervene in the capitalist economy, the greater the likelihood that effective actions can be taken to facilitate investment.

Not every extension of state power will survive beyond those periods in which state managers have special opportunities to expand the state's role. After a war, depression, or period of reconstruction, the business community is likely to campaign for a restoration of the *status quo ante*. State managers in these new periods will be forced to make some concessions to the business community in order to avert a decline in business confidence. However, the state managers also want to avoid the elimination of certain reforms important for the stabilization of the economy and the integration of the working class. Self-interest also leads them to resist a complete elimination of the state's expanded powers. The consequence is a selection process by which state managers abandon certain reforms while retaining others. In this process, reforms that are most beneficial for capitalism will be retained, while those whose effects are more questionable will be eliminated.[15] Again, the ultimate outcome is determined by intense political struggle.

Conclusion

The purpose of this essay has been to argue that a viable Marxist theory of the state depends on the rejection of the idea of a conscious, politically directive ruling class. By returning to Marx's suggestions that the historical process unfolds "behind the backs" of the actors (including the ruling-class actors), it is possible to locate the structural mechanisms that shape the workings of the capitalist state. These mechanisms operate independently of any political consciousness on the part of the ruling class. Instead, capitalist rationality emerges out of the three-sided relationship among capitalists, workers, and state managers. The structural position of state managers forces them to achieve some consciousness of what is necessary to maintain the viability of the social order. It is this consciousness that explains both the reluctance of state managers to offend business confidence, and their capacity to rationalize a capitalist society. However, the fact of consciousness does not imply control over the historical process. State managers are able to act only in the terrain that is marked out by the intersection of two factors—the intensity of class struggle and the level of economic activity.

This framework has implications for a wide range of theoretical and political questions. One of the most critical of these concerns capitalism's capacity to overcome its current economic difficulties. Analysts on the left have predicted that the forward-looking segment of the American ruling class will favor a further extension of the state's role in regulating the economy as a means to solve the problems of stagflation.[16] This perspective exaggerates the capacity of capitalism to reform itself in "normal" periods, and is unable to account, for example, for the inability of British capitalism to rationalize itself during the long period of decline since the nineteen-fifties. The framework developed here predicts that while the working class and the state managers themselves might favor an expansion of state intervention, business confidence will effectively veto such changes. It is therefore quite possible that the American economy will continue in its present state of crisis for many years to come.

Notes

1. For two surveys of recent Marxist work on the state—one polemical and the other dispassionate—see Alan Wolfe, "New Directions in the Marxist Theory of Politics," *Politics and Society* 4, 2 (1974), and David Gold, Clarence Y. H. Lo, and Erik Olin Wright, "Recent Developments in Marxist Theories of the Capitalist State," parts 1 and 2, *Monthly Review* (Oct. and Nov. 1975).

2. For critiques of such interpretations of Watergate, see Steve Weissman, "Cowboys and Crooks," in *Big Brother and the Holding Company; The World Behind Watergate*, ed. Steve Weissman (Palo Alto: Ramparts, 1974), 297–310; and Stephen Johnson, "How the West Was Won: Last Shootout for the Yankee-Cowboy Theory," *Insurgent Socialist* (Winter 1975): 61–93.

3. My analysis has been influenced by the arguments of Nicos Poulantzas, particularly in his "Problems of the Capitalist State," *New Left Review* 58 (Nov.–Dec. 1969). However, my analysis differs from Poulantzas' in two important respects. He tends to attribute consciousness to particular fractions of the ruling class and he fails to explain adequately the mechanisms by which the state is structurally a capitalist state. In this regard, my position is closer to that of Claus Offe in a number of articles, including "Structural Problems of the Capitalist State," in *German Political Studies*, ed. Klaus von Beyme (Beverly Hills, Calif.: Sage Publications, 1976); and Claus Offe and Volker Ronge, "Theses on the Theory of the State," *New German Critique* 6 (fall 1975).

4. By "rationalization" and "capitalist reform," I am referring primarily to the use of the state in new ways to overcome economic contradictions and to facilitate the integration of the working class. Rationalization must be distinguished from strategies of forcing the working class to bear the costs of economic contradictions through dramatic reductions in living standards combined with severe political repression.

5. Each of these categories requires some definition: "Capitalist class" or "ruling class" is used to refer to the individuals and families that own or control a certain quantity of capital. The cut-off point would vary by country or period, and it would necessarily be somewhat arbitrary, but the point is to distinguish between small businesses and large capitalist firms. The "managers of the state apparatus" include the leading figures of both the legislative and executive branches. This includes the highest-ranking civil servants, as well as appointed and elected politicians. "Working class" is being used in the broad sense. It includes most of those who sell their labor for wages, unwaged workers, and the unemployed.

6. In *The German Ideology*, Marx and Engels talk about a division of labor and of interests between capitalists and the producers of bourgeois ideology; "so that inside this class one part appears as the thinkers of the class (its active, conceptive ideologists, who make the perfection of the illusion of the class about itself their chief source of livelihood), while the others' attitude to these ideas and illusions is more passive and receptive, because they are in reality the active members of this class and have less time to make up illusions and ideas about themselves." In

Robert C. Tucker, ed., *The Marx-Engels Reader* (New York: Norton, 1972), 136–137. This suggests an analogous division of labor between capitalists and state managers. In both cases, however, treating ideologists or state managers as part of the ruling class violates the idea that class is determined by one's relation to the means of production. In short, Marx and Engels in this passage are using the notion of the ruling class in a polemical sense.

7. "The Eighteenth Brumaire," in ibid., 502.

8. Ibid., 462.

9. It is beyond the scope of this essay to explore the dynamics of authoritarian rule in capitalist societies. However, it is important to give some content to the familiar Marxist thesis that authoritarian rule is a second-best solution for capitalism, as compared with parliamentarism, and is only resorted to when the threat of revolution is serious. Part of the answer is that authoritarian regimes are less reliable in serving the general interests of capital because the structural mechanisms described here do not operate in the same way in the absence of parliamentarism.

10. [...].

11. An obvious example here is the commitment to maintaining "full employment. "This was a concession granted to the working class in the aftermath of the Great Depression, but it has proved increasingly costly for the developed capitalist nations.

12. They also have the option of responding to pressures through severe repression. The choice between concessions and repression is made by the state managers on the basis of their perceptions of the general environment and their political orientations.

13. These arguments all assume that some significant degree of national mobilization has occurred. In this sense, the business confidence veto was far stronger during Vietnam than during Korea. (In fact, it can be argued that the Johnson administration's desire to continue escalating in Vietnam ran afoul of declining business confidence.) In some cases, the business community's lack of enthusiasm for a war can prevent mobilization efforts from getting off the ground in time. This was clearly an element in the French collapse during World War II. But how does business confidence evaluate wars? I would suggest that the answer lies in terms of short-term considerations rather than an evaluation of the nation's long-term international position. In conditions of weak demand, the outbreak of major wars generally leads to a decline in business confidence.

14. This was the case with the New Deal. The Roosevelt administration simply stumbled on some of the elements necessary for a rationalization of the economy. The open-ended nature of the process is indicated by the fact that full recovery was not achieved until the mobilization for World War II.

15. This kind of selection process was carried out by the Conservative government that came to power in Britain in 1951 after Labour had presided over postwar reconstruction. The dangers

involved in the selection process are indicated by the fact that Britain's long-term prospects as a capitalist nation might have been improved by the retention of more of the Labour reforms.

16. See, for example, Stanley Aronowitz, "Modernizing Capitalism," *Social Policy* (May–June 1975), and James Crotty and Raford Boddy, "Who Will Plan the Planned Economy?" *The Progressive* (Feb. 1975). Such analyses tend to assume that the contradictions of advanced capitalism can be solved or effectively eased through state action. The possibility exists that this is not the case. While it is virtually impossible to reach a conclusion on that issue, one can debate whether such expanded state intervention will even be attempted.

Reading 5.4

China vs. America: Managing the Next Clash of Civilizations

Graham Allison

A S AMERICANS AWAKEN TO A RISING China that now rivals the United States in every arena, many seek comfort in the conviction that as China grows richer and stronger, it will follow in the footsteps of Germany, Japan, and other countries that have undergone profound transformations and emerged as advanced liberal democracies. In this view, the magic cocktail of globalization, market-based consumerism, and integration into the rule-based international order will eventually lead China to become democratic at home and to develop into what former U.S. Deputy Secretary of State Robert Zoellick once described as "a responsible stakeholder" abroad.

Samuel Huntington disagreed. In his essay "The Clash of Civilizations?," published [...] in 1993, the political scientist argued that, far from dissolving in a global liberal world order, cultural fault lines would become a defining feature of the post–Cold War world. Huntington's argument is remembered today primarily for its prescience in spotlighting the divide between "Western and Islamic civilizations"—a rift that was revealed most vividly by the 9/11 attacks and their aftermath. But Huntington saw the gulf between the U.S.-led West and Chinese civilization as just as deep, enduring, and consequential. As he put it, "The very notion that there could be a 'universal civilization' is a Western idea, directly at odds with the particularism of most Asian societies and their emphasis on what distinguishes one people from another."

The years since have bolstered Huntington's case. The coming decades will only strengthen it further. The United States embodies what Huntington considered Western civilization. And tensions between American and Chinese values, traditions, and philosophies will aggravate the fundamental structural stresses that occur whenever a rising power, such as China, threatens to displace an established power, such as the United States.

The reason such shifts so often lead to conflict is Thucydides' trap, named after the ancient Greek historian who observed a dangerous dynamic between a rising Athens and ruling Sparta. According to Thucydides, "It was the rise of Athens, and the fear that this instilled in Sparta, that made war inevitable." Rising powers understandably feel a growing sense of entitlement and demand greater influence and respect. Established powers, faced with challengers, tend to become fearful, insecure, and defensive. In such an environment, misunderstandings are

Graham Allison, "China vs. America: Managing the Next Clash of Civilizations," *Foreign Affairs*, vol. 96, no. 5, pp. 80–89.

magnified, empathy remains elusive, and events and third-party actions that would otherwise be inconsequential or manageable can trigger wars that the primary players never wanted to fight.

In the case of the United States and China, Thucydidean risks are compounded by civilizational incompatibility between the two countries, which exacerbates their competition and makes it more difficult to achieve rapprochement. This mismatch is most easily observed in the profound differences between American and Chinese conceptions of the state, economics, the role of individuals, relations among nations, and the nature of time.

Americans see government as a necessary evil and believe that the state's tendency toward tyranny and abuse of power must be feared and constrained. For Chinese, government is a necessary good, the fundamental pillar ensuring order and preventing chaos. In American-style free-market capitalism, government establishes and enforces the rules; state ownership and government intervention in the economy sometimes occur but are undesirable exceptions. In China's state-led market economy, the government establishes targets for growth, picks and subsidizes industries to develop, promotes national champions, and undertakes significant, long-term economic projects to advance the interests of the nation.

Chinese culture does not celebrate American-style individualism, which measures society by how well it protects the rights and fosters the freedom of individuals. Indeed, the Chinese term for "individualism"—*gerenzhuyi*—suggests a selfish preoccupation with oneself over one's community. China's equivalent of "give me liberty or give me death" would be "give me a harmonious community or give me death." For China, order is the highest value, and harmony results from a hierarchy in which participants obey Confucius' first imperative: Know thy place.

This view applies not only to domestic society but also to global affairs, where the Chinese view holds that China's rightful place is atop the pyramid; other states should be arranged as subordinate tributaries. The American view is somewhat different. Since at least the end of World War II, Washington has sought to prevent the emergence of a "peer competitor" that could challenge U.S. military dominance. But postwar American conceptions of international order have also emphasized the need for a rule-based global system that restrains even the United States.

Finally, the Americans and the Chinese think about time and experience its passage differently. Americans tend to focus on the present and often count in hours or days. Chinese, on the other hand, are more historical-minded and often think in terms of decades and even centuries.

Of course, these are sweeping generalizations that are by necessity reductive and not fully reflective of the complexities of American and Chinese society. But they also provide important reminders that policymakers in the United States and China should keep in mind in seeking to manage this competition without war.

We're Number One

The cultural differences between the United States and China are aggravated by a remarkable trait shared by both countries: an extreme superiority complex. Each sees itself as exceptional—indeed, without peer. But there can be only one number one. Lee Kuan Yew, the former prime minister of Singapore, had doubts about the United States' ability to adapt to a rising China. "For America to be displaced, not in the world, but only in the western Pacific, by an Asian people long despised and dismissed with contempt as decadent, feeble, corrupt, and inept is emotionally very difficult to accept," he said in a 1999 interview. "The sense of cultural supremacy of the Americans will make this adjustment most difficult."

In some ways, Chinese exceptionalism is more sweeping than its American counterpart. "The [Chinese] empire saw itself as the center of the civilized universe," the historian Harry Gelber wrote in his 2001 book, *Nations Out of Empires*. During the imperial era, "the Chinese scholar-bureaucrat did not think of a 'China' or a 'Chinese civilization' in the modern sense at all. For him, there were the Han people and, beyond that, only barbarism. Whatever was not civilized was, by definition, barbaric."

To this day, the Chinese take great pride in their civilizational achievements. "Our nation is a great nation," Chinese President Xi Jinping declared in a 2012 speech. "During the civilization and development process of more than 5,000 years, the Chinese nation has made an indelible contribution to the civilization and advancement of mankind." Indeed, Xi claimed in his 2014 book, *The Governance of China*, that "China's continuous civilization is not equal to anything on earth, but a unique achievement in world history."

Americans, too, see themselves as the vanguard of civilization, especially when it comes to political development. A passion for freedom is enshrined in the core document of the American political creed, the Declaration of Independence, which proclaims that "all men are created equal" and that they are "endowed by their Creator with certain unalienable Rights." The declaration specifies that these rights include "Life, Liberty and the pursuit of Happiness" and asserts that these are not matters for debate but rather "self-evident" truths. As the American historian Richard Hofstadter wrote, "It has been our fate as a nation not to have ideologies, but to be one." In contrast, order is the central political value for Chinese—and order results from hierarchy. Individual liberty, as Americans understand it, disrupts hierarchy; in the Chinese view, it invites chaos.

Do As I Say ... And As I Do?

These philosophical differences find expression in each country's concept of government. Although animated by a deep distrust of authority, the founders of the United States recognized that society required government. Otherwise, who would protect citizens from foreign threats or violations of their rights by criminals at home? They wrestled, however, with a dilemma: a government powerful enough to perform its essential functions would tend toward tyranny. To manage this challenge, they designed a government of "separated institutions sharing power," as the historian Richard Neustadt described it. This deliberately produced constant struggle among the executive, legislative, and judicial branches, which led to delay, gridlock, and even dysfunction. But it also provided checks and balances against abuse.

The Chinese conception of government and its role in society could hardly be more different. As Lee observed, "The country's history and cultural records show that when there is a strong center (Beijing or Nanjing), the country is peaceful and prosperous. When the center is weak, then the provinces and their counties are run by little warlords." Accordingly, the sort of strong central government that Americans resist represents to the Chinese the principal agent advancing order and the public good at home and abroad.

For Americans, democracy is the only just form of government: authorities derive their legitimacy from the consent of the governed. That is not the prevailing view in China, where it is common to believe that the government earns or losses political legitimacy based on its performance. In a provocative ted Talk delivered in 2013, the Shanghai-based venture capitalist Eric Li challenged democracy's presumed superiority. "I was asked once, 'The party wasn't voted in by election. Where is the source of legitimacy?'" he recounted.

> In some ways, Chinese exceptionalism is more sweeping than its American counterpart.

"I said, 'How about competency?'" He went on to remind his audience that in 1949, when the Chinese Community Party took power, "China was mired in civil war, dismembered by foreign aggression, [and] average life expectancy at that time [was] 41 years. Today [China] is the second-largest economy in the world, an industrial powerhouse, and its people live in increasing prosperity."

Washington and Beijing also have distinctly different approaches when it comes to promoting their fundamental political values internationally. Americans believe that human rights and democracy are universal aspirations, requiring only the example of the United States (and sometimes a neoimperialist nudge) to be realized everywhere. The United States is, as Huntington wrote in his follow-on book, *The Clash of Civilizations*, "a missionary nation," driven by the belief "that the non-Western peoples should commit themselves to the Western values ... and should embody these values in their institutions." Most Americans believe that democratic rights will benefit anyone, anywhere in the world.

Over the decades, Washington has pursued a foreign policy that seeks to advance the cause of democracy—even, on occasion, attempting to impose it on those who have failed to embrace it themselves. In contrast, although the Chinese believe that others can look up to them, admire their virtues, and even attempt to mimic their behavior, China's leaders have not proselytized on behalf of their approach. As the American diplomat Henry Kissinger has noted, imperial China "did not export its ideas but let others come to seek them." And unsurprisingly, Chinese leaders have been deeply suspicious of U.S. efforts to convert them to the American creed. In the late 1980s, Deng Xiaoping, who led China from 1978 until 1989 and began the country's process of economic liberalization, complained to a visiting dignitary that Western talk of "human rights, freedom, and democracy is designed only to safeguard the interests of the strong, rich countries, which take advantage of their strength to bully weak countries, and which pursue hegemony and practice power politics."

Thinking Fast and Slow

The American and Chinese senses of the past, present, and future are fundamentally distinct. Americans proudly celebrated their country turning 241 in July; the Chinese are fond of noting that their history spans five millennia. U.S. leaders often refer to "the American experiment," and their sometimes haphazard policies reflect that attitude. China, by contrast, sees itself as a fixture of the universe: it always was; it always will be.

Because of their expansive sense of time, Chinese leaders are careful to distinguish the acute from the chronic and the urgent from the merely important. It is difficult to imagine a U.S. political leader suggesting that a major foreign policy problem should be put on the proverbial shelf for a generation. That, however, is precisely what Deng did in 1979, when he led the Chinese side in negotiations with Japan over the disputed Diaoyu/Senkaku Islands and accepted an eventual, rather than an immediate, solution to the dispute.

Ever more sensitive to the demands of the news cycle and popular opinion, U.S. politicians take to Twitter or announce alliterative, bullet-point policy plans that promise quick solutions. In contrast, Chinese leaders are strategically patient: as long as trends are moving in their favor, they are comfortable waiting out a problem. Americans think of themselves as problem solvers. Reflecting their short-termism, they see problems as discrete issues to be addressed now so that they can move on to the next ones. The American novelist and historian Gore Vidal once called his country "the United States of Amnesia"—a place where every idea is an innovation and every crisis is unprecedented. This contrasts sharply with the deep historical and institutional memory of the Chinese, who assume that there is nothing new under the sun.

Indeed, Chinese leaders tend to believe that many problems cannot be solved and must instead be managed. They see challenges as long term and iterative; issues they face today resulted from processes that have evolved over the past year, decade, or century. Policy actions they take today will simply contribute to that evolution. For instance, since 1949, Taiwan has been ruled by what Beijing considers rogue Chinese nationalists. Although Chinese leaders insist that Taiwan remains an integral part of China, they have pursued a long-term strategy involving tightening economic and social entanglements to slowly suck the island back into the fold.

Who's the Boss?

The civilizational clash that will make it hardest for Washington and Beijing to escape Thucydides' trap emerges from their competing conceptions of world order. China's treatment of its own citizens provides the script for its relations with weaker neighbors abroad. The Chinese Communist Party maintains order by enforcing an authoritarian hierarchy that demands the deference and compliance of citizens. China's international behavior reflects similar expectations of order: in an unscripted moment during a 2010 meeting of the Association of Southeast Asian Nations, then Chinese Foreign Minister Yang Jiechi responded to complaints about Chinese assertiveness in the South China Sea by telling his regional counterparts and U.S. Secretary of State Hillary Clinton that "China is a big country and other countries are small countries, and that's just a fact."

By contrast, American leaders aspire to an international rule of law that is essentially U.S. domestic rule of law writ large. At the same time, they also recognize the realities of power in the Hobbesian global jungle, where it is better to be the lion than the lamb. Washington often tries to reconcile this tension by depicting a world in which the United States is a benevolent hegemon, acting as the world's lawmaker, policeman, judge, and jury.

Washington urges other powers to accept the rule-based international order over which it presides. But through Chinese eyes, it looks like the Americans make the rules and others obey Washing-ton's commands. General Martin Dempsey, former chairman of the Joint Chiefs of Staff, became familiar with the predictable resentment this elicited from China. "One of the things that fascinated me about the Chinese is whenever I would have a conversation with them about international standards or international rules of behavior, they would inevitably point out that those rules were made when they were absent from the world stage," Dempsey remarked in an interview [...] last year.

You Can Go Your Own Way

The United States has spent nearly three decades as the world's most powerful country. During that time, Washington's massive influence on world affairs has made it crucial for elites and leaders in other nations to understand American culture and the U.S. approach to strategy. Americans, on the other hand, have often felt that they have the luxury of not needing to think too hard about the worldviews of people elsewhere—a lack of interest encouraged by the belief, held by many American elites, that the rest of the world has been slowly but surely becoming more like the United States anyway.

In recent years, however, the rise of China has challenged that indifference. Policymakers in the United States are beginning to recognize that they must improve their understanding of China—especially Chinese strategic thinking. In particular, U.S. policymakers have begun to see distinctive traits in the way their Chinese counterparts think about the use of military force. In deciding whether, when, and how to attack adversaries, Chinese leaders have for the most part been rational and pragmatic. Beyond that, however, American policymakers and analysts have identified five presumptions and predilections that offer further clues to China's likely strategic behavior in confrontations.

First, in both war and peace, Chinese strategy is unabashedly driven by realpolitik and unencumbered by any serious need to justify Chinese behavior in terms of international law or ethical norms. This allows the Chinese government to be ruthlessly flexible, since it feels few constraints from prior rationales and is largely immune to criticisms of inconsistency. So, for example, when Kissinger arrived in China in 1971 to begin secret talks about a U.S.-Chinese rapprochement, he found his interlocutors unblinkered by ideology and brutally candid about China's national interests. Whereas Kissinger and U.S. President Richard Nixon felt it necessary to justify the compromise they ultimately reached to end the Vietnam War as "peace with honor," the Chinese leader Mao Zedong felt no need to pretend that in establishing relations with the capitalist United States to strengthen communist China's position vis-à-vis the Soviet Union, he was somehow bolstering a larger socialist international movement.

Just as China's practical approach to international politics arguably gives China an edge over the United States, so, too, does China's obsessively holistic strategic worldview. Chinese planners see everything as connected to everything else. The evolving context in which a strategic situation occurs determines what the Chinese call *shi*. This term has no direct English translation but can be rendered as the "potential energy" or "momentum" inherent in any circumstance at a given moment. It comprises geography and terrain, weather, the balance of forces, surprise, morale, and many other elements. "Each factor influences the others," as Kissinger wrote in his 2011 book, *On China*, "giving rise to subtle shifts in momentum and relative advantage." Thus, a skilled Chinese strategist spends most of his time patiently "observing and cultivating changes in the strategic landscape" and moves only when everything is in optimal alignment. Then he strikes swiftly. To an observer, the result appears inevitable.

War for Chinese strategists is primarily psychological and political. In Chinese thinking, an opponent's perception of facts on the ground may be just as important as the facts themselves. For imperial China, creating and sustaining the image of a civilization so superior that it represented "the center of the universe" served to deter enemies from challenging Chinese dominance. Today, a narrative of China's inevitable rise and the United States' irreversible decline plays a similar role.

Traditionally, the Chinese have sought victory not in a decisive battle but through incremental moves designed to gradually improve their position. David Lai, an expert on Asian military affairs, has illustrated this approach by comparing the Western game of chess with its Chinese equivalent, *weiqi* (often referred to as go). In chess, players seek to dominate the center of the board and conquer the opponent. In *weiqi*, players seek to surround the opponent. If the chess master sees five or six moves ahead, the *weiqi* master sees 20 or 30. Attending to every dimension in the broader relationship with an adversary, the Chinese strategist resists rushing prematurely toward victory, instead aiming to build incremental advantage. "In the Western tradition, there is a heavy emphasis on the use of force; the art of war is largely limited to the battlefields; and the way to fight is force on force," Lai wrote in a 2004 analysis for the U.S. Army War College's Strategic Studies Institute. By contrast, "the philosophy behind *go* ... is to compete for relative gain rather than seeking complete annihilation of the opponent forces." In a wise reminder, Lai warns that "it is dangerous to play *go* with the chess mindset."

Let's Make a Deal

Washington would do well to heed that warning. In the coming years, any number of flash points could produce a crisis in U.S.-Chinese relations, including further territorial disputes over the South China Sea and tensions over North Korea's burgeoning nuclear weapons program. Since it will take at least another decade or more for China's military capabilities to fully match those of the United States, the Chinese will be cautious and prudent about any lethal use of force against the Americans. Beijing will treat military force as a subordinate instrument in its foreign policy, which seeks not victory in battle but the achievement of national objectives. It will bolster its diplomatic and economic connections with its neighbors, deepening their dependency on China, and use economic leverage to encourage (or coerce) cooperation on other issues. Although China has traditionally viewed war as a last resort, should it conclude that long-term trend lines are no longer moving in its favor and that it is losing bargaining power, it could initiate a limited military conflict to attempt to reverse the trends.

The last time the United States faced extremely high Thucydidean risks was during the Cold War—especially during the Cuban missile crisis. Reflecting on the crisis a few months after its resolution, U.S. President John F. Kennedy identified one enduring lesson: "Above all, while defending our own vital interests, nuclear powers must avert those confrontations which bring an adversary to a choice of either a humiliating retreat or nuclear war." In spite of Moscow's hard-line rhetoric, Soviet Premier Nikita Khrushchev ultimately concluded that he could compromise on nuclear arms in Cuba. Likewise, Kissinger and Nixon later discovered that the Chinese ideologue Mao was quite adept at giving ground when it served China's interests.

Xi and U.S. President Donald Trump have both made maximalist claims, especially when it comes to the South China Sea. But both are also dealmakers. The better the Trump administration understands how Beijing sees China's role in the world and the country's core interests, the better prepared it will be to negotiate. The problem remains psychological projection: even seasoned State Department officials too often mistakenly assume that China's vital interests mirror those of the United States. The officials now crafting the Trump administration's approach to China would be wise to read the ancient Chinese philosopher Suntzu: "If you know the enemy and know yourself, you need not fear the result of a hundred battles. If you know yourself but not the enemy, for every victory gained you will also suffer a defeat. If you know neither the enemy nor yourself, you will succumb in every battle."

Chapter 5

1. What theories are implicit in the idea of distinguishing dictatorship and democracy by the following: "government by a minority" differs from "government by minorities"?
2. Identify two of the leading advocates of pluralist democracy, and summarize their contribution.
3. In what way is the bureaucratic firm a Trojan horse of a neoliberal oligarchy? Why does bureaucratic organization entrench a neoliberal elite?
4. How can a capitalist ruling class dominate a political system? Why is class-consciousness irrelevant in this power system?
5. Summarize why Graham Allison foresees the rise of Chinese power as likely to lead to war between America and China.

Chapter 6

Weakening State Formations
Sources of Political Disorder

T HE READINGS IN THIS CHAPTER POSE significant questions about the legitimacy and functioning of political systems today. They highlight the emergence of internal conflicts in political systems that are causing stalemate, ideological fixation, bitter political conflict, and disregard for democratic civility. The first reading by David Lake focuses on internal and external factors that weaken political authority. He points to the diminished US control of the global economy and the incapacity to facilitate economic growth and equality. These trends, he suggests, are due to technology, globalization, and their effect in generating global specializations rather than homogeneity, changing the nature of global capitalism. More precisely, he points out that developments are making life for working people more precarious, undercutting living conditions for the majority. Lake characterizes this situation as the end of "embedded capitalism," referring to the post–World War II era political settlement providing the population with full employment, rising living standards, social benefits, and educational opportunities. By the 1970s, the full employment paradigm faltered, growth slowed, inflation skyrocketed, and workers' wages began to stagnate. These factors led to an erosion of the authority of the state. The end of the post–World War II class compromise caused a major political and economic crisis that undermined the state's ability to govern. In addition, Lake briefly notes another major threat, the rise of China as challenger to American domination of global economy and military hegemony.

The second article also argues that globalization is fomenting social divisions that weaken political order. Frances Fox Piven argues that the loss of working-class organizational influence and prospects of positive futures generated cultural conflict. In contrast to class conflicts that involve a vertical social divide between the owners of businesses and workers, cultural conflict is horizontal, dividing society into antagonistic identity groups. With the economic stagnation and the rise in inequality, society becomes ever more fragmented, conflictual, and frustrated. Finally, social divisions also weaken citizens' capacity to challenge the power elite.

The third reading examines sources of conflict and generation of pressures for disintegration of the European Union. Starting with the British effort to leave the European Union (Brexit), Matthias Matthijs notes rightward movements in Poland and Hungary, the effects of the refugee crisis, and the rise of anti-establishment political parties as evidence of disintegration. He reports that the pressures for fragmentation originate from the effects of policies that undermined the standard of living in and political power of member states. He identifies three key policy initiatives prompting the backlash. In the 1980s, there was an elite-driven move to establish an internal market; in the early 1990s, there was the decision establishing the European Union; and then by 2000, the introduction of the Eurozone, imposing a common currency and monetary controls. The problems became apparent after the financial crisis of 2009, resulting in economic stagnation, unpayable debts, and the emigration of talented young people. The refugee crisis that peaked in 2015 made member states realize that they could no longer shape key policies affecting their own societies. The result, Matthijs argues, is the widespread and growing agreement among the citizens of many member states that they need to take back the powers that would enable them to help themselves.

Reading 6.1

Crises of Authority: Domestic Structures and the Changing American Imperium

David A. Lake

[...]

JENTLESON AND PAULY DESCRIBE A WORLD beset by change, challenges, and hard choices. Many of the challenges they identify are rooted in two global crises of authority, which in turn derive from the constraints and opportunities of the domestic structures of leading states. How well the international community copes with change will be determined in large measure by such structures and how they evolve in the decades ahead.

The first crisis arises from the steady erosion of embedded liberalism by the very process of globalization that it supports. Following World War II, the United States successfully generalized its own "liberal" domestic structure through the American "imperium," creating interests in most advanced industrialized states (AIS) vested in an open international economy.[1] Over time, however, the cross-class compromise that supported free trade and factor flows has come under increasing threat, especially since the dawn of the Great Recession that began in 2008.

The second crisis is the growth of China as a world power. The rise of economic challengers is not inherently dangerous. Although there were significant stumbles, most notably the failure of collective action in the Great Depression of the 1930s, Britain passed the torch of economic leadership to the United States without major changes in preferred economic policies.[2] China's politically dominated market economy, however, suggests that its preferences on the rules of a future international economic order will differ considerably from those of the United States. The potential for conflict depends on these differences in domestic structure, and specifically whether China will embrace the American imperium or resist and eventually challenge that imperium.

This chapter makes four points necessary to understand the origins and likely consequences of the crises of authority. First, domestic structures vary from failed states, in which authority is completely dispersed to the private sphere, to totalitarian states, in which authority is centralized and concentrated in the state. Truncating variation in domestic structure to that found only in the AIS confounds our estimates of its role and importance in politics. Second, as "congealed" authority, domestic structure is nonetheless negotiated, dynamic, and a product of politics. Earlier conceptions tended to see domestic structure as largely static. In actuality, structure is variable but made real through vested interests. As these interests evolve, domestic structure is also renegotiated and adapted. Third, for all but the most powerful states, domestic structures are at least in part a product of their international environment. Since 1945, the United States has attempted to project its own domestic structure onto other states through a liberal international economy. These targets of American hierarchy have evolved domestic structures that vest their economies, perhaps unwittingly, into the American-led international order. Finally, the challenges of the twenty-first century will be driven by differences in the domestic structures of its two likely superpowers, the United States and China.

Domestic Structure Revisited

Domestic structure is both a product of the international political system and a constraint on foreign policy and policy making. In its simplest form, it is the distribution and differentiation of political authority within state and society.[3] This discussion begins with some basic definitions and builds a view of domestic structures from the ground up.

Authority

Political authority is legitimate power embodied in the right by A to command B to alter his actions. This right, in turn, implies a correlative obligation by B to comply, if possible, with A's command. B's obligation, finally, implies a further right by A to enforce her commands in the event of B's noncompliance. In any authority relationship, B chooses whether to comply with A's commands, but is bound by the right of A to discipline or punish his noncompliance.[4]

The centralization of the state refers directly to how authority is distributed within the governing apparatus. In the United States, for instance, authority is divided across three branches of government, including two coequal legislative houses. In the United Kingdom and Japan, political authority is centralized in the lower house of the legislature and the majority party, with other branches playing subordinate roles.[5]

Although not commonly acknowledged, social groups also possess political authority. Weber's definition of the modern state has focused attention on the coercive powers of political authorities and blinded analysts to the broad range of private authorities in many sectors of social life.[6] Some social groups, such as families and clans, do use violence, sometimes legitimately, to enforce rules governing members; "honor killings" are a powerful disciplinary device to enforce traditional rules and societal roles, especially for women. More often, though, social groups enforce rules by various degrees of exclusion. Hunter-gatherer societies ostracize individuals who cannot or will not obey the elders. Parents threaten to disown their unruly children. Religions shun or excommunicate sinners, and threaten apostates and nonbelievers with eternal damnation. Professional associations disbar, decertify, or discharge incompetents and transgressors. Exclusion from a group can be an enforcement mechanism equal in power to the legitimate violence wielded by a state. In this way, private actors can often wield political authority over their members in ways that are as binding as the state.

The centralization of society refers implicitly to the distribution of political authority among private actors. Peak associations of business or labor, for instance, centralize authority over their members and thereby speak with a single voice in policy circles. Individuals and units exert influence within the associations, just as voters do in a democratic government, but must ultimately conform to the policy positions adopted by the organization. Those who disagree with the association's majority on an issue often have no other place to go for the benefits provided by the group. Multiple, competing business or labor associations are decentralized and usually have less power over their members because ostracism has less impact on dissatisfied individuals or groups who can simply join another association or form one of their own. The same can be said for clan and tribal structures, religious or sectarian bodies, and other economic or identity groups within society. All exercise more or less authority over their members, and are more or less centralized in structure.

The differentiation of state and society describes how authority is distributed within the polity between the public and private sectors, on the one hand, and across the ruling coalition, on the other. In polities with large public spheres (small private spheres), the state possesses authority over a wide range of issues and practices. At an extreme, in totalitarian societies the state claims the authority to regulate legitimately all human interactions, although this is usually not possible in practice. In polities with small public spheres (large private spheres), the state possesses only limited and highly constrained authority. Liberal states, for instance, possess only limited powers, and are explicitly denied the right to regulate many social, religious, "personal," and even political practices. In fragile or failed states, at the opposite extreme, the public sphere is extremely small to nil, with the state unable to exercise authority beyond the border of the capital city and sometimes, as in Somalia, not even there.

The nature of the ruling coalition also matters.[7] Large coalition systems must be responsive to a broad range of social forces, and the boundary between state and society is ultimately more porous as competing elites mobilize different constituencies. Small coalition systems create access for some, but exclude other social groups from the political arena and limit political participation. The size of the coalition interacts with social structure. Large selectorate systems with centralized societies limit points of access in the political process. Peak associations of any denomination have an interest and the ability to regulate access and they channel social demands through their institutions. In large coalition systems with decentralized societies, on the other hand, associations cannot successfully regulate access and the result is an extremely porous border between state and society.

Finally, where the divide between public and private authority lies is a fundamental determinant of the policy instruments available to the state. With decentralized societies and large private spheres, the United States and Britain have fewer legitimate rights to regulate social practices and largely depend on market mechanisms to cope with globalization and change. With few policy instruments, they can cushion disruptions but must ultimately let them flow through and reshape society over time.[8] Centralized states with more centralized societies, in turn, can solve collective action problems more effectively, have more policy instruments, and can direct change, especially in an extensive growth phase where the future is relatively clear and technocratic elites can reap the advantages of backwardness. These more centralized polities, in turn, acquire more vested interests (see below), and are easily cartelized over time; as the "lost decades" in Japan make clear, this can impede adjustment, and especially so when approaching the technological frontier where innovation counts.

Variation in Domestic Structures

The causes and consequences of domestic structure are difficult to identify, in part, because the range of variation has been unduly truncated. Compared to other states, the AIS all occupy a middle range wherein state and society are sufficiently balanced that policy is reasonably coherent and effective. Indeed, this may be why the AIS are, in fact, advanced industrialized states. As the discussion here suggests, the centralization of state and society can take on more extreme values than commonly found in the AIS.

North Korea and Myanmar, along with the historical cases of Nazi Germany and Soviet Russia, are totalitarian and highly centralized states that focus power in small ruling cliques that, as the label implies, adopt a totalizing view of their authority and negate the private sphere.[9] The centralization of state authority in totalitarian states far exceeds anything experienced in the AIS. Even authoritarian governments over time intentionally undercut private authorities, lest they compete with the state or provide mechanisms for solving collective action problems within society. After thirty years of rule by Saddam Hussein, for instance, Iraqi society was completely gutted, a fact that the United States did not anticipate in planning for its invasion and the state-building challenges that followed. A similar problem exists in Egypt following political changes after the Arab Spring.

Conversely, the problem of failed states typically arises when societies are too strong relative to the state. Although sometimes treated as a disease that befalls unsuspecting victims, state weakness is commonly endogenous, with multiple private authorities—primarily clans, tribes, or sectarian groups—remaining the locus of traditional social, economic, and political life. Either state authority was never consolidated because of these preexisting private authorities—as in Afghanistan throughout most of its history or many postcolonial African states[10]—or because political entrepreneurs reactivated ethnic or religious cleavages that had waned or been suppressed, as during the breakup of the former Yugoslavia.

Despite this great variation, most attention to domestic structure has occurred within the study of AIS. This focus truncates the range of actual variation in the world. As King, Keohane, and Verba remind us, truncating a dependent variable "attenuates estimates of causal effects on average," while limiting the range of variation in an independent variable increases the uncertainty of the estimate.[11] With domestic structure often being used in typological holistic analyses, studies may suffer from both effects simultaneously. Expanding the range of variation in both state and society promises to reveal more about the sources and effects of domestic structure.

Too much authority vested in the state (a large public sphere, with high state centralization) appears to lead to rent-seeking, economic distortions, slow economic growth, and possibly state collapse. Without a vibrant society to balance state power, abuse may be inevitable. This describes the path of the former Soviet Union, as well as the one North Korea appears to be following today.[12] Too much authority vested in a moderately to highly centralized society (a large private sphere, without a monopoly group) may be equally dangerous, leading to factionalism, rivalry, and possibly violence. Without a state that can act authoritatively and impose a rule of law on powerful social groups, competition may pull apart the society. Domestic structure matters to the fundamental stability of countries in ways not appreciated when limited to the AIS. Indeed, the AIS may exist in a "sweet spot" where state and society are sufficiently balanced that the extremes of state rent seeking and social rivalry are avoided. Variations among the AIS are likely to be overwhelmed by their similarities. Analyzing the full range of variance is especially important in considering future competition between the United States, with its decentralized state and society, and China, with its highly centralized state fused with society.

Stasis and Change in Domestic Structures

Structure matters only if it is relatively stable and fixed. If the distribution of political authority sways in the wind—turning this way and that with the shifting breeze—it will have little effect, or at least not one that we can easily discern. Fortunately for analysts, domestic structure is a product of long-term historical developments, especially the timing of industrialization and political crises.[13] Similarly, the differences between Europe, centered on

Germany, and Asia, centered on Japan, despite the integrative pull of the American imperium, suggests the persistence of domestic structure.[14] Domestic structure does have an enduring quality, and thus is an object worthy of study.

The Structure of Domestic Structures

That institutions are "sticky" is a commonplace observation, but not one that actually explains why institutions endure. The problem is a deep one. We know that, in any two-dimensional issue space, nearly any outcome can be an equilibrium under majority rule. Faced with this potential policy chaos, scholars have argued that institutions, and especially rules of agenda setting, "induce" an equilibrium, privileging some outcomes over others. Yet if institutions matter, then cycling between policy alternatives is likely to be displaced onto cycling between institutions; rather than fighting over alternative policies, this implies that political actors will fight over the choice of institutions.[15] The political chaos is merely shifted down one level from policy to institutions. The critical point is that if institutions are a choice, then they are an output of the political process like any other, subject to the same pushing and hauling as other issues. How and why institutions congeal remains a mystery in the literature, and especially problematic in explaining the robustness of domestic structures.

The distribution of political authority within and between state and society—itself an institution—is largely self-enforcing because of the vested interests that accumulate in society. Institutions are not stable because they are institutions; rather, they become stable because social forces that benefit from the policies they produce develop interests in those institutions and their privileged position within them. We can see the effect of vested interests most easily, perhaps, in the contrast between liberal market economies (LMEs) and organized market economies (OMEs).[16] LMEs have large private spheres of authority, rely more on market-based allocation systems, and offer fewer social protections. In turn, both firms and workers develop flexible economic strategies that discourage investments in specific processes or skills, creating a large pool of "generic" capital and labor that flows (relatively) easily across sectors. Having invested in flexible production and skills, however, society has little motivation to press government for policies that encourage long-term holding of assets, apprenticeship programs tailored to long-term employment contracts, and other features common in OMEs. Adapted for flexibility, changing policies are of less import and the political arena is characterized by institutions that amplify political swings, such as single-member electoral districts and majority party rule. The economy and its political actors are vested in a particular, self-reinforcing mode of production. Liberal markets beget more liberal markets.

OMEs, by contrast, have larger public spheres, rely less on market forces, and have more countercyclical social protection programs. Both firms and workers expect to be engaged in long-term relationships, so both have incentives to invest in specific skill and asset acquisition. Having invested in high skill-oriented production, in turn both firms and workers have incentives to press government for a steady flow of equally well-trained workers and countercyclical social programs that will tide them through market downturns and sustain investment in these specific assets. Since policy instability threatens to undermine these incentives, the political system is structured for centrism, either through proportional representation electoral systems or coalition governments in which centrist parties are pivotal. Organized markets beget organized markets.

Having adapted to life within either an LME or OME model, few in each type of society have an interest in disrupting those relationships. Flexible workers in LME systems have an interest in ensuring that business remains flexible, while highly skilled and firm-specific workers in OME systems have a vested interest in maintaining relations of long-term employment. The same goes for firms. Unless one model or the other is clearly superior—and this appears not to be the case, since both gain from specialization and trade[17]—there is little pressure to change once actors are vested into their respective systems.

Vested interests are found throughout politics. Social Security is the "third rail" of American politics, for instance, because so many individuals have premised their lifetime consumption and savings patterns on its future. Farm subsidies everywhere are hard to reform because any reduction would not only affect the current income of farmers but also the value of their land, often their single biggest asset. Vested interests are, of course, the bane of political reformers everywhere. Yet we often do not appreciate the positive role that vested societal interests play in producing political stability and institutionalization. Institutions themselves do not breed stability. Rather, it is their effects and the interests that accumulate around those institutions that create order out of the potential chaos of constantly shifting policies and institutions. This vesting of interests does lead to stasis and makes political reform difficult, even when necessary and likely Pareto improving. As the vested interests accumulate over time, change becomes harder and harder.[18] It is these same vested interests, however, that make domestic structures enduring and stable despite the winds of change that blow around them.

Domestic Structures Reversed

Although vested interests make domestic structure hard to change, such structures are continually renegotiated and evolving. In the United States, for example, the imperial presidency saw authority shift from Congress to the executive, changing the centralization of the state. Evolving society, and especially the decline of large-scale manufacturing and labor unions, may have led to a further decentralization of society (although we lack systematic measures). Much of contemporary politics is actually a struggle over the division between the public and private spheres, including whether the state should regulate business, on the one hand, and social practices such as reproductive freedom and marriage, on the other. Who has authority over what is always contested and, at least at the margin, always in flux.

There are at least two sources of change in domestic structures, both of which affect the value of assets and thus the interests of the various groups within society. Technology is largely exogenous and affects politics by changing the demand for certain factors of production and, over time, factor endowments. Technological innovations typically make labor more productive, thereby freeing labor from previous uses and lowering rates of return for unskilled labor. This has always been the motive behind "Luddite" policies aimed to slow the rate of technological change in large organizations and protect the least-skilled workers in an economy. Conversely, to operate the new technologies often requires more skilled workers, increasing the demand and real rates of return for human capital and, thus, encouraging the creation of more human capital over time. As technology "progresses," different factors of production are privileged and harmed, and the balance between factors will evolve.

More important in the short term is globalization, which is at least partly endogenous. Globalization is, in major part, the product of past policy choices, especially the progressive lowering of barriers to trade, investment, and information flows across national borders begun after World War II. Through these policies, and the resulting rules constructed at the international level for economic liberalization, the largest and most powerful countries have slowly generalized their particular domestic structures in the American imperium. Having adapted to a highly market-oriented political economy at home, it is only "natural" for hegemons to seek isomorphic institutions abroad.[19] Unsurprisingly, the most liberal and powerful states of the last two hundred years have also led the most liberal international economies during the Pax Britannica and Pax Americana.[20] In turn, what is a choice for hegemons becomes a common environmental constraint for other states that shapes their domestic structures. This was true for all the AIS after World War II, but it is found in its most acute form in the former Axis powers. As defeated countries, Germany and Japan were highly malleable after 1945. The war itself destroyed enormous economic assets, "divesting" domestic interests of much of their prior wealth and political interests. The old regimes were also strongly delegitimated. The United States, in turn, dangled significant rewards before them if they would join the American-led international hierarchy. This favored the rise of politically moderate, capitalist, and Western-oriented elites surrounding Konrad Adenauer in Germany and Shigeru Yoshida in Japan. Spreading the rewards of the American imperium broadly across the populations of these countries also brought the masses onboard and allowed for international subordination and democracy to coexist.[21] In the end, it was an American empire, but it was an "empire by invitation."[22] Although structural differences remained, both Germany and Japan became willing members of the American imperium.

Over time, states and more important societies within the American imperium became vested in that international hierarchy. As within countries, groups develop interests in sustaining the political order to which they have adapted and prospered. In this way, the international order becomes self-enforcing. Imagine the political outcry from industries around the world that have adapted their production and sales to a global market if the WTO were, say, to come under threat from more protectionist forces. Previous collapses notwithstanding, globalization appears to have created sufficiently vested interests that it is now a one-way bet: it does not require homogenization of economies and polities, but does reward winners and punish losers, tilting the political playing field increasingly in favor of the winners. Export interests and others that benefit from an open world economy gain, prosper, and expand their political influence, while import-competing sectors and others that lose steadily shrink in size and influence. Exporters become ever more dependent on world markets and the national economy becomes increasingly specialized. These "internationalist" interests, in turn, develop stronger interests in maintaining market openness, both at home and abroad. International liberalism becomes self-sustaining and perhaps even expands. Thus, the American imperium has slowly but inexorably reshaped the domestic political economies of its members, an effect that is deeper and more dramatic the higher the level of integration.

As globalization expands, the balance of political power shifts within countries. Globalization is a process of specialization, not homogenization. Small initial differences accumulate as the division of labor deepens.[23] The winners grow faster and invest some portion of their gains in lobbying for more favorable policies, while the losers shrink and, though highly motivated, steadily lose resources with which to invest in politics. Textiles and shoes, though politically important in the 1970s, are no longer a force in American trade policy.[24] As relative prices shift over time, the interests of groups change and coalitions that were once aligned come under pressure. If the changes become large enough, the coalitions eventually fracture in political "crises," often associated with critical realignments in politics.[25] Shifting relative prices are like the tectonic plates of the earth, in which small movements build pressure that eventually ruptures in an earthquake—or, in politics, in a crisis. Out of these crises, by means we do not yet understand well, a new political coalition emerges that renegotiates the distribution of political authority to lock in its conception of the interests of its constituent groups, starting the cycle anew.[26]

The Future of the American Imperium

The question today is, how robust is the American imperium? Has it become sufficiently vested that it is self-perpetuating? Or will it be reconfigured through some new international crisis? There are, at least, two significant threats to the American imperium as we know it.

Both are the product of that imperium's success. Whether these crises will lead to revolutionary change is an open question.

The Triumph of Neoliberalism

The first threat is the political triumph of the winners from globalization, manifested in the end of embedded liberalism and the new fiscal crisis of the state.[27] The threat is more to the substance of the American imperium than to the position of the United States itself, but it is nonetheless significant. As discussed, globalization has slowly but inexorably reshaped the domestic structures of constituent states by creating winners who invest their gains in political institutions favorable to their interests and losers who are slowly winnowed out. Globalization is a self-perpetuating system that destroys the political compromise that was its original foundation.

Globalization rests on a cross-class coalition of comparatively advantaged sectors or factors who, in exchange for policies of freer trade, agree to insulate comparatively disadvantaged sectors or factors from the full effects of economic change. This compromise does not halt the process of economic realignment, but it slows the pace through which comparatively disadvantaged producers depreciate their existing assets. Ruggie called this cross-class compromise "embedded liberalism."[28] In the AIS, capital is the big winner from economic openness, and it has shared its gains with labor, the big loser, through enhanced social welfare programs and a modicum of income redistribution. This implies high and progressive taxes, at least by historical standards, and social programs directed to the middle class (subsidies for higher education, in one form or another, unemployment insurance, etc.) and the poor (income subsidies). Rodrik and Garrett showed that more open AIS did, indeed, possess larger social welfare states.[29] This bargain was relatively stable through the mid-1980s.

As the winners win, however, over time they expand their political clout, become more vested in favorable institutions, and ultimately need the losers less to support their economic program. In the United States, labor and labor-intensive industries have shrunk over time. With new workers upgrading their skills and entering more capital-intensive occupations or securing less well-paying jobs in the nontradables sector (largely services), the number of "protectionist" voters has steadily declined. With downward pressure on wages, more intense competition for jobs, and greater political influence for capital, unions have slowly declined and "right to work" policies have spread, further weakening and fracturing an already-decentralized labor movement. As their numbers and political strength contract, in turn, the comparatively disadvantaged become politically less important and less necessary to the former political coalition. Technological change, of course, continues "churning" at the bottom of the division of labor as some previously "high-skilled" industries now become "low skilled." But with each new industry thrown into the maelstrom of change, fewer workers are displaced relative to capital (which remains relatively more mobile) and fewer "anti-globalization" voters are created than in the past. Through globalization, the political equipoise eventually tips toward the winners and erodes the political foundations of the cross-class compromise necessary to earlier policies of globalization. Liberalism eventually undercuts the "embedded" part of the original compromise, creating neoliberalism.

This political shift was first manifested in the Thatcher and Reagan revolutions of the 1980s in Britain and the United States, respectively. Taxes were lowered and rendered less progressive, industries were deregulated, social welfare policies were reformed, and labor unions were assaulted. Hall describes this as the end of the "Fordist regime."[30] The economic and social consequences of the shift were papered over, for a time, by capital market openness beginning in the mid-1980s which allowed for new borrowing by the AIS. Accumulating substantial foreign reserves in trying to keep their exchange rates artificially low, the export-led growth economies in Asia have been only too willing to lend to the AIS, with the risk of default being a small price to pay for continued exports. Importantly, this international borrowing permitted the AIS to run substantial fiscal deficits, thus enabling them to lower taxes while sustaining some—albeit reduced—social spending. Where in the previously closed economies savings had to equal investment plus fiscal deficits, almost by definition, with open capital markets public sector borrowing did not crowd out private investment, allowing continued private sector growth despite the increase in government deficits. And although real wages have been stagnant since the 1970s for most of the workforce in the AIS, consumer borrowing also increased and allowed standards of living, on average, to continue their upward growth through the new millennium. Borrowing thus held the cross-class compromise of embedded liberalism together for another two decades. As former Vice President Dick Cheney famously said of the Bush-era tax cuts, "Reagan proved that deficits don't matter," at least politically.[31]

This strategy of papering over the cracks in the political foundations of embedded liberalism by increased borrowing shattered in the financial crisis of 2008 and the ensuing Great Recession. The prior fiscal deficits in the United States and several key European economies led to inevitable current account deficits and, predictably, asset bubbles, especially in the non-tradables sector and, even more specifically, in real estate.[32] When the asset bubbles burst, capital markets dried up. Unable to borrow or even pay the debts on their now-depreciated assets, consumers cut back spending and tried, where possible, to rebuild their savings and credit. As consumer demand fell, and industry itself found it more difficult to borrow, new private investment fell dramatically and production and employment plummeted. As more workers were laid off, consumer demand fell further. Although fiscal stabilizers (i.e. unemployment insurance) kicked in and central banks moved quickly to stave off another Great Depression, and international institutions inhibited a return to the beggar-thy-neighbor policies of the 1930s, the net result was the Great Recession and continuing expectations of a prolonged period of economic stagnation.[33]

With accumulated fiscal debts now approaching unsustainable levels in southern Europe and the United States, the ability to prop up embedded liberalism through continued borrowing has finally ended. This brings the politics of winners and losers from globalization into sharp relief. In the United States, the Republican Party, under pressure from its Tea Party wing, refuses to countenance new taxes to close the budget deficit, forcing President Barak Obama to settle for trifling increases in taxes on the most wealthy Americans. The Democratic Party is on the defensive, seeking only to slow the rate of contraction in social welfare and so-called entitlement programs. Focusing attention on the dramatic increase in economic inequality in recent decades, the Occupy Movement has subsumed some of the antiglobalization forces that first appeared in 1999 in the "Battle for Seattle," though it has not yet turned explicitly into an antiglobalization movement. In Europe, the fiscal crisis has hit the Mediterranean countries especially hard. The European Union, led by Germany, has imposed devastating austerity on them in return for small amounts of stabilization funding. With draconian cuts in fiscal spending, the resulting tensions have shattered the myth of an emerging European identity and threaten the very foundations of the union.

How this crisis will play out is still unclear.[34] I am less sanguine about the situation in Europe than are Abdelal and Krotz [...], but we are obviously in the midst of a potentially significant change. The most likely outcome is that neoliberalism will indeed triumph, leading to a corresponding shift in the domestic structures of the AIS and, especially, further contracting the role of the state in the economy. This will open the way for major private centers of power in large corporations to exercise even more authority over their workers and, in turn, the economy as a whole. In this case, the pain will fall primarily on the upper working- and lower-middle classes through a combination of higher unemployment/lower wages and reduced government services/higher taxes. These class segments are among the most decentralized in the United States and the most politically disenfranchised. On this path, the winners from globalization continue to win and they will become even more vested in the neoliberal state. This would simply exacerbate a trend that has already been underway for decades.

Alternatively, a different line of political cleavage could emerge. As Gourevitch famously recognized, crises render politics more "plastic."[35] Under high uncertainty, as at present, political coalitions may be put together in new and presently unforeseen ways by political entrepreneurs carrying different ideas and agendas. What these new ideas may be remains to be seen. Left parties in the AIS appear largely on the defensive. The winners from globalization may already be too vested in neoliberalism to permit a wider range of alternatives from being seriously considered. But precisely because crises exert a profound effect on politics, it is too early to rule out an alternate future.

The New Chinese Imperium?

The second and more direct threat to the American imperium is the rise of China. The American imperium rests on the dominant position of the United States in the world economy. By promoting policies it favors, especially economic liberalism, the United States has realigned the domestic structures of constituent states and built interests vested in its continued imperium. These vested interests suggest, on the one hand, that the American imperium will not be easily dislodged. Even if the United States is challenged, groups within other states will continue to support its favored policies and will press their own governments to support liberalism as well. Nonetheless, as China becomes more powerful in the decades ahead, it is widely expected to challenge the United States either because it can (which is the traditional realist view), or because it favors a different package of policies and international economic rules, although the content of this package is typically left unspecified. Examining China's domestic structure, however, can give us some broad hints about its likely policy preferences and, thus, its potential challenge to the United States.

China is a highly centralized state dominated by a single political party that fuses state and society.[36] Local governors may appear to have substantial authority, but it is clearly delegated from the center and monitored to ensure local actions are consistent with central policy and needs.[37] In turn, the party retains a parallel structure to the state and its cadre system permeates all levels of society, both channeling issues upwards to the center for resolution and ensuring that directives from the center are appropriately implemented at the local level. Factions within the party compete, though programmatic differences appear limited and personal relationships among party elites are more important.[38] Critically, the party and state stand above the law, not subject to it, and personal connections and influence apparently figure large in political decisions. In an oft-repeated phrase, China is characterized by rule by law but not the rule of law. Finally, after decades of near-totalitarian rule and single-party dominance, private authorities able to restrain the state have either been fractured, coopted, or purged from the political system.[39] Although new social forces are arising in China and penetrating politics, they remain highly fragmented.[40] This highly decentralized society leaves a relatively open playing field for the state and its new private-sector allies.

Though significantly liberalized from the past, the state and party retain significant control over the economy through continued government planning and price setting, state-owned enterprises in key sectors, control over access to scarce finance, access to factors of production, industry siting and the development of new enterprises, and a variety of other economic levers.[41] The fusion of public and private authority in China ensures reciprocal influence between business and the state and relatively harmonious interests between government and private elites.[42] Promoting export-led growth since the economic reforms of 1978, China's economy has grown rapidly. Business has profited handsomely, and the state has enjoyed increased legitimacy by its ability to deliver higher standards of living to the average citizen.[43] More directly, and reflecting the importance of personal ties in a state-dominated economy, family members of high-ranking party officials have amassed large fortunes either as favored entrepreneurs or as intermediaries between business and the state.[44]

The mutual dependence of public and private elites on export-led growth suggests, at one level, that China will continue to support international economic liberalism. Like Europe and the rest of Northeast Asia, China has been integrated into the American imperium. For those in the West who see China as more a partner than a competitor in world politics, the expectation is that the vesting of its export industries in the state, and vice versa, will lock China into the liberal international economy.

At another level, however, China's personalist regime and political control of the economy will fit poorly with free and open competition and the rules embedded in the institutions of the American imperium. China's ideal international economy might look a lot like its domestic economy with markets functioning widely but in the interests of its political leaders. A Chinese-led international regime would likely not operate under the impersonal rules of the American imperium but under personal ties and to the advantage of individual political leaders. In this view, the United States and China might not clash over whether the international economy should be liberal, but would differ significantly on whether markets would be governed by the rule of law. This is less of an ideological distance, perhaps, than that which separated the liberal United States and communist Soviet Union at the height of the Cold War, but it is still a substantial distance in preferred rules for the international economy.

Whether or not China chooses to accommodate or challenge the American imperium will depend in large measure on the gains for its leaders from a liberal, market-based international economy versus a liberal, politically based international economy. The challenge, if it occurs, will be rooted in the differing domestic structures of the two twenty-first-century superpowers. Given the vesting of business in the state, and vice versa, the most likely prospect is for at least a degree of challenge. Personalist rule conflicts with an international rule of law and, like the United States before it, China will seek to promote its domestic system abroad.

The brightest future for the American imperium is for China's growing middle class to demand a rule of law within China. This is, in part, what the United States and the West more generally hope to achieve in pressing China on human rights and other "internal" political practices. Such reforms would restrain the state and its high-ranking officials and reduce their rent-seeking abilities. The United States and others, in turn, are limited in the pressure they can bring to bear on the regime for fear that it will provoke a backlash and the very challenge they hope to avoid. The international balance hangs on the domestic balance between the forces of resistance in China currently vested in the state and popular forces of reform calling for greater rule of law. Without significant private authorities able to help the masses overcome their collective action problems, the vested interests are likely to prevail and the challenge to the American imperium is likely to be a serious one.

Conclusion

Domestic structures vary in their centralization of public and private authority and in the differentiation between the two. These structures are quite stable, otherwise they would be of little analytic interest. Their stability is created by interests vested in their particular patterns of authority and the policies they produce, and in turn is reproduced by the actions of those same vested interests. Yet despite their stability, domestic structures are continually pressed by technological change and, today, globalization in ways that may lead to fissures and ultimately crises that can produce dramatic political change.

Under the American imperium, globalization has realigned the domestic structures of countries around the world, creating interests vested in that imperium. The beneficiaries of globalization, however, threaten the political bargain of embedded liberalism that underlies globalization. Though unlikely, those excluded from the gains of economic interdependence and those increasingly marginalized politically may rise up in a new coalition to challenge the dominance of neoliberalism. Likewise, although it too has been reshaped by the American imperium and globalization, China's domestic structure remains well outside the range of the other AIS. As it rises in international power defined in terms of control, [...] it will likely seek to alter the rules of the international economy to its advantage. Although the United States and China agree on far more than commonly feared, including the need for a fundamentally liberal international economy, the real question for the years ahead is whether China's domestic structure is reshaped quickly enough to coexist with the American-sponsored rule of law embodied in the World Trade Organization and other international institutions or whether the interests vested in the personalist regime will pursue a new set of rules better suited to their domestic political economy. For both threats, understanding how domestic structures persist and change remains a major and important topic.

Notes

1. On domestic structures, see Katzenstein 1978; on the American imperium, see Katzenstein 2005.
2. Gilpin 1977.
3. Katzenstein 1978.
4. Flathman 1980.
5. See Waltz 1967.

6. See Lake 2010.

7. Katzenstein 1978.

8. See Ikenberry 1988.

9. Friedrich and Brzezinski 1965.

10. Herbst 2000; Boone 2003.

11. King, Keohane, and Verba 1994.

12. Haggard and Noland 2009.

13. Katzenstein 1985.

14. Katzenstein 2005.

15. McKelvey 1979; Shepsle 1979; and Riker 1980.

16. Hall and Soskice 2001; see also Gourevitch and Shinn 2005.

17. Gourevitch 2003; Rogowski 2003.

18. Olson 1982.

19. Lake 1999.

20. Gilpin 1977.

21. See Lake 2013.

22. Lundestad 1990.

23. Rogowski 2003.

24. Hathaway 1998.

25. Frieden *et al.* 2011.

26. See Gourevitch 1999 and Katzenstein and Nelson 2013.

27. On the "first" fiscal crisis of the state, see Block 1981.

28. Ruggie 1983.

29. Rodrik 1997; Garrett 1998.

30. Hall 2013.

31. Suskind 2004, 291.

32. Chinn and Frieden 2011.

33. Kahler 2013.

34. See Kahler and Lake 2013.

35. Gourevitch 1986. He also argues, however, that with each successive crisis, institutions play a greater role in structuring interests and coalitions, narrowing the range of choice.

36. See Guo 2003.

37. Landry 2008.

38. The factions are sometimes described as the elitist faction, of officials rising through the party from the more prosperous provinces, and the populist faction, of officials from the rural interior. See Li 2009; also Zhiyue 2007.

39. See Yu and Guo 2012.

40. Saich 2000; Yang 2006; and Mertha 2009.

41. On China's "bamboo economy," see "Entrepreneurship in China: Let a Million Flowers Bloom," *The Economist*, 10 March 2011, http://www.economist.com/node/18330120 (accessed 18 January 2013).

42. Shirk 1993; Chen and Dickson 2010.

43. Businesses associated with party members do better on average than others. See Li *et al.* 2008. On growth as the foundation for legitimacy in contemporary China, see Laliberte and Lanteigne 2008 and Guo 2010.

44. See Manion 2004 and Sun 2004.

References

Block, Fred (1981) 'The Fiscal Crisis of the Capitalist State.' *Annual Review of Sociology* 7: 1–27.

Boone, Catherine (2003) *Political Topographies of the African State: Territorial Authority and Institutional Choice*. New York: Cambridge University Press.

Chen, Jie and Bruce J. Dickson (2010) *Allies of the State: China's Private Entrepreneurs and Democratic Change*. Cambridge, MA: Harvard University Press.

Chinn, Menzie and Jeffry A. Frieden (2011) *Lost Decades: The Making of America's Debt Crisis and the Long Recovery*. New York: W.W. Norton.

Flathman, Richard E. (1980) *The Practice of Political Authority: Authority and the Authoritative*. Chicago: University of Chicago Press.

Frieden, Jeffry A., David A. Lake, Michael Nicholson, and Aditya Ranganath (2011) 'Crisis Politics: Uncertainty, Relative Prices and Political Change.' Presented at the *Annual Meeting of the International Political Economy Society*, Madison, WI.

Friedrich, Carl J. and Zbigniew Brzezinski (1965) *Totalitarian Dictatorship and Autocracy*. Cambridge, MA: Harvard University Press.

Garrett, Geoffrey (1998) *Partisan Politics in the Global Economy*. New York: Cambridge University Press.

Gilpin, Robert (1977) 'Economic Interdependence and National Security in Historical Perspective.' In *Economic Issues and National Security*, edited by Klaus Knorr and Frank N. Trager, 19–66. Lawrence, KS: Regents Press of Kansas.

Gourevitch, Peter (1986) *Politics in Hard Times: Comparative Responses to International Economic Crises*. Ithaca, NY: Cornell University Press.

———(1999) 'The Governance Problem in International Relations.' In *Strategic Choice and International Relations*, edited by David Lake and Robert Powell, 137–64. Princeton, NJ: Princeton University Press.

———(2003) 'Corporate Governance, Global Markets, National Politics.' In *Governance in a Global Economy: Political Authority in Transition*, edited by Miles Kahler and David Lake, 305–31. Princeton, NJ: Princeton University Press.

Gourevitch, Peter A. and James Shinn (2005) *Political Power and Corporate Control: The New Global Politics of Corporate Governance*. Princeton, NJ: Princeton University Press.

Guo, Baogang (2010) *China's Quest for Political Legitimacy: The New Equity-Enhancing Politics*. Lanham, MD: Rowman and Littlefield.

Guo, Xiaoqin (2003) *State and Society in China's Democratic Transition: Confucianism, Leninism, and Economic Development*. New York: Routledge.

Haggard, Stephan and Marchs Noland (2009) *Famine in North Korea: Markets, Aid, and Reform*. New York: Columbia University Press.

Hall, Peter A. (2013) 'The Political Origins of Our Economic Discontents: Contemporary Adjustment Problems in Historical Perspective.' In *Politics in the New Hard Times: The Great Recession in Comparative Perspective*, edited by Miles Kahler and David A. Lake, 129–49. Ithaca, NY: Cornell University Press.

Hall, Peter A. and David Soskice, eds. (2001) *Varieties of Capitalism: The Institutional Foundations of Comparative Advantage*. New York: Oxford University Press.

Hathaway, Oona (1998) 'Positive Feedback: The Impact of Trade Liberalization on Industry Demands for Protection.' *International Organization* 52 (3): 575–612.

Herbst, Jeffrey (2000) *States and Power in Africa: Comparative Lessons in Authority and Control*. Princeton, NJ: Princeton University Press.

Ikenberry, G. John (1988) *Reasons of State: Oil Politics and the Capacities of American Government*. Ithaca, NY: Cornell University Press.

Jentleson, Bruce W. and Louis W. Pauly (2014) 'Political Authority, Policy Capacity, and Twenty-First-Century Governance.' This volume.

Kahler, Miles (2013) 'Economic Crisis and Global Governance: The Stability of a Globalized World.' In *Politics in the New Hard Times: The Great Recession in Comparative Perspective*, edited by Miles Kahler and David Lake, 27–51. Ithaca, NY: Cornell University Press.

Kahler, Miles and David A. Lake, eds. (2013) *Politics in the New Hard Times: The Great Recession in Comparative Perspective*. Ithaca, NY: Cornell University Press.

Katzenstein, Peter J., ed. (1978) *Between Power and Plenty: Foreign Economic Policies of Advanced Industrial States*. Madison, WI: University of Wisconsin Press.

———(2005) *A World of Regions: Asia and Europe in the American Imperium*. Ithaca, NY: Cornell University Press.

Katzenstein, Peter J. and Stephen C. Nelson (2013) 'Worlds in Collision: Uncertainty and Risk in Hard Times.' In *Politics in the New Hard Times: The Great Recession in Comparative Perspective*, edited by Miles Kahler and David A. Lake, 233–52. Ithaca, NY: Cornell University Press.

King, Gary, Robert O. Keohane, and Sidney Verba (1994) *Designing Social Inquiry: Scientific Inference in Qualitative Research*. Princeton, NJ: Princeton University Press.

Lake, David A. (1999) 'Global Governance: A Relational Contracting Approach.' In *Globalization and Governance*, edited by Aseem Prakash and Jeffrey A. Hart, 31–53. New York: Routledge.

———(2010) 'Rightful Rules: Authority, Order, and the Foundations of Global Governance.' *International Studies Quarterly* 54 (3): 587–613.

———(2013) 'Legitimating Power: The Domestic Politics of U.S. International Hierarchy.' *International Security* 38 (2): 74–111.

Laliberte, Andre and Marc Lanteigne, eds. (2008) *The Chinese Party-State in the Twenty-First Century: Adaptation and the Reinvention of Legitimacy*. New York: Routledge.

Landry, Pierre F. (2008) *Decentralized Authoritarianism in China: The Communist Party's Control of Local Elites in the Post-Mao Era*. New York: Cambridge University Press.

Li, Cheng (2009) 'China's Team of Rivals.' *Foreign Policy* 171: 88–93.

Li, Hongbin, Lingsheng Meng, Qian Wang, and Li-An Zhou (2008) 'Political Connections, Financing and Firm Performance: Evidence from Chinese Private Firms.' *Journal of Development Economics* 87 (2): 283–99.

Lundestad, Geir (1990) *The American 'Empire.'* New York: Oxford University Press.

Manion, Melanie (2004) *Corruption by Design: Building Clean Government in Mainland China and Hong Kong*. Cambridge, MA: Harvard University Press.

McKelvey, Richard D. (1979) 'General Conditions for Global Intransitivities in Formal Voting Models.' *Econometrica* 47 (5): 1085–112.

Mertha, Andrew (2009) 'Fragmented Authoritarianism 2.0: Political Pluralization in the Chinese Policy Process.' *The China Quarterly* 200: 995–1012.

Olson, Mancur (1982) *The Rise and Decline of Nations: Economic Growth, Stagflation, and Social Rigidities*. New Haven, CT: Yale University Press.

Riker, William H. (1980) 'Implications from the Disequilibrium of Majority Rule for the Study of Institutions.' *American Political Science Review* 74 (2): 432–46.

Rodrik, Dani (1997) *Has Globalization Gone Too Far?* Washington, DC: Institute for International Economics.

Rogowski, Ronald (2003) 'International Capital Mobility and National Policy Divergence.' In *Governance in a Global Economy: Political Authority in Transition*, edited by Miles Kahler and David A. Lake, 255–74. Princeton, NJ: Princeton University Press.

Ruggie, John G. (1983) 'International Regimes, Transactions, and Change: Embedded Liberalism in the Postwar Economic Order.' In *International Regimes*, edited by Stephen D. Krasner, 195–231. Ithaca, NY: Cornell University Press.

Saich, Tony (2000) 'Negotiating the State: The Development of Social Organizations in China.' *The China Quarterly* 161: 124–41.

Shepsle, Kenneth A. (1979) 'Institutional Arrangements and Equilibrium in Multidimensional Voting Models.' *American Journal of Political Science* 23 (1): 27–59.

Shirk, Susan (1993) *The Political Logic of Economic Reform in China*. Berkeley, CA: University of California Press.

Sun, Yan (2004) *Corruption and Market in Contemporary China*. Ithaca, NY: Cornell University Press.

Suskind, Ron (2004) *The Price of Loyalty: George W. Bush, the White House, and the Education of Paul O'Neill*. New York: Simon and Schuster.

Waltz, Kenneth N. (1967) *Foreign Policy and Democratic Politics: The American and British Experience*. Berkeley, CA: Institute of Governmetal Studies Press.

Yang, Dali L. (2006) 'Economic Transformation and Its Political Discontents in China: Authoritarianism, Unequal Growth, and the Dilemmas of Political Development.' *Annual Review of Political Science* 9: 143–64.

Yu, Jianxing and Sujian Guo, eds. (2012) *Civil Society and Governance in China*. New York: Palgrave Macmillan.

Zhiyue, Bo (2007) *China's Elite Politics: Political Transition and Power Balancing*. Hackensack, NJ: World Scientific.

Reading 6.2

Globalizing Capitalism and the Rise of Identity Politics

Frances Fox Piven

Source: Socialist Register, 1995, pp. 102–16.

Fox Piven focuses on the ways in which the globalization of capitalism intersects with 'identity polities', creating new and often intractable political divisions. One of the effects of global capitalism is to penetrate and subordinate nationally based political organizations, especially those based in the working class, and to create a fluid constellation of culturally or ethnically based movements. Fox Piven argues that this creates new forms of insecurity and exploitation of vulnerable groups, and that the result is subordination of working-class movements globally to supranational institutions created by capitalism. The result is increasing fragmentation and insecurity, exacerbated by large-scale dislocations and processes such as migration.

[Fox Piven begins by noting that hopes for the universalization of working class politics have been dashed because of the new cleavages promoted by globalization.]

A GOOD DEAL OF THE RECENT DISCUSSION of identity politics takes the form of arguments about whether to be for it, or against it. The dispute is in one sense pointless. Identity politics is almost surely inevitable, because it is a way of thinking that reflects something very elemental about human experience. Identity politics seems to be rooted quite simply in attachments to the group, attachments that are common to humankind, and that probably reflect primordial needs that are satisfied by the group, for material survival in a predatory world, as well as for recognition, community, security, and perhaps also a yearning for immortality. Hence people construct the 'collective identities' which define the common traits and common interests of the group, and inherit and invent shared traditions and rituals which bind them together. The mirror image of this collective identity is the invention of the Other, whoever that may be, and however many they may be. And as is often pointed out, it is partly through the construction of the Other, the naming of its traits, the demarcation of its locality, and the construction of a myth-like history of struggle between the group and the Other, that the group recognizes itself. All of this seems natural enough.

If identification with the group is ubiquitous, it is also typically the case that groupness and Otherness are understood as the result of biological nature. Perhaps this is simply because nature provides the most obvious explanation of groupness that is available to people. Even when groups are demarcated by their religion or culture, these mentalities are often regarded as traits so deeply rooted as to be virtually biological, inevitably passed on to future generations. Moreover, the pernicious traits attributed to the Other can easily be woven into explanations of the travails that people experience, into theories of why the rains don't come, or why children sicken and die, or why jobs are scarce and wages fall. This sort of racial theorizing makes the world as people experience it more comprehensible. Even labour politics, ideas about a universalistic proletarian class notwithstanding, was riddled with identity politics. Thus Hobsbawm makes the sensible point that the very fact that 20th century political movements preferred religious, nationalist, socialist and confessional credos suggests that their potential followers were responsive to all these appeals.[1] Politicized workers were bonded together not only and perhaps not mainly by common class position, but by the particularisms of maleness, of whiteness, and of diverse European ethnic and religious identities. In short, features of the human condition seem to drive people to identity politics and, if it is not an inevitable way of thinking, it is surely widespread.

But if identity politics is ubiquitous because of what it offers people in protection, comfort and pride, it has also been a bane upon humankind, the source of unending tragedy. The fatal flaw in identity politics is easily recognized. Glass politics, at least in principle, promotes vertical cleavages, mobilizing people around axes which broadly correspond to hierarchies of power, and which promote challenges to these hierarchies. By contrast, identity politics fosters lateral cleavages which are unlikely to reflect fundamental conflicts over societal power and resources and, indeed, may seal popular allegiance to the ruling classes that exploit them. This fatal flaw at the very heart of a popular politics based on identity is in turn regularly exploited by elites. We can see it dramatically, for example, in the unfolding of the genocidal tribal massacres in Rwanda, fomented by a Hutu governing class which found itself losing a war with Tutsi rebels. And of course the vulnerability to manipulation resulting from identity politics is as characteristic of modern societies as tribal societies.

Thus identity politics makes people susceptible to the appeals of modern nationalism, to the bloody idea of loyalty to state and flag, which is surely one of the more murderous ideas to beset humankind. State builders cultivate a sort of race pride to build allegiance to an abstract state, drawing on the ordinary and human attachments that people form to their group and their locality, and drawing also on the animosity to the Other that is typically the complement of these attachments. The actual group that people experience, the local territory that they actually know, comes to be joined with the remote state and its flag, just as the external enemy of the state comes to be seen as the menacing Other, now depicted as a threat not only to the group and its locale, but as a threat to the nation state. I hardly need add that this melding of identity politics with state patriotism can stir people to extraordinary acts of destruction and self-destruction in the name of mystical abstractions, and the identity politics that energizes them. Napoleon was able to waste his own men easily in his murdurous march across Europe because they were quickly replaced with waves of recruits drawn from a French population enthused by their new attachment to the French nation. And World War I showed that modern states could extract even more extraordinary contributions of life and material well-being from their citizenry, as Europeans seized by nationalist passions joined in a frenzy of destruction and death in the name of state patriotism.

In the United States, popular politics has always been primarily about race, ethnicity and religion. Perhaps a population of slaves and immigrants of diverse origins, captive and free, provided some objective basis for the cultivation of identity politics, constructed by ordinary people themselves, and of course by political and economic elites who have never been slow to see that division ensured domination. From the colonial era, public policy engraved distinctions among whites, blacks and native Americans by enshrining elaborate racial hierarchies by law, by prohibiting sexual liaisons across racial lines, and by punishing with particular ferocity the insurrections in which humble people of different races joined together.

The institutions of the American South, especially the post reconstruction South, are illustrative, for they can be understood as a vast complex of social arrangements which, by strictly segregating Afro-Americans, and specifying their obligations of deference, made factitious racial differences real. Similar practices by industrialists had similar if less total consequences in inscribing difference. Employers deliberately drew from diverse ethnic groups for their workforce, and then artfully arranged job assignments, wage scales and residential quarters in company towns so as to maintain and underline those differences. Or note the strident emphasis on ethnic, religious, and later racial identities in the organizations, the mobilizing strategies and the policy outcomes of big city politics. The labour movement was riddled by these influences and, if it was sometimes strengthened by the gender, racial and ethnic solidarities that flourished within it, particularistic identities also blinded workers to their commonalities, making them vulnerable to employers who pitted one group against another, and leading them also to engage in terrible episodes of labour fratricide. Needless perhaps to add, this history still marks American politics today.

All this notwithstanding, identity politics can also be a potentially liberating and even equalizing development, especially among subordinate groups, and the more so in a political culture already dominated by identity politics. This possibility has sometimes been difficult for liberals honed on ideals of universalism to appreciate. Certainly it has been difficult for a Left preoccupied with class to appreciate.

Contemporary complaints about identity politics would be more understandable if they were aimed at elites who help foment and manipulate divisions. Instead, however, they are often directed at the subordinate groups who assert fractious identities. It may well be, however, that identity politics is especially necessary to lower status peoples, to those who are more insecure, and who are more likely to be deprived of recognition and respect by wider currents of culture and social interaction. Subordinate groups try to construct distinctive and sometimes defiant group identities, perhaps to defend themselves against dominant definitions, at least when they are allowed the cultural space to do so. Moreover, the construction of distinctive identities may be a necessary prelude to self-organization and political assertion, and particularly so in a political culture organized by identity politics. Indeed, in the cauldron of an American politics based on difference, immigrants who had previously recognized only a village or a locale as their homeland invented new national identities the better to survive and do battle in contests among nationalities. For them, the construction of new identities was a vehicle of at least psychic emancipation, and sometimes of political empowerment as well.

The black movement of the post World War II era, which is often (unreasonably) blamed for heightened identity politics, is a good example of the emancipatory construction and assertion of group identity. The celebration of Blackness was in the first instance reactive to the racism of American society: to the experience of racial subordination and terror in the South, to the extreme subordination imposed by the North whose cultural imagery at its most benign featured minstrels in blackface, Sambos, and so on. Blacks reconstructed their identity in the face of these imposed identities, and this was almost surely essential to the rise of a movement demanding racial liberation—and to the substantial achievements of that movement in dismantling the caste arrangements which had engraved racial identity politics.

However, these achievements set in motion a train of repercussions that were not simple. The new assertions of Black pride and the political demands that pride fuelled provoked alarmed and angry reactions from other groups whose own identities depended on the subordination of blacks. And of course political elites, especially but not only Republican party operatives, who stood to benefit from the politics of backlash, worked to sharpen these reactions, making such code words of race hatred as 'quotas,' or 'law and order,' or 'welfare dependency,' focal to their popular appeals. Still, the very emergence of far-reaching race conflict reflected the fact that subordination had come to be contested. Blacks were no longer allowing others to define their identity, repress their interests, and stamp out their aspirations. That was an achievement.

The rise of gender politics followed a similar course. While women do not have what is recognized as a distinctive language or turf, the understanding of gender has in other ways been prototypical of the understanding of group identity. Gender identities are closely similar to racial identities, because the traits which were thought to be feminine or masculine, and the social roles to which women and men were consigned, were always understood as the natural consequence of biological difference. Necessarily, therefore, the emergence of a liberatory movement among women was preceded and accompanied by an effort to cast off this inherited identity and construct new identities that disavowed biological fatalism or, in some variants, celebrated biological difference. Indeed, Zaretsky writes of 'the profundity and the intensity of the identity impulse among women that emerged in the early seventies.'[2] The most salient issues of the women's movement—the struggle for the Equal Rights Amendment, for reproductive rights, and the campaigns against rape and sexual harassment—are closely reflective of this effort to reconstruct the meaning of gender by challenging the biological underpinnings of traditional meanings. The mounting of such a challenge to the most ancient of subordinations, and a subordination rooted in understandings of nature itself, is surely a stunning accomplishment.

As with Blacks, the consequences were not simple. Liberatory reconstructions of gender struck at deeply imprinted understandings, threatening and arousing people still embedded in more traditional relationships, including many women embedded in traditional relationships. And as had been the case with conflict over racial identities, the contest over understandings of gender became the focus of elite manipulations in electoral politics. By 1980, the Republicans had taken notice, and in an effort to turn the widening anxieties provoked by gender conflict to electoral advantage, struck support for ERA from their platform, and initiated a campaign that culminated in the odd spectacle of American Presidents—leaders of the richest and most technologically advanced nation in the world—casting themselves as leaders of a holy war against abortion.

While identity politics may always be with us, the contemporary world appears to be engulfed by particularistic conflicts of rising intensity and destructiveness, in a pattern reminiscent of the rising tide of nationalist furies of the late 19th century. The main reasons for this, then and now, can be traced to the transformation of world capitalism. First, in the contemporary period, capitalist expansion is at least partly responsible for the weakening or collapse of nation states, with horrific consequences for ethnic and religious conflict. Second, economic restructuring is enfeebling existing forms of working class political organization which in the past sometimes restrained particularistic conflicts in the interests of class solidarity. Finally, even while the restraining capacities of governments and working class organizations are diminishing, capitalist restructuring is aggravating group conflict, by accelerating the migration of peoples, by intensifying competition for scarce resources, and by creating the widespread economic and social insecurity which always accompanies large-scale change, and particularly so when the changes for many people are for the worse.

Of course, not every instance of the weakening or collapse of central governments that had previously restrained group conflict can be traced to the current global capitalist transformation. Ancient animosities can erupt whenever central governments no longer hold them in check. The withdrawal of the British Raj unleashed bloody conflicts in India which persist to this day, and the withdrawal of the colonial powers from Africa also spurred tribal conflicts. But other instances of central government collapse cannot easily be disentangled from the changes wrought by world capitalism. Waves of anarchic warfare in the developing world are at least partly the result of saddling third world governments with debt through the imposition of neo-liberal credit policies. The fall of the Yugoslavian government, and the ethnic wars that resulted, was similarly at least partly the result of the shock therapy administered by the IMF. And other Eastern European governments were undermined by the spread of a consumer culture which fuelled popular discontent with state provision. (The Eastern European revolutions, says Benjamin R. Barber, were less over the right to vote than the right to shop.)[3]

Other consequences of capitalist tranformation for the intensification of identity politics are more direct. In a sense, the old prediction has proved true; the bourgeoisie is on the move with a series of universalizing projects which promise utterly to transform the world, penetrating and homogenizing social life across the globe. But instead of nourishing a growing proletariat, a missionary capitalism is destroying the working class formations of the older industrial order, at least in the rich countries of the West.

I do not want to overstate the unifying influence of the labour movement at its peak. I have already pointed out that worker mobilizations were riven by the particularistic divisions of race and ethnicity, and sometimes gender. Nevertheless, the promise of the labour movement was that class solidarity would override particularisms, and even that proletarian internationalism would override state patriotism. And in instance after instance, where the successful use of the strike power demanded it, labour did indeed override the divisions of identity politics, even in the United States. Now that moderating influence has weakened.

The basic lines of capitalist restructuring and the impact on organized labour are familiar. First, the expansion of global trade, itself promoted by the internationalizing of markets in finance and production, as well as by improvements in transportation and communications, has lead to the intensified exploitation of labour and resources across the globe. From Indonesia to China to Haiti, previously peripheral peoples and places are being incorporated into capitalist markets, with the consequence that organized workers in the mother countries find themselves competing with products made by low wage workers across the globe, including workers made docile by coercive authoritarian governments.

Second, the power constellations patterning the policies of national governments have shifted. Organized labour has lost ground dramatically to new supra-national institutions created by capital. It is true, as Panitch says, that the nation states are major authors of these institutions, and also continue to serve important functions for internationalizing capital.[4] Nevertheless, once in existence, international organizations and networks, including multinational corporations and international banking organizations, together with their domestic corporate and financial allies who freely use the threat of disinvestment as leverage in their dealings with governments, become major constraints on the policy options of the state. Constraints on the state are also constraints on the ability of democratic publics, including the organized working class, to exert influence through electoral-representative arrangements. The trade unions and political parties constructed by organized workers in the mother countries gained what influence they had through their leverage on governments, where strike power, trade union organization and working class voting numbers made them a force with which to be reckoned. If capitalist internationalism circumscribes what national governments can do, it inevitably also circumscribes working class political power.

Third, as a consequence of both internationalism and the shifting power constellations within nations, the economies and polities of the mother-counties of industrial capitalism are being restructured, with dire consequences for the old working class. This process is most advanced in England and the United States where unions are weaker and welfare state protections less adequate. The old mass production industries which created the industrial working class are being dismantled or reorganized and decentralized, with the consequence that the numbers of blue collar workers are shrinking. And as communities disperse and the mass media supplants the local pub, the old working class culture also crumbles. Those who remain have become excruciatingly vulnerable to the threat power of a mobile capital, unable to resist shrinking wages and benefits, and the worsening terms of work, including speedup, and forced overtime for some, and involuntary part-time or temporary work for others, all of which undermines union organization. At the same time, capitalists have launched a specifically political project to dismantle the institutional supports created by working class politics, by attacking unions, and slashing welfare state income and service protections which shielded workers from the market, and by discrediting Keynesian macro-economic political regulation.

Finally, a capitalist class on the move has launched an ideological campaign to justify and promote its expansionary mission. International markets exist, but they have also been cast as a superordinate order, operating according to a kind of natural law, penetrating national economies more deeply than they actually do, and beyond the reach of politics. In fact, this neo-laissez faire doctrine cloaks the capitalist class with the mantle once claimed by the proletariat. Capital is forging the way to the future, it is the great force for progress, the hope of humankind. And as with 19th century laissez faire notions to which this doctrine owes its main tenets, the ideology is touched with fanaticism, with a zealous utopianism that ignores the actual needs of the human subjects of any world order. Of course, this ideological campaign is as persuasive as it is because international markets are also real, and the palpable evidence of capital and goods mobility lends the sweeping doctrine of neo-laissez faire a certain material reality.

In all of these ways a universalizing capitalism has weakened the old industrial working class as a political force. No wonder unions and labour parties that were the instrument of this class have also lost their ideological footing. The imagery which gave working-class politics its elan, the idea that the future belonged to the workers, and that workers acted for all humankind, has collapsed. That universalizing myth now belongs to a capitalist class on the move.

The surge of identity politics is not just the result of a collapsing central government or a receding class politics. It is also the result of the massive dislocations of people set in motion by capitalist restructuring. More and more people are being drawn into the orbit of capitalism. Considered abstractly, that process is universalizing. In the actual experience of people, it has had the effect of heightening particularistic identities and conflicts. Gellner, writing of an earlier phase of capitalist transformation and the nationalist furies it helped to set loose, showed how an 'explosive blend of early industrialism (dislocation, mobility, acute inequality *not* hallowed by time and custom) seeks out, as it were, all the available nooks and crannies of cultural differentiation, wherever they be.'[5] The pattern is being repeated in the contemporary era. In other words, instead of wiping out the 'train of ancient and venerable prejudices,' the advance of global capitalism is whipping ancient prejudices to fever pitch.

Identity politics is pervasive, and probably inevitable. But group conflict is likely to rise under some conditions, and subside under others. One important source of disturbance has to do with the large-scale migration of people spurred by capitalist penetration of subsistence agricultural economies, with the consequence that conflicts over land escalate, and people no longer able to survive in agriculture migrate to urban centres. At the same time, the spread of consumer culture also attracts people from the periphery, while the development of globe-spanning circuits of communication and transportation facilitates the recruitment of cheap labour to the metropole. 'Every migration,' says Enzensberger, 'no matter what triggered it, what motive underlies it, whether it is voluntary or involuntary, and what scale it assumes, leads to conflicts.'[6] Or as Jean Daniel, editor of *Le Nouvel Observateur*, warns about population movements and the 'unprecedented' mingling of peoples, we should remember that 'Babel [...] was a curse.'[7]

If unfamiliar proximity is likely to intensify group consciousness and fractionalism, this is especially so when outsider groups are seen as competitors for limited jobs, neighbourhood space, honour and influence. In his last book, Ralph Miliband wrote that intra-class conflicts among wage-earners involving race or gender or ethnicity or religion can reasonably be understood as the effort to find scapegoats to explain insecurity and alienation.[8] If he was not entirely right, he was surely at least significantly right. Group conflict is far more likely when people feel growing uncertainty about their own future and as is true in many instances, are experiencing real declines in living standards. When times get harder, and competition for scarce resources intensifies, theories about the Other, and how the Other is to blame for these turns in events, being ubiquitous, are readily available. And, of course, such interpretations are more likely to be seized upon when alternative and perhaps more systemic explanations of the troubles people face are not available, or when such explanations yield no practicable line of action. No wonder there has been a spread of an identity politics, often a hate-filled identity politics, in the metropole. As Vaclav Havel says, 'The world of our experiences seems chaotic, confusing [...] And the fewer answers the era of rational knowledge provides [...] the more deeply it would seem that people behind its back as it were, cling to the ancient certainties of their tribe.'[9]

Finally, as so many times before, the group divisions of identity politics are being worsened by political elites who seize the opportunity for gaining advantage from popular division. In particular, politicians on the Right—Le Pen's Front National in France, the Christian Right in the United States, the Freedom Party in Austria, the Falangists in Spain, the Lombard League in Italy, or the Republicans in Germany where half a million immigrants arrived in 1992 alone—work to stoke the anger against outsiders. They draw popular attention away from the economic transformations underway, and try to hold or win anxious voters by directing resentment against outsiders. Or, as a retired Russian officer commented to a *New York Times* reporter about the conflict between the Tatars and ethnic Russians, 'Half the population is building mosques, the other half is building churches. And the bosses are building big brick houses for themselves.'

Notes

1. On the overlap and tension between the appeals of national identity and class in working class political mobilization, see Eric Hobsbawm, *Nations and Nationalism Since 1789* (Cambridge University Press, Cambridge, 1990).
2. E. Zaretsky, 'Responses', *Socialist Review*, vol. 23(3), 1994.
3. B. Barber, 'Jihad vs. McWorld', *Atlantic Monthly*, March 1992.
4. L. Panitch, 'Globalization and the State', *The Socialist Register*, 1994.
5. E. Gellner, cited in Hobsbawm, *Nations and Nationalism*, p. 112.
6. Hans Enzensberger, *Civil Wars from L.A. to Bosnia* (The New Press, 1994).
7. See J. Daniel, 'God is Not a Head of State', *New Perspectives Quarterly*, vol. 11(2), Spring 1994.
8. R. Miliband, *Socialism for a Sceptical Age* (Polity Press, Cambridge, 1994), pp. 22, 192–3.
9. V. Havel, 'The New Measure of Man', *New York Times*, July 8, 1994.

Reading 6.3

Europe After Brexit: A Less Perfect Union

Matthias Matthijs

THE UNITED KINGDOM'S VOTE TO LEAVE the European Union has triggered the worst political crisis the EU has ever faced. Since the early 1950s, the EU has steadily expanded, but on June 23, 52 percent of British voters ignored the experts' warnings of economic misery and opted to leave the bloc. At the annual British Conservative Party conference in October, Prime Minister Theresa May promised to invoke Article 50, which formally begins negotiations and sets a two-year deadline for leaving the EU, by March 2017. Now, given her determination to regain control of immigration and the stiffening resolve of other EU leaders to make an example of the United Kingdom, a so-called hard Brexit—an exit from both the single market and the customs union—is looking increasingly likely. This prospect should lay to rest the once dominant idea that European integration is an irreversible process.

When the United Kingdom leaves, as it almost certainly will, the EU will lose its largest military power, one of its two nuclear weapons states, one of its two veto-wielding members of the UN Security Council, its second-largest economy (representing 18 percent of its GDP and 13 percent of its population), and its only truly global financial center. The United Kingdom stands to lose even more. Forty-four percent of British exports go to EU countries; just eight percent of the EU's exports head to the United Kingdom. The United Kingdom will also face much less favorable terms with the rest of the world when negotiating future trade and investment deals on its own, and British citizens will lose their automatic right to study, live, work, and retire in the 27 other EU member states. What's more, the process of disentangling the country from 44 years of membership will consume a mind-boggling amount of human and financial resources. But the British people have made their decision, and it would be hard, if not impossible, to reverse course.

For the EU, the timing could not be worse. More than seven years after the eurozone debt crisis hit, Europe's economies remain fragile. Russia continues its saber rattling on the eastern periphery. Two of the EU's member states, Hungary and Poland, are rapidly sliding toward illiberal democracy. The refugee crisis has exposed deep divisions across the continent over immigration. Europe seems to be in a perpetual state of crisis. Antiestablishment parties on both the right and the left that question the value of the EU have gained ground, mainly at the expense of centrist Christian democratic and social democratic parties, which have never wavered in their support for further European integration. In the 1957 Treaty of Rome, which established the EU's predecessor, Europe's leaders envisioned "an ever closer union among the peoples of Europe." Six decades on, that notion has never seemed more distant.

The roots of the EU's current crisis can be traced to the 1980s. In the first four decades after World War II, leaders saw the European project primarily as a means of restoring the political legitimacy of their war-torn nation-states. In the 1980s, however, Europe's elites set their sights on a loftier goal: forging a supranational economic regional order over which an enlightened technocracy would reign supreme. The creation of the single market in 1986 and then the introduction of a single currency a decade later seemed to herald a glorious new era of economic growth and political integration.

In reality, however, these steps sowed the seeds of Europe's current crisis. Leaders on the continent failed to set up the institutions that would be necessary to make both the single market and the single currency function properly. They brought about monetary union without fiscal and financial union, leaving countries such as Greece and Italy vulnerable after the Great Recession struck in 2008. Today, Greece's economy is 26 percent smaller than it was in 2007 and remains mired in debt. Youth unemployment there stands at just below 50 percent; in Spain, it remains above 45 percent, and in Italy, it hovers around 40 percent. Europe's leaders always assumed, incorrectly, that future shocks would lead to further integration. But the economic crisis, followed closely by an ongoing political crisis over immigration, has brought the EU to the brink of disintegration.

If the EU is to survive, it must restore the original division of labor between Brussels and Europe's capitals, in which national governments retained discretion over key areas of economic policy, such as the ability to conduct fiscal stimulus and defend national champions. The nation-state is here to stay, and national policies still have far more democratic legitimacy than those imposed by technocrats in Brussels or Frankfurt. The EU needs to give Europe's national governments more, not less, freedom to act.

From the Ashes

The founders of the EU would be disheartened to see what their creation has morphed into. As the British historian Alan Milward argued in his 1992 book *The European Rescue of the Nation-State*, Europe's ruling elites established the European Economic Community (EEC) in the 1950s not to build a new supranational power but to rehabilitate the system of European nation-states after the horrors of World War II. They realized that if their countries were to survive, they would need some degree of continental coordination to help provide economic prosperity and political stability.

Milward argued that increased European cooperation required some surrender of sovereignty, but not the wholesale replacement of the nation-state with a new form of supranational governance. Instead, the EEC was designed in keeping with the idea of "embedded liberalism": the postwar consensus that sovereign countries would gradually liberalize their economies but maintain enough discretion over their economic policies to cope with hard domestic times. The EEC's founding fathers left most political and economic powers with national governments, leaving the EEC to coordinate coal and steel production, agricultural support, and nuclear research, as well as internal trade relations and common foreign economic policies.

This political bargain ushered in three decades of successful European integration by guaranteeing peace and stability and fostering increased trade and prosperity. In the early 1990s, when Milward published his book, European integration had reached its zenith. In 1991, according to Eurobarometer polls, a record 71 percent of EU citizens considered their country's membership in the union "a good thing"; just seven percent thought it was "a bad thing."

Yet no sooner had Milward's thesis appeared than it became outdated. Starting in the mid-1980s, Europe's elites had begun to transform the nature of the European political project. Led by Jacques Delors, the president of the European Commission, and backed by French President François Mitterrand and German Chancellor Helmut Kohl, they set out to create a new form of supranational governance, rather than using European integration to strengthen the continent's old system of nation-states. Pan-European rules would take precedence over national policy discretion. Economic integration would trump domestic democratic politics. Europe's leaders would turn their countries "from nation-states to member states," as the political scientist Chris Bickerton has put it, as they progressively dismantled the postwar national corporatist state. Delors' federalist vision required the EU's member states to surrender ever more sovereignty and gradually weaken the privileged bonds that had existed between national governments and their people. Membership in the EU would no longer entail reinvigorating the nation-state; it would mean caging it.

The Great Experiment

The first landmark in the transformation of the European political project came in 1986, when French socialists such as Delors and Mitterrand joined forces with conservatives such as Kohl and British Prime Minister Margaret Thatcher to sign the Single European Act. The SEA represented a response to the "Eurosclerosis" of the 1970s and 1980s, Europe's protracted disease of low growth, labor unrest, and high unemployment and inflation. The Treaty of Rome had already established a common market and enshrined "four freedoms" into European law: the free movement of people, services, goods, and capital. But countless national regulations still held back cross-border trade. Only through more deregulation and liberalization, European policymakers argued, could Europe escape its economic doldrums. And indeed, by 1992, the EEC would become a genuine single market.

The roots of the EU's current crisis can be traced to the 1980s.

But as the Hungarian economic sociologist Karl Polanyi warned in the mid-twentieth century, there is nothing natural about the creation of markets. They require major acts of state power, so that activities that were once "embedded" in local social and political relationships become tradable commodities among anonymous participants. Exchanges need to become "disembedded" from their social context to become market transactions. The SEA was a major exercise in disembedding countries' markets from their national protections, regulations, and traditions.

The SEA was extraordinarily ambitious. Most countries require people to hold national licenses when they provide services, whether they are designing a house, performing surgery, or offering financial advice. Many governments still monitor and restrict capital and financial flows into and out of their national jurisdictions. All kinds of nontariff barriers, such as national health, safety, and environmental standards, still hold back international trade in goods. But after the sea, European citizens could move easily among national labor markets, capital could flow freely across European borders, and manufacturers no longer had to deal with a raft of conflicting product standards. A Portuguese pilot could fly for Air France, a Belgian bank could now invest in Greece, and a German driver could buy an Italian Lamborghini without having to worry if it complied with Germany's technical and safety standards. Intra-EEC trade in goods soared. The single market remained incomplete—fatally, it lacked a unified system for supervising and resolving Europe's most important banks and monitoring mechanisms to warn of sudden interruptions to international capital flows—but it went much further than any similar exercise in modern history.

Indeed, the political scientists Leif Hoffmann and Craig Parsons have observed that in many instances, the United States' single market has more rules than Europe's. In public procurement, for example, the state of California or the city of Chicago can give preference to state or local service providers. Member states of the EU cannot favor national companies. Similarly, the regulation of many services in the United States takes place at the state, rather than the federal, level. A licensed hairdresser who moves from Ohio to Pennsylvania must undergo 2,100 hours of training and pass written and practical exams to obtain a new license. A barber from Berlin, on the other hand, can set up shop in Paris the very next day.

> The EU's experiment in creating a truly free market has come at a price.

But the EU's experiment in creating a truly free market has come at a price. The increased market competition that the SEA introduced brought widespread benefits, but it also created winners and losers, such as the local producers and service providers in France or the United Kingdom who now faced stronger competition from cheaper Slovakian manufacturers, Polish plumbers, and Romanian contractors. In the boom years, Europe's economies generated enough wealth to compensate the losers. As growth has stagnated, however, large swaths of national electorates have begun to clamor for more protection from the market that the EU built.

Yet because the SEA uprooted European markets from their nationally based democratic politics and social institutions, Europe's governments have given up much of their power to intervene in their countries' economies. To some extent, this process has happened everywhere due to globalization, but European countries embraced the primacy of international markets over domestic politics to a much greater extent than countries anywhere else in the advanced industrial world. As a result, they have found themselves with much less control over their domestic economies than any of their Western peers. And because regulations concerning the EU's single market require only a qualified majority of member states, rather than unanimity, to become law, they can sometimes directly conflict with national interests. For instance, in August 2016, the EU ordered the Irish government to collect $14.5 billion in unpaid taxes from Apple, despite protestations by the Irish government that low corporate taxes were a key component of its economic model and a "fundamental matter of sovereignty."

"Someday There Will Be a Crisis"

The creation of the euro in the Treaty of Maastricht in 1992 represented an even more serious loss of power for Europe's national governments. Elites introduced the euro because they believed that a single market would function properly only with a single currency. They also argued that countries as open and integrated as the EU member states would benefit from ending exchange-rate fluctuations with one another. More quietly, they dreamed of building a common currency that could challenge the global supremacy of the U.S. dollar.

Federalists hailed the euro as another great leap forward toward European unification, but it took Europe even further away from the postwar embedded liberalism that had underpinned Milward's grand bargain. That bargain had left nation-states in control of European integration and had presupposed that democracies needed leeway when times were tough to rebalance their economies toward higher growth or lower unemployment, even if that meant temporarily pausing further liberalization.

Yet the design of the euro gave Europe's democracies no such freedom. The introduction of the common currency and the European Central Bank, which has a sole mandate to maintain price stability, prevented member states from pursuing their own monetary policies. Austere fiscal requirements, meanwhile, which Germany insisted on, made it much harder for governments to stimulate economic growth by boosting spending during a downturn. The 1997 Stability and Growth Pact mandated low public deficits and declining sovereign debt ratios, but the agreement's name is a misnomer: the pact has undermined social stability and generated little growth. Although national governments often ignored the pact, especially in the early years of the single currency, the EU, at Germany's behest, tightened the rules in response to the euro crisis and rendered any activist fiscal policy all but illegal.

Germany has been the biggest winner from the euro. Because Germany's currency can't appreciate in relation to the currencies of its European trading partners, Germany has held down the real cost of its exports, resulting in a massive trade surplus. But the euro has been a disaster for the rest of Europe. When they created the currency, Europe's elites removed the economic shock absorbers that their countries had traditionally relied on without creating any new adjustment mechanisms. Europe's leaders thought it unwise to establish a genuine fiscal, financial, and political union to complement the monetary union. They rightly judged that their electorates would not accept it, and they assumed that future crises would propel the EU toward further integration. As Romano Prodi, a former prime minister of Italy and then president of the European Commission, observed in 2001, on the eve of the launch of the euro notes and coins, "I am sure the euro will oblige us to introduce a new set of economic policy instruments. It is politically impossible to propose that now. But someday there will be a crisis and new instruments will be created."

But when the crisis struck, the European Central Bank initially refused to ease monetary policy and in fact raised interest rates; meanwhile, national governments could no longer devalue their currencies in relation to those of their main trading partners to boost exports, nor launch fiscal stimulus programs. That left harsh austerity measures as their only option. In the short term, this response only worsened the crisis. Since then, the EU has created some new instruments, including a banking union and a new fiscal compact, which have transferred responsibility for supervising the eurozone's biggest banks from national authorities to the European Central Bank, created a single resolution board to wind up failing banks, and established more intrusive monitoring of national budgets. But the logic of European integration has remained the same: more supranational rules, less national discretion. The German government, for example, could not step in to rescue Deutsche Bank, once a symbol of Germany's financial prowess, if Berlin judged it to be in the national interest to do so, nor can the Italian government run larger fiscal deficits to counter its chronic lack of economic growth.

Ins and Outs

It is the crisis over immigration, however, that threatens to trigger the union's demise. The free movement of people within the single market used to be a minor political issue. Most people saw it as a chance for the young to study abroad through the EU's Erasmus and Socrates programs and for the educated and upwardly mobile to get work experience in a different European country. Until the early years of this century, EU-wide migration remained very low.

But when the EU expanded its membership in 2004 to include the former communist countries of central and eastern Europe, intra-EU migration started to grow. EU enlargement to the east created "a Europe whole and free," as U.S. President George H. W. Bush phrased it in 1989, but it also made the union's membership much more economically unequal. In 2004, when Poland joined the EU, its GDP per capita stood at around $6,600; in the United Kingdom, the figure was $38,300. These vast differences in income levels encouraged millions of eastern Europeans to head westward. Between 2004 and 2014, for example, over two million people moved from Poland to Germany and the United Kingdom, and almost another two million moved from Romania to Italy and Spain. Such large movements of people have put pressure on the public services and safety nets of the countries receiving them.

Then, in 2015, more than one million migrants and refugees from Afghanistan, Iraq, Syria, and sub-Saharan Africa poured across Europe's borders. The single market had no mechanism to deal with sudden movements of people within it, nor did the EU have any common external migration policy to help absorb a large influx of refugees. National governments, constrained by EU rules over fiscal spending and unable to agree on how to share the burden, have struggled to respond. True, the overall migration numbers remain relatively low, and the net contribution of migrants to their host countries is mainly positive. But many citizens feel that their own governments are powerless and that the EU fails to represent their interests, and so anti-immigrant parties have surged across Europe. For the first time, the EU's commitment to the free movement of people has begun to waver.

Eastern European governments, such as those of Viktor Orban in Hungary and Beata Szydlo in Poland, have ferociously defended their citizens' rights to live and work across the EU while refusing EU requests to take in a quota of refugees. Many western European governments are prepared to begrudgingly accept EU quotas on refugees but increasingly question the unlimited nature of migration within the EU. Fears of unlimited emigration from countries such as Turkey, a candidate for EU membership, played a major role in the United Kingdom's decision to leave the EU, and the desire to regain control over immigration to the United Kingdom will likely result in that country's departure from the single market altogether.

Taking Back Control

So where does the EU go from here? Since the United Kingdom has always been its most reluctant member state, many Europhiles will be tempted to argue that Brussels can now finally push forward with further integration. But that would be a misreading of the current mood in Europe's capitals and a misdiagnosis of Europe's ailment. More Europe is not the answer to the EU's problems.

Instead, Europe's leaders need to return to Milward's basic idea that Europe was meant not to cage its nation-states but to rescue them. Democratic legitimacy, for better or worse, remains with Europe's national governments. There are no technocratic solutions to Europe's political problems. "I don't wish to suggest that there is something inherently superior about national institutions over others," the historian Tony Judt observed in 1996. "But we should recognize the reality of nations and states, and note the risk that, when neglected, they become an electoral resource of virulent nationalists."

> The EU does not need any more rules; it needs political leadership.

European integration has taken so many policy levers away from governments that many citizens have started to wonder what their governments are still there for. As the political economist Mark Blyth and I argue in *The Future of the Euro*, "Without developing a political process to legitimately embed [the eurozone's] economic and financial institutions, the future of the euro will be fragile at best." Restoring growth in the eurozone, fighting youth unemployment, and championing EU political reforms that return some economic power to member states should take precedence over austerity and one-size-fits-all structural reforms.

Distributive policies that create winners and losers need to be legitimized democratically through regular elections and should therefore remain the sole preserve of national governments. Such policies include setting budgetary priorities, determining the generosity of the welfare state, regulating labor markets, controlling immigration, and directing industrial policy. Permitting countries to occasionally break the rules of both the single market and the single currency—by temporarily letting them protect and financially support key industries, for instance, or institute an emergency break on immigration under certain strict conditions—would empower national elites to deal with specific national problems and respond to voters' legitimate concerns by giving them a democratic choice over policy.

The EU, meanwhile, should focus on the things that member states cannot do efficiently on their own and that create mutual gains: negotiating international trade deals, supervising systemically important banks and other financial institutions, responding to global warming, and coordinating foreign and security policy. In Euro barometer polls, about two-thirds of European citizens surveyed consistently say that they support a common foreign policy for the EU. National governments could start with a much more effective pooling of their military resources to conduct joint peacekeeping and humanitarian missions overseas.

The EU does not need any more rules; it needs political leadership. Germany must give up its opposition to eurobonds, or jointly guaranteed eurozone debt instruments, and common deposit insurance, which would go a long way toward providing long-term financial stability in the eurozone by preventing future sovereign bond market contagion and bank runs. It must relax its insistence on tough fiscal rules to allow countries such as Italy and Portugal to engage in aggregate demand stimulus. And it must take the lead in setting up new mechanisms for promoting solidarity within the EU, such as a joint refugee and migration fund, which could make up the difference in temporary shortfalls in local funding and help member states more effectively share the burden of integrating new migrants across Europe.

Germany needs to finally embrace its leadership role. If Germany can overcome its parochialism and recognize that it is in its long-term interest to act as a benign hegemon for Europe—not unlike the role the United States played in the Western world after World War II—there is no reason why the EU cannot emerge stronger from its current malaise. The leaders of the other remaining large member states—especially France, Italy, Poland, and Spain—must reassure Berlin that they are committed to reforming their economies once growth returns, pledge to actively contribute to EU-wide solidarity, and reaffirm that the European project is in their national interests. Collectively, Europe's leaders need to reimagine what Europe is for and regain control of the process of European integration. Sixty years on from the signing of the foundational Treaty of Rome, Europe needs a new grand bargain, now more than ever.

Chapter 6

1. Why does David Lake argue that full employment is needed to maintain democratic government?

2. Do you agree with Frances Fox Piven that the decline of working-class influence and the hope of a positive future lead to rising horizontal social divisions and a reduction in vertical conflict?

3. Does economic decline constitute a significant source of cultural conflict?

4. Do you agree with Matthijs's view that the European Union is in decline due to the multiplicity of conflicts among members?

Chapter 7

A Future for Comparative Politics?

Social and Environmental Threats to the
Current Political Order

O UR FINAL CHAPTER LOOKS AT THE institutional, cultural, and environmental challenges
facing humanity in the twenty-first century, indirectly questioning the future of comparative politics. The first reading highlights the crisis of capitalism. In his review article, Mark Blyth
notes that capitalism and democracy have a long history of rebalancing their inherently antagonistic relationship. Blyth starts with Jürgen Kocha's short history of capitalism, asking whether
this pattern will continue. Kocha documents the self-correcting advance of property rights,
markets, and a capitalism producing and selling goods. By the 1980s, a crisis emerged. Finance
displaced industrial capitalism, and the manipulation of monetary assets became primary. Next,
Blyth turns to Wolfgang Streeck's more pessimistic analysis. In *Buying Time*, Streeck agrees that
the economic crisis of 2008 resulted from a crisis of finance capitalism and that financialization
continues in the form of permanent austerity and lack of real growth. More strikingly, Streeck
argues that this situation portends the slow decay and death of capitalism. Finally, Blyth turns
to Paul Mason's *Postcapitalism*, the most pessimistic of the three books. Mason assures us that
capitalism is dying, citing the confluence of destructive factors, namely, the use of fiat money,
financialization, lack of regulation, new technologies, and climate change.

A second reading examines population growth, identifying four megatrends that will change
the balance among human populations on earth. Aging and diminishing populations in the
West, in China, and in South Korea will reduce wealth creation and their political leadership.
At the same time, expanding populations will flourish in Africa, in Latin America, the Middle
East, and Southeast Asia. These areas, however, suffer from a combination of dilemmas that
limit their capacity for wealth creation and global domination. Global population growth presents unprecedented political challenges.

The third article summarizes the daunting complexity of addressing the problems caused by
climate change. The chapter reviews studies of the challenges and efforts to face up to climate
change, highlighting the everchanging, disorganized, and uncertain nature of such programs.

Real solutions require cooperation and coordination among the vast array of institutions, states, and individuals and an agreed and enforceable plan. Who and how states will collectively formulate and enforce the monumental programs needed to meet the challenge, identifying solutions, assigning duties, and generating organizational and resource capabilities, is becoming ever more pressing. This report challenges readers to appreciate the daunting, perhaps impossible, task of forging a new comprehensive policy program of global governance. Such a system would have to supersede all current forms of state, being simultaneously complex, systemic, adaptable, inclusive, and transactional in nature. Such a political order would be unlike any system of governance humanity has so far devised.

Reading 7.1

Capitalism in Crisis: What Went Wrong and What Comes Next

Mark Blyth

E VER SINCE THE EMERGENCE OF MASS democracy after World War II, an inherent tension has existed between capitalism and democratic politics; capitalism allocates resources through markets, whereas democracy allocates power through votes. Economists, in particular, have been slow to accept that this tension exists. Instead, they have tended to view markets as a realm beyond the political sphere and to see politics as something that gets in the way of an otherwise self-adjusting system. Yet how democratic politics and capitalism fit together determines today's world. Politics is not a mistake that gets in the way of markets.

The conflict between capitalism and democracy, and the compromises the two systems have struck with each other over time, has shaped our contemporary political and economic world. In the three decades that followed World War II, democracy set the rules, taming markets with the establishment of protective labor laws, restrictive financial regulations, and expanded welfare systems. But in the 1970s, a globalized, deregulated capitalism, unconstrained by national borders, began to push back. Today, capital markets and capitalists set the rules that democratic governments must follow.

But the dominance of capital has now provoked a backlash. As inequality has widened and real wages for the majority of people have stagnated—all while governments have bailed out wealthy institutions at the first sign of trouble—populations have become less willing to accept the so-called costs of adjustment as their lot. A "double movement," in the words of the Hungarian historian Karl Polanyi, occurs in such moments as these, when those who feel most victimized by markets reclaim the powers of the state to protect them. The rise of Bernie Sanders and Donald Trump in the United States is a product of this reaction, as is the strengthening of populist parties in Europe.

Three recent books shed light on this continuing tension between the imperatives of the market and the desires of the people. Together, they offer a biography of capitalism: where it came from, what went wrong, and where it may be going in a world of stagnant living standards, widening inequality, and rising carbon emissions. And the picture they paint is a bleak one.

The Rise of Capitalism

Capitalism: A Short History, by the German historian Jürgen Kocka, is aptly named. In just 169 pages, it tells the story of capitalism from its origins in the ancient long-distance trade routes of Mesopotamia to the 2008 financial crisis. This is no mean feat. Yet such brevity requires some simplification, which comes at a cost.

For Kocka, capitalism is "an essential concept for understanding modernity." More important, it is a set of institutions that enshrine property rights, promote the use of markets to allocate resources, and protect capital. And it is also an ethos, he claims, a set of principles and ideas. Defining capitalism so expansively allows Kocka to see its earliest forms developing among traders in Mesopotamia, in the eastern Mediterranean, and along Asia's Silk Road, until, by the eleventh century, the beginnings of a merchant capitalist bourgeoisie had emerged on the Arabian Peninsula and in China.

Capitalism developed later in Europe, boosted by long-distance trade with Asia and the Arab world, between the twelfth and fifteenth centuries. Merchants formed cooperative institutions that led to greater risk sharing, which encouraged the accumulation of capital. This development, Kocka writes, led to "the formation of enterprises with legal personalities of their own," rudimentary capital markets, and, finally, banks whose fortunes became intimately connected with the rise of modern states through the management of their debts.

This alliance between merchant capitalism and the emergent state helped usher in the age of colonialism. Merchants, entrepreneurs, and conquistadors, with increasingly powerful states backing them, propelled European expansion. Critical to this expansion was the triangular trade, in which European merchants brought finished goods to Africa, traded them for slaves, and then exchanged those slaves in the New World for sugar and cotton that went back to Europe. This process helped embed capitalism deeper in Europe than in the Middle East and China: the scale of investment that such ventures required led to the rise of what would become known as "joint-stock companies" and the beginnings of what economic historians call "finance capitalism"—stock exchanges opened in Antwerp in 1531 and Amsterdam in 1611.

Much of the profits that early European capitalists enjoyed came from these profoundly illiberal activities. As Kocka points out, "capitalism ... contains little in the way of resistance against inhumane practices." Yet in the long run, capitalism laid the groundwork for democracy, because the wealth it generated, and the possibilities that came with its new institutions, disrupted the guilds, helped cities expand, and allowed nineteenth-century industrialization to evolve into twentieth-century managerial capitalism.

Blame the Bankers

In Kocka's narrative, each stage of capitalism begets the next, in an almost natural progression. Capitalism simply marches onward, for the most part benevolently—at least once the reformers abolished slavery and colonialism. But beginning around 1980, he writes, some thing started to go wrong. Firms started to derive a larger share of their profits from the financial sector than they did from real investments, a process economists call "financialization." This process, according to Kocka, "imparted a new quality to the system."

Modern finance, in contrast to the earlier, "productive" forms of finance that Kocka admires, seems to mainly consist of unproductive "locust" hedge funds that "cannibalize" good firms, contributing nothing to production in the wider economy. Meanwhile, Kocka insists, since the 1980s, governments have failed to exercise self-restraint, and publics have lived beyond their means. Massive growth in public and private debt in the developed world has been the result, which represents "a lasting source of destabilization for capitalism."

But this trenchant critique of modern finance sits oddly alongside the rest of the book. For Kocka, the system was doing just fine until the rot of modern finance set in. He insists that financialization represents a break in the evolution of capitalism. But he fails to explain where it came from, if it didn't emerge directly from those earlier forms of capitalism.

After all, the modern finance that Kocka condemns is not so different from the earlier, "productive" finance that he lauds. The financiers that got Germany into trouble in 2007 through their exposure to U.S. subprime mortgages were not "locust" hedge funds but traditional German development banks. And one of the world's largest derivatives traders at the time of the crisis was Deutsche Bank—hardly a new institution on the financial scene. In short, the idea that financialization may be not a perversion of capitalism but the next stage in its evolution seems to be a little too uncomfortable for Kocka to fully consider.

In the Red

The German sociologist Wolfgang Streeck also sees modern capitalism as flawed. Yet its current plight is not an aberration, he argues in *Buying Time*, but a direct consequence of the unraveling of the postwar marriage of capitalism and democracy.

Streeck's account focuses on Michal Kalecki, a Polish economist who came to prominence in the interwar period. Kalecki published a remarkable article in 1943 that predicted the economic turmoil of the 1970s. Kalecki argued that if full employment ever became the norm, workers would be able to move freely from job to job. Not only would this undermine traditional authority relationships within firms; it would also push wages up regardless of productivity levels, since workers would have more leverage to demand higher wages.

In response, firms would have to raise prices, creating a spiral of inflation that would eat into profits and lower real wages, which would, in turn, promote greater labor unrest. Kalecki argued that to restore profits, capitalists would rebel against the system that promoted full employment. In its place, they would seek to create a regime in which market discipline, with a focus on price stability rather than full employment, would be the primary goal of policy. Welfare protections would be rolled back, and the discipline that unemployment provides would be restored.

Kalecki's predictions proved astonishingly accurate. By the 1970s, as Kalecki had foreseen, inflation had risen dramatically, profits had fallen, and capital began its rebellion. Organizations as diverse as the Swedish Employers' Confederation and the Business Roundtable in the United States pressured governments to reduce taxes, especially on high earners. But cutting taxes in the recessionary early 1980s meant that revenues fell, deficits widened, and real interest rates rose as those deficits became harder to finance. At the same time, conservative governments, especially in the United Kingdom and the United States, set out to weaken labor and shrink the role of the state as they dismantled the regulations that had reined in the excesses of finance since the 1940s.

The financial industry could now grow unchecked, and as it expanded, investors sought safe assets that were highly liquid and provided good returns: the debt of developed countries. This allowed governments to plug their deficits and spend more, all without raising taxes. But the shift to financing the state through debt came at a cost. Since World War II, taxes on labor and capital had provided the foundation of postwar state spending. Now, as governments began to rely more and more on debt, the tax-based states of the postwar era became the debt-based states of the contemporary neoliberal era.

This transformation has had profound political consequences. The increase in government debt has allowed transnational capitalists to override the preferences of domestic citizens everywhere: bond-market investors can now exercise an effective veto on policies they don't like by demanding higher interest rates when they replace old debt with new debt. In the most extreme cases, investors can use courts to override the ability of states to default on their debts, as happened recently in Argentina, or they can shut down an entire country's payment system if that country votes against the interests of creditors, as happened in Greece in 2015. The financial industry has become, Streeck writes, "the second constituency of the modern state," one more powerful than the people.

This shift from taxes to debt initially bought time for capitalism: it restored profits, destroyed labor's ability to demand wage increases, tamed inflation to the point of deflation (which increases the real value of debt), and even seemed to provide prosperity for all after the crisis of the 1970s. Mortgages and credit cards allowed private citizens to rack up deficits of their own—a process the sociologist Colin Crouch has described as "privatized Keynesianism." But it was all an illusion. Credit sustained the appearance of prosperity for the lower classes. In reality, the rich captured most of the newly created wealth. In the United States, for example, the top one percent more than doubled their share of the national income over the last three decades, as wages for the bottom 60 percent stood still.

In 2008, the financial crisis shattered this illusion. Governments bailed out the banks and transferred the costs of doing so to public budgets. Public debt exploded as governments bailed out the rich, and austerity measures, intended to reduce this new debt, have only compounded the losses of the majority of citizens. Capital continues to dominate democracy, especially in the eu: in Greece and Italy in 2011, technocrats replaced democratically elected governments, and in 2015, the so-called troika—the European Central Bank, the European Commission, and the International Monetary Fund—bulldozed Greek democracy.

So where Kocka blames profligate governments and debt-laden citizens for the current crisis, Streeck instead sees them as the victims. It's not lavish public spending, he shows, but rather falling tax revenues and financial bailouts that have created so much government debt and empowered capital. If states are spending extravagantly on voters, as Kocka and those who fetishize austerity maintain, there is precious little to show for it. "Had the rise in public debt been due to the rising power of mass democracy," Streeck writes, "it would be impossible to explain how prosperity … could have been so radically redistributed from the bottom to the top of society."

Streeck foresees a prolonged period of low growth and political turmoil ahead, in which states commanded by creditors, allied with transnational investors, struggle to get resisting debtor states into line: think of Germany and Greece. "The clock is ticking for democracy," Streeck writes, but "it must remain an open question … whether the clock is also ticking for capitalism."

"Neoliberalism Is Broken"

For the British journalist Paul Mason, that question is closed: capitalism's current condition is terminal. In *Postcapitalism*, Mason writes that capitalism is "a complex, adaptive system which has reached the limits of its capacity to adapt." The roots of capitalism's demise, Mason argues, lie in the 1980s (also when Kocka saw problems arise), when capitalism was taken over by neoliberalism: an ideology and a set of policies that recognize no limits to the commodification of the world. Unfortunately for capitalism, "neoliberalism is broken." To explain why, Mason turns to the work of Nikolai Kondratieff, a brilliant Soviet economist whom Stalin had murdered in 1938.

According to Kondratieff, capitalism goes up and down in 50-year cycles. At the bottom of a cycle, old technologies and business models cease to function. In response, entrepreneurs, both public and private, roll out new technologies to open up untapped markets, and an upswing begins. This leads to a loosening of credit, which accelerates the upswing. These cycles bring to mind the concept of "creative destruction" popularized in the 1940s by the economist Joseph Schumpeter. But Mason downplays the importance of the entrepreneur, whom Schumpeter cast in a central role, and focuses instead on the effect of class-based politics on productivity.

Mason's first cycle runs from 1790 to 1848. The upswing began when British entrepreneurs first harnessed steam power to run their factories, and it ended with the depression of the 1820s. The subsequent downswing produced the revolutions of 1848, when the emergent bourgeois classes of Europe burst onto the historical stage. Mason's second cycle runs from 1848 to the mid-1890s. The spread of railways, the telegraph, and shipping drove growth until the depression of the 1870s. In the decades that followed, strong labor movements gained momentum all over the world, and capital, in response, became more concentrated. Electricity and mass production then powered a third upswing that crashed in the Great Depression and the massive capital destruction of World War II. After the war, a fourth cycle began with innovations in electronics and synthetics, improvements in the organization of production, and labor's relative victory over capital in the institutions of the welfare state. That cycle's upswing peaked in the mid-1970s, but this time, there was no major depression. The fourth cycle stalled.

The End of Capitalism

Mason's argument about why a major depression has not arrived during the past 40 years, the Great Recession notwithstanding, is partly conventional and partly surprising. The conventional explanation has four components. First, after U.S. President Richard Nixon took the dollar off the gold standard in 1971, the United States moved to a paper standard, which eliminated the constraints on deficit financing that the gold standard entailed. Second, the financialization of the developed economies masked the reality of stagnant incomes by substituting credit for wage increases. Third, the emergence of global imbalances in finance and trade allowed the United States to keep consuming as Asian countries stepped in as producers. Finally, advances in information technology empowered capital and weakened labor, and helped spread neoliberal practices across the globe.

That is a fairly familiar analysis. The unconventional part of Mason's answer harks back to Marx and Kalecki and stresses how neoliberalism managed to prevent profits from falling more effectively than any previous economic system. Mason borrows from Marx and

Kalecki the idea that average profits in any market will fall due to both competition and the flood of capital into a new market, which reduce returns on investment. As a result, capitalists will always try to replace human labor with machines to protect their share of profits. During a downswing, as profits shrink, capitalists will do everything they can to boost their share of profits at the expense of labor: they will force employees to work intensively and will accelerate their attempts to replace workers with machines.

In the past, such attempts to restore profits simply by crushing labor failed. In each of the first three waves, one way or another, workers managed to resist. The best examples of such resistance were the postwar constraints on capitalism: strong unions, rigorous regulations, and generous welfare systems. When workers defy capitalists' attempts to squeeze profits from them by building such institutions, firms have to adapt. Rather than fight labor over the fixed distribution of income, they are forced to invest in improving workers' productivity, to the benefit of both parties: this was the post–World War II growth story.

But under neoliberalism, capitalists have managed to squeeze labor in an entirely new way. Globalization obliterated the power of workers to resist, because if they did, capital—and jobs—could easily flow elsewhere. This explains why the number of labor strikes has declined so steeply all over the world. As Mason writes, "The fourth long cycle was prolonged, distorted and ultimately broken by factors that have not occurred before in the history of capitalism: the defeat ... of organized labour, the rise of information technology and the discovery that once an unchallenged superpower exists, it can create money out of nothing for a long time."

Still, Mason believes that these factors have only delayed capitalism's inevitable collapse. Where Marx thought that organized labor would rise up and overthrow the system, Mason bets that information technology will destroy it from within. Digital goods, such as music files and software, create a real problem for markets: they destroy the role of price in balancing supply and demand. People can copy digital goods freely forever: they have zero marginal cost and are nonrival in consumption. When one person downloads a music file or a piece of code from the Internet, for example, she makes it no harder for anyone else to do the same. So the only way that firms can maintain their profits is by enforcing monopoly property rights: consider Apple and Samsung suing each other for the right to profit from patents or the need for major pharmaceutical companies to keep drugs prohibitively expensive.

Mason is optimistic about what will replace the profit motive. He points to decentralized networks such as Wikipedia, the "biggest information product in the world ... made by 27,000 volunteers, for free," and the rise of the so-called sharing economy: nonmarket peer production systems, where work has value but cannot be priced in a traditional manner. The result is a "contradiction in modern capitalism ... between the possibility of free, abundant socially produced goods, and a system of monopolies, banks and governments struggling to maintain control over power and information." In such a world, the central battle will be between those who want to preserve property rights and those who wish to destroy them in the name of democracy. The stakes, Mason argues, could not be higher. Without the revolution he calls for, the world will be vulnerable to a much greater threat: catastrophic climate change.

What Comes Next?

Mason's chapter "The Rational Case for Panic" confronts what most economists and politicians tend to shy away from: the idea that capitalism in its current form is going to kill everyone. Of course, people have predicted an environmental apocalypse before. A group of experts called the Club of Rome famously published *The Limits to Growth* in the 1970s, forecasting economic and environmental crises—and those predictions have failed to come to pass. But this time may be different.

The science behind climate change is better this time around, and it's conclusive. The world is in trouble. As Mason notes, in 2012, the International Energy Agency predicted that even if world leaders implemented all the announced emissions-reduction plans, carbon dioxide emissions would rise by another 20 percent by 2035. The world cannot burn 60 to 80 percent of remaining known carbon fuel stocks without causing catastrophic warming. But under capitalism, this is exactly what the world will do. Carbon taxes will do little to change this reality.

Add to this mix an aging developed world with huge pension liabilities and a climate-shocked developing world of young people who have nowhere to go, and it's little wonder that the Organization for Economic Cooperation and Development has forecast stagnant growth for the global economy for the next 50 years and an almost 40 percent rise in inequality in the world's rich countries. But despite this stark warning, Mason emphasizes an aspect of capitalism that both Kocka and Streeck underplay: its adaptive potential.

It is highly likely, for instance, that statistics such as GDP underestimate the impact of new information-based technologies. Hal Varian, Google's chief economist, might be exaggerating when he claims that the free search engine is worth $150 billion to users in the United States every year, but there is no doubt that Google has transformed the economics of finding information. Google saves everyone time and money—but that doesn't show up in gdp. Although capitalism may be reaching its adaptive limits, it has been more robust than most doomsayers realize.

Nonetheless, Mason thinks that climate change may be the one bullet that capitalism cannot dodge. Neoliberals often naively assert that capitalism will generate a miracle technology at just the right moment to stave off catastrophe. But Mason argues that previous

Hail Mary passes, such as geoengineering and carbon capture, have failed to pay off. What gives him hope is that large-scale technological innovations may not be as important as micro-level changes in the structure of property rights themselves.

Whether or not such a restructuring will be enough to save the world remains unclear. But Mason is right to hold out hope. Capitalism, in its current form, has reached a dead end. If ever there were a time for pessimism of the intellect and optimism of the will, it is now.

Reading 7.2

The New Population Bomb: The Four Megatrends That Will Change the World

Jack A. Goldstone

FORTY-TWO YEARS AGO, THE BIOLOGIST Paul Ehrlich warned in *The Population Bomb* that mass starvation would strike in the 1970s and 1980s, with the world's population growth outpacing the production of food and other critical resources. Thanks to innovations and efforts such as the "green revolution" in farming and the widespread adoption of family planning, Ehrlich's worst fears did not come to pass. In fact, since the 1970s, global economic output has increased and fertility has fallen dramatically, especially in developing countries.

The United Nations Population Division now projects that global population growth will nearly halt by 2050. By that date, the world's population will have stabilized at 9.15 billion people, according to the "medium growth" variant of the UN's authoritative population database World Population Prospects: The 2008 Revision. (Today's global population is 6.83 billion.) Barring a cataclysmic climate crisis or a complete failure to recover from the current economic malaise, global economic output is expected to increase by two to three percent per year, meaning that global income will increase far more than population over the next four decades.

But twenty-first-century international security will depend less on how many people inhabit the world than on how the global population is composed and distributed: where populations are declining and where they are growing, which countries are relatively older and which are more youthful, and how demographics will influence population movements across regions.

These elements are not well recognized or widely understood. A recent article in *The Economist*, for example, cheered the decline in global fertility without noting other vital demographic developments. Indeed, the same un data cited by *The Economist* reveal four historic shifts that will fundamentally alter the world's population over the next four decades: the relative demographic weight of the world's developed countries will drop by nearly 25 percent, shifting economic power to the developing nations; the developed countries' labor forces will substantially age and decline, constraining economic growth in the developed world and raising the demand for immigrant workers; most of the world's expected population growth will increasingly be concentrated in today's poorest, youngest, and most heavily Muslim countries, which have a dangerous lack of quality education, capital, and employment opportunities; and, for the first time in history, most of the world's population will become urbanized, with

Jack A Goldstone, "The New Population Bomb," *Foreign Affairs*, vol. 89, no. 1, pp. 31–43. Copyright © 2010 by Council on Foreign Relations, Inc. Reprinted with permission.

the largest urban centers being in the world's poorest countries, where policing, sanitation, and health care are often scarce.

Taken together, these trends will pose challenges every bit as alarming as those noted by Ehrlich. Coping with them will require nothing less than a major reconsideration of the world's basic global governance structures.

Europe's Reversal of Fortunes

At the beginning of the eighteenth century, approximately 20 percent of the world's inhabitants lived in Europe (including Russia). Then, with the Industrial Revolution, Europe's population boomed, and streams of European emigrants set off for the Americas. By the eve of World War I, Europe's population had more than quadrupled. In 1913, Europe had more people than China, and the proportion of the world's population living in Europe and the former European colonies of North America had risen to over 33 percent.

But this trend reversed after World War I, as basic health care and sanitation began to spread to poorer countries. In Asia, Africa, and Latin America, people began to live longer, and birthrates remained high or fell only slowly. By 2003, the combined populations of Europe, the United States, and Canada accounted for just 17 percent of the global population. In 2050, this figure is expected to be just 12 percent—far less than it was in 1700. (These projections, moreover, might even understate the reality because they reflect the "medium growth" projection of the un forecasts, which assumes that the fertility rates of developing countries will decline while those of developed countries will increase. In fact, many developed countries show no evidence of increasing fertility rates.)

The West's relative decline is even more dramatic if one also considers changes in income. The Industrial Revolution made Europeans not only more numerous than they had been but also considerably richer per capita than others worldwide. According to the economic historian Angus Maddison, Europe, the United States, and Canada together produced about 32 percent of the world's GDP at the beginning of the nineteenth century. By 1950, that proportion had increased to a remarkable 68 percent of the world's total output (adjusted to reflect purchasing power parity).

This trend, too, is headed for a sharp reversal. The proportion of global GDP produced by Europe, the United States, and Canada fell from 68 percent in 1950 to 47 percent in 2003 and will decline even more steeply in the future. If the growth rate of per capita income (again, adjusted for purchasing power parity) between 2003 and 2050 remains as it was between 1973 and 2003—averaging 1.68 percent annually in Europe, the United States, and Canada and 2.47 percent annually in the rest of the world—then the combined GDP of Europe, the United States, and Canada will roughly double by 2050, whereas the GDP of the rest of the world will grow by a factor of five. The portion of global GDP produced by Europe, the United States, and Canada in 2050 will then be less than 30 percent—smaller than it was in 1820.

These figures also imply that an overwhelming proportion of the world's GDP growth between 2003 and 2050—nearly 80 percent—will occur outside of Europe, the United States, and Canada. By the middle of this century, the global middle class—those capable of purchasing durable consumer products, such as cars, appliances, and electronics—will increasingly be found in what is now considered the developing world. The World Bank has predicted that by 2030 the number of middle-class people in the developing world will be 1.2 billion—a rise of 200 percent since 2005. This means that the developing world's middle class alone will be larger than the total populations of Europe, Japan, and the United States combined. From now on, therefore, the main driver of global economic expansion will be the economic growth of newly industrialized countries, such as Brazil, China, India, Indonesia, Mexico, and Turkey.

Aging Pains

Part of the reason developed countries will be less economically dynamic in the coming decades is that their populations will become substantially older. The European countries, Canada, the United States, Japan, South Korea, and even China are aging at unprecedented rates. Today, the proportion of people aged 60 or older in China and South Korea is 12–15 percent. It is 15–22 percent in the European Union, Canada, and the United States and 30 percent in Japan. With baby boomers aging and life expectancy increasing, these numbers will increase dramatically. In 2050, approximately 30 percent of Americans, Canadians, Chinese, and Europeans will be over 60, as will more than 40 percent of Japanese and South Koreans.

Over the next decades, therefore, these countries will have increasingly large proportions of retirees and increasingly small proportions of workers. As workers born during the baby boom of 1945–65 are retiring, they are not being replaced by a new cohort of citizens of prime working age (15–59 years old). Industrialized countries are experiencing a drop in their working-age populations that is even more severe than the overall slowdown in their population growth. South Korea represents the most extreme example. Even as its total population is projected to decline by almost 9 percent by 2050 (from 48.3 million to 44.1 million), the population of working-age South Koreans is expected to drop by 36 percent (from 32.9 million to 21.1 million), and the number of South Koreans aged 60 and older will increase by almost 150 percent (from 7.3 million to 18 million). By 2050, in other words, the entire working-age population will barely exceed the 60-and-older population. Although South Korea's case is extreme, it represents an increasingly common fate for developed countries.

Europe is expected to lose 24 percent of its prime working-age population (about 120 million workers) by 2050, and its 60-and-older population is expected to increase by 47 percent. In the United States, where higher fertility and more immigration are expected than in Europe, the working-age population will grow by 15 percent over the next four decades—a steep decline from its growth of 62 percent between 1950 and 2010. And by 2050, the United States' 60-and-older population is expected to double.

All this will have a dramatic impact on economic growth, health care, and military strength in the developed world. The forces that fueled economic growth in industrialized countries during the second half of the twentieth century—increased productivity due to better education, the movement of women into the labor force, and innovations in technology—will all likely weaken in the coming decades. College enrollment boomed after World War II, a trend that is not likely to recur in the twenty-first century; the extensive movement of women into the labor force also was a one-time social change; and the technological change of the time resulted from innovators who created new products and leading-edge consumers who were willing to try them out—two groups that are thinning out as the industrialized world's population ages.

Overall economic growth will also be hampered by a decline in the number of new consumers and new households. When developed countries' labor forces were growing by 0.5–1.0 percent per year, as they did until 2005, even annual increases in real output per worker of just 1.7 percent meant that annual economic growth totaled 2.2–2.7 percent per year. But with the labor forces of many developed countries (such as Germany, Hungary, Japan, Russia, and the Baltic states) now shrinking by 0.2 percent per year and those of other countries (including Austria, the Czech Republic, Denmark, Greece, and Italy) growing by less than 0.2 percent per year, the same 1.7 percent increase in real output per worker yields only 1.5–1.9 percent annual overall growth. Moreover, developed countries will be lucky to keep productivity growth at even that level; in many developed countries, productivity is more likely to decline as the population ages.

A further strain on industrialized economies will be rising medical costs: as populations age, they will demand more health care for longer periods of time. Public pension schemes for aging populations are already being reformed in various industrialized countries—often prompting heated debate. In theory, at least, pensions might be kept solvent by increasing the retirement age, raising taxes modestly, and phasing out benefits for the wealthy. Regardless, the number of 80- and 90-year-olds—who are unlikely to work and highly likely to require nursing-home and other expensive care—will rise dramatically. And even if 60- and 70-year-olds remain active and employed, they will require procedures and medications—hip replacements, kidney transplants, blood-pressure treatments—to sustain their health in old age.

All this means that just as aging developed countries will have proportionally fewer workers, innovators, and consumerist young households, a large portion of those countries' remaining economic growth will have to be diverted to pay for the medical bills and pensions of their growing elderly populations. Basic services, meanwhile, will be increasingly costly because fewer young workers will be available for strenuous and labor-intensive jobs. Unfortunately, policymakers seldom reckon with these potentially disruptive effects of otherwise welcome developments, such as higher life expectancy.

Youth and Islam in the Developing World

Even as the industrialized countries of Europe, North America, and Northeast Asia will experience unprecedented aging this century, fast-growing countries in Africa, Latin America, the Middle East, and Southeast Asia will have exceptionally youthful populations. Today, roughly nine out of ten children under the age of 15 live in developing countries. And these are the countries that will continue to have the world's highest birthrates. Indeed, over 70 percent of the world's population growth between now and 2050 will occur in 24 countries, all of which are classified by the World Bank as low income or lower-middle income, with an average per capita income of under $3,855 in 2008.

Many developing countries have few ways of providing employment to their young, fast-growing populations. Would-be laborers, therefore, will be increasingly attracted to the labor markets of the aging developed countries of Europe, North America, and Northeast Asia. Youthful immigrants from nearby regions with high unemployment—Central America, North Africa, and Southeast Asia, for example—will be drawn to those vital entry-level and manual-labor jobs that sustain advanced economies: janitors, nursing-home aides, bus drivers, plumbers, security guards, farm workers, and the like. Current levels of immigration from developing to developed countries are paltry compared to those that the forces of supply and demand might soon create across the world.

These forces will act strongly on the Muslim world, where many economically weak countries will continue to experience dramatic population growth in the decades ahead. In 1950, Bangladesh, Egypt, Indonesia, Nigeria, Pakistan, and Turkey had a combined population of 242 million. By 2009, those six countries were the world's most populous Muslim-majority countries and had a combined population of 886 million. Their populations are continuing to grow and indeed are expected to increase by 475 million between now and 2050—during which time, by comparison, the six most populous developed countries are projected to gain only 44 million inhabitants. Worldwide, of the 48 fastest-growing countries today—those with annual population growth of two percent or more—28 are majority Muslim or have Muslim minorities of 33 percent or more.

It is therefore imperative to improve relations between Muslim and Western societies. This will be difficult given that many Muslims live in poor communities vulnerable to radical appeals and many see the West as antagonistic and militaristic. In the 2009 Pew Global Attitudes Project survey, for example, whereas 69 percent of those Indonesians and Nigerians surveyed reported viewing the United States favorably, just 18 percent of those polled in Egypt, Jordan, Pakistan, and Turkey (all U.S. allies) did. And in 2006, when the Pew survey last asked detailed questions about Muslim-Western relations, more than half of the respondents in Muslim countries characterized those relations as bad and blamed the West for this state of affairs.

But improving relations is all the more important because of the growing demographic weight of poor Muslim countries and the attendant increase in Muslim immigration, especially to Europe from North Africa and the Middle East. (To be sure, forecasts that Muslims will soon dominate Europe are outlandish: Muslims compose just three to ten percent of the population in the major European countries today, and this proportion will at most double by midcentury.) Strategists worldwide must consider that the world's young are becoming concentrated in those countries least prepared to educate and employ them, including some Muslim states. Any resulting poverty, social tension, or ideological radicalization could have disruptive effects in many corners of the world. But this need not be the case; the healthy immigration of workers to the developed world and the movement of capital to the developing world, among other things, could lead to better results.

Urban Sprawl

Exacerbating twenty-first-century risks will be the fact that the world is urbanizing to an unprecedented degree. The year 2010 will likely be the first time in history that a majority of the world's people live in cities rather than in the countryside. Whereas less than 30 percent of the world's population was urban in 1950, according to UN projections, more than 70 percent will be by 2050.

Lower-income countries in Asia and Africa are urbanizing especially rapidly, as agriculture becomes less labor intensive and as employment opportunities shift to the industrial and service sectors. Already, most of the world's urban agglomerations—Mumbai (population 20.1 million), Mexico City (19.5 million), New Delhi (17 million), Shanghai (15.8 million), Calcutta (15.6 million), Karachi (13.1 million), Cairo (12.5 million), Manila (11.7 million), Lagos (10.6 million), Jakarta (9.7 million)—are found in low-income countries. Many of these countries have multiple cities with over one million residents each: Pakistan has eight, Mexico 12, and China more than 100. The UN projects that the urbanized proportion of sub-Saharan Africa will nearly double between 2005 and 2050, from 35 percent (300 million people) to over 67 percent (1 billion). China, which is roughly 40 percent urbanized today, is expected to be 73 percent urbanized by 2050; India, which is less than 30 percent urbanized today, is expected to be 55 percent urbanized by 2050. Overall, the world's urban population is expected to grow by 3 billion people by 2050.

This urbanization may prove destabilizing. Developing countries that urbanize in the twenty-first century will have far lower per capita incomes than did many industrial countries when they first urbanized. The United States, for example, did not reach 65 percent urbanization until 1950, when per capita income was nearly $13,000 (in 2005 dollars). By contrast, Nigeria, Pakistan, and the Philippines, which are approaching similar levels of urbanization, currently have per capita incomes of just $1,800–$4,000 (in 2005 dollars).

According to the research of Richard Cincotta and other political demographers, countries with younger populations are especially prone to civil unrest and are less able to create or sustain democratic institutions. And the more heavily urbanized, the more such countries are likely to experience Dickensian poverty and anarchic violence. In good times, a thriving economy might keep urban residents employed and governments flush with sufficient resources to meet their needs. More often, however, sprawling and impoverished cities are vulnerable to crime lords, gangs, and petty rebellions. Thus, the rapid urbanization of the developing world in the decades ahead might bring, in exaggerated form, problems similar to those that urbanization brought to nineteenth-century Europe. Back then, cyclical employment, inadequate policing, and limited sanitation and education often spawned widespread labor strife, periodic violence, and sometimes—as in the 1820s, the 1830s, and 1848—even revolutions.

International terrorism might also originate in fast-urbanizing developing countries (even more than it already does). With their neighborhood networks, access to the Internet and digital communications technology, and concentration of valuable targets, sprawling cities offer excellent opportunities for recruiting, maintaining, and hiding terrorist networks.

Defusing the Bomb

Averting this century's potential dangers will require sweeping measures. Three major global efforts defused the population bomb of Ehrlich's day: a commitment by governments and nongovernmental organizations to control reproduction rates; agricultural advances, such as the green revolution and the spread of new technology; and a vast increase in international trade, which globalized markets and thus allowed developing countries to export foodstuffs in exchange for seeds, fertilizers, and machinery, which in turn helped them boost production. But today's population bomb is the product less of absolute growth in the world's population than of changes in its age and distribution. Policymakers must therefore adapt today's global governance institutions to the new realities of the aging of the industrialized world, the concentration of the world's economic and population growth in developing countries, and the increase in international immigration.

During the Cold War, Western strategists divided the world into a "First World," of democratic industrialized countries; a "Second World," of communist industrialized countries; and a "Third World," of developing countries. These strategists focused chiefly on deterring or managing conflict between the First and the Second Worlds and on launching proxy wars and diplomatic initiatives to attract Third World countries into the First World's camp. Since the end of the Cold War, strategists have largely abandoned this three-group division and have tended to believe either that the United States, as the sole superpower, would maintain a Pax Americana or that the world would become multipolar, with the United States, Europe, and China playing major roles.

Unfortunately, because they ignore current global demographic trends, these views will be obsolete within a few decades. A better approach would be to consider a different three-world order, with a new First World of the aging industrialized nations of North America, Europe, and Asia's Pacific Rim (including Japan, Singapore, South Korea, and Taiwan, as well as China after 2030, by which point the one-child policy will have produced significant aging); a Second World comprising fast-growing and economically dynamic countries with a healthy mix of young and old inhabitants (such as Brazil, Iran, Mexico, Thailand, Turkey, and Vietnam, as well as China until 2030); and a Third World of fast-growing, very young, and increasingly urbanized countries with poorer economies and often weak governments.

To cope with the instability that will likely arise from the new Third World's urbanization, economic strife, lawlessness, and potential terrorist activity, the aging industrialized nations of the new First World must build effective alliances with the growing powers of the new Second World and together reach out to Third World nations. Second World powers will be pivotal in the twenty-first century not just because they will drive economic growth and consume technologies and other products engineered in the First World; they will also be central to international security and cooperation. The realities of religion, culture, and geographic proximity mean that any peaceful and productive engagement by the First World of Third World countries will have to include the open cooperation of Second World countries.

Strategists, therefore, must fundamentally reconsider the structure of various current global institutions. The G-8, for example, will likely become obsolete as a body for making global economic policy. The G-20 is already becoming increasingly important, and this is less a short-term consequence of the ongoing global financial crisis than the beginning of the necessary recognition that Brazil, China, India, Indonesia, Mexico, Turkey, and others are becoming global economic powers. International institutions will not retain their legitimacy if they exclude the world's fastest-growing and most economically dynamic countries. It is essential, therefore, despite European concerns about the potential effects on immigration, to take steps such as admitting Turkey into the European Union. This would add youth and economic dynamism to the EU—and would prove that Muslims are welcome to join Europeans as equals in shaping a free and prosperous future. On the other hand, excluding Turkey from the EU could lead to hostility not only on the part of Turkish citizens, who are expected to number 100 million by 2050, but also on the part of Muslim populations worldwide.

NATO must also adapt. The alliance today is composed almost entirely of countries with aging, shrinking populations and relatively slow-growing economies. It is oriented toward the Northern Hemisphere and holds on to a Cold War structure that cannot adequately respond to contemporary threats. The young and increasingly populous countries of Africa, the Middle East, Central Asia, and South Asia could mobilize insurgents much more easily than NATO could mobilize the troops it would need if it were called on to stabilize those countries. Long-standing NATO members should, therefore—although it would require atypical creativity and flexibility—consider the logistical and demographic advantages of inviting into the alliance countries such as Brazil and Morocco, rather than countries such as Albania. That this seems far-fetched does not minimize the imperative that First World countries begin including large and strategic Second and Third World powers in formal international alliances.

The case of Afghanistan—a country whose population is growing fast and where NATO is currently engaged—illustrates the importance of building effective global institutions. Today, there are 28 million Afghans; by 2025, there will be 45 million; and by 2050, there will be close to 75 million. As nearly 20 million additional Afghans are born over the next 15 years, NATO will have an opportunity to help Afghanistan become reasonably stable, self-governing, and prosperous. If NATO's efforts fail and the Afghans judge that NATO intervention harmed their interests, tens of millions of young Afghans will become more hostile to the West. But if they come to think that NATO's involvement benefited their society, the West will have tens of millions of new friends. The example might then motivate the approximately one billion other young Muslims growing up in low-income countries over the next four decades to look more kindly on relations between their countries and the countries of the industrialized West.

Creative Reforms at Home

The aging industrialized countries can also take various steps at home to promote stability in light of the coming demographic trends. First, they should encourage families to have more children. France and Sweden have had success providing child care, generous leave time, and financial allowances to families with young children. Yet there is no consensus among policymakers—and certainly not among demographers—about what policies best encourage fertility.

More important than unproven tactics for increasing family size is immigration. Correctly managed, population movement can benefit developed and developing countries alike. Given the dangers of young, underemployed, and unstable populations in developing countries, immigration to developed countries can provide economic opportunities for the ambitious and serve as a safety valve for all. Countries that embrace immigrants, such as the United States, gain economically by having willing laborers and greater entrepreneurial spirit. And countries with high levels of emigration (but not so much that they experience so-called brain drains) also benefit because emigrants often send remittances home or return to their native countries with valuable education and work experience.

One somewhat daring approach to immigration would be to encourage a reverse flow of older immigrants from developed to developing countries. If older residents of developed countries took their retirements along the southern coast of the Mediterranean or in Latin America or Africa, it would greatly reduce the strain on their home countries' public entitlement systems. The developing countries involved, meanwhile, would benefit because caring for the elderly and providing retirement and leisure services is highly labor intensive. Relocating a portion of these activities to developing countries would provide employment and valuable training to the young, growing populations of the Second and Third Worlds.

This would require developing residential and medical facilities of First World quality in Second and Third World countries. Yet even this difficult task would be preferable to the status quo, by which low wages and poor facilities lead to a steady drain of medical and nursing talent from developing to developed countries. Many residents of developed countries who desire cheaper medical procedures already practice medical tourism today, with India, Singapore, and Thailand being the most common destinations. (For example, the international consulting firm Deloitte estimated that 750,000 Americans traveled abroad for care in 2008.)

Never since 1800 has a majority of the world's economic growth occurred outside of Europe, the United States, and Canada. Never have so many people in those regions been over 60 years old. And never have low-income countries' populations been so young and so urbanized. But such will be the world's demography in the twenty-first century. The strategic and economic policies of the twentieth century are obsolete, and it is time to find new ones.

Reading 7.3

Conclusions to *Governing Climate Change*

Harriet Bulkeley and Peter Newell

ONCE UPON A TIME STUDYING AND keeping track of the world of climate governance was relatively simple. By attending the UN climate change negotiations or reading *Earth Negotiations Bulletin*[1] and the NGO newsletter *ECO* you could keep up to date with what was going on. If you take the view that international institutions continue to be the primary and most important site of climate governance, your task continues to be a relatively straight-forward one, even if the range of issues on the negotiating table has grown more complex. If, however, you adopt a broader view of climate governance—one that raises more open questions about how and where it happens and who is engaged in it—[...] your task is altogether more complex. In this [...] chapter [...] we summarize some of the key crosscutting themes that have emerged [...], what they imply for governing climate change, and how we can make sense of them.

The Shifting Terrain of Governance

Claiming that the landscape of climate governance is more plural, diverse and multifaceted is not to say that the governance of climate change by and through international institutions and nation-states does not continue to be a central part of the story. Key decisions about over-all targets and the means of delivering them continue to be made at the international level by nation-states operating within global institutions. [...] [H]istorical and contemporary conflicts along North–South and other lines continue to get played out in the UN negotiations through debates about responsibility for the problem and the appropriate responses to it.

However, we have also seen examples of a tremendous proliferation in governance initiatives around the world at all scales of politics (from the local to the global) that enroll a vast array of state, non-state, public and private actors in different dimensions of governing. These have taken the form of public-private and hybrid initiatives (such as REEEP and CDM), of private codes and standard-setting (such as the VCS or Gold Standard) or community-based initiatives such as Transition Town projects. As the dimensions of the challenge of tackling climate change become clearer and the debate moves from setting goals to implementation, it has become increasingly obvious that climate governance can no longer be achieved by the actions and initiatives of international institutions or national governments alone. Rather, the growth of new "sites" of climate politics [...] is testament to the increasing mainstreaming of climate change—its integration in other policy domains (biodiversity, trade, energy) and its increasing uptake by a range of organizations (be they corporate, donor or civil society) beyond the realm of what was traditionally considered as climate governance.

We have seen, though, that with this shifting terrain come a number of critical challenges. Governing across so many scales and through so many dispersed but overlapping networks presents huge problems of coordination and policy coherence. [...] [T]he number of banks, donors, and NGOs clamoring to define a leading role for themselves in the delivery of carbon finance is creating problems of duplication and turf wars over who funds what. As a premium is placed on the delivery of clean energy we have seen the REEEP initiative set up, the APP created and numerous energy investments overseen by the World Bank and regional development banks in Asia and Latin America. In such a crowded field, there are challenges of ensuring a rational division of labor which allows each actor to do what it does best.

Just as actors beyond the traditional world of climate policy are becoming increasingly involved in its governance, so too though the nature of climate change as an issue means that it spills over into the governance of other sectors, such as energy, trade, industry, agriculture and housing, to name but a few. This creates problems of policy coherence at the national level; ensuring that actions in such areas are compatible with and do not undermine climate policy goals. But these issue linkages are also apparent at the international level in debates about the compatibility of climate policy measures with the international trade regime, for example. Tentative US and EU proposals to use border tax adjustment measures against imported goods that have been produced in an energy or carbon-intensive manner (such as Chinese steel) could well face a legal challenge in a dispute under the remit of the WTO.[2] How this issue, and others, is resolved will be shaped by who wields the most power and whose rules rule. Managing the shifting terrain and multiple sites of climate governance is not just a matter of improved coordination. The power of key actors with interests at stake will be brought to bear in determining what counts as climate governance, and how and where particular issues such as this get resolved.

New Actors, Old Politics?

The shifting terrain of climate governance is in part a reflection of the realization that the resources, capacity, expertise, networks, and power of actors as diverse as states, firms, cities, communities, civil society organizations, and individuals are required to effectively address all aspects of the problem. While nation-states and international institutions remain critical actors, what we have found is that the delivery of the targets and agreed commitments often implies an important role for many other actors, such as businesses and cities, and in reality is dependent on their support and engagement if it is to be effective. As David Levy argues, "if an agreement cannot be crafted that gains the consent of major affected industries, there will likely be no agreement at all."[3] They are after all the "street level bureaucrats" that will be expected to put regulation into practice.[4] Often, however, as well as helping to realize the goals of the regime through their own independent actions, these actors are going beyond the formal climate regime by setting more ambitious targets than those contained in Kyoto. For example, the 2007 Bali World Mayors and Local Governments Climate Protection Agreement states that municipal authorities will seek to reduce GHG emissions by 60 percent worldwide by 2050, with an 80 percent reduction in emissions from industrialized countries.[5] Non-state actors also engage in forms of governance innovation that precede and predate those adopted by government. The oil giants Shell and BP had both developed intra-firm emissions trading schemes from 2000, for example, three years before the EU ETS was established.

The involvement of multiple actors in the governing of climate change has not been a harmonious and consensual process, however. We have seen how actors with conflicting interests in the debate compete to assert their preferred understanding of the nature of the challenges associated with climate change. [...] [T]here has been fierce contestation over whether sufficient scientific consensus exists to justify potentially costly forms of action. Conflicts over which evidence is highlighted in the policy makers' summaries produced by the IPCC reflect what is at stake in the recommendations that flow from how the risks associated with acting or not acting are presented. [...] [T]he business community throughout much of the 1990s sought to present climate change as a threat to economic growth rather than an opportunity to develop new forms of low-carbon business. Battles continue today among and within firms about whether climate change is a threat or an opportunity to their business.

The issue of who governs directly impinges upon the question of who benefits from current governance arrangements. [...] [D]isputes over whether the Global Environment Facility was the appropriate institution to oversee the delivery of aid and technology transfer to developing countries as part of the UNFCCC agreement reflected concerns that the body is too tightly controlled by the World Bank to be responsive to developing country concerns. We have also seen how many smaller developing countries, those most vulnerable to the effects of climate change in many cases, are poorly represented in the international negotiations and lack the legal and scientific capacity to engage fully in the discussions taking place. We [...] [use] the example of the legal support given by FIELD, the environmental legal NGO, to the Alliance of Small Island States most affected by sea-level rise to bolster their negotiating capacity vis-à-vis more powerful countries and regions. At the same time, the mutual dependence of state and non-state actors in realizing climate governance goals is leading to compromises and new forms of partnership. [...] [V]arious forms of community are being mobilized by states and international institutions in order to address climate change. This can bring benefits, both in terms of addressing climate change and for wider goals of social and environmental justice, but can also lead to the exclusion of those actors' interests and goals that do not fit with particular interpretations of the climate governance "project." Attending to the politics of who governs, and on whose behalf, will be critical to ensuring that addressing climate change does not come at a cost to those least able to represent their interests.

The Rise of Market and Voluntary Governance

[...] [W]ho governs, and importantly how they govern, is in a continual state of flux in the world of climate politics. What is possible and likely from climate governance is a feature of the health of the economy, the nature of relations between states, and which other issues compete with climate change for resources and attention, all of which are subject to change. This broader political and economic context shapes and is shaped by climate governance. [...] [T]he popularity of market-based mechanisms in climate governance can best be understood within a prevailing context of neo-liberalism: an ideology and set of practices which construct a minimal role for the state and view the market as the main provider of welfare and efficient outcomes. The embrace of emissions trading and the creation of the CDM, where earlier they had been opposed, can be understood as part of the deepening hold of neo-liberalism throughout the 1990s as well as the ability of its most powerful proponent, the USA, to insist that such solutions be part of the global deal. Likewise, the call for communities to govern themselves in order to address climate change [...] and the growth in partnership approaches [...] are also modes of governance that fit with neo-liberal ideas about the respective roles of the state, of the private sector, and of individuals.

[...] [There is] a dynamic relationship between formal and informal forms of soft regulation. The CDM Gold Standard is a private non-governmental initiative that provides "compliance plus" incentives for investments in projects that meet certain sustainable development criteria. It does not compete with the CDM rules agreed under the Kyoto Protocol, but rather provides the incentives and means for those who want to go beyond that to do so. [...] [V]oluntary governance experiments, such as with forestry projects in voluntary carbon offset markets, can prepare the way for their acceptance into the formal climate regime. On the other hand, [...] some initiatives are seen as a threat to the climate regime. The APP was interpreted as an attempt by the United States to develop an alternative approach to a global legally binding emissions reductions framework by focusing on clean technology cooperation among a select number of leading states, rather than overall emissions reductions targets.

The normalization of market and voluntary approaches to climate governance as a legitimate and appropriate response to the threat of climate change has, therefore, not been without contest. In particular, with the rise of carbon markets as a means of allowing wealthier countries to meet their emissions reductions obligations, we have seen contestation over their consequences, particularly for poorer communities whose resources (land and forests) become subject to an international trade in emissions reductions [...]. This has resulted in instances of displacement and conflict that critics refer to as "carbon colonialism"[6] as local regimes of resource management are brought into the realm of global climate governance. Likewise, [...] local institutions are [important] in ensuring that local communities can capture some of the benefits of engagement with the carbon economy. These examples suggest the importance of the link between the procedural and distributional aspects of climate governance: who participates and who decides exercises a powerful influence over who wins and who loses.

Consequences and Contestations in Climate Governance

Amid such diversity among actors and practices of climate governance, it is difficult to form definitive judgments about what is working and for whom. One answer is that it is difficult to know in quantitative terms who is reducing by how much as more actors get involved in setting their own standards employing different baselines and covering different GHG [...]. As responsibility is diffused and governance tools proliferate, maintaining a clear view of what is being achieved overall is very difficult. Symbolically, the fact that governments advance slowly towards a successor to the Kyoto Protocol, [...], or the fact that many of the world's leading firms now endorse the idea of action of climate change, [...] represents success on one level. Key actors are engaged and the momentum is there.

And yet despite the enormous proliferation of initiatives aimed at reporting, benchmarking, and measuring performance, at funding projects and trading credits, that we have seen throughout the book, it would be difficult to argue that the world is showing genuine progress in moving away from a model of development that is fueling climate change. Continued emissions growth tells a different story. Economic growth and emissions trajectories of GHG continue to be closely aligned and governments and corporations alike continue to scour the earth for new sources of fossil fuels, in spite of full knowledge of the human and ecological consequences of burning them into the atmosphere. Rather than prioritize fundamental changes in production and consumption of energy, the world's most industrialized countries are seeking to locate the lowest-cost ways of reducing emissions by identifying emissions reductions projects in the global South or to make more money by trading their way out of trouble through the buying and selling of emissions permits. We have seen how climate justice movements and critics of carbon trading in particular have sought to question the assumed efficiency and effectiveness of such market-based governance instruments, as well as highlight the inequalities and injustices that they create or reinforce. But in a context of such power inequalities within and between societies, the means of holding to account those that benefit most from what has been called the "un-governance" of climate change by those that are or will suffer the worst consequences of inaction are often just not there.

One conclusion that can surely be drawn from the evidence [...], however, is that the landscape of climate governance is ever changing, and interesting and unpredictable alliances between actors, even former adversaries, are increasingly common. It is to be hoped that enough powerful allies in the world of finance and business can be brought on board alongside enough governments with the will and power to lead on action on climate change, pressured, cajoled and shamed into action by an increasingly active public and civil society, to adequately address perhaps the greatest collective action problem the world currently faces.

Theoretical Implications

How then are we to explain and make sense of the patterns of governance described above? [...] Here, we gather some of the key insights that emerge [...].

If we accept that climate governance now takes place in many more places and is produced by a greater range of actors, it is clear that we need to adopt theoretical tools and concepts that allow us to go beyond the state as the primary focus of analysis. Emphasizing the role of non-state actors and explaining their influence on international climate policy is one important aspect of this.[7] But given that many of these actors are cooperating and working together in ways which bypass the climate regime altogether, we need to explore their roles as governance actors in ways that are not defined by whether and when they affect state policy. [...] [O]rganizations such as the Climate Group have been able to bring together novel coalitions of cities, businesses, and civil society organizations to share and build on successful initiatives to reduce

GHG emissions. An emphasis on networks that cut across divisions of national and international is useful here.[8] [...] [W]ork on public-private partnerships can also usefully be applied to governance innovation in the climate arena.[9] A key challenge that remains is how to account for the fact that some partnerships are more successful and more powerful than others.

The political economy approaches [...] offer promising ways forward for understanding the relations of power that underpin political coalitions which seek to deliver or frustrate change. They emphasize in particular the role of economic actors in the very processes which are subject to regulation, where powerful interests are at stake and from whence change ultimately has to come. By focusing on the dependencies and material and political alliances that bind together state, market, and civil society actors, they provide a sense of how much autonomy, "policy space" and scope for effective action they have.[10] This could be the developing country governments dependent on World Bank finance, or developed country governments reluctant to regulate the emissions of businesses that threaten to relocate their operations elsewhere. But it could also be the coalitions formed between financial capital in the city of London and NGOs pushing business to commit to action, or conflicts between different business interests which create openings for change. This provides us with a useful way to understand why climate is governed as it is and on whose behalf, by placing power at the heart of governance analysis.

All of this implies broader understandings of power than have traditionally been used in the study of climate governance. Notions of "power over" and the ability to demand actions of others continue to be important: the power of states over firms and local authorities is critical to their ability to ensure they enforce actions on climate change. But many of the forms of private governance [...] show that even without sanctions, forms of peer and consumer or activist pressure often provide incentives for compliance.[11] We have also seen how power operates in more subtle ways, through the presentation of knowledge; the inclusion or exclusion of emphasis on some aspects of climate science and economics and not others. Appeals to moral authority are strongly made by developing countries, as well as underpinning NGO-led proposals on contraction and convergence or the greenhouse development rights framework [...]. Considering power in these terms means understanding how it works through discourse and in the everyday practice of policies and actions to address climate change.

The power that actors wield in climate governance is not just visible within the self-proclaimed arenas of climate policy, nor does it derive primarily from the power they wield in that area, however. As Susan Strange argues in her critique of regime theories of international governance:

since the chain of cause and effect so often originates in technology and markets, passing through national policy decisions to emerge as negotiating postures in multilateral discussions, it follows that attention to the resultant international agreement of some sort is apt to overlook most of the determining factors on which agreement may, in brief, rest.[12]

Likewise, the World Bank is an increasingly central actor in climate governance, not primarily because of its role in developing the Prototype Carbon Fund or the Climate Investment Funds, but because it exerts such influence over the overall development strategies of so many developing countries. Separating its role as the world's largest lender from its role as one among many actors in climate governance makes little sense, because how developing countries engage with it as a climate actor is shaped by the knowledge of the power the institution wields over all other aspects of their economies.

Climate governance is ironically both a microcosm of a larger global political economy, but also a meta-feature of that system in so far as virtually all areas of political activity have an impact on, or might be understood as forms of, climate governance. For instance, the WTO or the World Bank would not consider themselves environmental organizations or climate agencies, but the mandates they have and the influence they wield mean they have a tremendous impact on the level of GHG emissions that pass into the atmosphere. Trade agreements that mean goods are transported over larger distances and financial loans for coal-fired power stations in the case of the World Bank make the work of the official climate regime that much harder. Ultimately, whether we have the collective capacity and will to address climate change in the time frames available to avoid its most dangerous consequences will depend on fundamental change in policy areas beyond the direct control of many of the actors and initiatives [...].

Last but not least, [...] it takes on a much broader range of forms in reality than many theoretical accounts allow for. We have clearly observed, as others have done in other areas, a shift from government to governance in which more actors are involved in processes of governing.[13] The tools of governance have not only broadened from law and regulation to voluntary standards, codes, and partnerships, but also to day-to-day supply chain management within firms whose decisions often dwarf those made in the traditional arenas of climate governance in terms of their impact on emissions of GHG. While the tremendous diversity and dynamism of climate governance generates huge challenges of coordination, accountability and effectiveness, a fact which in itself makes it hard to get a handle on how effective action is and who is benefiting, the plurality of sites of action could also be a positive thing as actors move between arenas trying to advance action in the fastest and most effective way they can, working with whom they need to, wherever that happens to be. We surely have to hope for all our sakes that the forms of climate governance we are now busy constructing are up to the scale of the challenge we are faced with, and can deliver change within the time we have available to us to prevent the very worst scenarios of uncontrolled climate change.

Notes

1. Back issues of *Earth Negotiations Bulletin* can be found at: www.iisd.ca/voltoc.html

2. Aaron Cosbey, *Border Carbon Adjustment* (Winnipeg, Canada: International Institute for Sustainable Development, 2008).

3. David Levy, "Business and the Evolution of the Climate Regime: The Dynamics of Corporate Strategies," in *The Business of Global Environmental Governance*, eds David Levy and Peter Newell (Cambridge, Mass.: MIT Press, 2005), 73–105.

4. Michael Lipskey, *Street-level Bureaucracy* (New York: Russell Sage Foundation, 1983).

5. The World Mayors and Local Governments Climate Protection Agreement, www.globalclimateagreement.org/

6. Heidi Bachram, "Climate Fraud and Carbon Colonialism: The New Trade in Greenhouse Gases," *Capitalism, Nature, Socialism* 15, no. 4 (2004): 10–12.

7. Bas Arts, "Non-State Actors in Global Environmental Governance: New Arrangements Beyond the State," in *New Modes of Governance in the Global System: Exploring Publicness, Delegation and Inclusiveness*, eds Mathias Koenig-Archibugi and Michael Zürn (Basingstoke, UK: Palgrave Macmillan, 2006): 177–201; Peter Newell, *Climate for Change: Non-State Actors and the Global Politics of the Greenhouse* (Cambridge: Cambridge University Press, 2000); Michele Betsill and Elizabeth Correll, "NGO Influence in International Environmental Negotiations: A Framework for Analysis," *Global Environmental Politics* 1, no. 4 (2001): 65–85.

8. Harriet Bulkeley, "Reconfiguring Environmental Governance: Towards a Politics of Scales and Networks," *Political Geography* 24, no. 8 (2005): 875–902.

9. Karin Backstränd and Charlotte Streck, "New Partnerships in Global Environmental Policy: The Clean Development Mechanism," *Journal of Environment and Development* 13, no. 3 (2004): 295–322.

10. Kevin Gallagher, ed., *Putting Development First* (London: Zed Books, 2005).

11. Peter Newell, "Civil Society, Corporate Accountability and the Politics of Climate Change," *Global Environmental Politics* 8, no. 3 (2008): 124–55.

12. Susan Strange, "Cave! Hic Dragones: A Critique of Regime Analysis," *International Organization* 36, no. 2 (1983): 488–90.

13. James Rosenau and Ernst Otto Czempiel, eds, *Governance Without Government: Order and Change in World Politics* (Cambridge: Cambridge University Press, 1992); Vasudha Chhotray and Gerry Stoker, *Governance Theory: A Cross-Disciplinary Approach* (Basingstoke, UK: Palgrave Macmillan, 2008); Rod A. W. Rhodes, "The New Governance: Governing Without Government," *Political Studies* 44, no. 4 (1996): 652–67.

Chapter 7

1. Can the complexity confronting projects of reversing climate change be resolved?
2. Identify and critically assess the megatrends affecting population growth.
3. Is there anything optimistic about Mark Blyth's conclusions of advanced economies?

CPSIA information can be obtained
at www.ICGtesting.com
Printed in the USA
LVHW050026260821
696099LV00005B/65